THE MOSQUITO

ALSO BY TIMOTHY C. WINEGARD

The First World Oil War

For King and Kanata: Canadian Indians and the First World War

Indigenous Peoples of the British Dominions and the First World War

Oka: A Convergence of Cultures and the Canadian Forces

THE MOSQUITO

A Human History of Our Deadliest Predator

TIMOTHY C. WINEGARD

DUTTON

DUTTON
An imprint of Penguin Random House LLC
www.penguinrandomhouse.com

LIBRARY OF CONGRESS CATALOGING-IN-PUBLICATION DATA
Names: Winegard, Timothy C. (Timothy Charles), 1977– author.
Title: The mosquito : a human history of our deadliest predator / Timothy C. Winegard.
Description: New York : Dutton, [2019] | Includes bibliographical references and index.
Identifiers: LCCN 2019005477 | ISBN 9781524743413 (hardcover) | ISBN 9781524743437 (ebook) | ISBN 9781524745608 (export)
Subjects: LCSH: Mosquitoes—Ecology—History. | Human ecology.
Classification: LCC QL536 .W56 2019 | DDC 595.77/2—dc23
LC record available at https://lccn.loc.gov/2019005477

Printed in the United States of America
1 3 5 7 9 10 8 6 4 2

Book design by Nancy Resnick

To my parents, Charles and Marian,
who filled my formative years
with knowledge, travel, curiosity, and love

Contents

Introduction

We are at war with the mosquito.

A swarming and consuming army of 110 trillion enemy mosquitoes patrols every inch of the globe save Antarctica, Iceland, the Seychelles, and a handful of French Polynesian micro-islands. The biting female warriors of this droning insect population are armed with at least fifteen lethal and debilitating biological weapons against our 7.7 billion humans deploying suspect and often self-detrimental defensive capabilities. In fact, our defense budget for personal shields, sprays, and other deterrents to stymie her unrelenting raids has a rapidly rising annual revenue of $11 billion. And yet, her deadly offensive campaigns and crimes against humanity continue with reckless abandon. While our counterattacks are reducing the number of annual casualties she perpetrates, the mosquito remains the deadliest hunter of human beings on the planet. Last year she slaughtered *only* 830,000 people. We sensible and wise Homo sapiens occupied the runner-up #2 spot, slaying 580,000 of our own species.

The Bill & Melinda Gates Foundation, which has contributed nearly $4 billion to mosquito research since its creation in 2000, releases an annual report that identifies the animals most lethal to humans. The contest is not even close. The heavyweight champion, and our apex predator in perpetuity, is the mosquito. Since 2000, the annual average number of human deaths caused by the mosquito has hovered around 2 million. We come in a distant second at 475,000, followed by snakes (50,000), dogs and sand flies (25,000 each), the tsetse fly, and the assassin or kissing bug (10,000 each). The fierce killers of lore and Hollywood celebrity appear much further down our list. The crocodile is ranked #10 with 1,000 annual deaths. Next on the list are hippos with 500, and elephants and lions with 100 fatalities each. The much-slandered shark and wolf share the #15 position, killing an average of ten people per annum.*

The mosquito has killed more people than *any* other cause of death in human history. Statistical extrapolation situates mosquito-inflicted deaths approaching *half of all humans that have ever lived*. In plain numbers, the mosquito has dispatched an estimated 52 billion people from a total of 108 billion throughout our relatively brief 200,000-year existence.†

Yet, the mosquito does not directly harm anyone. It is the toxic and highly evolved diseases she transmits that cause an endless barrage of desolation and death. Without her, however, these sinister pathogens could not be transferred or vectored to humans nor continue their cyclical contagion. In fact, without her, these diseases would not exist at all. You cannot have one without the other. The nefarious mosquito, roughly the size and weight of a grape seed, would be as innocuous as a generic ant or housefly and you would not be reading this book. After all, her dominion of death would be erased from the historical record and I would have no wild and remarkable tales to tell. Imagine for a moment a world without deadly mosquitoes or any mosquitoes for that matter? Our history and the world we know, or think we know, would be completely unrecognizable. We might as well live on a foreign planet in a galaxy far, far away.

As the pinnacle purveyor of our extermination, the mosquito has consistently been at the front lines of history as the grim reaper, the

* For this time period, annual death statistics for mosquito-borne diseases vary between 1 and 3 million. The consensus usually straddles an average of 2 million.

† These are estimates and extrapolations based on the following factors and scientific models: the origin and longevity of both Homo sapiens and mosquito-borne diseases in Africa; the time frame and patterns of the migrations of humans, mosquitoes, and mosquito-borne diseases out of Africa; the first appearance and evolution of numerous genetic hereditary defenses to distinct strains of malaria; historical death rates from mosquito-borne disease; human population growth and demography; historic periods of natural climate change and global temperature fluctuations, among other contributing considerations and components.

harvester of human populations, and the ultimate agent of historical change. She has played a greater role in shaping our story than any other animal with which we share our global village. Within these bloody and disease-plagued pages, you will embark on a chronological mosquito-tormented journey through our tangled communal history. Karl Marx recognized in 1852 that "men make their own history, but they do not make it as they please." It was the steadfast and insatiable mosquito that manipulated and determined our destiny. "It is perhaps a rude blow to the *amour propre* of our species," writes acclaimed University of Georgetown history professor J. R. McNeill, "to think that lowly mosquitoes and mindless viruses can shape our international affairs. But they can." We tend to forget that history is not the artifact of inevitability.

A common theme throughout this story is the interplay between war, politics, travel, trade, and the changing patterns of human land use and natural climate. The mosquito does not exist in a vacuum, and her global ascendancy was created by corresponding historical events both naturally and socially induced. Our relatively short human journey from our first steps in and out of Africa to our global historical trails is the result of a coevolutionary marriage between society and nature. We as humans have played a large role in the transmission of mosquito-borne diseases through population migrations (involuntary or otherwise), densities, and pressures. Historically, our domestication of plants and animals (which are reservoirs of disease), advancements in agriculture, deforestation, climate change (natural and artificially encouraged), and global war, trade, and travel have all played a part in nurturing the ideal ecologies for the proliferation of mosquito-borne illnesses.

Historians, journalists, and modern memories, however, find pestilence and disease rather dull, when compared to war, conquest, and national supermen, most often legendary military leaders. The literary record has been tainted by attributing the fates of empires and nations, the outcome of pivotal wars, and the bending of historical events to individual rulers, to specific generals, or to the larger concerns of human agencies such as politics, religion, and economics. The mosquito has been written off as a sidelined spectator, rather than an active agent within the ongoing processes of civilization. In doing so, she has been defamed by this slanderous exclusion of her enduring influence and impact in changing the course of history. Mosquitoes and her diseases that have accompanied traders, travelers, soldiers, and settlers around the world have been far more lethal than any man-made weapons or inventions. The mosquito has ambushed humankind with unmitigated fury since time immemorial and scratched her indelible mark on the modern world order.

Mercenary mosquitoes mustered armies of pestilence and stalked battlefields across the globe, often deciding the outcome of game-changing wars. Time and time again, the mosquito laid waste to the greatest armies of her generations. To borrow from acclaimed author Jared Diamond, the endless shelves of military history books and Hollywood fanfare lionizing famed generals distort the ego-deflating truth: Mosquito-borne disease proved far deadlier than manpower, materials, or the minds of the most brilliant generals. It is worth remembering, as we navigate the trenches and tour historic theaters of war, that a sick soldier is more taxing to the military machine than a dead one. Not only do they need to be replaced but they also continue to consume valuable resources. During our warring existence, mosquito-borne diseases have been prolific battlefield burdens and killers.

Our immune systems are finely tuned to our local environments. Our curiosity, greed, invention, arrogance, and blatant aggression thrust germs into the global whirlwind of historical events. Mosquitoes do not respect international borders—walls or no walls. Marching armies, inquisitive explorers, and land-hungry colonists (and their African slaves) brought new diseases to distant lands, but, on the other hand, were also brought to their knees by the microorganisms in the foreign lands they intended to conquer. As the mosquito transformed the landscapes of civilization, humans were unwittingly required to respond to her piercing universal projection of power. After all, the biting truth is that more than any other external participant, the mosquito, as our deadliest predator, drove the events of human history to create our present reality.

I think I can safely say that most of you reading this book have one thing in common—a genuine hatred for mosquitoes. Bashing mosquitoes is a universal pastime and has been since the dawn of humanity.

Across the ages, from our hominid ancestral evolution in Africa to the present day, we have been locked in an unsurpassed life-or-death struggle for survival with the not-so-simple mosquito. In this lopsided battle and unequal balance of power, historically, we did not stand a chance. Through evolutionary adaptation, our dogged and deadly archnemesis has repeatedly circumvented our efforts of extermination to continue her feverish uninterrupted feeding and her undefeated reign of terror. The mosquito remains the destroyer of worlds and the preeminent and globally distinguished killer of humankind.

Our war with the mosquito is *the* war of our world.

CHAPTER I

Toxic Twins: The Mosquito and Her Diseases

It has been one of the most universally recognizable and aggravating sounds on earth for 190 million years—the humming buzz of a mosquito. After a long day of hiking while camping with your family or friends, you quickly shower, settle into your lawn chair, crack an ice-cold beer, and exhale a deep, contented sigh. Before you can enjoy your first satisfying swig, however, you hear that all-too-familiar sound signaling the ambitious approach of your soon-to-be tormentors.

It is nearing dusk, her favorite time to feed. Although you heard her droning arrival, she gently lands on your ankle without detection, as she usually bites close to the ground. It's always a female, by the way. She conducts a tender, probing, ten-second reconnaissance, looking for a prime blood vessel. With her backside in the air, she steadies her cross-hairs and zeros in with six sophisticated needles. She inserts two serrated mandible cutting blades (much like an electric carving knife with two blades shifting back and forth), and saws into your skin, while two other retractors open a passage for the proboscis, a hypodermic syringe that emerges from its protective sheath. With this straw she starts to suck 3–5 milligrams of your blood, immediately excreting its water, while condensing its 20% protein content. All the while, a sixth needle is pumping in saliva that contains an anticoagulant preventing your blood from clotting at the puncture site.* This shortens her feeding time, lessening the

* For this reason, mosquitoes cannot transmit HIV or any other blood-borne virus. The mosquito injects only saliva, which does not and cannot contain HIV, through a specific tube separate from the tube used to take in blood. No blood is transmitted during her bite.

likelihood that you feel her penetration and splat her across your ankle.* The anticoagulant causes an allergic reaction, leaving an itchy bump as her parting gift. The mosquito bite is an intricate and innovative feeding ritual required for reproduction. She needs your blood to grow and mature her eggs.†

Please don't feel singled out, special, or view yourself as a chosen one. She bites everyone. This is just the inherent nature of the beast. There is absolutely no truth to the persistent myths that mosquitoes fancy females over males, that they prefer blondes and redheads over those with darker hair, or that the darker or more leathery your skin, the safer you are from her bite. It is true, however, that she does play favorites and feasts on some more than others.

Blood type O seems to be the vintage of choice over types A and B or their blend. People with blood type O get bitten twice as often as those with type A, with type B falling somewhere in between. Disney/Pixar must have done their homework when portraying a tipsy mosquito ordering a "Bloody Mary, O-Positive" in the 1998 movie *A Bug's Life*. Those who have higher natural levels of certain chemicals in their skin, particularly lactic acid, also seem to be more attractive. From these elements she can analyze which blood type you are. These are the same chemicals that determine an individual's level of skin bacteria and unique body odor. While you may offend others and perhaps yourself, in this case being pungently rancid is a good thing, for it increases bacterial levels on the skin, which makes you less alluring to mosquitoes. Cleanliness is not next to godliness, except for stinky feet, which emit a bacterium (the same one that ripens and rinds certain cheeses) that is a mosquito aphrodisiac. Mosquitoes are also enticed by deodorants, perfumes, soap, and other applied fragrances.

While this may seem unfair to many of you, and the reason remains a mystery, she also has an affinity for beer drinkers. Wearing bright

---

* This amazing three-minute video from PBS Deep Look provides an actual up-close view and explanation of a mosquito feeding: https://www.youtube.com/watch?v=rD8SmacBUcU. It is well worth the watch.

† Recent studies suggest that, as a survival mechanism, Aedes mosquitoes can be trained to avoid unpleasant interactions such as swatting for up to twenty-four hours, making a repeat strike less likely.

colors is also not a wise choice, since she hunts by both sight and smell—the latter depending chiefly on the amount of carbon dioxide exhaled by the potential target. So all your thrashing and huffing and puffing only magnetizes mosquitoes and puts you at greater risk. She can smell carbon dioxide from over 200 feet away. When you exercise, for example, you emit more carbon dioxide through both frequency of breath and output. You also sweat, releasing those appetizing chemicals, primarily lactic acid, that invite the mosquito's attention. Lastly, your body temperature rises, which is an easily identifiable heat signature for your soon-to-be tormentor. On average, pregnant women suffer twice as many bites, as they respire 20% more carbon dioxide, and have a marginally elevated body temperature. As we will see, this is bad news for the mother and the fetus when it comes to infection from Zika and malaria.

Please don't go on a shower, deodorant, and exercise strike or shelve your beloved beer and bright T-shirts just yet. Unfortunately, 85% of what makes you attractive to mosquitoes is prewired in your genetic circuit board, whether that be blood type; natural chemical, bacteria, or CO_2 levels; metabolism; or stink and stench. At the end of the day, she will find blood from any exposed target of opportunity.

Unlike their female counterparts, male mosquitoes do not bite. Their world revolves around two things: nectar and sex. Like other flying insects, when ready to mate, male mosquitoes assemble over a prominent feature, ranging from chimneys to antennas to trees to people. Many of us grumble and flail in frustration as that dogged cloud of bugs droning over our heads shadows us when we walk and refuses to disperse. You are not paranoid, nor are you imagining this phenomenon. Take it as a compliment. Male mosquitoes have graced you with the honor of being a "swarm marker." Mosquito swarms have been photographed extending 1,000 feet into the air, resembling a tornado funnel cloud. With the cocksure males stubbornly assembled over your head, females will fly into their horde to find a suitable mate. While males will mate frequently in a lifetime, one dose of sperm is all the female needs to produce numerous batches of offspring. She stores the sperm and dispenses them piecemeal for each separate birthing of eggs. Her short moment of passion has provided one of the two necessary components for procreation. The only ingredient missing is your blood.

Returning to our camping scenario, you just finished your strenuous hike and proceed to the shower, where you richly lather up with soap and shampoo. After toweling off, you apply a healthy dose of body spray and deodorant before finally putting on your bright red-and-blue beachwear. It is nearing dusk, dinnertime for the Anopheles mosquito, and you sit down in your lawn chair to relax with that well-deserved cold beer. You have done everything in your power to lure a famished female Anopheles mosquito (and by the way, I just moved to the seat that is farthest from you). Having just mated in a swarming frenzy of eager male suitors, she willingly takes your bait and makes off with a few drops of your blood.

She has taken a blood meal three times her own body weight, so she quickly finds the nearest vertical surface and, with the aid of gravity, continues to evacuate the water from your blood. Using this concentrated blood, she will develop her eggs over the next few days. She then deposits roughly 200 floating eggs on the surface of a small pool of water that has collected on a crushed beer can that was overlooked during cleanup as you and your party headed home. She always lays her eggs in water, although she does not need much. From a pond or stream to a minuscule collection in the bottom of an old container, used tire, or backyard toy, any will suffice. Certain types of mosquitoes desire specific types of water—fresh, salt, or brackish (a mixture)—while for others, any water will do the trick.

Our mosquito will continue to bite and lay eggs during her short life span of an average one to three weeks to an infrequent maximum longevity of five months. While she can fly up to two miles, she, like most mosquitoes, rarely ranges farther than 400 meters from her birthplace. Although it takes a few days longer in cool weather, given the high temperatures, her eggs hatch into wiggling water-bound worms (children) within two to three days. Skimming the water for food, these quickly turn into upside-down, comma-shaped tumbling caterpillars (teenagers) who breathe through two "trumpets" protruding from their water-exposed buttocks. A few days later, a protective encasement splits and healthy adult mosquitoes take to flight, with a new generation of succubus females anxious to feed on you once more. This impressive maturation to adulthood takes roughly one week.

The repetition of this life cycle has been uninterrupted on planet Earth since the first appearance of modern mosquitoes. Research suggests that mosquitoes, identical in appearance to those of today, surfaced as early as 190 million years ago. Amber, which is essentially petrified tree sap or resin, represents the crown jewels of fossilized insects, for it captures minute details such as webs, eggs, and the complete intact innards of its entombed. The two oldest fossilized mosquitoes on record are those preserved in amber from Canada and Myanmar dating from 105 to 80 million years ago. While the global environments these original bloodsuckers patrolled would be unrecognizable to us today, the mosquito remains the same.

Our planet was vastly different from the one we currently inhabit, as were most of the animals that called it home. If we navigate the evolution of life on earth, the devious partnership between insects and disease becomes strikingly clear. Single-cell bacteria were the first life-form to appear not long after the creation of our planet roughly 4.5 billion years ago. Spawning from a cauldron of gases and primordial oceanic ooze, they quickly established themselves, forming a biomass twenty-five times larger than all other plants and animals combined, and the foundation of petroleum and other fossil fuels. In one day, a single bacterium can spawn a culture of over four sextillion (twenty-one zeros), more than all other life on the planet. They are the essential ingredient and building block for all other life on earth. As specification commenced, asexual, cell-dividing bacteria adapted and found safer and more favorable homes as permanent guests on or in other host creatures. The human body contains one hundred times as many bacterial cells as it does human cells. For the most part, these symbiotic relationships are generally beneficial to the host as well as to the bacterial boarders.

It is the handful of negative pairings that cause problems. Currently, over one million microbes have been identified, yet only 1,400 have the potential to cause harm to humans.* Twelve ounces (a standard-size pop can) of the toxin produced by the bacterium that causes botulism food poisoning, for example, is enough to kill every human being on the planet. Viruses then arrived, quickly followed by parasites, both mirroring the housing arrangements of their bacterial parent, ushering in the potent combinations for disease and death. The sole parental responsibility of these microbes is to reproduce . . . and . . . to reproduce.† Bacteria, viruses, and parasites, along with worms and fungi, have triggered untold misery and have commanded the course of human history. Why have these pathogens evolved to exterminate their hosts?

If we can set aside our bias for a moment, we can see that these microbes have journeyed through the natural selection voyage just as we have. This is why they still make us sick and are so difficult to eradicate. You may be puzzled: It seems self-defeating and detrimental to kill your host. The disease kills us, yes, but the symptoms of the disease are ways in which the microbe conscripts us to help it spread and reproduce. It is dazzlingly clever, when you stop to think about it. Generally, germs guarantee their contagion and replication *prior* to killing their hosts.

Some, like the salmonella "food poisoning" bacteria and various worms, wait to be ingested; that is one animal eating another animal. There is a wide range of water-borne/diarrhea transmitters, including giardia, cholera, typhoid, dysentery, and hepatitis. Others, including the common cold, the twenty-four-hour flu, and true influenza, are passed on through coughing and sneezing. Some, like smallpox, are transferred directly or indirectly by lesions, open sores, contaminated objects, or coughing. My personal favorites, strictly from an evolutionary standpoint of course, are those that covertly ensure their reproduction while we intimately ensure our own! These include the full gamut of microbes

---

* It is estimated that there are about one trillion species of microbes on our planet, meaning 99.999% have yet to be unearthed.

† Unlike bacteria, viruses are not cells—they are a collection of molecules and genetic hardwiring. Viruses are not considered "alive" because they lack three fundamental properties associated with living organisms. Viruses lack the ability to reproduce without the aid of a host cell. They hijack the reproductive equipment of a host cell, redirecting it to "photocopy" its own viral genetic code. Viruses also cannot multiply through cell division. Finally, they do not have a metabolism of any kind, meaning that they do not need or consume energy to survive. Given the absolute necessity to have a host in order to reproduce, viruses affect nearly every life-form on earth.

that trigger sexually transmitted diseases. Many sinister pathogens are passed from mother to fetus in utero.

Others that germinate typhus, bubonic plague, Chagas, trypanosomiasis (African sleeping sickness), and the catalogue of diseases that are the concern of this book, catch a free ride provided by a vector (an organism that transmits disease) such as fleas, mites, flies, ticks, and our darling mosquito. To maximize their chances of survival, many germs use a combination of more than one method. The diverse collection of symptoms, or modes of transference, assembled by microorganisms is expert evolutionary selection to effectively procreate and ensure the existence of their species. These germs fight for their survival just as much as we do and stay an evolutionary step ahead of us as they continue to morph and shape-shift to circumvent our best means of extermination.

Dinosaurs, whose long progeny lasted from 230 to 65 million years ago, ruled the earth for an astounding 165 million years. But they were not alone on the planet. Insects and their illnesses were present before, during, and after the reign of dinosaurs. First appearing some 350 million years ago, insects quickly attracted a toxic army of diseases, creating an unprecedented lethal alliance. Jurassic mosquitoes and sand flies were soon armed with these biological weapons of mass destruction. As bacteria, viruses, and parasites continued to insidiously and expertly evolve, they expanded their living space and real estate portfolio to include a zoological Noah's Ark of animal safe houses. In classic Darwinian selection, more hosts increase the probability of survival and procreation.

Undaunted by these behemoth dinosaurs, belligerent hordes of mosquitoes sought them out as prey. "These insect-borne infections together with already long-established parasites became more than the dinosaurs' immune systems could handle," theorize paleobiologists George and Roberta Poinar in their book *What Bugged the Dinosaurs?*. "With their deadly weapons, biting insects were the top predators in the food chain and could now shape the destiny of the dinosaurs just as they shape our world today." Millions of years ago, also just like today, insatiable mosquitoes found a way to secure their blood snack—this buzz-and-bite happy meal remains unchanged.

Thin-skinned dinosaurs, equivalent to modern-day chameleons and

Gila monsters (both of which carry numerous mosquito-borne diseases), were ripe quarry for tiny, inconspicuous mosquitoes. Even the heavily armored beasts would have been vulnerable, since the skin flanked by the thick keratin (like our fingernails) scales of plated dinosaurs was an easy target, as was the skin of feathered, downy dinosaurs. In short, they were all fair game, just as birds, mammals, reptiles, and amphibians all are today.

Think about our mosquito seasons, or your personal, often protracted, skirmishes with these tenacious enemies. We cover up our skin, we soak ourselves in repellent, we light citronella candles and burn coils, huddle around a fire, we swat and flail, and we fortify our positions with nets, screens, and tents. Yet, no matter how hard we try, the mosquito will always find the chink in our armor and nip our Achilles heel. She will not be denied her self-evident, unalienable right to procreate by way of our blood. She will target that one exposed area, pierce our clothing, and outmaneuver our best efforts to stymie her unrelenting assault and celebratory meal. It was no different for the dinosaurs, only they had no defensive measures.*

Given the tropical, wet conditions, during the age of dinosaurs, mosquitoes would have bred and been active all year round, increasing their numbers and potency. Experts liken it to swarms of mosquitoes in the Canadian Arctic. "There aren't a lot of animals for them to eat in the Arctic, so when they finally find one, they are ferocious," says Dr. Lauren Culler, an entomologist at Dartmouth's Institute of Arctic Studies. "They are relentless. They do not stop. You can be completely covered in a matter of seconds." The more time reindeer and caribou spend fleeing the onslaught of mosquitoes, the less time they spend eating, migrating, or socializing, causing a severe decline in populations. Ravenous mosquito swarms literally bleed young caribou to death at a bite rate of 9,000 per minute, or by way of comparison, they can drain half the blood from an adult human in just two hours!

* It is scientific speculation as to whether they were equipped with retractable, folding skin on their backs like our wrinkled modern-day elephants. When a swarm of mosquitoes settles on the smooth skin of an elephant, it suddenly contracts its skin into a series of accordion-like waves, crushing the unsuspecting mosquitoes. Since elephants cannot reach their backs with their tail or trunk, this ingenious evolutionary adaptation solves the problem.

Amber-encased mosquito specimens contain the blood of dinosaurs infected with various mosquito-borne diseases, including malaria, a forerunner to yellow fever, and worms similar to those that now cause heartworm in dogs and elephantiasis in humans. After all, in Michael Crichton's novel *Jurassic Park,* dinosaur blood/DNA was extracted from the guts of amber-encased mosquitoes. CRISPR-like technology genetically engineered new living dinosaurs, creating a lucrative prehistoric theme park version of African Lion Safari. There is one small but important detail amiss with this script—the mosquito depicted in Steven Spielberg's 1993 blockbuster movie adaptation is one of the few species that *does not* require blood to reproduce!

Many of the mosquito-borne illnesses that afflict humans and animals today were present during the age of the dinosaurs and ravaged populations with deadly precision. A blood vessel from a T. rex revealed the unmistakable signs of both malaria and other parasitic worms, as does coprolite (petrified dinosaur dung) from numerous species. Mosquitoes currently transmit twenty-nine different forms of malaria to reptiles, although symptoms are absent or tolerable, as reptiles have built up an acquired immunity to this ancient disease. Dinosaurs, however, would have been void of such a shield, because at that time, malaria was a new recruit, joining the team of mosquito-borne diseases roughly 130 million years ago. "When arthropod-borne malaria was a relatively new disease," hypothesize the Poinars, "the effects on dinosaurs could have been devastating until some degree of immunity was acquired . . . malarial organisms had already evolved their complicated life cycle." Recently, when a handful of these diseases were injected into chameleons, the entire batch of test subjects died. While many of these diseases are not generally lethal, they would have been debilitating, like they are today. Dinosaurs would have been left incapacitated, sick, or lethargic, and vulnerable to attack or easy prey for carnivores.

History does not warehouse well in neatly labeled boxes, for events do not exist in quarantined isolation. They exist on a broad spectrum, and all influence and shape each other. Historical episodes are rarely built on the ground of a single foundation. Most are the product of a tangled web of influences and cascading cause-and-effect relationships within a broader historical narrative. The mosquito and her diseases are no different.

Take, for example, our dinosaur collapse model. While the dinosaur-disease extinction theory has gained traction and credibility over the last decade, it does not supplant or supersede the common and long-held earth-shattering-meteor collapse model. There is ample evidence and data from a breadth of scientific fields to indicate that a deep impact, leaving a crater the size of the state of Vermont, did occur 65.5 million years ago just west of Cancun in Mexico's now touristy Yucatan Peninsula.

Dinosaurs, however, were already in drastic decline. It is theorized that up to 70% of regional species were already extinct or endangered. The asteroid strike, with the subsequent nuclear winter and cataclysmic climate change, was the knockout punch, accelerating their inevitable disappearance. Sea levels and temperatures plunged and the earth's ability to sustain life was harshly destabilized. "Whether a catastrophist or gradualist, you cannot discount the probability that diseases," conclude the Poinars, "especially those vectored by miniscule [*sic*] insects, played an important role in exterminating the dinosaurs." Long before the emergence of modern Homo sapiens, the mosquito was wreaking havoc and substantially altering the course of life on earth. Aided by her role in eliminating these top-tier dinosaur predators, mammals, including our direct prehominid ancestors, evolved and flourished.

The relatively sudden disappearance of the dinosaurs allowed the few dazed but determined survivors to rise from the ashes to eke out an existence in a dark, unforgiving wasteland of wildfires, earthquakes, volcanoes, and acid rain. Patrolling this apocalyptic landscape were legions of heat-seeking mosquitoes. After the asteroid impact, smaller animals, many equipped with night vision, prospered. They required less food, were not finicky eaters, had more options for shelter from the raging inferno, and no longer had to fear for their safety. Two of the most adaptable groups to survive, thrive, and ultimately spawn a variety of new species were mammals and insects. Another was beaked birds, the only animal living today that is thought to be a direct descendant of dinosaurs. Given this unbroken family tree, birds harbored and disseminated numerous mosquito-borne diseases to a vast array of other animal species. Birds are still a primary reservoir for numerous mosquito-induced viruses, including West Nile and an assortment of encephalitides. Within this maelstrom of rebirth, regeneration, and evolutionary expansion, the ongoing war between man and mosquito was made.

While dinosaurs perished, the bugs that aided in their demise endured to inject death and disease into humanity throughout our history. They are the ultimate survivors. Insects remain the most prolific and diverse catalogue of creatures on our planet, accounting for 57% of all living organisms, and an astounding 76% of all animal life. When compared to mammals, which comprise a paltry 0.35% of species, these numbers heighten the overall impact of insects. They quickly became asylums and the optimal hosts for various bacteria, viruses, and parasites. The sheer volume and variety of insects offered these microorganisms a greater chance for continued existence.

The natural transmission of diseases from animals to humans is termed zoonosis ("animal sickness" in Greek) or more commonly referred to as "spillover." Currently, zoonosis accounts for 75% of all human diseases, and is on the rise. The group that has seen the sharpest increase over the last fifty years is the arboviruses. These are viruses that are transmitted by arthropod vectors like ticks, gnats, and mosquitoes. In 1930, only six such viruses were known to cause disease in humans, with mosquito-borne yellow fever being by far the most deadly. The current total now stands at 505. Many older viruses have been formally identified, and new ones, including West Nile and Zika, made the swing from animal to human hosts through an insect vector, in this case the mosquito.

Given our genetic similarities and common origin, 20% of our diseases are shared by, and transferred from, our ape cousins through various vectors, including mosquitoes. She and her diseases have stalked us through our evolutionary tree with dexterous Darwinian precision. Fossil evidence suggests that a form of the malaria parasite, which made its first appearance in birds 130 million years ago, plagued our primary human ancestors as early as 6 to 8 million years ago. It was precisely at this time that early hominids and chimpanzees, our closest relative with 96%

identical DNA, shared a final common ancestor, and the humanoid line diverged from that of the great apes.*

Our primordial malaria parasite companion shadowed both evolutionary lines and is currently shared by humans and all great apes. In fact, it is theorized that our hominid line gradually shed our thick fur to keep cool on the African savannah while making it easier to find and combat body parasites and biting insects. "Malaria, the oldest and cumulatively the deadliest of the human infectious diseases, seeped into our very earliest human history," emphasizes historian James Webb in *Humanity's Burden*, offering a sweeping account of the disease. "Malaria is thus an ancient and a modern scourge. For much of its career it left little trace. It sickened us in early epochs, long before we were able to record our experiences. Even in recent millennia, it has frequently lain silent in the diverse records of our pasts, too common a disease to claim much notice. At other times, epidemic malaria has careened violently across the landscapes of world history, leaving death and suffering in its wake." Dr. W. D. Tiggert, an early malariologist at Walter Reed Army Medical Center, bemoaned, "Malaria, like the weather, appears to have always been with the human race, and as Mark Twain said about the weather, it seems that very little has been done about it." Compared to mosquitoes and malaria, Homo sapiens is a new kid on the Darwinian block. It is generally accepted that we began our rapid ascent as modern Homo sapiens ("wise man") only roughly 200,000 years ago.† At any rate, we are a relatively new species.

To understand the sprawling and stealthy influence of the mosquito on history and humanity, it is first necessary to appreciate the animal itself and the diseases it transmits. I am not an entomologist, a malariologist, or a physician of tropical medicine. Nor am I one of the countless unsung heroes fighting in the trenches of the ongoing medical and

* Currently humans and chimps share 99.4% of critical nonsynonymous or "functionally important" DNA and are ten times more closely related than are mice and rats. Given this close genetic relationship, some scientists have argued that the two living species of chimpanzees (the bonobo and the common chimpanzee) belong in the genus Homo currently occupied only by modern humans.

† Adhering to acclaimed historian Alfred W. Crosby's paradigm, these dates and others cited are subject to discrepancy and controversy. For our purposes, we will focus on chronology and relative time frames, not absolute dates.

scientific war against mosquitoes. I am a historian. I leave the complex scientific explanations of the mosquito and her pathogens in the hands of these experts. Entomologist Dr. Andrew Spielman advises us, "To meet the health threats that are growing worse in many corners of the world, we must know the mosquito and see clearly her place in nature. More importantly, we should understand many aspects of our relationship to this tiny, ubiquitous insect, and appreciate our long, historical struggle to share this planet." In order to best appreciate the rest of our story, however, we first must know what we are up against. To encapsulate Chinese general Sun Tzu's timeless fifth-century BCE treatise, *The Art of War*: "Know your enemy."

According to an orthodox quotation erroneously attributed to Charles Darwin, "It is not the strongest of the species that survives, nor the most intelligent that survives. It is the one that is most adaptable to change."* Regardless of its origin, the mosquito and its diseases, most notably malaria parasites, are the quintessential example of this passage. They are masters of evolutionary adaptation. Mosquitoes can evolve and adapt quickly to their changing environments within a few generations. During the Blitz of 1940–1941, for example, as German bombs rained down on London, isolated populations of Culex mosquitoes were confined to the air-raid tunnel shelters of the Underground Tube along with the city's resilient citizens. These trapped mosquitoes quickly adapted to feed on mice, rats, and humans instead of birds and are now a species of mosquito distinct from their aboveground parental counterparts.† What should have taken thousands of years of evolution was accomplished by these mining sapper mosquitoes in less than one hundred years. "In another 100 years time," jokes Richard Jones, former president of the British Entomological and Natural History Society, "there may be separate Circle Line, Metropolitan Line and Jubilee Line mosquito species in the tunnels below London."

While the mosquito is miraculously adaptable, it is also a purely

* This often-referenced quotation does not appear in any of Darwin's published writings, journals, or letters.

† The British fighter-bomber aircraft Mosquito entered service in late 1941 shortly after the Battle of Britain.

narcissistic creature. Unlike other insects, it does not pollinate plants in any meaningful way or aerate the soil, nor does it ingest waste. Contrary to popular belief, the mosquito does not even serve as an indispensable food source for any other animal. She has no purpose other than to propagate her species and perhaps to kill humans. As the apex predator throughout our odyssey, it appears that her role in our relationship is to act as a countermeasure against uncontrolled human population growth.

In 1798, English cleric and scholar Thomas Malthus published his groundbreaking *An Essay on the Principle of Population*, outlining his ideas on political economy and demography. He argued that once an animal population has outpaced its resources, natural catastrophes or checks such as drought, famine, war, and disease will force a return to sustainable population levels and restore a healthy equilibrium. Malthus bleakly reasons, "The vices of mankind are active and able ministers of depopulation. They are the precursors in the great army of destruction, and often finish the dreadful work themselves. But should they fail in this war of extermination, sickly seasons, epidemics, pestilence, and plague advance in terrific array, and sweep off their thousands and tens

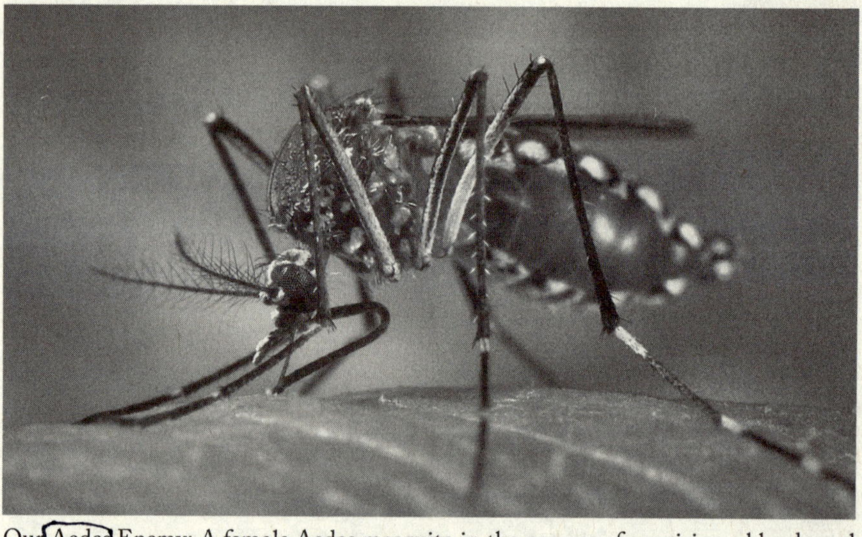

Our Aedes Enemy: A female Aedes mosquito in the process of acquiring a blood meal from her human host. Aedes mosquito species transmit a catalogue of mosquito-borne disease including the viruses that cause yellow fever, dengue, chikungunya, West Nile, Zika, and various encephalitides. *(James Gathany/Public Health Image Library-CDC)*

Our Anopheles Enemy: A female Anopheles mosquito obtaining a blood meal from a human host through her pointed proboscis. Note the secretion droplet being expelled to condense the protein content of the blood in her abdomen. Anopheles mosquito species are the sole vectors of the five human types of malaria plasmodium. *(James Gathany/ Public Health Image Library-CDC)*

of thousands. Should success be still incomplete, gigantic inevitable famine stalks in the rear." Enter the mosquito as the main human Malthusian check in this grim apocalyptic vision. This unrivaled dealing in death is primarily inflicted by only two perpetrators with no harm to themselves—Anopheles and Aedes mosquitoes. The leading ladies of these two species circulate the entire catalogue of more than fifteen mosquito-borne diseases.

Throughout our existence, the mosquito's toxic twins of malaria and yellow fever have been the prevailing agents of death and historical change and will largely play the role of antagonists in the protracted chronological war between man and mosquito. "It is not always easy to remember to give yellow fever and malaria their due. Mosquitoes and pathogens left no memoirs or manifestos. Before 1900, prevalent understanding of disease and health did not recognize their roles, and no one grasped their full significance," upholds J. R. McNeill. "Subsequently historians, living in the golden age of health, normally failed to see their significance either . . . But the mosquitoes and pathogens were there . . . and they had effects on human affairs that we can see reflected in archives and memoirs."

Yet malaria and yellow fever are only two of over fifteen diseases that the mosquito bestows upon humans. The others will provide the supporting ensemble cast in our story. Mosquito-borne pathogens can be separated into three groupings: viruses, worms, and protozoans (parasites).

The most abundant are the viruses: yellow fever, dengue, chikungunya, Mayaro, West Nile, Zika, and various encephalitides, including St. Louis, Equine, and Japanese. While debilitating, these diseases, aside from yellow fever, are generally not prolific killers. West Nile, Mayaro, and Zika are relatively new entries to the index of mosquito-borne disease. There are currently no vaccines, save that for yellow fever, but for the most part, survivors are blessed with lifetime immunity. Since they are closely related, common symptoms include fever, headaches, vomiting, rashes, and muscle and joint pain. These symptoms usually begin three to ten days after contagion from a mosquito bite. The vast majority of those infected recover within a week. Although exceptionally rare, severe cases can result in death caused by viral hemorrhagic fevers and a swelling of the brain (encephalitis). The old and young, pregnant women, and those with escorting medical issues make up the disproportionate bulk of casualties from these viral infections, which are all spread predominantly by the Aedes mosquito. Although globally present, the highest infection rates occur in Africa.

Occupying the top tier of the virus class is yellow fever, which often amplified and accompanied endemic malaria. It is an accomplished killer, first stalking humans in Africa about 3,000 years ago. Until recently, it was a global historical game-changer. This adversary targets healthy, young adults in the prime of life. Although a successful vaccine was discovered in 1937, between 30,000 and 50,000 people still die annually of yellow fever, with 95% of fatalities occurring in Africa. For about 75% of those infected with yellow fever, symptoms mirror those of its viral cousins mentioned above, and usually last three to four days. For the unlucky 25% or so, after a day of respite, they enter a second toxic phase of the disease complete with fever-induced delirium, jaundice due to liver damage, severe abdominal pain, diarrhea, and bleeding from the mouth, nose, and ears. The internal corrosion of the gastrointestinal tract and kidneys induces vomit of bile and blood, the consistency and color of coffee grounds—giving rise to the Spanish name for yellow fever, *vómito negro* (black vomit)—which is followed by coma and death. The latter, usually occurring two weeks after initial symptoms, might well have been the last pleading wish of many victims.

While this portrayal paints a grisly picture, it also embodies the gnawing terror that yellow fever implanted in pacing and brooding populations across the world, especially in the European colonial outposts of the New World. The first definitive outbreak in the Americas occurred in 1647, disembarking with African slaves and fugitive mosquitoes.* It must have been agonizing to wonder when and where "Yellow Jack," as the British christened it, would strike next. While fatality rates from yellow fever averaged around 25%, depending on the strain and conditions of an epidemic, it was not uncommon for death rates to reach 50%. A handful of outbreaks reached 85% in the Caribbean. The salty sea stories of ghost ships like the *Flying Dutchman* are based on true accounts; whole crews might succumb to yellow fever, months passing before the aimlessly drifting ships were corralled. Boarding parties were greeted with nothing but the stench of death and the rattle of skeletons with no revealing clues as to the cause. Luckily for survivors, who are left incapacitated for weeks, yellow fever is a one-shot deal. Lifetime immunity is imparted to those who defang the dogged virus. Although dengue, thought to have its 2,000-year-old ancestral origins in monkeys of Africa or Asia (or both), is far more benign than its close cousin, yellow fever, the two viruses can provide limited and partial cross-immunization.

Spread by the Aedes, Anopheles, and Culex mosquito breeds, the sole member of the worm category is filariasis, commonly referred to as elephantiasis. The worms invade and obstruct the lymphatic system, causing an accumulation of fluids resulting in extreme, if not spectacular, swelling of the lower extremities and genitals, while also frequently causing blindness. Engorged scrotums, easily surpassing the size of large beach

* Academics still debate the first appearance of yellow fever in the Americas, with some suggesting outbreaks as early as 1616.

Stigmata: This engraving from a 1614 British medical textbook depicts a woman showing the unmistakable symptoms of filariasis or "elephantiasis." *(Diomedia/Wellcome Library)*

balls, are not unusual. For women, the labia can become almost as grotesque. Although this stigmatizing disease is treatable with inexpensive modern medicine, unfortunately, 120 million people annually still suffer from filariasis, predominantly in the tropics of Africa and Southeast Asia.

Malaria stands alone in the protozoan, or parasite, classification. In 1883, Scottish biologist Henry Drummond called parasites "a breach in the laws of Evolution and the greatest crime against humanity." Malaria is *the* unsurpassed scourge of humankind. Currently, almost 300 million unlucky people annually contract malaria from the bite of an Anopheles mosquito, the very same one that bit you and stole your blood during your camping vacation. Without your having the slightest clue, the malaria parasite has entered your bloodstream and is making a mad dash for your liver, where it can rest and recuperate while it plans its procreative assault on your body. You, however, are back home from your camping trip, madly scratching your mosquito bites with the malaria parasite furtively hibernating in your liver. How sick you become, and your likelihood of death, is dependent upon which strain of malaria you have contracted.

It is possible to be infected with more than one species at a time, although usually within this battle the deadliest strain outperforms the others. They are all perpetrated by 70 of the 480 species of your Anopheles offender. There are over 450 different types of malaria parasites vexing animals across the world, with five of them afflicting humans. Three types, *knowlesi*, *ovale*, and *malariae*, are not only extremely rare but have a comparatively low mortality rate. *Knowlesi* recently made the zoonotic jump from the macaque monkey in Southeast Asia, while the uncommon *ovale* and *malariae* now exist almost exclusively in West Africa. We can rule out that you have contracted any of these three, which leaves us with the two most dangerous and widespread contenders battling for hegemony of your health and life—*vivax* and *falciparum*.

The malaria parasite roosting in your liver will traverse through an impressive seven-stage life cycle. It must have multiple hosts to survive and procreate—the mosquito and an army of secondary vectors: humans, apes, rats, bats, rabbits, porcupines, squirrels, a volery of birds, a congress of amphibians and reptiles, and a swarm of others. Unfortunately, you are that host.

Following that fateful mosquito bite, this miscreant will mutate and reproduce inside your liver for one to two weeks, during which time you will show no symptoms. A toxic army of this new form of the parasite will then explode out of your liver and invade your bloodstream. The parasites attach to your red blood cells, quickly penetrate the outer defenses, and feast on the inner hemoglobin. Inside the blood cell, they undergo another metamorphosis and reproductive cycle. Engorged blood cells eventually burst, spewing both a duplicate form, which marches forward to attack fresh red blood cells, and also a new "asexual" form that relaxedly floats in your bloodstream, waiting for mosquito transportation. The parasite is a shape-shifter, and it is precisely this genetic flexibility that makes it so difficult to eradicate or suppress with drugs or vaccines.

You are now gravely ill with an orderly, clockwork progression of chills followed by a mercury-driving fever touching 106 degrees. This full-blown cyclical malarial episode has you in its firm grip and you are at the mercy of the parasite. Lying prostrate and agonizingly helpless on sweat-soaked sheets, you twitch and fumble, curse and moan. You look down and notice that your spleen and liver are visibly enlarged, your skin has the yellowing patina of jaundice, and you vomit sporadically. Your mind-melting fever will relapse at precise intervals with each new burst and invasion of the parasite from your blood cells. The fever then subsides while the parasite eats and reproduces inside new blood cells.

The parasite uses sophisticated signaling to synchronize its sequencing, and this entire cycle adheres to a very strict schedule. This new smart hub asexual form transmits a chemical "bite me" signal in our blood, significantly boosting the chances of being picked up by a mosquito from an infected human to complete the reproductive cycle. Inside the stomach of the mosquito, these cells mutate once more, into both male and female varieties. They quickly mate, producing threadlike offspring versions of the parasite, which make their way out of the gut and into the salivary glands of the mosquito. Within the saliva glands, the malaria parasite shrewdly manipulates the mosquito to bite more frequently by suppressing the production of her anticoagulant to minimize her blood intake during a single feeding. This forces her to bite more frequently to get her required fill. In doing so, the malaria parasite ensures that it maximizes its rate and range of transfer, its procreation, and its survival. Malaria is a remarkable example of evolutionary adaptation.

It was this salivary configuration of the parasite that was transferred to you by that damned mosquito on the camping trip you took over two weeks ago. But the question remains: What type of malaria has left you incapacitated with enervating recurrent symptoms? If it is the dreaded *falciparum*, you may recover, or you may enter a second phase of the disease called cerebral or severe malaria. Within a day or two, you will experience seizures, coma, and death. The fatality rate from *falciparum* is dependent upon strain, location, and numerous other factors, but nevertheless straddles 25% to 50% of those infected. Of those who survive cerebral malaria, roughly 25% will have permanent neurological damage, including blindness, loss of speech, severe learning disabilities, or paralysis of the limbs. Malaria takes a life every thirty seconds. Sadly, 75% of the deceased are children under five years of age. *Falciparum* is the vampiric serial killer, accounting for 90% of malarial deaths, and Africa currently houses 85% of all global malarial deaths. Unlike yellow fever, malaria hunts the young and immunologically weak. Pregnant women also suffer disproportionately.

In this unfortunate scenario, if you are lucky enough to have contracted *vivax*, you probably will not die. *Vivax* is the most common form of malaria, especially outside of Africa, and is responsible for 80% of all malaria cases, but it is not generally a killer. Its mortality rate hovers around 5% in Africa, with an even lower 1–2% in the rest of the world.

It is almost impossible to describe the scale of the devastation the malarial Anopheles mosquito can wreak. Even today, the horror of malaria is hard to comprehend. So it is near unfathomable to imagine malaria in the historical context when causes were unknown and treatments did not exist. J. A. Sinton, an early-twentieth-century malariologist, conceded that the disease "constitutes one of the most important causes of economic misfortune, engendering poverty, diminishing the quantity and quality of the food supply, lowering the physical and intellectual standard of the nation, and hampering increased prosperity and economic progression in every way." Add to this description the physical, emotional, and psychological effects of such an enormous death toll. Currently, it is estimated that endemic malaria costs Africa roughly $30–$40 billion a year in lost commercial output. Economic growth in malarious countries is 1.3% to 2.5% lower than the adjusted global average. Cumulatively, spanning the modern era after the Second World War, this equates to a 35% lower gross domestic product (GDP) than it would have been in the absence of malaria. Malaria sickens and cripples economies.

Thankfully for you, the odds were in your favor and you shook off your stint of *vivax* malaria within a month. I am sorry to tell you, however, that your suffering is likely not over. Neither *falciparum* nor *knowlesi* causes malarial relapse. A second communicable bite from a malarious mosquito is required for reinfection. Regiments of parasites from the other three types of malaria, including *vivax*, however, lie in ambush in the liver, and can generate repeated relapses for up to twenty years. A British veteran of the Second World War had a malarial encore forty-five years after his infection in 1942 during the Burma campaign. In your case, the time frame for *vivax* is generally one to three years. Nevertheless, you can always be reinjected by another mosquito bite.

Temperature is an important element for both mosquito reproduction and the life cycle of malaria. Given their symbiotic relationship, they are also both climate-sensitive. In colder temperatures, it takes longer for mosquito eggs to mature and hatch. Mosquitoes are also cold-blooded and, unlike mammals, cannot regulate their own body temperatures. They simply cannot survive in mercury-dipping environments below 50 degrees. Mosquitoes are generally at their prime health and peak performance in temperatures above 75 degrees. A direct heat of 105 degrees will boil mosquitoes to death. For temperate, nontropical zones, this means that mosquitoes are seasonal creatures with breeding, hatching, and biting taking place from spring through fall. Although never seeing the outside world, malaria needs to contend with both the short life span of the mosquito and temperature conditions to ensure replication. The time frame of malaria reproduction is dependent upon the temperature of the cold-blooded mosquito, which itself is dependent upon the temperature outside. The colder the mosquito, the more sluggish malaria reproduction becomes, eventually hitting a threshold. Between 60 and 70 degrees (depending on the type of malaria), the reproductive cycle of the parasite can take up to a month, exceeding the average life span of the mosquito. By then, she is long dead and brings malaria down with her.

In your case, you might have avoided this whole bloody malarial ordeal if you had decided on either a frigid or a blisteringly hot vacation destination, or elected not to brave the wilds during the mosquito's peak campaigning season (in most temperate zones) of late spring to early fall. Alternatively, you could have opted out of your camping vacation altogether.

In short, warmer climates can sustain year-round mosquito populations promoting *endemic* (chronic and ever-present) circulation of her diseases. Abnormally high temperatures from the effects of La Niña or El Niño can cause seasonal *epidemics* (a sudden outbreak of a disease that burns through populations before fading away) of mosquito-borne diseases in regions where they are generally absent or fleeting. Intervals of natural or artificially induced global warming also allow the mosquito and her diseases to broaden their topographical range. As temperatures rise, disease-carrying species, usually confined to southern regions and lower altitudes, creep north and into higher elevations.

The dinosaurs could not survive the meteoric crashing climate change, and they could not evolve quickly enough to outrun the onslaught of mosquito-borne disease. The tiny mosquito helped pave the way for their destruction, escorting in the evolutionary age of mammals, our hominid ancestors, and, eventually, modern Homo sapiens. As a survivor, she also set the table for her historic flight to global ascendancy. Unlike the dinosaurs, however, humans evolved to fight back. Through hasty natural selection, suits of hereditary immunological armor against the mosquito have been passed down through our Homo sapien family tree. Our DNA displays these genetically encoded keepsakes as reminders of the deadly and protracted war for survival our early ancestors fought against a merciless mosquito enemy.

CHAPTER 2

Survival of the Fittest: Fever Demons, Footballs, and Sickle Cell Safeties

Ryan Clark Jr. was the epitome of health and in the prime of his life. As a starting safety in the National Football League (NFL), the thirty-one-year-old Clark was a famous, finely tuned professional athlete, lean and muscular at five feet eleven and 205 pounds. He was married to his high school sweetheart and had three beautiful young children. He had recently signed a lucrative new contract with the Pittsburgh Steelers to open the 2007 season. Life was good.

Midway through the season, he and the Steelers headed to Denver to play the Broncos and lost in a heartbreaker—brought down by a last-minute field goal. A disheartened Clark boarded the plane for the long flight home. Just before takeoff, he experienced an acute stabbing pain under his left ribs. He was accustomed to the routine wear and tear and bumps and bruises on his body following a tough, physical football game. This, however, was something different, a piercing and wrenching pang he had never experienced before. "I called my wife and told her I didn't think I was going to make it," he remembered. "I'd never been in that much pain." His concerned teammates and the Steelers medical staff acted quickly. The flight was immediately halted on the tarmac and Clark was rushed to a Denver hospital. A few days later, after being stabilized, Clark flew back home to Pittsburgh and was placed on injured reserve, although his doctors had not yet identified the cause of his puzzling symptoms.

Over the next month, he had nightly teeth-chattering chills melting into fevers reaching 104 degrees. Clark lost forty pounds, transforming into a sickly skeleton of his former strapping self. One night, his pain was so severe, he was certain he was going to die. Clark recalls uttering a silent prayer, "God, if it's my time, let my wife find a good husband. Let him not be as good-looking as me, but let him be a good guy. Take care of my family. Please forgive me for my sins. I'm ready." He survived that terrifying night and eventually after another month of inconclusive medical examinations, his doctors finally intercepted the cause of his distress and agony. Clark was diagnosed with splenetic infarction—that is, the tissue death of his spleen. He was rushed into surgery and his rotting spleen and gall bladder were removed. The underlying cause of organ failure in such a healthy, young adult still needed to be isolated and identified.

As athletes have known for decades, playing in Denver can be strenuous and exacting. The city sits 5,280 feet above sea level, and unlike their home-field opponents, visiting players are not acclimatized to the thin air. They struggle to catch a full breath and to provide enough oxygen to their working muscles, compounded by the physical exertion of professional competition. While a slight shortness of breath is anticipated, no one expects to die from a road trip to Denver's Mile High Stadium.

Unbelievably, Clark returned to football and a year later won the 2009 Super Bowl with the Steelers. His celebration was unfortunately cut short. Two weeks later, his twenty-seven-year-old sister-in-law died of a congenital blood disease. After thirteen years of NFL football, Clark retired in 2014 on his own terms. To understand what happened to Ryan Clark in Denver we need to travel back thousands of years into prehistory.

Hooded and cloaked in his DNA at the time of his health crisis, Clark's hereditary sickle cell trait, commonly called sickle cell anemia, triggered his near-death experience. As a genetic mutation of the red blood cells, sickle cell impedes the transport and delivery of oxygen to muscles and organs. In Denver's oxygen-reduced atmosphere, and with its amplified demand by an elite athlete, Clark's body tissues were starved of oxygen. His spleen and gall bladder simply shut down, and necrosis set in.

Advanced by natural selection, sickle cell is a hereditary genetic mutation passed on precisely because it was originally a net *benefit* to the people who carried it. Yes, you read that correctly. The evolutionary design that nearly killed Ryan Clark was initially a lifesaving human genetic adaptation. Clark's sickle cell, which first appeared in Africa 7,300 years ago in a female known to anthropologists as "Sickle Cell Eve," is the most recent and well-known genetic response to *falciparum* malaria.

This first appearance of sickle cell was a direct result of expansive agriculture encroaching on formerly undisturbed mosquito habitats. Roughly 8,000 years ago, pioneering Bantu farmers began concentrated yam and plantain cultivation. This pastoral intensification in West Central Africa along the Niger River delta, slashing south to the Congo River, awoke the mosquito from her isolated slumber. The consequences could hardly have been more catastrophic: Vampiric *falciparum* malaria was unleashed on its new human host. Within only 700 years, our immediate evolutionary counteroffensive, which bewildered the parasite, was to promote a random mutation of the hemoglobin—the cell became sickle (or crescent) shaped. Normally, healthy red blood cells are cast from a donut or oval template. The malaria parasite cannot latch on to the strange-shaped sickle cell.

Children inheriting sickle cell from one parent and the normal gene from the other, known as sickle cell trait, of which Ryan Clark is a carrier, are blessed with 90% immunity from *falciparum* malaria. The downside (prior to modern medicine) was that the average life span of those carrying sickle cell trait was a brief twenty-three years. This would have been a great trade-off, however, in what anthropologists call our "ancestral environment," where life spans were relatively short—twenty-three years is certainly long enough to pass on the trait to 50% of any offspring. In the modern era, however, this genetic interceptor and safety against *falciparum* malaria turns out to be a severe health impediment for modern NFL players, or anyone else who is a carrier and would like to live to the ripe old age of, say, twenty-four. The other downside within this Punnett square hereditary matrix is that 25% of offspring would receive no sickle cell and therefore no immunity, with the other 25% receiving two sickle cell genes. Those born with sickle cell from both parents, or sickle cell disease (which killed Ryan Clark's sister-in-law two weeks after he hoisted the NFL championship Lombardi Trophy), inherit a death sentence, with the vast majority dying in infancy.

While it now seems inconceivable, in areas of Africa that were devastated by unremitting *falciparum* malaria, the death toll from sickle cell resulted from *an advantage*, or alternatively was an acceptable cost, for survival, compared to what must have been apocalyptic rates of malarial mortality. Despite the influx of sickle cell, the preadult death rate prior to 1500 was upwards of 55% in sub-Saharan Africa.

Given that sickle cell both gives and takes away life, it was a hasty and imperfect evolutionary response to mosquito-borne malaria. What it reveals, though, is the sheer scale of the threat *falciparum* malaria posed to early humans and by extension our very existence: It was arguably the paramount evolutionary survival pressure on our species. It is almost as if the biological architect of our selective genetic sequencing implicitly understood, "There is no time for research and clinical trials. Hurry up and make a quick fix to ensure the survival of our species. We will worry about the rest later." Desperate times called for desperate measures.

The genetic distribution of sickle cell shadowed the spread of humans, mosquitoes, and malaria in and out of Africa. Today, there are about 50–60 million carriers of sickle cell worldwide, with 80% still living in its birthplace, sub-Saharan Africa. Regionally, there are pockets in Africa, the Middle East, and South Asia where upwards of 40% of the population harbor the sickle cell gene. The modern global diffusion of sickle cell is a hereditary reminder of our deadly and protracted war with the mosquito.

One in twelve, or 4.2 million, African Americans currently possess the sickle cell trait, creating a safety issue for the National Football League, in which 70% of its players are potential carriers. With Clark's terrifying and perilous experience, the league finally was provided the scare and the impetus to study sickle cell. It was quickly discovered that other players were also genetic receivers of this ancient guard against *falciparum* malaria. Each year a handful of competitors, like Ryan Clark, are unable to participate at the high-altitude stadium of the Denver

Broncos because they possess the sickle cell trait. "The good thing is people are living longer and being a lot more productive," Clark told reporters in 2015. "People are starting to understand sickle cell a little bit more. People have gained the knowledge to know how to take care of themselves."

He created the charity organization Ryan Clark's Cure League in 2012 to raise awareness and research about sickle cell. The former All-Pro, Super Bowl champion now makes the rounds giving frequent lectures and making guest appearances to discuss the disease and educate his audiences about its deep-rooted, mosquito-reared human history. While Clark's northern home of Pittsburgh is hardly a malarial mecca, one of his three children inherited the sickle cell trait, a living legacy of their African ancestors' fierce fight for survival against the mosquito and of the long trajectory of her genetic impact across time. The mosquito and her pathogens, which are at least 165 million years old, have hitchhiked on board our wild evolutionary ride.

In this primal lopsided battle, however, the mosquito and her malarial parasite have had the overwhelming advantage. She had millions of years' head start on the journey of evolution and natural selection. The malaria parasite, for instance, began its life as a form of aquatic algae 600 to 800 million years ago, and still contains vestiges of photosynthesis machinery. As we evolved, these viruses and parasites, eager for new outlets, met our challenge and adapted to ensure their survival. Thankfully, for us, Lucy and her successive hominid offspring managed to outlast the onslaught of mosquito-borne diseases.* To safeguard our own species, we fought back through natural selection, giving rise to a series of genetically encoded antimalarial armors, including sickle cell. These immunological defenses are all human evolutionary survival responses to inescapable and menacing malaria exposure.

In this never-ending cyclical war for survival linking man and mosquito we retaliated by way of genetic malaria-shielding mutations of our red blood cells. Approximately 10% of humans have inherited some

* The famous hominin skeleton Lucy, dating from 3.2 million years ago, acquired her household name from the 1967 song *"Lucy in the Sky with Diamonds"* by the Beatles, which played loudly on repeat the day she was discovered in the Ethiopian Awash Valley in 1974 by Donald Johanson.

degree of genetic protection against the two most common and deadly types of the five human malaria plasmodia: *vivax* and *falciparum*. There is a catch, however. These malarial screens, as revealed by Ryan Clark's sickle cell, also carry serious, sometimes fatal, health-related penalties.

First appearing in the African population roughly 97,000 years ago, red blood cell Duffy antigen negativity, or simply Duffy negativity, was the inaugural human genetic response to the scourge of *vivax* malaria. The *vivax* parasite uses the antigen receptor on the hemoglobin molecule as a gateway to invade our red blood cells (like a shuttle docking at a space station or a sperm entering an egg). The absence of this antigen, that is, Duffy negativity, closes the portal, denying the parasite entrance to the red blood cell. Currently, an astonishing 97% of West and Central Africans carry the mutation for Duffy negativity, making them impervious to *vivax* and *knowlesi* infection. Some communities, such as the Pygmy, are effectively 100% Duffy negative. While Duffy negativity was the first of the four genetic human malaria responses to arise, it was the last to be scientifically unmasked. Despite this shorter research life, a few negative health correlations have been detected. Current studies have revealed a higher predisposition to asthma, pneumonia, and various cancers in those with Duffy negativity. Even more alarming is that Duffy negativity also increases the susceptibility to HIV infection by 40%.

As both man and malaria ventured out of Africa, isolated and pocketed populations developed their own genetic answers to the malaria question. Thalassemia, which is an abnormal production or mutation of the hemoglobin, reduces the risk of *vivax* malaria by 50%. Today, thalassemia occurs in roughly 3% of the global population and is particularly prevalent among peoples from southern Europe, the Middle East, and North Africa. Historically, malaria had a firm grip on this Mediterranean expanse, which led to another fascinating genetic mutation to combat the far more lethal *falciparum* strain.

Identified in the early 1950s, and usually called G6PDD (an abbreviation for the tongue-twisting mouthful of Glucose-6-phosphate dehydrogenase deficiency), this modification robs red blood cells of an enzyme that protects the cell against oxygen-raiding substances known as oxidants. Antioxidants in trendy "superfoods" that include blueberries, broccoli, kale, spinach, and pomegranate, combat oxidants by promoting the healthy oxygen maintenance and transport capacity of our red blood cells. Similar to thalassemia, G6PDD offers partial immunity to malaria but not near-complete immunity as do Duffy negativity and sickle cell. Carriers do not show any negative symptoms unless their red blood cells are exposed to a trigger, prompting what has been called "Baghdad Fever" for centuries, which has a range of symptoms, from lethargy, fever, and nausea, to death on rare occasions.

Unfortunately, the triggers include antimalarial drugs such as quinine, chloroquine, and primaquine. *M*A*S*H* aficionados may well remember the episode where Corporal Klinger develops a serious illness after being prescribed primaquine. Given Klinger's Lebanese ancestry, this is cinematically accurate, for G6PDD primarily affects those of Mediterranean and North African origin. The most common trigger is fava beans, which is why the condition is commonly known as favism. As a precaution, it became customary across the Mediterranean world to cook fava beans with rosemary, cinnamon, nutmeg, garlic, onion, basil, or cloves, all of which dull the effects of favism and soften its symptomatic blow. In fact, the famed Greek philosopher and mathematician Pythagoras was warning his people of the dangers of eating fava beans in the sixth century BCE.

The final resistance to malaria in our defensive arsenal, enlisted alongside Duffy negativity, thalassemia, G6PDD, and sickle cell, is repeated infection, commonly labeled "seasoning." Those who suffer chronic malarial infections build up a marginal tolerance to the parasite, producing milder symptoms with each infection, while nullifying the risk of death. I hardly suggest that this is a positive or pleasant inoculation strategy, but in areas with rampant malaria rates, it might be argued that the more you suffer, the less you suffer. "Seasoning" will be an important ingredient in our story. Local seasoning to mosquito-borne disease was a critical factor during the wars of colonization and liberation in the Americas in the shadows of the Columbian Exchange. The origins of both malaria and our various evolutionary shields against it occurred in Africa. The longer association of Africans with mosquito-borne diseases and their corresponding full or partial acquired immunities bent by natural selection would have severe repercussions during the dark days of slavery.

Natural selection, including our genetic buffers against malaria, is a process of trial and error. As Charles Darwin surmised, those genetic mutations that aid in the survival of a species are passed down the family tree. Those lacking these mutations, or inheriting other undesirable modifications, simply die off within the constant competitive clash for survival or what Darwin declared "the preservation of the favoured races in the struggle for life." Individuals who possess these advantageous mutations, like sickle cell, persist or live just long enough to procreate and continue their genetic inheritance and, more important, the preservation of their species. Gradually, the adaptable survivors "breed out" those who do not possess these favorable traits—simple and uncomplicated survival of the fittest.*

The healing properties of medicines, both natural and now synthesized, are also unearthed through an experimental trial-and-error form of natural selection. When our hungry hominid ancestor perished because of eating appetizing but poisonous berries, this forbidden fruit was quickly scratched from the grocery lists of their observant and insightful companions. Over time, our hominid and human hunter-gatherer grandparents catalogued a lengthy mental Rolodex of do and do-not eats and treats. In the process, they also realized the medicinal properties of certain plants. Theirs was an austere and unforgiving existence and they experimented with the natural world around them to assuage their afflicting maladies and ward off the hungry hordes of mosquitoes.

Like the malaria parasite itself, knowledge of naturopathic remedies survived the evolutionary jump from ape to human. Chimpanzees still chew the mululuza shrub, as did our ancestors, to provide relief from malaria. It is still a common ingredient in soups and stews among the peoples of equatorial Africa, the epicenter of malaria's stretching

* The term "survival of the fittest" is commonly, and mistakenly, attributed to Darwin. English biologist and anthropologist Herbert Spencer first used and coined the catchphrase in his 1864 book *Principles of Biology* after reading Darwin's book *On the Origin of Species*, first published in 1859. Darwin then used/borrowed the term from Spencer for the 5th edition of his book, released in 1869.

domain. Interestingly, the mululuza shrub comes from the same family of plants as chrysanthemums, or pyrethrum—the first known commercial pesticide. The dried and pulverized flowers found their insecticidal use in China around 1000 BCE before spreading to the Middle East around 400 BCE and acquiring the nickname "Persian Powder." When ground and mixed with water or oil and sprayed, or applied in powdered form, the active ingredients (called pyrethrins) attack the nervous system of insects, including mosquitoes.

As a result, the symbolism associated with chrysanthemums in global cultures has been directly prejudiced by the mosquito. In countries with high historical rates of mosquito-borne disease, they are associated with death and grieving or are tendered only as funeral and gravestone offerings. Conversely, in locations largely void of mosquito-borne disease, the flower symbolizes love, joyfulness, and vitality. As evidenced in the United States, the flower has a positive connection in the North but a ghoulish connotation in the South, specifically in New Orleans, the nation's epicenter of yellow fever and malaria epidemics until the early twentieth century. Its vast cemetery complexes are collectively known as the "Cities of the Dead" and the "Necropolis of the South" and are the primary setting for the modern vampire craze feeding on both fiction and film.

While the insecticidal properties of chrysanthemums targeted the mosquito directly, humans have also experimented with a cornucopia of organic remedies to combat mosquito-borne illness. As a result, even our taste buds have been tainted and trained by the mosquito. Cloves, nutmeg, cinnamon, basil, and onions all soften malaria's symptoms, which may explain why, for millennia, people have added these nutritionally hollow flavorings to their diets. In Africa, coffee was also whispered to assuage malarial fevers, while in ancient China, it was alleged that tea held these same magical malaria-assailing powers.

In China, agriculture germinated both endemic malaria and also the rise of tea culture around 2700 BCE. According to tradition, Shen Nung, the second of China's legendary emperors, is credited with the invention of the plow and industrial export agriculture as well as the discovery of numerous medicinal herbs, including the first cup of homeopathic tea to treat malaise and malarial fever. Prior to being steeped as a drink, however, boiled tea leaves fused with garlic, dried fish, salt, and animal fats were consumed as a medicinal gruel. The leaves were also chewed much like mululuza, or the stimulant amphetamine-laced coca leaves in South America and khat in the Horn of Africa. Masticated tea leaves were also applied to wounds as a dressing. Although tea is impotent against the malaria parasite, modern research has shown that the tannic acid found in tea can kill the bacteria that cause cholera, typhoid, and dysentery. Aided by Buddhist and Taoist monks who drank copious amounts of tea to enhance meditation, the drink went from an obscure medicinal beverage to the favored drink of China by the first century BCE.

Tea's popularity continued to rise and to be exported, along with its cultivation and malaria, to neighboring countries until the Mongol invasions in the thirteenth century. The Mongols banned tea in favor of koumiss (fermented mare's milk churned into alcohol). Venetian traveler and trader Marco Polo, who spent years at the Mongol court during this time, makes no mention of tea but does contend that koumiss was "like white wine and a very good drink." The spouted silver drinking fountain at the Mongol capital of Karakorum, intended to illustrate the extent and diversity of the vast Mongol Empire, dispensed four drinks (rice beer from China, grape wine from Persia, Slavic honey mead, and, of course, Mongolian koumiss), but no tea.

While on the topic of tea, hidden inside a 2,200-year-old Chinese medical text blandly called "52 Prescriptions" is a brief description of the medical and fever-curing benefits of consuming bitter tea made from the small, unassuming *Artemisia annua*, or the sweet wormwood plant. Its chemical compound of artemisinin is truly a malaria assassin. Unfortunately, the killer antimalarial properties of this invasive weedlike shrub, which can grow just about anywhere, were forgotten by the world until it was rediscovered in 1972 by Mao Zedong's top secret Chinese medical venture code-named Project 523. This covert think tank, detailed later in our story, was sanctioned to find a solution to the dire, manpower-draining malaria rates eating away at the North Vietnamese Army and their Vietcong allies in their drawn-out war against the Americans. As one of both the oldest and the newest in the arsenal of antimalarial drugs, artemisinin, as we will learn later, is for now the antimalarial drug of choice for wealthy Western backpackers and travelers who can afford its prohibitive cost.

Not to be topped by its caffeinated companion, tea, coffee also has its roots firmly grounded in malaria. According to legend, during the eighth century, Kaldi, an Ethiopian goatherd, noticed that his sick or lackadaisical goats perked up after eating the bright caffeine-laced red berries of a specific bush. Inquisitive at their sudden vigor, and believing it could suppress his malarial fevers, Kaldi ate some himself. His euphoria prompted him to bring a handful of the berries to a nearby Islamic Sufi monastery. Thinking the shepherd foolish, the imam tossed the beans into the fire, filling the room with the billowing aroma so many of us now associate with the best part of waking up—coffee in your cup. Kaldi scooped the now roasted beans out of the fire, ground them up, and added boiling water. In the year 750, the first cup of coffee was born and brewed.

While the story of Kaldi, his goats, and his coffee is often dismissed as apocryphal, there are usually embers of truth within the smoke screen shrouding most legends. The coffee shrub is from the Rubiaceae family of plants often referred to as the madder, coffee, or bedstraw family. Coffee plants are systematically avoided by insects, which seem to possess a fierce disdain for the caffeine-laden shrubbery. Like our berry-eating hominid ancestors, through their own processes of trial and error, insects developed an ardent aversion to coffee. Caffeine, like pyrethrins, acts as a natural insecticide by disrupting the nervous system of insects, including mosquitoes. The cinchona tree, the source of the first successful antimalarial drug, quinine, is also a member of the coffee plant's Rubiaceae family. As we will discover, quinine was administered as a suppressant by Europeans since its discovery by Spanish Jesuits in Peru (through observing the indigenous Quechua peoples) in the mid-seventeenth century.

The chronicle of Kaldi's adventures in coffee, like his drink itself, has staying power. The Ethiopian goatherd and his animals are often featured in the names of coffee shops and roasting companies, represented by Kaldi's Coffee Roasting Company, Kaldi Wholesale Gourmet Coffee

Roasters, Wandering Goat Coffee Company, Dancing Goat Coffee Company, and Klatch Crazy Goat Coffee among others. Coffee is the world's second most valuable (legal) commodity after petroleum, and the most widely used psychoactive drug, with Americans consuming 25% of the market share. It also provides employment for over 125 million people worldwide, with another 500 million people involved directly or indirectly with the coffee trade. In 2018, Starbucks hauled in a whopping annual revenue of $25 billion from roughly 29,000 locations in over seventy-five countries. The phenomenon that is Starbucks and the all-consuming global coffee culture has the mosquito to thank for its grip on caffeine addicts the world over. Given the properties and effects of caffeinated coffee, it certainly would have been considered a viable antimalarial.

Coffee is first mentioned in a tenth-century Arabian medical text written by the renowned Persian physician Rhazes. The "Wine of Arabia," as it was once known, quickly spread to Egypt and Yemen and, in a short time, conquered Muslim lands. The prophet Muhammad, the founder of Islam, professed that with the stimulating inspiration and medicinal virtues of coffee, he could "unhorse forty men and possess forty women." Soon after Kaldi's revelations, coffee went viral across the Middle East and, upon its European discovery in the mid-sixteenth century as a result of the African slave trade, coffee sailed on the winds of the worldwide Columbian Exchange.

The coffee-malaria-mosquito connection filters throughout our story. Coffee added a dash of revolutionary flavor to America and France. It became the favored drink of intellectual Europe during the Scientific Revolution. Coffeehouses, fittingly conceived in Oxford, England, in 1650 and in the colonies in Boston in 1689, became the hotbed of avant-garde conversation, and steeped an unprecedented period of academic advancement across Europe, and revolutionary philosophies in the American colonies. In short, coffeehouses provided the medium for the exchange and dialogue of information and ideas.

The mosquito's infusion of coffee, however, brewed a far more sinister and enduring bond. As the drink went global, and coffee plantation colonies percolated throughout the post-Columbian world, coffee became invariably connected to the African slave trade and to the spread of mosquito-borne diseases. As we will see, the transatlantic slave trade introduced Africans and deadly mosquitoes and their diseases to the Americas. These African slaves, fortified with their hereditary genetic immunities to malaria, including sickle cell, withstood the wrath of mosquitoes as compared to defenseless and vulnerable European laborers and indentured servants. Enslaved Africans became a valuable commodity on colonial outposts and plantations in the Americas. Africans survived mosquito-borne diseases to produce profit, thereby becoming profitable entities themselves.

Ryan Clark's personal struggle with sickle cell is a tiny aftershock of the mosquito's seismic entry onto the global platform and our attempts through genetic design to persevere against her persistent bombardment of disease. His individual story is embedded within the larger historical events that occurred in and out of Africa. Prior to European imperial mercantilist expansion in the mid-fifteenth century, Africans had always lived *in* Africa. During the Columbian Exchange, African slaves and their genetic shields against malaria were carried to distant fields across the Americas. For those currently living and contending with sickle cell in the United States, like Ryan Clark, this is not history at all. For them, it is everyday routine and reality. The influence and impact of the mosquito is not confined to the pages of history, and straddles all stages and ages of humanity. The first appearance of sickle cell in Bantu yam farmers, for example, kick-started a chain of sweeping events in which Ryan Clark was caught up, with influential echoes that are still reverberating today.

The advent of sickle cell had immediate impacts and enduring repercussions for Africa and its people. Mosquito populations boomed with the emergence of Bantu-speaking plantain and yam farmers in West Central Africa around 8000 BCE. Devastating year-round *falciparum* malaria quickly took root. Human natural selection countered by affording Bantu peoples protection through hereditary sickle cell. As malaria spread and began to raze nonimmune populations, the Bantu, armed with their immunological advantage and iron weapons, slashed south and east across Africa. The yams they cultivated also reinforced their genetic resistance to the malaria parasite. Yams release chemicals that inhibit the reproduction of *falciparum* malaria in the blood.

During two large Bantu migrations between 5000 and 1000 BCE, they drove the malaria-ridden survivors of hunter-gatherer groups with limited or no immunities, such as the Khoisan, San, Pygmy, and Mande peoples, to the fringes and peripheries of the continent. This land did not suit Bantu agricultural requirements, nor was it suitable for grazing their itinerant wealth in the form of cattle. The ousted Khoisan survivors found refuge on the Cape of Good Hope at the tip of Africa. "The immunological fence that *P. falciparum* built around the Bantu repelled incursions by outsiders as effectively as a standing army," decodes malaria researcher Sonia Shah. "The Bantu villagers didn't have to be bigger or stronger to beat back the nomads: a couple bites from their mosquitoes did the trick." The mosquito and the Bantu genetic adaptations to her malarial disease carved out mighty, southern African empires for the Xhosa, Shona, and Zulu. The ecological interference by human pastoral pursuits, embodied by the Bantu plotline, was the key to unlocking Pandora's Box, letting loose deadly plagues of gleaning and reaping mosquitoes.

The derivation of our escalating war with mosquitoes was the relatively recent human shift from small hunter-gatherer clan-based cultures to larger densely populated settled societies based upon the domestication of plants and animals during the Agricultural Revolution. "The past 200 years, during which ever increasing numbers of Sapiens have obtained their daily bread as urban labourers and office workers, and the preceding 10,000 years, during which most Sapiens lived as farmers and herders," explains Yuval Noah Harari in his bestseller *Sapiens: A Brief History of Humankind*, "are a blink of an eye compared to the tens of thousands of years during which our ancestors hunted and gathered." Husbandry and its human interference and manipulation of local environments brought early farmers face-to-face with deadly mosquitoes while inadvertently expanding their living space through deforestation and land clearance. The addition of irrigation and the deliberate diversion of waterways maximized the mosquito's ability to procreate, generating the perfect storm for the proliferation of mosquito-borne disease.

While agriculture led to a bounty of advancements across human sociocultural systems, including the written word, it also tampered with and unleashed nature's biological weapon of mass destruction—the mosquito. Cultivation was shackled to a corpse.

By 4000 BCE, intense agriculture was being practiced in the Middle East, China, India, Africa, and Egypt, giving rise to all the trappings of modern civilization. As author H. G. Wells put it, "civilization was the agricultural surplus." This was the principal contributor to the commencement of *the* war of our world between man and mosquitoes. In fact, between 12,000 and 6,000 years ago, there were at least eleven independent sites of agricultural origin.

This agricultural ripening, which led to the expansion of mosquito habitats and breeding sites, also required beasts of burden, quickly followed by other barnyard livestock, including sheep, goats, pigs, fowl, and cattle. These animals were teeming reservoirs of disease. As Alfred W. Crosby argues, "When humans domesticated animals and gathered them to the human bosom—sometimes literally, as human mothers wet-nursed motherless animals—they created maladies their hunter and gatherer ancestors had rarely or never known." Domesticated animals that did not require intimate human management, such as donkeys, yaks, and water buffalo, did not make many, if any, zoonotic contributions. Those animals that were collected and nurtured within the human environment, however, delivered with dire consequences. To inventory just a few examples, horses conveyed the common cold virus; from chickens came "bird flu," chickenpox, and shingles; pigs and ducks donated influenza; and from cattle arose measles, tuberculosis, and smallpox.

While farming flourished in South and Central America as early as 10,000 years ago, as we will see, unlike the rest of the world, it was not accompanied by extensive domestication of livestock or by the unimpeded conquest of disease. In the Americas, the farming package, or pairing of agriculture and animals, did not occur. As a result, zoonosis was incompatible with their pastoral practices, and indigenous peoples of the Americas remained sheltered from the storm of all zoonotic diseases, including those rained down by the mosquito. While the Western Hemisphere was swarming and abuzz with the largest mosquito populations on the planet, these New World mosquito species followed a self-determining evolutionary path for 95 million years, one that liberated them from the burden of vectoring disease—for the time being. Throughout the rest of the pre-Columbian world, however, malaria was the only mosquito-borne disease to yet escape the clutches of Africa.

Mirroring the Bantu in Africa, the evidence we have from antiquity authenticates this intersection between the rise of agriculture and the domestication of animals, and the proliferation of mosquito-borne diseases. Japan, for example, imported both rice agronomy and malaria from China around 400 BCE. "Both falciparum and vivax probably emerged as truly chronic infections with expanding cultural and economic consequences," acknowledges historian James Webb, "only when human beings began to settle in the earliest subtropical and tropical river basins—along the banks of the Nile, the Tigris-Euphrates, the Indus, and the Yellow rivers—and founded the first great seed-based societies." Human domestication of plants and animals accelerated the mosquito's ascent to global domination and presented her diseases with beckoning untapped frontiers and unblemished horizons of opportunity.

In the heart of the ancient world, centered on Mesopotamia, imperialism in some form has existed since the dawn of agronomy around 8500 BCE at the confluence of the Tigris and Euphrates Rivers near the ancient city of Qurnah (300 miles southeast of Baghdad and the purported site of the Garden of Eden). Agricultural pursuits fostered the emergence of the first Sumerian city-states around 4000 BCE, while also allowing a relatively isolated Egypt to flourish on the banks of the Nile. Throughout history, great empires expanded through imperialism, conquest, and political or economic leverage. Each was defeated in time and replaced by another, continuing a cyclical rise and fall of ancient kingdoms.

The Agricultural Revolution led to the creation of modern city-states, drastically increasing populations, and more importantly for the spread of contagion, escalating population densities. By 2500 BCE, some cities in the Middle East topped 20,000 inhabitants. The advent of farming led to a surplus of crops and an accumulation of wealth. Greed is a powerful stimulus. This innate human lust for prosperity and power led to complex social stratification, local economic specialization, sophisticated and tiered spiritual, legal, and political structures, and most significantly, to trade. Statistically, throughout history, societies that were engaged in elevated trade also had a higher propensity for war. Political power and military might were wielded through the accumulation of wealth, which was chained to commerce and control of vital ports, trade routes, and transportation choke points. The reality of economics is quite simple: Why trade when you can invade? The success or failure of early empires in their drive for territorial expansion and wealth largely rested on the mosquito.

Inside the ancient Mediterranean compass, just as the malaria-mosquito axis shaped our very DNA, the mosquito also assembled the historical chromosomes of civilization itself. With reckless abandon, "General Anopheles" razed armies and decided the outcome of countless course-altering wars. Just as the Russians had "General Winter" during the Napoleonic Wars and the Second World War, General Anopheles has been a fertile and rapacious guerrilla force throughout the history of warfare and in the creation of nations and empires. She plays the role of mercenary, alternating between friend and foe. As we will see, she does not pick sides but attacks indiscriminate targets of opportunity, with one side usually benefiting from the other's suffering. With industrial farming penetrating global landscapes and giving rise to budding empires, the mosquito became the destroyer of worlds. Ancient scribes of these early agrarian societies in Mesopotamia, Egypt, China, and India documented—through symptomatic descriptions of disease—the mosquito's projection of power across antiquity.

Theirs was a world stalked by mysterious disease and death. Within the physical and psychological world our ancestors moved through, sicknesses and suffering were an uncanny, supernatural, terrifying specter. As English philosopher Thomas Hobbes announced in his 1651 treatise, *Leviathan*, humankind "is naturally punished with diseases; rashness, with mischances; injustice, with violence of enemies; pride, with ruin; cowardice, with oppression; and rebellion, with slaughter . . . and which is worst of all, continual fear, and danger of violent death; And the life of man, solitary, poor, nasty, brutish, and short." Imagine for a moment: What if this dark, ominous, terrifying, and apocalyptic apparition morosely espoused by Hobbes was your everyday reality? Our predecessors were operating under, and interpreting from, a wholly foreign and superstitious concept of illness. They were adrift in uncharted waters within a worldview governed by mysticism, miracles, and the wrath of gods.

The ancients looked to the elements of earth, water, air, and fire for answers, and beheld their vengeful deities as a cause of disease, suffering, and death. They prayed and sacrificed to these very same smiting spirits to end their sufferings, annul their tormenting symptoms, and forgive them their trespasses. It is difficult, perhaps impossible, for us to summon a world without scientific reason, deficient in concrete cause-and-effect relationships, and deprived of prevention and treatment for most diseases. "But for the moment," invokes J. R. McNeill, "we must recognize how unusual the last century has been for human health, and for our human ability to bend the rest of the biosphere to our will—within limits and not without unintended consequences—and remember that it was not always so."

To be fair, our ancient ancestors did experiment with organic treatments, as we have seen, and, quite shrewdly, even scratched the surface of exposing the true cause of mosquito-borne diseases. The established medical consensus, known as the miasma theory, attributed most diseases to noxious fumes, particles, or simply "bad air" leaching and misting from stagnant water, marshes, and swamps. This reasoning was so tantalizingly close to unmasking the real culprit, the mosquito that dwelled and multiplied in these very same bodies of water at blame. But close only counts in horseshoes and hand grenades, or so the saying goes. To better understand their ailments and the workings of their biological world, our ancient ancestors did document the symptoms of numerous diseases, including those messengered by mosquitoes.

Decrypting diseases in this deep historical record, however, is daunting. Ancient chronicles usually reference fevers, but given the embryonic state of medical knowledge before Louis Pasteur's revolutionary germ theory in the 1850s, descriptions are vague, lacking in specifics and, unquestionably, in cause. Most illnesses are accompanied by a fever, including cholera and typhoid, both of which were relatively generic. Thankfully, the diseases themselves provide some help in decoding documented plagues and pestilence throughout our past.

The symptoms of filariasis and yellow fever are unmistakable and are generally authenticated by our earliest scribes. Fever-producing malarias, however, are more problematic to isolate from other diseases, yet they, too, leave us with clues as to their historical whereabouts and implications. Of the five human malaria parasites, the deadly *falciparum* and the rare newcomer *knowlesi* start with a twenty-four-hour fever cycle of chills, high fever, and profuse sweating, meaning that the fever peaks once a day. Historically, this was referred to as quotidian fever. These two types of malaria then join the *ovale* and *vivax* strains by settling into a forty-eight-hour fever schedule dubbed tertian fever. *Malariae* adheres to a seventy-two-hour regimen referenced as quartan fever.* All malarial attacks also produce a visibly distended spleen. This begs mention, for if the reporter, like the famed Greek physician Hippocrates or his Roman successor Galen, was savvy enough to include details about the behavior of the fever itself, then, along with other archeological evidence, including skeletal remains, the shroud of mystery can be lifted to reveal the mosquito at work.

The earliest written endorsement of a mosquito-borne disease dates to 3200 BCE. These Sumerian tablets, unearthed from the "cradle of civilization" between the Tigris and Euphrates Rivers of ancient Mesopotamia, unquestionably describe malarious fevers attributed to Nergal, the Babylonian god of the underworld, depicted as a mosquito-like insect. The Canaanite and Philistine god Beelzebub (lord of the flies or insects) was reflected in the devil of early Hebrew and Christian scriptures. The evil demons of the ancient fire-worshipping Zoroastrians clustered in Persia and the Caucasus were represented as flies and mosquitoes, as was Baal, the Chaldean spirit of sickness. Hobbes borrowed his ominous incarnation of Leviathan from the Hebrew (and Christian) scriptures of the Old Testament, where the sea monster Leviathan

* The fever names adhere to the Roman practice of starting with day one, not zero. For example, tertian is two days, even though it represents the number three, if we start counting at one, and quartan, meaning four, is for us three.

spreads evil and disorder by stirring up the waters of chaos. This Leviathan character sure sounds an awful lot like our own sprightly mosquito, who has dined on mayhem and bedlam across history. Even today, the fictional portrayal of the Christian devil, with its bloodred wings, probing horns, and sweeping pointed tail, conjures lingering insect-like visions.

Malaria—"Behold a pale horse: and his name that sat on him was Death, and Hell followed with him": A Chinese antimalaria poster mimicking the death rider of the Pale Horse from the Book of Revelation alerting the public that "Prevention means killing the mosquito; frightening diseased mosquito carries hell to planet Earth and spreads epidemic disease." *(U.S. National Library of Medicine)*

The Old Testament frequently depicts divine judgments as plagues of insects and their deadly pestilence. Sickness was wrought by a vengeful god upon its disobedient subjects or their enemies, chiefly the Egyptians and Philistines. As part of their spoils of war after defeating the Israelites at the Battle of Ebenezer around 1130 BCE, for example, the Philistines seized the Ark of the Covenant. Vengeance was served by smiting the Philistines with devastating afflictions until the Ark was returned to its rightful owners. As I write, my mind is projecting the final scene of the 1981 movie *Indiana Jones and the Raiders of the Lost Ark* when God unleashes phantom angels of death upon the plundering Nazis for unsealing the Ark. Of the Four Horsemen of the Apocalypse outlined in the Book of Revelation, the rider of the pale horse was Death, who had authority "to kill with sword and with famine and with pestilence and by the wild beasts of the earth."

The Bible is one of the most studied and scrutinized texts in the world, and yet experts from across academic fields, including epidemiology, theology, linguistics, archeology, and history, cannot positively identify the exact causes or diseases that consume the Old Testament. The general consensus among scholars is that malaria or plagues of mosquitoes are mentioned at least four times, one of which is the destruction of the Assyrian army under King Sennacherib in 701 BCE, lifting the siege of Jerusalem. This event was later immortalized in Lord Byron's rousing 1815 poem.* The romantic politician and poet died of malarial fever in 1824 while fighting the Greek War of Independence against the Ottoman Empire. Shortly before his death at thirty-six, Byron conceded that "I staid [sic] out too late for this malaria season."

We do know, however, that malaria, and possibly filariasis, already had a strong foothold in Egypt and across the Middle East during and after the presumed Exodus around 1225 BCE. Based on reliefs carved into Egyptian funeral temples at Thebes, now Luxor's Valley of the Kings, and subsequent descriptions left by both ancient Persian and Indian observers, there is evidence to suggest that filariasis first engorged humanity as early as 1500 BCE. Residual evidence of malaria was

* Byron's famous rhythmic poem, "The Destruction of Sennacherib," is based on the biblical account of the battle.

In the Valley of the Kings: the mosquito among the hieroglyphs on the Temple of Ramesses III in Luxor, Egypt. The construction of the temple around 1175 BCE coincided with the invasions of the "Sea People" and the collapse of the early micro-empires of Mesopotamia and Egypt. *(Shutterstock Images)*

recently confirmed in 9,000-year-old bones from the Neolithic town of Catalhoyuk in southern Turkey, and in Egyptian and Nubian remains as old as 5,200 years, including King Tutankhamen (Tut). The death of eighteen-year-old King Tut from *falciparum* malaria in 1323 BCE marked the beginning of the end of Egyptian imperial power and cultural achievement.* Never again was Egypt an esteemed international player.

The unification of Egyptian city-states and agricultural expansion from the Nile River delta began around 3100 BCE. Given its geographic isolation and austere desert surroundings, Egypt was a minor player in the higher echelons of external geopolitical affairs. While the Egyptians invaded the eastern shores of the Mediterranean, bringing them into conflict with the Israelites and others, they never secured a lasting foothold. Early Egyptian civilization generally evolved outside of the perpetual imperial political and military concerns to the east. Essentially, Egypt was an empire unto itself, reaching its territorial and cultural zenith during the era known as the New Kingdom from 1550 to

* It has been suggested that King Tut was born of an incestuous brother-sister relationship causing numerous congenital deformities, including a club foot. It was common for Egyptian nobility to marry siblings and even their children. For example, Cleopatra was the wife, sister, and co-ruler to both her adolescent brothers Ptolemy XIII and Ptolemy XIV. Of the fifteen marriages of Ptolemaic Egyptian rule, ten were between brother and sister and two were with a niece or a cousin.

1070 BCE, noted for some of the most well-known pharaohs, including Akhenaten and his wife Nefertiti, Ramesses II, and Tutankhamen. Over the next two hundred years, Egyptian territorial holdings, wealth, and influence markedly diminished. Egypt ultimately became a vassal state for a series of conquering empires, beginning with the Libyans around 1000 BCE, followed by Cyrus the Great's Persians, Alexander's Greeks, and Augustus Caesar's Romans.

Predating the malarious mummy of King Tut by a millennium, malaria or "swamp fever" is also mentioned in the earliest Egyptian papyrus medical text of 2200 BCE. The renowned fifth-century BCE Greek historian Herodotus tells us Egyptians battled "against the mosquitoes, being in great numbers, these are the means they have invented: the towers are of service to those who inhabit the upper parts of the marshes, and ascending into them, they sleep there; for the mosquitoes, on account of the winds, are not able to fly high. But those who live around the marshes have invented other means instead of towers. Every man of them possesses a casting-net, with which, during the day, he catches fish, and at night he makes use of it in the bed where he reposes, round which he places the net, and then having crept under it, he sleeps. But the mosquitoes, if he sleeps wrapped up in a woolen or linen garment, bite through these, but through the net they do not even attempt to bite." He also reveals that the prevailing Egyptian practice for treating malarial fevers was to bathe in fresh human urine. Having never contracted malaria, I can only assume that its symptoms are so unbearably severe that a pampering soak in sparkling, steaming urine issuing from your thoughtful and upstanding servants is worth a shot for some well-deserved relief.

Ancient Chinese records, including the famed *Nei Ching* (Yellow Emperor's Canon of Medicine, 400–300 BCE), clearly distinguish the ebb-and-flow fever patterns of the various types of malaria and articulate the enlargement of the spleen. It was believed that the symptoms of "the mother of all fevers" were brought on by disturbances of *chi* (energy force) and the balance between *yin* and *yang* (dark and light dualism of the natural world), concepts seemingly borrowed by *Star Wars* creator and guru George Lucas. Malaria was represented in Chinese folklore and medical texts by a demonic trio, with each evil spirit signifying a stage of the fever cycle. The demon of chills was armed with a bucket of ice water, the subsequent fever demon stoked a blazing fire, and the ensuing demon of perspiration and pounding headaches holstered a sledgehammer.

The grip of these malarial demons is recounted in legend when a Chinese emperor asked his most trusted emissary to pacify and become governor of an outlying southern province. The ambassador thanked the emperor and began preparing himself for his new post. When the time came to leave, however, he refused to go, stating that his purpose meant certain death as the province in question was teeming with malaria. He was quickly beheaded by his enraged ruler.

Ssu-ma Ch'ien, considered the father of Chinese historical writing for his *Records of the Grand Historian* (94 BCE), confirms that "in the area south of the Yangtze the land is low and the climate humid; adult males die young." Accordingly, in ancient China, men traveling to the malarious south arranged for their wives' remarriage before departing. Award-winning historian William H. McNeill reveals, "Another mosquito-borne disease, dengue fever, which is closely related to yellow fever though not as lethal . . . also affects southern parts of China. Like malaria, dengue fever may have been present from time immemorial, lying in wait for immigrants from more northerly climes . . . such afflictions mattered a good deal in the early centuries of Chinese expansion . . . probably among the major obstacles to Chinese penetration southwards." This unequal burden of disease plagued economic development in southern China for centuries, leaving it stagnant and lagging far behind the prosperous north.

The commercial disparity between north and south imparted by endemic malaria, with looming future ramifications, was mirrored in other countries, such as Italy, Spain, and the United States, and was often referred to as the "Southern Question" or the "Southern Problem." Malaria, according to an early-twentieth-century Italian politician, "has the most serious social consequences. Fever destroys the capacity to work, annihilates energy, and renders a people sluggish and indifferent. Inevitably, therefore, malaria stunts productivity, wealth and well-being." For Americans, the mosquito's uneven geographic economic impact would eventually engulf the United States in the momentous issues of slavery and civil war.

Indian medical texts also mention the differing malarial fevers by 1500 BCE. The "king of diseases" was personified by the fiery fever demon Takman, who arises from lightning during the rainy season. Not only did Indians recognize that water was somehow affiliated with mosquitoes, they also seem to have been the first to identify mosquitoes as the source of malaria. In his detailed sixth-century BCE compendium on medicine, Indian physician Sushruta singled out five mosquito species of the northern Indus River Valley: "Their bite is as painful as that of a serpent, and causes diseases . . . accompanied by fever, pain of limbs, hair standing on end, pain, vomiting, diarrhea, thirst, heat, giddiness, yawning, shivering, hiccups, burning sensations, intense cold." He also alludes to an enlarged spleen, "which distends the left side, is as hard as stone, and is arched like the back of a turtle." While he suspected the mosquito as a vector for disease, medical practitioners, scientists, and the casual observer lacked scientific evidence until recently, so the theory remained just that, a theory. Dr. Sushruta's astute reasoning and keen observations went unheeded for millennia.

The mosquito's influence and impact travel unregulated and unfettered across the historical space-time continuum. The agricultural expansion of Bantu yam farmers in Africa 8,000 years ago was a link in the chain of African chattel slavery, and also led directly to Ryan Clark's near-death experience following his participation in an NFL football game in Denver in 2007. "We are not makers of history," conceded the esteemed Dr. Martin Luther King Jr. "We are made by history." The mosquito prods our human journey along its uncharted course and stimulates our swing through time in mysterious, if not macabre, ways. She connects historical, at times seemingly unrelated, events separated by distance, epochs, and space. Hers is a long and warped reach.

If we pick up the trail of our Bantu yam farmers, we can see the mosquito's unshakable manipulation of history across millennia. We last left our Bantu friends around 3,000 years ago, when, with the advantage of their sickle cell and iron weapons, they drove the malaria-badgered Khoisan, Mande, and San peoples to the coastal fringes of southern

Africa. "The much heavier consequence," contends anthropologist and acclaimed author Jared Diamond, "was that the Dutch settlers in 1652 had to contend only with a sparse population of Khoisan herders, not with a dense population of steel-equipped Bantu farmers." During the European colonization of southern Africa, beginning with the Dutch, who were quickly chased by the British, these African ethnic arrangements created by the mosquito thousands of years earlier would shape and fashion apartheid oppression and the modern nations of South Africa, Namibia, Botswana, and Zimbabwe.

When Dutch Afrikaners arrived at the Cape in 1652 alongside the Dutch East India Company, they met a small, fragmented Khoisan population that was easily defeated by military conquest and European disease. Europe secured a beachhead on the Cape, and Afrikaner treks through southern Africa gained traction. As the Afrikaners, and eventually the British, spread north and east from the Cape Colony, they ran into denser Bantu populations, such as the Xhosa and Zulu, who had fashioned their societies into mighty military-agricultural packages complete with steel weapons. It took the Dutch and British nine wars spanning 175 years to finally conquer the Xhosa in 1879. In bare, tactical military topographical terms, this was a Dutch/British rate of advance of less than one mile per year.

A relatively bloodless coup backed by the majority of the Zulu population had allowed Shaka to seize the throne in 1816. He united or incorporated neighboring tribes through merciless military forays and cunning diplomacy and instigated comprehensive cultural, political, and military reforms. Armed by Shaka's sweeping social and military-industrial revolution, the Zulu fiercely resisted British incursion until their final defeat, also in 1879, during the Anglo-Zulu War.

British malaria rates during the Anglo-Zulu War, spanning January to July 1879, uncover an alternate plotline. From a military strength of 12,615 British troops, during this seven-month period, 9,510 received medical treatment for disease, including 4,311 (45%) for malaria. While the mosquito's deliverance of malaria was still a mystery to medicine, during the Anglo-Zulu War, the British were fortified with the recently developed germ theory of disease and, more importantly, by stockpiles of the malaria suppressant quinine. I hazard to guess that had the Dutch (and British) met the Zulu and Xhosa instead of the Khoisan peoples at the onset of colonialism on the Cape in the mid-seventeenth century (without the aid of quinine), it would have been an ugly encounter for the European trespassers. "How could whites have succeeded in establishing themselves at the Cape at all, if those first few arriving Dutch ships had faced such fierce resistance?" questions Diamond. "Thus, the problems of modern South Africa stem at least in part from a geographic accident . . . Africa's past has stamped itself deeply on Africa's present." This long historical arc, including apartheid and its enduring legacy, whether by accident or design, was originally fabricated by the mosquito through malaria and the genetic response of sickle cell cultivated by Bantu agricultural expansion.

In this instance her penetration of history's layers pushed even deeper. These mosquito-engineered events in Africa, embracing the emergence of Sickle Cell Eve, found their way into the history logs of the Americas through the African slave trade and pierced the players of the modern NFL, including Ryan Clark. She has tormented and twisted humanity and our history across time. If I didn't know better, I would say she is satisfying her sadistic and narcissistic impulses at our expense.

Two and a half centuries after Dr. Sushruta exposed the deadly mosquitoes of the Indus River Valley, for instance, a young Macedonian warrior-king would feel the wrath of their bite. These mosquitoes would challenge his drive for global supremacy, quench his insatiable thirst for power, and shatter his dreams of conquest.

CHAPTER 3

General Anopheles: From Athens to Alexander

The Athenian philosopher Plato declared that "ideas are the source of all things." The ideas, observations, and writings of Plato and his pioneering academic contemporaries of "Golden Age" Greece, which included Socrates, Aristotle, Hippocrates, Sophocles, Aristophanes, Thucydides, and Herodotus, among a legendary list of others, are truly the source of all things as they cemented the eternal and immortal foundation of Western culture and modern academia. Their names are permanently emblazoned on the pages of humanity. Adhering to "the Athenian gadfly" Socrates's use of questioning to elicit more questions and eventually answers, known today as the Socratic Method, how did this come to pass?* How did the ideas from a handful of trailblazing Greeks, predominantly Athenians, from such a small space and time within the larger historical realm, come to dominate Western, if not global, civilization and thought? Our worldview 2,500 years later is still governed by their ideas, their concepts; and their groundbreaking works are a staple on bookshelves across the globe and still taught and dissected in the classrooms and laboratories of higher education. Aristotle gave us the answer when he resolved, "The one exclusive sign of thorough knowledge is the power of teaching."

Socrates tutored Plato, who founded the Academy in Athens, the first true institution of higher learning. Plato is considered the most

* Socrates, and his persistent questioning, was such an annoyance to the Athenian aristocracy and elite that they nicknamed him the Athenian *gadfly*. Gadfly is a generic term for a buzzing, blood-sucking insect.

pivotal figure in the development of Western philosophy and science. His most famous student, Aristotle, who studied under his mentor for twenty years, left his mark on every modern academic field from zoology and biology, including the study of insects, to physics, music, and theater, to political science and the collective and individual psychoanalysis of human beings. Aristotle coupled detailed investigation and the scientific method to biological reasoning, empiricism, and the order of the natural world. In plain terms, there is a reason why Plato, along with his master, Socrates, and his apprentice, Aristotle, among other Golden Age Greeks, is still so widely regarded, studied, and referenced today.

The torch of progress was passed from Socrates through the hands of Plato to Aristotle and eventually found its way from Aristotle into the ambitious grip of a young prince in the northern wilds of Macedon. In time, he would embolden and disseminate Greek culture, books, and ideas across the known world, where they would be warehoused in magnificent libraries and be enriched by the minds, literature, and innovations of subsequent scholars. Plato's observation that "books give a soul to the universe, wings to the mind, flight to the imagination, and life to everything" applies directly to his own time-tested publications, such as *The Republic*, and also to the vast collection of writings from his generation of Greek peers, including his pupil Aristotle.

Shortly after the death of Plato, Aristotle left Athens. He had been petitioned to tutor the thirteen-year-old son and heir of King Philip II of Macedon. Prior to summoning Aristotle to the Macedonian court, Philip had recognized his child's innate intellect, curiosity, and courage. When the prince was ten years old, a frustrated trader had abandoned a massive feral horse to roam the streets of the capital city. The muscular, raven-black stallion marked by a menacing white star on its brow and one penetratingly piercing blue eye, refused to be mounted, and chased off any attempt to be corralled. Originally interested in purchasing the magnificent creature, Philip quickly rescinded his offer after witnessing the ferocity of the wild animal. The one-eyed king had no use for an unruly, insubordinate steed. This hostile horse quickly drew a swelling audience of curious, riveted onlookers. The young prince, surveying the unfolding, stampeding spectacle, pleaded with his father to purchase the horse. Much to his son's disappointment, Philip could not be swayed.

Refusing to take no for an answer, the youthful heir to the throne of Macedon shrugged off his fluttering, wind-whipped cloak and silently crept toward the now hysterical and panic-stricken horse. As he approached the startled animal, the plucky prince quieted the raucous crowd. Sensing that the horse was afraid of its own shadow, he stunned the now silent spectators as he clutched the dangling reins and turned the horse toward the sun to shroud its silhouette. He had tamed the savage beast. "O my son," a proud and beaming Philip purportedly decreed, "look thee out a kingdom equal to and worthy of thyself, for Macedon is too little for thee." Eventually, the warhorse and loyal companion, which the prince named Bucephalus (ox-head), would carry his master across the known and unknown worlds as far as India, the eastern limit of his vast empire and one of the largest kingdoms in history.

From the smoldering cinders of the mosquito-ravaged Greco-Persian and Peloponnesian Wars, a new power arose, and the young horse-whispering prodigy would lead it beyond the summits of supremacy, prestige, and legend, filling the power vacuum left by the waning Greek city-states. He would go on to become a god on earth and one of the greatest leaders in the history of humankind, with the titles Hegemon of the Hellenic League, Shah of Persia, Pharaoh of Egypt, Lord of Asia, and Basileus of Macedon. To history, he is known simply as Alexander the Great.

Regardless of the futile academic squabbling over motivation and personality, there can be no questioning the pure, raw genius that was Alexander. It is also worth remembering just how young he was, and the relatively small size of his army, when he challenged Persian emperor Darius III for imperial command and carved out one of the largest domains in history.

There are few instances in our past when the spheres of civilization line up so perfectly to foster an environment in which one individual can single-handedly leave such a deep and indelible mark on humankind. This environment was fashioned by the events of the Greco-Persian and Peloponnesian Wars preceding Alexander's meteoric rise to conquering celebrity. These conflicts, pitted with mosquito-borne disease, left the weary war-torn world in financial decay and political disarray. What was left of the door to world domination was propped ajar by rubble and ruins, affording the entrance of Alexander onto the world stage. "An unexamined life," professed Plato, "is not worth living." To examine the life and legacy of Alexander, we must first take a step back into the mosquito-stalked affairs that created the atmosphere for his enduring imprint on the modern world. While Macedon was still a rugged mountainous tribal backwater, the continuing events of Western civilization were collected around Mesopotamia and Egypt.

Until 1200 BCE, a political and economic equilibrium and balance of power existed across the greater Middle East. Economic concentration and specialization of the various Babylonian, Assyrian, and Hittite micro-empires fostered trade, peace, and general prosperity. This was short-lived. Within fifty years, each of these empires, as well as Egypt, was brought to its knees by invasions from displaced mercenary plunderers, sundry Mediterranean islanders immortalized by their mythological Trojan Horse. These "Sea People," as they are collectively known, severed trade routes and ravaged crops and towns amid dire drought, famine, and a series of earthquakes and tsunamis, thrusting the region into the "Ancient Dark Ages." This complete cultural, political, and economic collapse was aided by the mosquito's circulation of a resolute malaria epidemic. On a Cypriot clay tablet, the cause was clearly etched: "the Hand of Nergal [the Babylonian mosquito devil] is now in my country; he has slain all the men of my country." Thanks in part to the mosquito, what remained of these inaugural human agricultural civilizations was charred relics and crumbling ruins, collapsing into a vacant power vacuum.

Out of these ashes arose two rival powers—Greece and Persia. These vying ancient superpowers laid the foundations for modern literature and the arts, engineering, politics and democratic governance, the art of war, philosophy, medicine, and all facets of Western civilization. In the wake of the wreckage left by the marauding Sea Peoples, while the majority of the Middle East drowned in the darkness of a cultural and developmental abyss, a new power quietly arose from the shadows in the East. Cyrus the Great's Persian Empire, the largest yet seen, embraced all the former imperial states of the Middle East, and extended into central Asia, the southern Caucasus, and the Ionian-Greek settler states of western Turkey.

Cyrus had founded the Persian Empire in 550 BCE through skilled diplomacy, benevolent intimidation, periodic military forays, and, above all else, a human rights policy the United Nations would applaud.* Across his burgeoning and flourishing empire, Cyrus promoted cultural, technological, and religious reciprocation and exchange, and nurtured artistic, engineering, and scientific innovation. The expansion of Persian power under Cyrus and his heirs, Darius I and Xerxes, who stretched his empire to include Egypt, the Sudan, and eastern Libya, led to a legendary showdown with another young power: Greece. In 440 BCE, Greek writer Herodotus, considered the "father of history," wrote that Cyrus brought together "every nation without exception." The exception, however, was Greece itself.

At this point, the singular "Greece" we commonly imagine did not exist. It was an assemblage of competing and warring city-states, with the coalitions of Sparta and Athens the two top contenders for military and economic supremacy. In fact, the original Olympic Games, initiated in Greece in 776 BCE, were a peace offering made by mimicking war in the form of battlefield athletics and soldierly skills, such as wrestling, boxing, javelin, discus, running, equestrian, and pankration, meaning "all of power and might" (an early form of the Ultimate Fighting Championship, or UFC, the only rules being no biting or eye gouging). Although the Olympics Games were intended to promote peace, the mutually hostile and sparring Greek city-states were drawn into a life-or-death struggle against the Persians, instigated by their Greek Ionian brethren who revolted against Persian rule.

Supported by the democratic city-state of Athens, in 499 BCE, the

* Written on the Cyrus Cylinder is his declaration of the restoration of temples and cultural edifices, and the repatriation of exiled peoples to their homelands, including the Jews, whom he freed from Babylonian bondage as outlined in the *Book of Ezra*. He is mentioned twenty-three times in the Bible and is the only non-Jewish figure referred to as messiah. Adding to his legend and impressive résumé, Cyrus died in battle on the steppes of Kazakhstan in 530 BCE. His body was returned to his beloved capital and buried in a modest limestone tomb, duly preserved and aptly recognized as a United Nations World Heritage site. Cyrus is regarded as one of the most important and illustrious leaders in recorded history and is truly deserving of his "Great" suffix.

Ionian Greeks mutinied against the regime of Persia's emperor Darius I, who ruled over 50 million people, almost half the global population. Darius quickly subdued the rebellion but vowed to punish Athens for its insolence. In addition to the punitive benefits of retaliation, the conquest of Greece would consolidate Persian power in the region and guarantee complete control of Mediterranean commerce. Seven years later, Darius's full-scale invasion of Greece, the last sovereign vestige in the known Western world, ignited the Greco-Persian Wars.

The Persian army crossed the Dardanelles Straits from Asia into Europe, and marched on Thrace and Macedonia, exacting the fidelity of local populations en route. Continuing south toward Athens, the avenging campaign of Darius quickly descended into disaster. Nearing the approaches to the city, the Persian naval fleet was destroyed by a violent storm, while Persian land forces retreated after being shredded by what historians hypothesize to be a lethal combination of dysentery, typhoid, and malaria.

Two years later, in 490 BCE, Darius unleashed a second campaign, circumventing the arduous northern overland route by launching an amphibious landing, 26,000-strong, at Marathon, roughly twenty-six miles north of Athens. Outnumbered two-to-one, the amateur but heavily armed and bronze-armored Athenians confined the Persians to low-lying marshy encampments. Within a week, the same toxic mixture of disease mentioned above thinned the Persian force. Given the position of the Persian fleet, the disembarkation grounds of the Persian troops, and the placement of the Athenian defenders, it would have been impossible for them to bivouac away from or to skirt the swamps. The terrain and Athenian posture dictated the battle. Following a decisive Athenian victory, the disease-riddled Persians withdrew and set sail to attack Athens itself. Herodotus records that 6,400 Persian corpses were strewn on the battlefield, with an unknown number perishing in the surrounding swamps. Messengers were quickly dispatched from Marathon to run the twenty-six miles to Athens to warn the city of the impending Persian attack.

The legend of the Athenian courier Pheidippides racing to Athens, commemorated by the modern marathon athletic event, did not happen.

This myth is a muddled and confused version of two truths. In a day and a half, Pheidippides did in fact cover the distance of over 140 miles from Marathon to Sparta to seek help prior to the battle. Although the rapport between Sparta and Athens was anything but cordial, the Spartans, as Herodotus mentions, were "moved by the appeal, and willing to send help to Athens." If Athens crumbled and surrendered to Persian power, Sparta would no doubt suffer the same fate. Better the devil you know, right? The 2,000 Spartans, however, arrived a day late as battlefield tourists just in time to survey the corpses of roughly 6,500 Persian and 1,500 Athenian dead. Immediately after their victory at Marathon, the Athenian army marched to Athens to successfully prevent a Persian landing. Sensing that the opportunity had been lost, and with the surviving soldiers demoralized by malarial infection and defeat, the Persians headed home. They would be back, though, under a new emperor, Darius's heir and son, Xerxes.

Determined to avenge his father, in 480 BCE, Xerxes personally commanded an unprecedented and alarming combined naval and land force nearing 400,000 men. To meet the daunting Persian invasion, the rival Greek states, led by Athens and Sparta, temporarily put aside their differences once again to marshal an allied defense of roughly 125,000 men. After marching into Europe across ingeniously engineered pontoon bridges spanning the Hellespont (Dardanelles), the Persians were blocked at the bottleneck pass of Thermopylae by a vastly outnumbered Greek force. The 1,500 Greeks left behind, including 300 Spartans led by King Leonidas, briefly checked the Persian advance by fighting to the death. While the military significance of the Battle of Thermopylae has been inflated and sensationalized, the delaying action of Leonidas and his band of brothers at this defile did allow the main Greek column to withdraw to Athens. With this last stand, the legend of the 300 was born, and subsequently exaggerated to the point where it has become unrecognizable, epitomized by the historically challenged *300* movie franchise.

When news of Thermopylae reached the Greek navy, it disengaged from the Persian fleet after two days of fighting. With the Persians marching unchecked on Athens, its citizens and the fleeing army were evacuated by the retreating fleet to the island of Salamis. When Xerxes entered the prized city and found it deserted, he impulsively put Athens to the torch. He immediately regretted his decision as it was out of character with the Persian tradition of tolerance and respect championed by Cyrus and Darius I. Realizing his error, he repeatedly offered to rebuild Athens, but it was too late for acts of contrition. The Athenians had already fled the city and the opportunity for negotiation and reconciliation had gone up in smoke. This was now total war. Outraged by this Athenian insolence, in September 480 BCE, Xerxes ordered his navy to destroy the coalition fleet at Salamis. There the Persian navy entered a brilliantly sprung trap conceived by the Athenian general Themistocles.

Luring the numerically superior but flimsier Persian vessels into a narrow strait, the bulkier Greek trireme ships quickly blocked both entries. In these tight quarters, the Persian ships became logjammed, unnavigable, and disorganized. The heavier, battering-ram Greek navy swept through, scoring a decisive victory. Undaunted by this defeat, a disgruntled Xerxes continued his campaign to conquer Greece and bring the alliance to its knees. It was the Persians, however, who would be brought to heel and disciplined by a late addition to the Greek coalition—flying columns of mosquitoes.

Persian ground forces were pressed and sieved to traverse swampy terrain and lay siege to numerous Greek towns girded by bristling marshes. With the Persian force now trespassing on her terrain, the mosquito quickly announced her presence to the hapless, unsuspecting foreign soldiers. Malaria compounded by dysentery soon swallowed the Persian ranks, with losses upwards of 40%. This straggling, scarecrow Persian force was shattered at the Battle of Plataea in August 479 BCE, effectively ending any future Persian intentions toward Greece. Salamis and Plataea marked the turning point in the Greco-Persian Wars. Accompanied by General Anopheles, these decisive victories propelled the balance of power and the center of civilization west to Greece. The initiative and momentum were wrested from Xerxes and his retreating Persians and were now permanently in the custody of the Greeks. With the Persian Empire weakened and its regional influence waning, the ensuing

"Golden Age" of Greece would be the substance from which modern Western society was built.

There was, however, still the lingering question of hegemony within Greece itself. The Persian threat had only temporarily paused the ongoing hostility between Athens and Sparta, which came to a head with the Peloponnesian Wars intermittently raging from 460 to 404 BCE. Aristophanes's satirical, sexually charged comedy *Lysistrata*, debuting in 411 BCE at the height of the Peloponnesian War and in the wake of the disastrous mosquito-spawned Athenian defeat in Sicily two years earlier, embodies the futile bloodbath washing across Greece and beyond. The rascal Athenian title character, Lysistrata, sets out on a mission to persuade the women of the warring city-states to withhold sexual relations, pleasures, and privileges from their husbands and lovers to broker a peace and put end to the brutal conflict and catastrophic butchery. The carnage of the Peloponnesian War could not be cured or pacified by a play, however, even one as brilliant and enduringly relevant as *Lysistrata*.

Ironically, this period, demonstrated by Aristophanes's play itself, coincided with a flurry of academic advancement shaped by men whose names are now commonplace and roll off the tongues of schoolchildren across the world. Despite this constant warfare, or perhaps because of it, fifth-century BCE Greeks, primarily Athenians, fashioned their most celebrated innovations in architecture, science, philosophy, theater, and the arts. Socrates, Plato, and Thucydides, for example, all fought for Athens during the Peloponnesian War.

All was not entirely golden, however, as malarial epidemics sapped and bled the Greek population, undermined military might, eroded economic influence, and eventually ended Greece's reign as the heart of Western civilization. Greek poet Homer mentions malaria in the *Iliad* (750 BCE) when he describes the autumn season: "burning breath taints the red air with fevers, plagues, and death." Numerous entries on the who's who list of golden age Greeks, including Sophocles, Aristophanes, Herodotus, Thucydides, Plato, and Aristotle, left exemplary depictions of malaria. "And we have made ourselves living cesspools," Plato noted, "and driven doctors to invent names for our diseases." The famed Greek physician Hippocrates (460–370 BCE), for example, likened the deadly malaria season of summer and early fall to the nightly arrival of Sirius the Dog Star, a period of sickness he branded the "dog days of summer."

Hippocrates, or the father of Western medicine, as he is often called, was clear to distinguish malaria from other types of fever. He noted in articulate detail the enlargement of spleens and the fever cycles, time frames, and severity of the different "tertian, quartan and quotidian" malarial infections, going so far as to note which strains were prone to relapse. Hippocrates conceded that malaria was the "worst, most protracted and most painful of all the diseases then occurring," adding that "the fevers that attack are of the acutest type while the earth is soaked by reason of the spring rains." He was the world's first malariologist since no one before him or for centuries afterward so methodically and patently diagnosed, studied, and recorded the symptoms of malaria.

Hippocrates removed medicine from under a religious umbrella, arguing that illness was not punishment inflicted by the gods, but rather was the product of environmental factors and internal disparities within the human body itself. This was an unprecedented, monumental shift in the balance between the supernatural and natural worlds. Hippocrates maintained that the best medicine was prevention, not cure. Benjamin Franklin later paraphrased this aphorism, insisting that "an ounce of prevention is worth a pound of cure," albeit that it pertained to the fire hazards of colonial Philadelphia rather than to mosquito-borne (and other) illnesses. Hippocrates also stressed the importance of clinical observation and documentation during which he correctly diagnosed and recorded numerous diseases, including malaria. His Hippocratic oath to "use treatment to help the sick according to my ability and judgment, but never with a view to injury and wrong-doing" is still observed by physicians to this day, accompanied by his caveat and vow to uphold the privilege of doctor-patient confidentiality.

In the miasmic tradition of the Hippocratic school of medicine, observers, writers, and health professionals believed until the late nineteenth century that diseases, including malaria, were caused by decaying debris and poisonous gases emanating from stagnant swamps, marshes, and wetlands, giving rise to the name malaria—literally "bad air" in Italian—discordant with Plato's musing that "they certainly give very strange names to diseases." Hippocrates and his predecessors came tantalizingly close to the source, for they did couple standing water to malaria, though not to the mosquitoes that bred in it. For example, Empedocles, a contemporary of Hippocrates and the author of the paradigm of the four elements of earth, water, air, and fire, successfully diverted two rivers near the Sicilian town of Selinus at his own expense to rid the area of "evil smelling" swamps that were "causing death and making pregnant women miscarry." His likeness was struck on a coin of currency so that residents would be continuously reminded of his miraculous and lifesaving humanitarian efforts. The mosquito, however, remained anonymous.

While Hippocrates was wrong about disease being caused by an imbalance of the four humors—black bile, yellow bile, phlegm, and blood—his vivid accounts of malaria provide us with context as to its rampant proliferation during the Peloponnesian War and its role in deciding the war's outcome. Mosquito-borne malaria, as biologist Dr. R. S. Bray affirms, "no doubt added to the burdens of the Peloponnesian War." In fact, it defined them. Zoology professor Dr. J. L. Cloudsley-Thompson goes one step further, recognizing that "Hippocrates knew malaria well: this insidious disease was afterwards to sap and rot the civilizations of ancient Greece and Rome." For those two superpowers, the mosquito was as skilled and capable at killing as any earthly soldier. On the battlefields of empire building, she prejudiced the results of clashes and campaigns during both the rise and fall of Greece and Rome.

While Hippocrates was studiously recording the many faces of malaria and observing the interplay between the natural world, disease, and the human body, the relationship between Sparta and his adopted home, Athens, was souring. Sensing impending hostilities, Sparta initiated the Peloponnesian War in 431 BCE by launching a preemptive strike on Athens, hoping for a quick victory before the dominant Athenians could summon their allies. The Athenian strategist Pericles advised a two-pronged plan to defeat the Spartans. The first was to prolong the conflict by avoiding decisive infantry battles, instead fighting smaller rearguard delaying actions to allow for a purposeful retreat to the fortified city of Athens. He was sure that the superior supplies and resources of Athens, and its ability to withstand a siege, would win a war of attrition. Second, Athenian naval supremacy permitted unrivaled command of the seas. Raiding the ports and commercial coastal cities of both Sparta and its allies would force a surrender of resource starvation. Pericles's genius might have won the day had it not been for the intervention of disease.

With an Athenian victory in reach, a devastating epidemic, known as the Plague of Athens, struck in 430 BCE, claiming the celebrated general as one of its first victims. This contagion ripped apart the cohesion and foundation of not only the Athenian military but also Athenian society. It struck a blow so powerful that any immediate salvage of the social, religious, and cultural antebellum status quo was untenable. The epidemic originated in Ethiopia and passed through the seaports of Libya and Egypt before being shuttled northbound across the Mediterranean by infected sailors, and entered Greece through the Athenian port of Piraeus. The sanctuary city of Athens was crawling with over 200,000 refugees and their livestock, adding to an already overpopulated city. This overcrowding inside the fortified city walls, when combined with appalling hygiene, a shortage of resources, clean water, and supplies, was an invitation to death by disease.

Within three years, the mysterious disease had killed upwards of 100,000 people, roughly 35% of the Athenian population. A vulnerable Athens ensnared in social and military anarchy should have made for an easy Spartan victory. The terror of the mystifying plague was so persistent, however, that Sparta abandoned its siege of the city. The Plague of Athens was a rare one-sided epidemic, for the Spartans escaped relatively unscathed. From a military perspective, the Plague of Athens leveled the playing field but brought neither side closer to victory. Eventually, in 421 BCE, as a result of this calamitous and enigmatic contagion magnified by years of attrition and mutual exhaustion, a tenuous peace was brokered.

More ink and academic sweat have been spilled on literature concerning the nature of the Plague of Athens than blood spilled during the Peloponnesian War. The never-ending clinical discussion of causality is surprising, given that the eyewitness description from acclaimed Athenian historian Thucydides is so exhaustively thorough. His firsthand written account of the Peloponnesian War, including the Plague of Athens of which he was a survivor, is the watershed of impartial scientific-based history and international relations theory. His unbiased research methods, analysis of cause and effect, recognition of strategy and the influence of individual initiative were innovative and groundbreaking. His text is still studied and scrutinized at universities and military colleges around the world. As a young army officer at the Royal Military College of Canada, I carried Thucydides on my mandatory reading list.

His exquisite symptomatic description of the disease, too lengthy to reproduce here, is so comprehensive as to be problematic. The symptoms mirror all the designer name-brand diseases, but not any particular one completely enough to be able to discount others. Historians and medical experts have bantered and debated the cause for centuries, tabling over thirty different pathogens as the architect of the plague. The initial considerations of bubonic plague, scarlet fever, anthrax, measles, or smallpox have generally been discredited. While typhoid is a candidate, the top contenders to claim this carnage are typhus, malaria, and some form of mosquito-borne viral hemorrhagic fever akin to yellow fever.

Given the myriad symptoms rendered by Thucydides, it could also have been a lethal concoction of these three diseases empowered by the cramped and unsanitary conditions in the besieged city of Athens. Harvard physician and biologist Dr. Hans Zinsser emphasizes that most historical epidemics are exacerbated by other complementary diseases: "Soldiers have rarely won wars. They more often mop up after the barrage of epidemics. . . . Very rarely is there a pure epidemic of a single malady. It is not unlikely that the description of Thucydides is confused by the fact that a number of diseases were epidemic in Athens at the time of the great plague. The conditions were ripe for it. . . . The plague of Athens, whatever it may have been, had a profound effect upon historical events."

A rejuvenated Athens broke the armistice in 415 BCE, launching the greatest and most expensive military campaign in Greek history, enflaming Aristophanes to write his antiwar protest play, *Lysistrata*. Feeling obligated to assist their allies in Sicily, the Athenians set sail to crush the Spartan pawn of Syracuse. Upon landing, the Athenian force dithered under clumsy leadership, and languished in marshy, mosquito-infested encampments surrounding Syracuse. Historians have mulled the idea that the defenders purposefully channeled and lured the Athenians into the malarial swamps, subjecting them to a brand of biological warfare. Given the accepted miasma theory that standing water and wetlands caused disease, it seems likely that this strategy was employed throughout the ancient world.

The Athenian army at Syracuse was crippled by malaria. As the two-year siege dragged on, malaria killed or incapacitated over 70% of the total force. The Athenians floundered into catastrophic defeat in 413 BCE. The Sicilian Expedition was an unqualified disaster. The entire Athenian force of 40,000 men died of disease or were killed, captured, or sold into slavery. The Athenian navy was in tatters. The Athenian treasury was bankrupt. The mosquito and soldierly bungling effected one of the greatest military blunders in history with global reverberations.

The Athenian democratic government was overthrown by an oligarchy, and in 404 BCE Athens surrendered to Spartan occupation under the draconian rule of a puppet government known as the Thirty Tyrants. The dream of Athens and its democracy died with the execution-suicide of the luminary thinker Socrates in 399 BCE. Like Athens, however, Sparta was also in an economic and military shambles. Fifty-six years of intermittent warfare had left Athens and Sparta, and their lesser allies of Corinth, Elis, Delphi, and Thebes, impoverished, tired, and weak. In addition, the war shattered religious, cultural, and societal taboos, vast amounts of the countryside and entire cities had been razed and lay in ruin, and populations had been devastated by war and disease.

This disintegration and collapse were bolstered by endemic malaria throughout southern Greece. Malaria interminably drained Greek health, vitality, and manpower. Consequently, fields, barnyards, mines, and ports were left fallow, untended, vacuous. Malaria attacked fertility by targeting pregnant women and young children, sending populations into a downward spiral. Endemic malaria was accompanied by stillbirths and miscarriages. Children with underdeveloped immune systems were easy targets for the parasitic predator. Malarial fevers often reaching 106 degrees sizzled and cooked sperm, draining male potency. Plato lamented that "what now remains compared with what then existed is like the skeleton of a sick man." The Peloponnesian War and General Anopheles put a harsh, abrupt end to the golden age of Greece. Every loss, however, is tethered to a gain. In this case, the ultimate victor was the relatively unsullied and isolated kingdom of Macedon.

While a teenage Alexander immersed himself in the teachings of Aristotle, his father, Philip, began to train and organize a formidable Macedonian army. Philip's innovative use of maneuver warfare with both heavy and light cavalry and infantry, accompanied by the alteration of existing weapons, produced a highly mobile, quick-striking Macedonian force. These military improvements, formations, and tactics were later tailored and refashioned by Alexander. While viewing themselves as Greek, the Macedonians were viewed by southern Greeks as lewd barbarians and uncivilized drunkards. Historical and archeological evidence supports the notion that the Macedonian aristocracy had a healthy penchant for alcohol and were a hard-drinking lot. Macedonia's rise to superpower status in the ancient world is regarded as one of the greatest wonders of antiquity. Given the economic and social plight of its battle-scarred and mosquito-spiked southern neighbors, however, it was no accident.

With the Greek city-states reeling from the devastation of the Peloponnesian Wars, throughout the 340s BCE, King Philip II persuaded the majority of northern and central Greece into alliance before taking the offensive. With his father away warring, sixteen-year-old Alexander was left as regent and heir apparent. When rebellion against Macedonian rule broke out in Thrace, Alexander raised a small army of local leftovers and dregs, and quickly crushed the revolt in a widely heralded event among his peers and subjects. Alexander's military prowess and reputation continued to grow as he put down subsequent revolts in southern Thrace and northern Greece. To counter the Macedonian southern offensive, in 338 BCE, Athens and Thebes subsequently rallied a defensive coalition that Philip and Alexander, whose flanking force was the first to break the enemy lines, summarily dispatched at the Battle of Chaeronea. Never again would the city-states of Greece be independent agents in international affairs.

Alexander quickly gained status as a fierce and admirable leader who inspired loyalty, courage, and devotion by fighting at the front of his ranks. He was the archetypal modern military commander in all facets of his strategic and tactical thought and implementation, in his generalship, and in his ability to relate directly to his troops. He ate with them, he slept with them, he placed a high priority on the treatment of the wounded and their families. Fighting alongside his father, Alexander gained invaluable training, confidence, and momentum. The young prince possessed the appetite, intellect, and ability for war, and his sudden and surprising ascension to the throne of Macedon was close at hand.

Having united Greece under his rule, save a recalcitrant but weak and largely irrelevant Sparta, whom Alexander ridiculed as "mice," an anxious Philip feared that without a mission his strengthened, but also bored and idle, army would be prone to revolt and instability. He smartly conjured up a common cause for all Greeks to rally behind by dredging up an old archenemy. It was time, he declared, for a united Greece to march on Persia. Philip, however, would not steer the invasion. In 336 BCE, Philip was murdered by one of his personal bodyguards. Legend and lore have swirled the scheme that Alexander and his mother, Olympias, cunningly devised the assassination. While this makes for a more colorful plot, in truth the slaying was most likely the act of a disgruntled lone wolf. Thus, unexpectedly, at twenty years old, Alexander assumed the throne and prepared to carry out his assassinated father's vision of conquest to unimagined heights.

Without hesitation, Alexander began his conquests in earnest, creating his legend in the process. Like most new leaders, his first move was to eliminate rivals and dissenters. When Thebes rebelled, for example, Alexander destroyed the disloyal city. After securing his domestic rule and his Balkan borders, he revived his father's collective campaign to strike at Darius III's Persia. In 334 BCE, Alexander mustered his combined Macedonian and Greek force of no more than 40,000 soldiers, crossed the Hellespont, and marched on Persia.

Outnumbered three-to-one, Alexander's force defeated the armies of Persian emperor Darius III at Granicus and Issus. After pausing briefly with a nasty bout of malaria, Alexander quickly conquered what is modern-day Syria, Jordan, Lebanon, and Israel/Palestine. He was anointed a god by the Egyptians, who viewed him as their liberator from Persian rule. Alexander then drove his forces into the Persian heartland. Although outnumbered as usual, he decisively defeated Darius in 331 BCE at Gaugamela, gaining control of the majority of the Persian Empire.

With little motivation to continue fighting, the Persian army rebelled against Darius, who was assassinated shortly after his defeat at Gaugamela. During his conquests, Alexander emulated his hero Cyrus the Great's promotion of cultural, technological, and religious reciprocation and exchange, and like Cyrus, he nurtured the arts, engineering, and scientific intrigue, and eventually shared his idol's "Great" epithet. Like Cyrus, Alexander did not subject his conquered lands to authoritarian rule. He retained local administrative systems and culture, constructed infrastructure and twenty-four cities (including Alexandria, Kandahar, Herat, and Iskenderun), gifted lands, and had his own military and political leadership marry into local populations. Alexander wed the daughter of the vanquished Darius.

It had been only three years since Alexander left Macedonia, and his battle record was a perfect 11-0. He proceeded east into previously unknown territory, including Turkmenistan, Uzbekistan, Tajikistan, Afghanistan, and through the Khyber Pass of the hostile Hindu Kush mountains into Pakistan and India. By this time, his forces had been fighting continuously without defeat (17-0) for eight years. And yet he remained restless. Stirred and swayed by his maniacal ego, Alexander was hell-bent on chasing and conquering "the ends of the world and the Great Outer Sea."

Alexander's drive to Asia began in the spring of 326 BCE with a seventy-day march through monsoon rains along the Indus River system. His tired and ailing army secured the Punjab in May after defeating King Porus and his Paurava troops and war elephants at the Battle of Hydaspes. After mourning the natural death of his old friend and faithful warhorse, Bucephalus (in whose honor he named a city in Pakistan), Alexander halted his forces along the Beas River. Soon after, his most reliable and trusted general, Coenus, reported that the soldiers "longed to see their parents, their wives and children, their homeland," and refused to advance any farther. On the banks of the Beas River, Alexander's India campaign ground to a halt, marking the eastern extent of his conquests and empire.

While this event is often sensationalized as a "mutiny," no such rebellion occurred. When Alexander was approached by Coenus, who relayed the message that the troops wished to return west, it does not appear that Alexander protested with any great zeal. The alleged mutiny, or more accurately the customary and typical airing of grievances by soldiers up the chain of command, was only one of many composite factors forcing Alexander's hand. His troops were simply exhausted, his supply lines overstretched, and his victories progressively harder to attain. His army was increasingly reliant on foreign conscripts and mercenaries rather than on Macedonians and Greeks. His next targets were the powerful Nanda and Gangaridai kingdoms; victory was not a foregone conclusion. The Nanda force that first awaited Alexander's 40,000 infantry and 7,000 cavalrymen was composed of 280,000 combined infantry and cavalry, 8,000 chariots, and 6,000 war elephants (which scared the Greek horses). And this was also not the only enemy standing in his way.

Along the Indus River Valley, Alexander's force came face-to-face with deadly mosquitoes and their "diseases . . . accompanied by fever" identified two centuries earlier by Indian physician Sushruta. Having traversed and camped among swamps and rivers during the rainy season of spring and into the mosquito season of summer, his troops were riddled and reduced by malaria. References to corrupt climate and enervating illnesses (along with venomous snakes) litter the historical record of Alexander's India campaign. The Greek historian Arrian, for instance, tells us that "the Greeks and the Macedonian forces have lost part of their number in battle; others have been invalided with wounds and have been left behind in different parts of Asia; but most have died of sickness, and of all that host few survive, and even they no longer enjoy bodily strength." Alexander's once pulsating army was now a walking skeleton of its former self. "The general health of the army had deteriorated," acknowledges Frank L. Holt in his study *Into the Land of Bones: Alexander the Great in Afghanistan*, "and maladies of one sort or another carried off many victims." Shortly after the about-face of Alexander's army, for example, Coenus died of what commentators posit to be malaria or, possibly, typhoid. Given the sapped and sickly state of his men, their low morale and wish to retreat west, and facing an intimidating and daunting enemy, among other military complexities and impediments, his India campaign was aborted. Not even Alexander the Great could circumvent these coalescing challenges.

Another theory suggests that egotistical Alexander engineered the entire event to avoid personal humiliation and to preserve his honor and perfect 20-0 battle record. Grasping the tactical and strategic situation and realizing he was holding an unwinnable hand, Alexander had absolutely no intention of pushing an attack deeper into India. Resolved to protect his reputation and legendary prowess, he planted rumors, intentionally made the proposed campaign unpalatable to his men, and stage-managed the entire "mutiny" to place blame for the retreat squarely on their insubordinate shoulders. Either way, the result was the same. Alexander knew that any further advance, given the circumstances, was unsustainable. The wishes of his troops to return home were only a small component of a much larger inauspicious and unflattering strategic situation.

As it turned out, soon after Alexander reversed his course, the Maurya Empire was established, uniting the Indian subcontinent and creating the largest empire in Indian history. This kingdom paved the way for a modern, unified Indian state, and nurtured the dissemination of Buddhism. In hindsight, given Alexander's untenable position, the abandonment of his India campaign proved to be a sensibly cautious decision.

Although Alexander turned his army toward Macedon, he was by no means satisfied with his exploits, nor was he ready to burn out or fade away. Upon his return to Persia, for example, after learning that ceremonial guards had desecrated the tomb of his hero, Cyrus the Great, he summarily had them executed. Continuing west toward Babylon, he gave orders to prepare for an invasion of Arabia and North Africa, with his eye trained on the western Mediterranean. Europe via the Rock of Gibraltar and Spain would have been in his sights. The history-altering possibilities here are boundless. Secondary reconnaissance missions were tasked to the shores of the Caspian and Black Seas to lay the foundation for the eventual rekindling of his Asian push. He was preparing marching orders for simultaneous operations into uncharted, nameless regions of the unknown world. Alexander, however, would never reach "the ends of the world," at least not in this lifetime tour.

In the spring of 323 BCE, Alexander halted in Babylon to plan these next campaigns, and to receive delegates from the Libyans and Carthaginians. While he had been seriously wounded no fewer than eight times, had recently lost his best friend (and possibly his lover), Hephaestion, most likely to malaria or perhaps typhoid, and was drinking heavily as usual, he was not a broken man. After he crossed the Tigris River, Chaldean locals warned Alexander of a premonition they had received from their god Baal. The prophecy, they explained, foretold that his current approach to the city from the east would be escorted by death. They suggested that he enter through the Royal Gate on the opposite western wall. Alexander heeded their omen and changed course. Approaching the perimeter of the city center, Alexander and his entourage zigzagged through a labyrinth of crawling marshes and concentric canals abuzz with swarms of stirred-up mosquitoes.

Alexander's initial days in Babylon were spent shaping his military campaigns, hosting feasts, fraternizing with dignitaries, conducting spiritual rituals, and, of course, binge drinking. Abnormal fatigue, however, was quickly followed by a crippling, but intermittent, fever. The sequence of Alexander's ailment was well documented by his inner circle and is logged in the "Royal Diaries" or "Royal Journal." The records are consistently clear that from the first symptoms to his death, Alexander's illness lasted twelve days. The recorded time frame, from Alexander's swampy miasmic Babylonian entry, through his symptoms and fever cycle, to his death all point to *falciparum* malaria. The larger-than-life Alexander the Great died on June 11, 323 BCE, at the age of thirty-two, his life cut short by an inconspicuous, tiny mosquito.

Had this malarious mosquito not sucked the life out of Alexander, all indications point toward an advance into the Far East, truly uniting the east and west for the first time. Had this occurred, it would have upended the course of history and humankind to the point where modern society would literally be unrecognizable. The unprecedented exchange of ideas, knowledge, disease, and technology, including gunpowder, is too much to fathom. As it was, the world would have to wait another 1,500 years for this to happen. During the thirteenth century, this unification would be solidified by European traders like Marco Polo trudging east, and the Mongol hordes under Genghis Khan sweeping west. Included in this multifarious cross-cultural exchange was the Black Death. But what if Alexander had . . . He didn't. The mosquito helped rob him of this opportunity and glory.

Numerous other causes of death have been proposed throughout the ages, but lack credibility and backing. While the assassination plot is irresistible for conspiracy theorists, it does not hold sway. There is simply no reliable documented evidence or scientific credibility to back the claim. This alluring murder mystery appears to have entered the corridors of the gossip circle roughly five years after his death. The conspiracy was enriched and perfected by rumors that the assassination was carried out by none other than his old master and tutor, Aristotle himself, or one of Alexander's jilted wives or lovers. Yet Alexander, who had become increasingly paranoid and unpredictable, never mentioned any fears of an assassination intrigue.* Other theories ranging from acute alcohol poisoning, liver disease caused by Alexander's alcoholism, to a lengthy list of natural causes, including leukemia, typhoid, and even an altogether strange diagnosis of West Nile (which became a distinct viral species only roughly 1,300 years after his death) have all largely been disqualified as candidates. While an autopsy of Alexander's remains would definitively mark malaria as the cause of death, as is commonly agreed upon, this is not possible. One of the greatest men in human history is absent without leave.

En route to Macedonia, Alexander's body was diverted to Egypt and interred at Memphis. In the late fourth century BCE, his remains were

* Given Alexander's erratic behavior toward the end of his life, it has been proposed, although can never be definitively substantiated, that he was suffering from Chronic Traumatic Encephalopathy (CTE) due to the recurrent head traumas he sustained in battle. With the intense scrutiny currently surrounding concussions and professional sports, specifically the National Football League and the National Hockey League, Alexander's demeanor seems to mirror that of former players suffering from CTE.

exhumed and relocated to a mausoleum in Alexandria, the city bearing his name. Roman generals Pompey and Julius Caesar both visited his tomb to pay homage. Cleopatra robbed gold and jewels from the tomb to finance her war against Octavian (Augustus Caesar), who visited Alexander's grave upon his triumphant entrance into Alexandria in 30 BCE after defeating the star-crossed lovers Cleopatra and Mark Antony. In the mid-first century, the sadistic and tyrannical Roman emperor Caligula allegedly poached Alexander's breastplate for his own.

By the fourth century, Alexander's resting place simply vanishes from the historical record, perpetuating myth to which the vainglorious Alexander would certainly have no objection. Over 150 large-scale archeological excavations have been launched in search of his remains. Alexander is one of those rare historical figures that still resonate in an age of cell phones, virtual reality, genetic engineering, and nuclear weapons, and has captured the imagination, intrigue, adoration, and respect of admirers across time.

According to legend, when asked who should inherit his empire, with his dying words Alexander muttered "the strongest" or "the best man." In reality, the mosquito ensured that his vast empire and accomplishments died with him. Immediately, an orgy of infighting among his generals quickly destroyed any semblance of cohesion or imperial governance. Alexander's direct bloodline was also exterminated. His mother, Olympias, his wife, Roxana, and his heir, Alexander IV, were all hunted down and murdered. Eventually, his empire was divided into three main but weak and competing territories. Two were summarily fragmented into minor impotent and forgettable enclaves. Egypt, however, endured as a Macedonian dynasty until 31 BCE, when Mark Antony and Cleopatra were decisively defeated by Octavian at the Battle of Actium.*

While the territorial gains of Alexander were quickly erased by infighting and the absence of centralized authority, the enlightening legacy of his Hellenistic empire endures to this day. Following his death, Greek

* The suicides of Mark Antony and Cleopatra were immortalized by William Shakespeare's tragedy *Antony and Cleopatra*. In August 30 BCE, believing that his lover Cleopatra had already committed suicide, Mark Antony stabbed himself with a sword. When he found out that she was still alive, he was quickly brought to Cleopatra and died in her arms. A grieving Cleopatra then committed suicide by inducing an Egyptian cobra to bite her repeatedly.

sociocultural influence peaked across Europe, North Africa, the Middle East, and western Asia. Exploding from the heart of his former empire, Greek literature, architecture, science, mathematics, philosophy, and military strategy and design were disseminated across a wider berth and flourished in an age of academic prosperity and progress. Great libraries were constructed across the Arab world and scholars pondered the principles and ideas of Socrates, Plato, Aristotle, Hippocrates, Aristophanes, Herodotus, and shelves of books from other Greek writers of the golden age.

When Europe languished in 400 years of a cultural and intellectual abyss during the Dark Ages, academia flourished across the newly christened Muslim expanse. During the cross-cultural exchange of the Crusades, Islamic academics extended Europe a scholarly ladder to climb out of the caverns of ignorance, by reintroducing Greek and Roman literature and culture, as well as their own refinements and academic advancements flowering from the illuminating Muslim Renaissance.

After the mosquito dispatched Alexander, however, the ensuing fragmentation and collapse of his empire left the Mediterranean world in a power vacuum. This void would be filled by the ascendance of a backwater city located on a mosquito-plagued peninsula 650 miles west of Athens. After layovers in Persia and Greece, the mantle of power and the epicenter of Western civilization continued its westward progression, eventually landing in Rome. "The fate of Rome was played out by emperors and barbarians, senators and generals, soldiers and slaves," emphasizes Kyle Harper in his acclaimed 2017 work, *The Fate of Rome: Climate, Disease, and the End of an Empire*. "But it was equally decided by bacteria and viruses. . . . The fate of Rome might serve to remind us that nature is cunning and capricious." After the mosquito reinforced the Greeks during the Persian onslaughts; helped shatter the belligerent city-states of Greece during the Peloponnesian War, emboldening the rise of Macedon; nibbled away at Alexander's once unassailable army and proved him to be a mortal man after all, she pointed her proboscis west. She unleashed her unquenchable thirst on Rome, cultivating both the creation and the destruction of the mighty Roman Empire.

Roman supremacy was not a foregone conclusion. The Romans eked out a surprising but unconvincing and pyrrhic victory against the

Carthaginians during the First Punic War. At the outbreak of the Second Punic War, however, the underdog and uninspiring Romans were pitted against an unnerving and seemingly invincible adversary commanded by a general who rivaled the genius of Alexander—the resourceful and brilliant Carthaginian warrior whose name still conjures fear—Hannibal Barca.

CHAPTER 4

Mosquito Legions: The Rise and Fall of the Roman Empire

Like Xerxes and Alexander before him, Hannibal inherited war from his father. The twenty-nine-year-old son of the vanquished Carthaginian leader Hamilcar Barca was determined to avenge his father's defeat at the hands of the Romans during the First Punic War and unburden himself of the humiliation of surrender that he had personally witnessed as a boy. Hannibal's meticulously planned route to infiltrate Rome, calculated to bypass robust Roman and allied garrisons and to negate Roman naval supremacy, would steer him straight through the most hostile terrain in the Mediterranean world and provoke the Second Punic War. The outcome of the Punic Wars, raging intermittently from 264 to 146 BCE, would pilot the course of history for the next 700 years. Hannibal and his Carthaginian parade of 60,000 troops, 12,000 horses, and 37 war elephants would navigate the precipices and passes of the Alps and penetrate the heart of Rome.

What Rome did not know is that she had a powerful ally inhabiting the 310 square miles of the Pontine Marshes surrounding and safeguarding the capital itself. The marshes, often referred to as the Campagna, flanking the city of Rome were home to legions of lethal mosquitoes and were the defensive equivalent to armies of men. According to a vivid description from an early Roman scholar, the Pontine "creates fear and horror. Before entering it you cover your neck and face well before the swarms of large bloodsucking insects are waiting for you in this great heat of summer, between the shade of the leaves, like animals thinking intently about their prey . . . here you find a green zone, putrid, nauseating where thousands of insects move around, where thousands of horrible marsh plants grow under a suffocating sun." Successive invading armies from the Punic Wars to the Second World War were literally swarmed to death in the Pontine Marshes surrounding Rome.

From their origins as small, isolated enclaves of farmers and traders, Rome and Carthage eventually squared off in a grudge match for hegemony of the Mediterranean world, refereed by the mosquitoes of the Pontine Marshes. Picking up the pieces of Alexander's mosquito-haunted dream of world domination, Carthage and Rome emerged as the heirs of empire and would vie for economic and territorial ascendency. Both Carthage and Rome, however, had humble pedigrees and isolated upbringings and remained relatively insulated from the imperial wars of the Persians and Greeks. Alexander's quests and longing gazes toward the horizons of the unknown "ends of the world" overlooked the two burgeoning city-states of Carthage and Rome.

According to legend, Rome was founded in 753 BCE by Romulus and Remus, who, after being abandoned as infants, were nursed by a she-wolf. Upon their reaching adolescence, their natural leadership gained them a community of local followers. During a dispute over who should be sole ruler, Romulus killed his twin brother, Remus, and became the first king of Rome. Unlike the city-states of Greece, Rome expanded by assimilating outsiders into its unified legal body. The Roman willingness to extend citizenship to foreigners was unique and played a central role in the growth and governance of empire. Initially a despotic monarchy, Rome became a democratic republic in 506 BCE after a popular uprising. Guided by the aristocratic members of the Senate, the Roman Republic slowly expanded to incorporate the isthmus of Italy south of the Po River by 220 BCE.

From a few scattered huts, the people of Rome steadily fashioned a state that fought numerous wars and relocated a staggering number of citizens, slaves, and traders to secure an empire encompassing most of Europe, England, Egypt, North Africa, Turkey, the southern Caucasus, and the Mediterranean region, extending east as far as the Tigris River to its mouth at the Persian Gulf by 117 BCE. The mosquito was also caught up in the company of traveling caravans and the snaking convoys and columns of traders and migrants crisscrossing Rome's commercial corridors and expanding domain. The vast geographic and ethnic composition of the Roman Empire, and its intersecting trade and slave routes, aided in the expansion of mosquito hunting grounds and a broader dissemination of malaria throughout Europe as far north as Scotland. For Rome to achieve the zenith of its domination, however, it would inevitably be thrust headlong into a collision course with Carthage, the only other imperialist power in the region.

Shortly before the founding of Rome by Romulus and Remus, seafaring Phoenician traders from modern-day Lebanon and Jordan (then Canaan) had established outposts across the Mediterranean world by 800 BCE as far west as Spain's Atlantic coast. One such port of call was the harbor city of Carthage in Tunisia. Given its central location and its proximity to Sicily, Carthage quickly became a major center of trade and culture. Carthage was soon embroiled in a contest with the Greek city-states for control of the Mediterranean.

Following the Athenian mosquito-triggered catastrophe at Syracuse in 413 BCE, and Aristophanes's theatrical rebuke, *Lysistrata*, Carthage launched its own Sicilian campaign in 397 BCE, its first major imperialistic foray. After successfully isolating Syracuse, the Carthaginians dug in along the marshy and swampy surroundings of the city and began their siege in the spring of 396 BCE. At the onset of summer, the Carthaginian force, like their Athenian predecessors, were racked by malaria, and this mission, like that of the Athenians, ended in mosquito-borne disaster. Livy, the esteemed Roman historian, recounts that the Carthaginians "perished to a man, together with their generals." Nevertheless, the Carthaginian Empire made headway in all other colonial enterprises, encompassing much of the Mediterranean coast of North Africa, southern Spain, including Gibraltar and the Balearic Islands, Sicily (aside from Syracuse), Malta, and the coastal haunts of the islands of Sardinia and Corsica. Rome, however, was also busy carving out its own burgeoning empire, transforming from an insignificant village into a world power. The stretching territorial and economic tentacles of Rome and Carthage became entangled over trade in the Mediterranean.

The First Punic War (264–241 BCE) erupted over Sicily, where

Carthage wanted to preserve its commercial leverage, while a jittery Rome wanted to limit Carthaginian power to the doorstep of Italy. Although the conflict witnessed limited ground campaigns in Sicily and North Africa, the war was primarily fought at sea. The Romans, inexperienced at naval warfare, poured vast amounts of capital, labor, and men into building a formidable navy based on a captured Carthaginian warship. Despite, or perhaps partly because of, having sacrificed over 500 ships and 250,000 men, Rome stubbornly prevailed in its first foreign campaign.

The Romans appropriated Sicily, Sardinia, and Corsica, and occupied the island-studded Dalmatian Coast of the Balkans. More importantly, victory and the corresponding economic boost from these new colonies whetted Rome's appetite for further expansion and conquest. While the war had crippled the Carthaginian navy and gave Rome command of the seas, it had done little to diminish Carthage's land forces. A revitalized and vengeful Carthaginian Empire decided to strike back. Hannibal was determined to bring the fight directly to Rome.

In the spring of 218 BCE, Hannibal departed New Carthage (Cartagena) on the southern coast of Spain and commenced his fighting advance to Italy through eastern Spain, over the Pyrenees mountain range, and across Gaul (France), reaching the western foothills of the Alps with 60,000 men and thirty-seven now legendary war elephants. His crossing of the Alps is considered one of the greatest logistical feats in military history. His army trudged forward through hostile Gallic tribal territory and unforgiving terrain at the onset of winter, with no viable supply line. Although Hannibal lost 20,000 men and all but a handful of elephants during the perilous passage over the rugged Alps, a battered, malnourished, and weathered Carthaginian force of 40,000 successfully navigated the steep decline and entered northern Italy in late November.

On the winter solstice of December 18, Hannibal's depleted and drained army, augmented by allied Celtic Gauls and Spaniards, engaged a Roman blocking force of 42,000 men at Trebia. With careful planning and innovative field craft, Hannibal provoked and outmaneuvered the Romans into conducting futile frontal assaults, ensnaring them in indefensible positions. Outflanking the center of the Roman line, his forces swept through and annihilated the disorganized defenders, inflicting at least 28,000 casualties and scattering the survivors from the field of battle.

Following this decisive Carthaginian victory at Trebia, the emaciated elephants, horses, and skeletal troops staggered forward to encamp and pasture on "the plains which are near the Po," providing Hannibal the "best means of reviving the spirits of his troops and restoring the men and horses to their former vigour and condition."* In March 217 BCE, Hannibal gave marching orders to conduct a cunningly calculated and crafty operation.

The success of this campaign rested on the element of surprise, preserved and safeguarded by a deliberate and demanding advance along an unexpected route over the Apennine Mountains, followed by a four-day trudge through malarial bogs. The Carthaginians cleared the sickly swamps, but at an enormous cost. The mosquito tapped into the health and morale of the Carthaginian ranks and of their exceptionally gifted leader. Hannibal contracted malaria, losing sight in his right eye as a result of his intense fevers. By this time, the disease had already claimed the lives of his Spanish wife and son. Beleaguered but not defeated, the Carthaginian general continued his predetermined, plotted line of approach.

With his brilliantly mapped but malaria-soaked route, Hannibal executed the first recorded "turning movement" in military history by purposefully skirting and evading the Roman left flank. By sidestepping the Roman boundaries, he flipped the actual front, or direction, of the battlefield, turning the advantageous Roman defensive positions and terrain against them. The Romans were now entrapped by their own defensive perimeter in an exposed pocket or kill zone. Hannibal's innovative preparations and strategy ensured a convincing Carthaginian victory at the Battle of Trasimene on June 21, 217 BCE. His skillful and timely use of concealment, ambush, cavalry, and flanking tactics led to the slaughter or capture of the entire Roman force of 30,000 soldiers. Following these

* There is debate over how many, if any, elephants survived the mountainous crossing of the Alps.

catastrophic defeats at Trebia and Trasimene, the Romans were wary of engaging Hannibal in pitched battles, opting instead to cut off his supply lines and resources. Once more, Hannibal outmaneuvered and bested the Romans at their own strategic game.

Before attacking Rome, Hannibal took the initiative in August 216 BCE to secure much-needed provisions at Cannae, which also starved Rome of its crucial lifeline to southern stores. Although outnumbered two-to-one, Hannibal engaged the center of the Roman force of 86,000 before a timely, stunning, and beautifully executed pincer, or double-flanking, movement that enveloped the Roman legions. The Carthaginians surrounded and slaughtered the Roman army, diminishing it to the point where it ceased to be an effective fighting force.* Hannibal's victory at Cannae is regarded as one of the most dazzling tactical feats in military history. His methods and maneuvers are still taught in military colleges across the world and have been mirrored in the battle plans and conduct of strategists and generals ever since.

German strategist and chief of the general staff Alfred von Schlieffen modeled his legendary plan for the invasion of France at the onset of the First World War "to the same plan devised by Hannibal in long forgotten times." As German field marshal Erwin Rommel's Afrika Korps scrambled the beleaguered British forces across Libya, he wrote in his diary that "a new Cannae was being prepared." At Stalingrad in 1942, General Friedrich Paulus, commander of the German 6th Army, arrogantly, and as it turned out quite erroneously, commented that he was close to completing "his Cannae." Supreme Allied Commander General Dwight D. Eisenhower sought to duplicate this battle of annihilation against Hitler's Nazi forces in Europe "in the classic example of Cannae." During the First Gulf War, General Norman Schwarzkopf modeled the coalition forces' 1990 liberation of Kuwait on Hannibal's "Cannae model."

Following Hannibal's devouring of the Roman legions at Cannae, his Carthaginians seemed unstoppable. With the Roman army shattered, the road to Rome itself lay unchecked. The prize of the "Eternal City"

* Roman casualties at Cannae are hotly debated among historians. From the 86,000 total Roman soldiers, estimates for those killed in battle range from 18,000 to 75,000. Most estimates and the relative consensus straddle 45,000 to 55,000 killed.

was within reach. Hannibal could finally realize his retribution on Rome and avenge his father for the dishonor of defeat during the First Punic War. There was, however, another unforeseen guardian of Rome waiting in the wings—the legions of faithful and famished mosquitoes patrolling the Pontine Marshes. After Rome's military machine was smashed at Cannae, the mosquito was drafted into service and thrust into action. She began her 2,000-year history-piercing reign as the messenger of misery and death in the Pontine Marshes. She acted as the unofficial ambassador of Rome, with the sole duty of hailing and devouring hostile foreign armies and invading dignitaries.

In the aftermath of Hannibal's convincing conquest at Cannae in 216 BCE, two events turned the tide of the Second Punic War and, with input from the mosquito, changed the course of history. The first was Hannibal's reluctance to attack Rome. Although campaigning on the Italian peninsula for more than fifteen years, the Carthaginians never secured the capital city. Historians chalk up Hannibal's refusal to take Rome to numerous factors. The city was protected by fresh, unsullied troops strong enough to defend its fortifications, negating the feasibility of a direct assault and forcing the Carthaginians to lay siege. This was not an option. Hannibal's forces engaged in quick-strike maneuver warfare and were not trained, equipped, or supplied for siege tactics.

More critical, however, was that the limited lines of approach and siege grounds would entrench the Carthaginian army in the mosquito-infested Pontine Marshes, where malaria flourished year-round. In his meticulously thorough study, *Malaria and Rome: A History of Malaria in Ancient Italy*, Robert Sallares affirms that wetlands across Italy, including the notorious Pontine Marshes of the Campagna, "were being seized by malaria." Throughout the Italian campaign, malarious mosquitoes slowly ate away at the Carthaginian ranks. Legendary Anopheles mosquitoes had made a permanent and comfortable home in Italy long before Hannibal's invasion and had earned themselves a fearsome reputation and accomplished résumé. Almost two centuries earlier, although the Gauls under King Brennus successfully sacked Rome in 390 BCE, malaria had so thinned their ranks that they settled for a payment of gold and withdrew from the area in sickly vagrant bands. Malaria killed so many in such a short duration that the Gauls were forced to abandon customary burial practices for mass funeral pyres. "Hannibal was too smart," emphasizes Sallares, "to spend the summer in an area subject to intense malaria if he could avoid it." The mosquito safeguarded Rome as much as her legions of human defenders.

The second war-altering event was the replacement of politically motivated Roman generals who lacked military training, with Publius Scipio (Africanus), heralded in the top tier of historical military minds. Scipio was a professional soldier, a survivor of the Battle of Cannae, and he possessed a reputation and record that quickly catapulted him into the higher echelons of leadership. Under Scipio, the Roman military underwent a sweeping transformation, becoming a professional and lethal war machine. He insisted on recruiting men into his legions from mountainous regions free from malaria. With the main Carthaginian army still ravaging the Italian countryside, Scipio decided to bring the war to Carthage itself.

In 203 BCE, his forces landed at Utica and advanced through Carthaginian territory, forcing Hannibal to quit Italy and return to defend his homeland. Despite mutual admiration, negotiations foundered between the two generals. The decisive blow was delivered by quick-striking Roman cavalry at the Battle of Zama in October 202 BCE. With this war-winning victory over Hannibal, Rome began its meteoric rise to superpower status. Historian Adrian Goldsworthy notes that "Hannibal has the sort of glamour which only surrounds those military geniuses who won stunning victories but ultimately lost the war, men such as Napoleon and Robert E. Lee. The march of his army from Spain via the Alps into Italy and the battles he won there were all epics in themselves."

At the hands of Scipio, Hannibal was finally defeated on the battlefield at Zama, marking the end of the seventeen-year conflict. The Carthaginian decline, however, had begun much earlier in the malarial marshlands of Italy. The mosquito helped safeguard Rome from Hannibal and his hordes, providing a stepping-stone for Rome's climb to command of the Mediterranean world and beyond. "The treacherous fleshpots of Campania," states Diana Spencer in her work *Roman Landscape: Culture and Identity*, "had diverted Hannibal from Rome, and therefore from victory." Both Hannibal and the Carthaginian culture were exiled and eventually perished as a result of the Roman triumph during the Punic Wars.

This mosquito-backed Roman victory had immeasurable and far-reaching implications across both space and time. The Greco-Roman culture that followed dominated Europe, North Africa, and the Middle East for the next 700 years and had a profound influence on the development of human civilization and Western culture. The world still lives among the mosquito-haunted shadows of the Roman Empire. Numerous countries currently speak a Latin-based, or heavily Latin-influenced, language; many legal and political systems are an adaptation of Roman law and republic-style democracy; and the Roman Empire first martyred and then eased the passage of Christianity across Europe.

Another immeasurably important by-product of the Roman victory during the Punic Wars was the emergence of Roman literature. There were few writings prior to 240 BCE. A perpetual state of war, contact with the outside world, and the adoption of Alexander's Hellenistic Greek culture stimulated Roman academia. Widely regarded authors left us with a paper trail of written works vividly portraying the mosquito's historical weight and potency across the Roman world. In the first century BCE, Varro, one of Rome's most celebrated scholars, warned that "precautions must be taken in the neighborhood of swamps, [they] breed certain minute creatures which cannot be seen by the eyes, but which float in the air and enter the body through the mouth and nose and cause serious diseases." He recommended for those who could afford it to build houses on high ground or hills free from swampy air, where the wind would blow away the invisible creatures. The house on the hill became fashionable for the Roman elite. This fad and practice was globally reinforced during the age of European colonization and continues to the present day. Hilltop houses in the United States are sought after by the wealthy as a status symbol and are 15–20% more expensive. Add the real estate market to the mosquito's portfolio of influence.

Continuing the Hippocratic tradition, Roman physicians and curious intellectuals, like Varro, reinforced the miasma or "mal aria," bad-air concept of disease. Conforming to the earlier musings of Hippocrates on the malarial "dog days of summer," for example, the month of

September in the Roman calendar was accompanied by a reference to the Dog Star and a cautionary description of the "bad air" disease. "There is a great disturbance in the air," it warned. "The bodies of healthy people, and especially those of sick people, change with the condition of the air." While the mosquito remained undetected, her diseases were not passed over or pardoned by the quills of Roman scholars and scribes.

The classical writers of ancient Rome, such as Pliny, Seneca, Cicero, Horace, Ovid, and Celsus, all reference mosquito-borne diseases. The most thorough accounts were written by the acclaimed physician, avid author, and surgeon to the gladiators, Galen, during the second century CE. His explanation of human physiology, although adhering to Hippocratic traditions, was a more nuanced and sophisticated interpretation. He left a detailed depiction of the various types of malaria fever, elaborating on the observations and deductions of Hippocrates. Galen recognized the distant and primitive origins of malaria, noting that he could fill three volumes with what had been previously written about the disease. "We no longer need the word of Hippocrates or anyone else as witness that there is such a fever," he wrote, "since it is right in our sight every day, and especially in Rome." Galen also candidly recorded a second mosquito-borne disease, logging definitively for the first time the unmistakable physical symptoms of filariasis, or elephantiasis.

Galen emphasized that health was related to habits, including diet, exercise, natural surroundings, and living conditions. He understood that the heart pumped blood through arteries and veins, and he practiced bloodletting as a practical cure for most diseases, including malaria. Another popular Roman malaria remedy was to wear a piece of papyrus or amulet inscribed with the powerful incantation "abracadabra." While the origin of the word is unclear, it appears to be borrowed from the Aramaic, meaning "I will create what I speak," essentially summoning a cure.* The Romans also prayed to the fever goddess, Febris, for malarial respite in three specifically detailed temples on the healthful hilltops surrounding the city. The cult of Febris, which had a

* During the Great Plague of London in 1665–1666, an outbreak of bubonic plague killing 25% of the city in just eighteen months, residents still believed in the magic word, posting it above their doorways to ward off sickness.

substantial number of adherents, attests to the expanse and impact malaria had on Rome and its larger imperial breadth.

As Roman legions and merchants swarmed across Europe, so, too, did malaria. The vast empire connecting Africa to northern Europe brought an unprecedented exchange of ideas, innovation, academia, and pestilence. As a direct result of Roman expansion, malaria's grip now extended as far north as Denmark and Scotland. Malaria was an ever-present and chronic partner to Roman expansion. While the mosquito assured Roman ascendancy over the Carthaginians, a century and a half later she also played a role in the demise of the democratic Roman Republic and the rise of the emperor era beginning with Julius Caesar.

Following a string of victories in Gaul, Julius Caesar turned his army south in 50 BCE to confront the Senate, who had given his military and political rival Pompey dictatorial powers as the emergency consul. The Senate also voted to strip Caesar of his command and disband his personally loyal army. Refusing to bow to these demands, Caesar crossed the frontier boundary of Italy at the Rubicon River and purportedly uttered his immortal phrase "The die is cast." There was no turning back. His army, however, was riddled with malaria, as was he, and was in no shape to fight. Caesar had a lifelong battle with the disease. Shakespeare wrote, "He had a fever when he was in Spain, And when the fit was on him, I did mark How he did shake: 'tis true this god did shake." Had Pompey, whose army was vastly larger, met Caesar on the field of battle instead of fleeing, Caesar's gamble in rolling the dice at the Rubicon would have ended in malarial, and martial, disaster.

As it turned out, Pompey was eventually defeated in a series of battles with Caesar's reinforced and healthy legions. Seeking asylum in Egypt, Pompey was assassinated by an agent of the Egyptian pharaoh Ptolemy XIII. Upon being presented with Pompey's head, a disgusted Caesar and his lover Cleopatra, who was also the sister of Ptolemy, deposed the pharaoh and placed Cleopatra on the throne of Egypt. In the wake of Julius Caesar's assassination during the 44 BCE Ides of March, a string of dictators guiding the Roman Empire all had malarial bouts, with a handful succumbing to the disease, including Vespasian, Titus, and Hadrian. Caesar's heir, Octavian (Augustus), and his successor,

Tiberius, both had recurrent malarial episodes, courtesy of the mosquitoes of the Pontine Marshes.

Ironically, prior to his twenty-three murderous stab wounds, Caesar had prepared an ambitious project aimed at draining the Pontine Marshes of the Campagna to increase agricultural productivity. The early-second-century Greek-Roman biographer Plutarch mentions that Caesar "designed to draw off the water from the marshes . . . and to make them solid ground, which would employ many thousands of men in the cultivation." If successful, this initiative would have inadvertently led to a momentous reduction in mosquito populations, overturning the events that followed, altering the historical arc of the Roman age. This alternative history expired with Julius Caesar. The ambitious scheme of reclaiming the Pontine Marshes, contemplated by Napoleon as well, would ultimately be realized 2,000 years later by another Italian dictator, Benito Mussolini.

While the malarious Campagna protected Rome from her enemies, malaria also dampened Rome's marauding armies. Similar to bacteria or viruses, malaria strains differ by region. Roman legionaries, administrators, and accompanying traders were unaccustomed and thus not acclimated or "seasoned" to foreign malaria parasites in distant lands. During the Germanic campaigns in the early first century CE, the Germans consistently forced the superior Roman legions to fight and camp among bogs and marshes, where malaria and filthy drinking water drastically reduced their combat effectiveness. Given that swamp-bred miasma was thought to cause sickness, this German tactic has the hallmark indicators of deliberate biological warfare. When General Germanicus Caesar passed through Teutoburg Forest, he reported that he found tangled masses of Roman skeletons, horses, and mutilated corpses rotting in the "sodden marshland and ditches." Adrienne Mayor, when writing about biological and chemical warfare in the ancient world, posits that "the German manipulation of the Roman legions . . . was most likely a biological stratagem." In keeping with the miasma theory, this was a weaponization of the marshes and not a premeditated biological use of the true assassins, the snubbed and marginalized mosquitoes themselves. The Battle of Teutoburg Forest in 9 CE, where the entire Roman force of three legions and auxiliaries was annihilated, is regarded as Rome's greatest military defeat. This disaster, coupled with indefatigable malaria, forced Rome to abandon its intentions east of the Rhine River. By the fifth century, these independent warring peoples of central and eastern Europe would eventually contribute to the fall of the Roman Empire.

The Roman attempt to subdue Scotland, known to them as Caledonia, was also thwarted by a local strain of malaria that killed half of the 80,000-man imperial force. Roman retreat behind the protection of Hadrian's Wall, begun in 122 CE, allowed for the preservation of independent Scottish peoples. In the Middle East, as in Scotland, malaria prevented Rome from securing a concrete foothold. The exotic forms of malaria feasted on new Roman arrivals to northern Europe or the Middle East until these trespassers were either seasoned or dead.

While the mosquito foiled Roman armies fighting on the front lines and fields of the far reaches of empire, on the home front she progressively turned her poison arrows inward on Rome itself. For Rome, she served as both a savior and, eventually, a killer, proving, as she often does, to be a fickle, fly-by-night ally. As a stalwart defender, the mosquito continued to patrol the Pontine Marshes protecting Rome from foreign invaders, but she also slowly began to consume those she sheltered and quartered. Malarious mosquitoes gradually gnawed at the foundations of the Roman Empire and drained the life from its subjects. Through their own advancements in engineering and agriculture, the Romans helped to convert the mosquito from friend to foe and choreographed the denouement of their own downfall.

Ironically, the Roman penchant for gardens, cisterns, fountains, baths, and ponds, in combination with the complex system of aqueducts, frequent natural floods, and a coinciding period of global warming, all provided a haven for mosquito propagation, turning the elements of urban beautification into death traps.* As the city grew from a population of 200,000 to over a million in the last two centuries BCE, rapid

* A fourth-century inventory of the city of Rome listed by Kyle Harper included: 28 libraries, 19 aqueducts, 423 neighborhoods, 46,602 apartment complexes, 1,790 mansions, 290 granaries, 254 bakeries, 856 public baths, 1,352 cisterns and fountains, and 46 brothels. The 144 public latrine facilities produced 100,000 pounds of human excrement per day!

deforestation and cultivation increased, fostering further mosquito ecologies on the rural fringes of the city, including the Pontine Marshes. "The Romans did not just modify landscapes; they imposed their will upon them. . . . Human encroachments on new environments is a dangerous game," emphasizes Kyle Harper. "In the Roman Empire, the revenge exacted by nature was grim. The prime agent of reprisal was malaria. Spread by mosquito bite, malaria was an albatross on Roman civilization . . . and made the eternal city a malarial bog. Malaria was a vicious killer in town and country, anywhere the *Anopheles* mosquito could thrive." Italy's malarial reputation was so well documented that outsiders referred to the disease simply as "Roman Fever." This disparaging moniker was merited and duly deserved.

The city of Rome was continuously imperiled and consumed by overwhelming malaria epidemics. In the aftermath of the "Great Fire of Rome," under Emperor Nero a hurricane tore through the Campagna in 65 CE, churning up moisture and mosquitoes, sparking a malaria epidemic that left upwards of 30,000 people dead. The mosquito was now attacking Rome itself. According to Tacitus, a Roman senator and historian, "the houses were filled with lifeless forms, and the streets with funerals." Again, in 79 CE, after the eruption of Mount Vesuvius, which petrified Pompeii, malaria ripped through Rome and the Italian countryside, forcing farmers to abandon their fields and villages, most notably in the Campagna. Tacitus witnessed refugees and commoners "with no regard even for their lives, a large proportion camped in the unhealthy districts of the Vatican, which resulted in many deaths." This massive area of bountiful farmland on Rome's doorstep, encompassing the Campagna and its Pontine Marshes, was left fallow until Il Duce Benito Mussolini's reclamation and relocation project prior to the outbreak of the Second World War.

In the wake of these natural disasters, the dearth of agriculture in the immediate vicinity of Rome allowed the marshes to expand, intensifying endemic malaria while also putting a dire strain on the food production required for the city's rising population. This chronic malarial snowball effect was a direct catalyst for the decline and fall of the Roman Empire. Society and its economic, agricultural, and political appendages cannot prosper, let alone maintain the status quo, when habitual malaria creates a merry-go-round of labor-draining illness. Roman society was hampered in all directions, with fewer than half of infants surviving childhood. Life expectancy for those who beat the odds was a dismal twenty to twenty-five years. The etching on the gravestone of Veturia, the wife of a centurion, relates the life of an average Roman: "Here I lie, having lived for twenty-seven years. I was married to the same man for sixteen years and bore six children, five of whom died before I did." Compounding the insidious presence of malaria was a series of catastrophic plagues that paralyzed the Roman Empire and hampered the progress of political and social life.

Livy, the Roman historian writing at the turn of the millennium, lists at least eleven distinct epidemics during the reign of the republic. Two now infamous plagues tore at the heart of the empire. The first, lasting from 165 to 189 CE, was brought by troops returning from the failed mosquito-ravaged campaigns in Mesopotamia. The Antonine Plague or the Plague of Galen, given his firsthand account, spread through the empire like wildfire. It first struck Rome, before spreading throughout Italy and causing large-scale depopulation and hordes of nomadic refugees and itinerant migrants. It took the life of Emperors Lucius Verus and Marcus Aurelius, whose family name, Antoninus, became associated with the outbreak. The disease then headed north as far as the Rhine, west to the shores of the Atlantic Ocean, and in the east, eventually reached India and China. At its peak, contemporary records reveal a death rate of 2,000 per day in Rome alone. Roman archives and the writings of Galen indicate a mortality rate of 25%, with an extrapolated death toll across the empire as high as five million. The severity suggests that it was a pathogen previously unknown to Europe. While Galen gives us symptomatic descriptions, they are uncharacteristically vague. While the true cause remains a mystery, the top candidate is smallpox, with measles as a distant runner-up.

The second epidemic, known as the Plague of Cyprian, originated in Ethiopia and then spread across North Africa and the eastern portion of the empire to Europe as far north as Scotland between 249 and 266 CE. Its name commemorates Saint Cyprian, the Catholic bishop of Carthage, who left an eyewitness interpretation of the misery, documenting a mortality rate of 25–30% and a daily death count in Rome nearing 5,000. Among them were the emperors Hostilian and Claudius Gothicus. The number of total deaths is not known, but estimates again reach as high as five to six million or one-third of the entire empire. Epidemiologists have proposed that both the Antonine and Cyprian Plagues were the first zoonotic transfers of smallpox and measles from their animal hosts to humans. Others view the first epidemic as one, or both, of these diseases. They ascribe the second, the Plague of Cyprian, to a mosquito-borne hemorrhagic fever similar to yellow fever or to a hemorrhagic virus akin to the dreaded Ebola (which is not transmitted by mosquitoes).

The lasting imprint of these plagues, in concert with universal malaria, was irreparable. The Roman Empire was an imploding superpower and could not be salvaged. Widespread manpower shortages for both agricultural labor and the Roman legions severely weakened Rome's hold on the surviving populations, cowering while the vast empire crumbled and collapsed around them. In addition to mass death, or because of it, this "Crisis of the Third Century" also witnessed widespread rioting, civil war, assassinations of emperors and politicians by rogue military commanders, and the rampant and sadistic persecution of Christian scapegoats. This unchecked hedonistic violence was compounded by economic depression, earthquakes and natural disasters, and the pressures of persistent incursions from relocated ethnicities within the empire and belligerents from beyond its borders during the "Era of Migrations" beginning around 350 CE. General Anopheles intervened as a lifesaving stopgap measure by humiliating a successive line of invaders, though only to prolong the inevitable outcome she was also simultaneously orchestrating—the fall of the Roman Empire.

Amid this upheaval during the Era of Migrations, a series of foreign aggressors, like the Gauls and Carthaginians before them, set their crosshairs directly on a weakened Rome, which by now was no longer the capital of a homogenous Roman Empire. Due to its strategic military and commercial location, in 330, Emperor Constantine moved the capital from Rome to Constantinople (Istanbul). The realignment and destabilization of empire continued under Emperor Theodosius, who made Nicene Christianity the official state faith in 380, before apportioning the empire between his two sons in 395, creating an enduring divide between East and West. This cleave reduced the military and economic clout of both halves. Constantinople remained the capital of the eastern portion until the collapse of the Byzantines at the hands of the Islamic Ottomans in 1453. In the Western Empire, due to unremitting malaria, Rome was replaced by a series of capitals, but the Eternal City retained its paramount position as the spiritual, cultural, and economic center of empire. It also remained the prize for pillaging raiders.

The first to strike at Rome were the Germanic Visigoths led by King Alaric. In 408, his "barbarians" swept south through Italy and laid siege to the city of roughly one million people on three separate occasions. Starvation and disease slowly eroded the Roman will to fight. When a Roman envoy asked what would be left for the besieged citizens of Rome, Alaric sardonically quipped, "Their lives." Zosimus, a Roman scribe tracking the events, woefully wrote, "all that remained of the Roman valor and intrepidity was totally extinguished." In 410, Alaric laid siege to the city for a third and final time. There would be no negotiations, quarter, or immunity. Once inside the city gates, his forces embarked on and reveled in three days of destruction and death. The citizens of Rome were robbed, raped, killed, and sold into slavery. Satisfied with their pillage and plunder, the Visigoths quit the city and headed south, subjecting the Campagna, Calabria, and Capua to the same fate, leaving a trail of wreckage in their wake. Rome's agricultural output, which was already unstable, was dealt another setback. Although intending to return to Rome, by this time Alaric's forces were ruined by malaria. The mighty King Alaric himself, the first to sack Rome in nearly 800 years, succumbed to malaria in the fall of 410. The mosquito had shielded Rome once again.

With his death, the mosquito-chased Visigoths consolidated their loot and retired north, establishing a kingdom in southwestern Gaul in 418. The locals flattered their new rulers, and as legend has it, the displaced Celtic nobility allowed the Visigoth leaders to win at the game of backgammon to curry their favor. In Star Wars vernacular, they always, and wisely, "let the Wookiee win." These new tenants of Gaul, however, would help defend the Western Empire from its next challenger—Attila and his plundering Huns.

The adroit, quick-striking Huns were skilled horsemen who terrified European populations with their fearsome tattooed arms, faces carved with patterned scars, and elongated skulls from having been bound between boards as infants. Originating in eastern Ukraine and the northern Caucasus, the Huns initiated their prolonged invasion of eastern Europe around 370, quickly reaching the Hungarian Danube River. By the late fourth century, as their raids intensified, a worried Constantinople began paying the Huns to spare the Eastern Roman Empire. With tribute payment arriving from the timorous east, a bold and ambitious new leader, Attila, projected his power westward over the Austrian Alps. It was only a matter of time before his skilled cavalry would attack Rome.

Yet, the Huns were not the only marauders coveting the Eternal City. The crown jewel at the heart of the Western Empire faced a dual threat, from the Huns and from another posse of despoiling pillagers, the Vandals. As the Huns cemented their presence in eastern Europe, the Vandals, a large group of Germanic tribes from Poland and Bohemia, cut a swath clear across northern Europe through Gaul and Spain. In 429, led by the warrior-king Geiseric, 20,000 Vandals were shuttled across the Strait of Gibraltar to North Africa. They further crippled the Western Empire and broadened the dearth of food production by seizing the North African tax payments of grains, vegetables, olive oil, and slaves. When the Vandals laid siege to the Roman harbor city of Hippo (modern-day Annaba in the northeastern corner of Algeria), the local bishop, Augustine, pleaded for mercy and begged that the cathedral and the immense library, housing a remarkable collection of Greek and Roman books, including his own writings, be spared the torch. The death of Augustine's piously Christian and venerated mother, Saint Monica, in 387 from malaria contracted in the Pontine Marshes inspired some of the finest passages of his autobiographical thirteen-volume masterpiece, *Confessions*.

Like his beloved mother before him, the future Saint Augustine, second only to Paul of Tarsus in influencing and shaping Western

Christianity, died of malaria in August of 430, soon after the Vandal siege of Hippo commenced. Shortly after his death, the Vandals reduced the city to rubble. The modern English word "vandal" meaning "deliberate destruction or defacement of property" perpetuates their reputation for "vandalism." During the destruction of Hippo, however, the Vandals did not quite live up to our dictionary definition. Augustine's cherished cathedral and library were granted clemency, standing immaculate amid the smoldering ruins. From North Africa the Vandals quickly secured Sicily, Corsica, Sardinia, Malta, and the Balearic Islands. Although Rome was within Geiseric's sight, Attila was the first to strike.

Attila's attempt to conquer Gaul was met with defeat near the Ardennes Forest in France/Belgium in June 451 by a coalition of Visigoths and Romans. He immediately turned his clattering Huns southward and commenced a swift invasion of northern Italy, despoiling town and country along the way. A small Roman shadow force, resembling the Spartans at Thermopylae, managed to stall the advancing Huns on the approaches to the Po River. Legions of mosquito reinforcements quickly entered the fray and secured a stalemate. Once more, the timely mediation of General Anopheles saved Rome.

Taking a page out of Hannibal's military aide-memoire, Attila also halted his emaciated troops at the Po, and entertained an audience with Pope Leo I. While it is a romantic bedtime story to tell of a pious Christian pope converting the barbarian Attila to forsake his intentions for Rome and retreat from Italy, this is stretching the bounds of poetic license. Like Brennus's Gauls, Hannibal's Carthaginians, and Alaric's Visigoths before them, Attila's ferocious Huns were steered and ultimately doomed by the mosquito. "The Huns," recorded the Roman bishop Hydatius, "were victims of divine punishment, being visited with heaven-sent disasters: famine and some kind of disease. . . . Thus crushed, they made peace with the Romans and all returned to their homes." Malaria rendered the Hun military impotent. Attila was also keenly aware of the malarial fate of Alaric and his Visigoths forty years earlier. To make matters worse, Hun stores were insufficient, food was in short supply, and living off the land had become increasingly fruitless. The Huns had ravaged the crops of northern Italy, North African imports had been hijacked by the

Vandals, the Campagna was a quagmire, and Rome was in the grips of famine as drought stalked local agriculture.

Attila's reception of the pope's entreaty was nothing more than a ruse to save face. Malarious mosquitoes had forced his hand. "The heartland of empire was a gauntlet of germs," explains Kyle Harper. "The unsung savior of Italy in this affair was perhaps even malaria. Pasturing their horses in the watery lowlands where mosquitoes breed and transmit the deadly protozoan, the Huns were easy prey for malaria. All in all, it may have been wise for the king of the Huns to turn his cavalry back toward the high steppe beyond the Danube, cold and dry, where the *Anopheles* mosquito could not follow." The mosquito successfully shielded Rome again, and forced Attila to abort his marauding mission. While Attila did not expire from malaria like Alexander or Alaric, his death two years later in 453 CE was just as inglorious. He died of complications triggered by acute alcoholism. Division and infighting quickly followed, and the temperamental tribal Huns abandoned their fragile unity and faded from history.

While Attila's campaign in Italy pinned down Roman legions, the Vandals were prowling the Mediterranean Sea, raiding ports and pirating trade. Vandal activity in the Mediterranean was so abundant and fierce that the Old English name for the sea was *Wendelsae* (Sea of Vandals). Given the dual threat from the Huns and the Vandals, Rome recalled its garrisons from Britain. Sensing an opportunity, the Angles from Denmark and the Saxons from northwestern Germany teamed up as the Anglo-Saxons and invaded Britain in the 440s, seizing territory from, and replacing the culture of, the indigenous Celtic peoples and the vestiges of Roman occupation.

Following Attila's mosquito-riddled retreat from Italy, the Romans could now concentrate exclusively on the Vandal threat amassing in North Africa and on the Mediterranean islands troublingly close to home. Political bungling and subversion among the Roman elite forced Geiseric's hand. In May 455, two years after the death of Attila, he landed in Italy with a Vandal force and marched on Rome. Pope Leo I, as he had done previously with Attila, beseeched Geiseric not to destroy the ancient city and slaughter its inhabitants, instead offering up loot as a conciliation prize. The gates of Rome were thrown open for Geiseric and his men.

While the Vandals honored their word, over the course of two weeks they gathered all the slaves and treasure they could find, including any precious metals adorning buildings or statues. When the mosquito began to eat away at the Vandal ranks, however, they quickly took their leave and returned to Carthage. The Vandal sack of Rome was not nearly as sadistic as legend would have us believe, simply because they did not overstay their malarial welcome. Like the disintegration and scattering of the Huns following the death of Attila, Vandal dominance in the Mediterranean region eroded after the passing of Geiseric in 477. Their residual and fragmented pockets were absorbed into the tartan collection of local populations.

The fall of the Western Roman Empire was a gradual decay, as it had been in decline since the third century. Over the final decades, however, Rome ultimately buckled under the weight and social pressures of endemic malaria, epidemics, famine, depopulation, war, and the scourge of sequential destabilizing invaders. Zoology professor J. L. Cloudsley-Thompson summarizes, "It would be mistaken to overstress an epidemic theory for the Roman decline, but bubonic plague and malaria clearly played an important part and, for the reasons given, it would appear that the role of malaria was the more significant." Philip Norrie, senior lecturer of medicine at the University of New South Wales, adds that the Roman Empire "ended in 476 in the grips of a falciparum malaria epidemic." The mosquito's continuous attrition unquestionably escorted Rome's gradual corrosion and ultimate collapse.

By the time the invading Ostrogoths carved out a kingdom in Italy in the 490s, there had not been a Western Roman emperor for nearly twenty years, and, as events unfolded, there never would be again. The Ostrogoths successfully sacked Rome in 546 during the twenty-year Gothic War of 535–554 between the Ostrogoths and their allies, and the Eastern Roman Empire or Byzantine Empire under the brilliant leadership of Emperor Justinian. The war was the final bid to salvage some of the lost territory of the west and resurrect a single unified Roman

Empire. It was not to be. A tidal wave of disease thwarted Justinian's dream of resuscitating the empire.

Beginning in 541, an unprecedented pandemic of bubonic plague, known as the Plague of Justinian, tore through the Byzantine Empire. Thought to have originated in India, the plague swiftly made call at every major port on the Mediterranean Sea and plunged northward into Europe, reaching Britain within three years. It is recorded as one of the deadliest epidemics in history, killing between 30 and 50 million people, or roughly 15% of the world's entire population. In Constantinople, half the population was wiped out in less than two years. This was not lost on contemporary commentators, who described the contagion as being global in nature and scope. Procopius, secretary to the brilliant and malaria-embattled Byzantine general Belisarius, shrewdly recognized that "during these times there was a pestilence, by which the whole human race came near to being annihilated . . . it embraced the whole world, and blighted the lives of all men." The only other epidemic in documented human history that approaches this calamity is a second serving of bubonic plague in the mid-fourteenth century known as the Black Death.

Emperor Justinian's cultural donations still resonate today through the resplendent buildings he constructed in Constantinople, including the imposing Hagia Sophia. His uniform rewriting of Roman law has also survived as the basis of codified civil law in most Western nations. Although his rule was not as popular during his own reign as it has become in modern times, his devotion to the arts, theology, and academia fostered the blossoming of Byzantine culture, and he is marked as one of the most visionary leaders of the late-antiquity period and is often praised as "the last Roman." The so-called Classical World—that of the Greek and Roman civilizations—had come to an abrupt halt. As William H. McNeill notes, the Justinian Plague led to "the perceptible shift away from the Mediterranean as the preeminent center of European civilization and the increase in the importance of more northerly lands." As such, the heart of Western civilization continued its westward migration to France, Spain, and eventually found an enduring residence in Britain.

For Rome, the mosquito ultimately proved to be a double-edged sword. Initially, she safeguarded Rome from the military genius of Hannibal and his conquering Carthaginians, encouraging and emboldening the construction of empire and the widespread dissemination of Roman cultural, scientific, political, and academic advancements, securing the enduring legacy of the Roman era. Over time, however, while she continued to defend Rome against foreign plunderers, including the Visigoths, Huns, and Vandals, from her headquarters in the Pontine Marshes, she was also busy piercing the heart of Rome itself.

For the Romans, shaking hands with the devil and striking a Faustian bargain with the mosquito proved to be an unpredictable alliance and a dangerous deal, one that ultimately ended in ruin. "I have never seen so bad of an appearance," wrote the author of the two-part tragic play *Faust*, Johann Wolfgang von Goethe, in 1787, "as they are usually described in Rome." In his play, Goethe mentions both the contaminating pollution and the potential bounty of the Pontine Marshes: "A marsh extends along the mountain chain, / That poisons what so far I've been achieving; / Were I that noisome pool to drain, / 'Twould be the highest, last achieving. / Thus space to many millions I will give / Where, though not safe, yet free and active they may live." Outside the pages of *Faust*, the mosquitoes of the Pontine Marshes flourished and were fickle allies to Rome, vacillating between friend and enemy. The mosquito scratched away the strength of Roman society, underpinning the collapse of one of the mightiest, vastest, and most influential empires in history. In the process, she also left her permanent and undying mark on human spirituality and the global religious order.

The rise and fall of the Roman Empire corresponded with the advent and proliferation of Christianity. This new faith, which began as a splinter camp or "Jesus Movement" within Judaism in the first century, broke away from its parental convictions, due in part to the treatment of, and rituals surrounding, what we now know to be mosquito-borne diseases, and the debate over the divinity and role of healers. After a rocky and violent start, Christianity soon found a home in the minds and ministries of populations across Europe and the Near East as a remedial religion, permanently realigning the balance of power around our planet.

Mostly, however, in the immediate aftermath of the collapse of the Roman Empire, Europe turned inward upon itself. The dictatorial feudalism of monarchies, lordships, and the papacy reigned supreme. Christianity reversed course from a healing faith and became fatalistic, loaded and burdened with fire and brimstone and sweeping spiritual and economic corruption. A recoiling European population bunkered down during the Dark Ages as progress, academia, and the knowledge of the ancients vanished from the collective memory. While Europe was blinded by disease and religious and cultural instability, another spiritual and political order flowered and flourished in the Middle East. The appearance of Islam in Mecca and Medina in the early seventh century spawned an inspired cultural and intellectual renaissance across the Middle East. As Europe slid into an intellectual abyss, education and advancement thrived across the maturing Muslim expanse. Inevitably, these two spiritual superpowers would vie for territorial and economic hegemony amid clouds of secular mosquitoes, igniting the clash of civilizations, the Crusades.

CHAPTER 5

Unrepentant Mosquitoes: A Crisis of Faiths and the Crusades

The emergence of the Christian faith was gradual. Two centuries after the crucifixion of Jesus, his converts were still a persecuted, scattered minority, viewed as a disloyal threat within the Roman Empire. The Romans were a diverse and malleable collective and were remarkably willing to assimilate a wide range of both peoples and practices into their system of beliefs and culture. Christianity, however, proved difficult to digest, and its disciples were slaughtered in creative ways. They were dressed in animal skins and torn to shreds by dogs, some were fastened to poles and set alight after dark, usually in groups, to enhance the fiery spectacle, while others suffered a standard crucifixion. However, the persecution of Christians not only failed to suppress the faith, but it also tempted the curiosity of eventual converts and, on a larger scale, undermined social stability in Rome and across an embattled empire hounded by disease and besieged by near-constant invasion.

During this "Crisis of the Third Century," Christianity saw a strengthening and development across Roman regions. This surge corresponds with the devastation wrought by the Plagues of Antonine and Cyprian, discussed earlier, and the broader dissemination of endemic malaria across Rome and realm. Christians were persecuted during both plagues. Their rejection of Roman polytheistic gods in favor of the monotheistic Yahweh or Jehovah was scapegoated as the cause. These two savage epidemics set against the dispiriting backdrop of endemic malaria, however, also brought a multitude of new converts who viewed the faith as a "healing" religion. After all, it was said that Jesus had performed miracle treatments, made the lame walk, made the blind see, cured leprosy, and brought Lazarus back from death itself. It was believed that these healing powers were transferred to the apostles and the subsequent disciples.

Within the cultural upheaval of the Crisis of the Third Century, and the ensuing foreign raids staved off by the mosquitoes of the Pontine Marshes during the Era of Migrations, chronic malarial infection was one of the challenges to the religious and social status quo and, as Sonia Shah writes, "shattered all the old certainties." The bane of malaria would have reinforced the shortfalls of traditional Roman spirituality, medicine, and mythology. Amulets, abracadabra, and offerings to Febris failed in the face of this newfound hope offered by therapeutic Christian rituals and philanthropic nursing practices.

While I would never be so historically reckless as to suggest that the mosquito single-handedly converted the masses to Christianity, malaria was, however, one of many factors that aided in its eventual dominion over the European expanse. "Christianity, unlike paganism, preached care of the sick as a recognized religious duty. Those who were nursed back to health felt gratitude and commitment to the faith, and this served to strengthen Christian churches at a time when other institutions were failing," explains Irwin W. Sherman, professor emeritus of biology and infectious disease at the University of California. "The capacity of Christian doctrine to cope with the psychic shock of epidemic disease made it attractive for the populations of the Roman Empire. Paganism, on the other hand, was less effective in dealing with the randomness of death. In time, the Romans came to accept the Christian view." The mosquito was one of the top dealers in "psychic shock" across the Roman Empire, and Christianity offered comfort, care, and perhaps even salvation, to its converts.

Early Christian communities regarded the nursing of the sick as an obligation of faith and established the first true hospitals. This concern, along with other charitable Christian practices, reinforced a strong sense of community and belonging, and a greater network for those in need. When Christians traveled for trade or business, they found a warm welcome among local congregations. By the year 300, the Christian diaspora in the city of Rome was caring for over 1,500 widows and orphans. During the unimpeded violence, famine, plagues, and rampant malaria spanning the third to fifth centuries, Christianity attracted followers as a remedial religion.

Microbiology professor David Clark sums up the connection between malaria and the diffusion of Christianity, cautioning, "Although modern-day Christianity dislikes admitting it, these early Christians practiced what can only be described as a form of magic. Spells were written on papyrus sheets, which were then folded into long strips and worn as amulets. . . . Similar spells were found down to the eleventh century, often containing magical formulas from the medieval Jewish cabala, mixed with more orthodox Christian terminology. These spells illustrate the great importance of malaria and magic among the Christians. . . . They also confirm that early Christianity was in many ways a healing cult."

The inscription on a fifth-century Roman Christian amulet, for example, was designed to cure a woman named Joannia from malaria: "Flee, hateful spirit! Christ pursues you; the son of God and the Holy Spirit have overtaken you. O God of the sheep-pool, deliver from all evil your handmaid Joannia. . . . O Lord, Christ, son and Word of the living god, who heals every disease and every infirmity, also heal and watch over your handmaiden Joannia . . . and chase away and banish from her every fever-heat and every kind of chill—quotidian, tertian, quartan—and every evil." In her chapter "A Gospel Amulet for Joannia" in the book *Daughters of Hecate: Women and Magic in the Ancient World*, AnneMarie Luijendijk, professor of religion at Princeton, forwards that "Irina Wandrey posits a connection between the large number of fever amulets from that period and the increase of malaria in Late Antiquity." She elaborates that malaria amulets and charms while "seemingly insignificant everyday objects participate in the larger discourse of healing, religion, and power . . . creating a legitimate and socially acceptable Christian practice." Dr. Roy Kotansky, historian of ancient religion and papyrology, cleverly detects that "during the Roman Empire the treatment of diseases with amulets seems to have required the proper diagnostic identification of the ailment, and we find that the texts found on amulets often indicate specific diseases for which they are written."

While the personal and malaria-specific plea on Joannia's amulet is hard to ignore, we do not know if the gods she invoked delivered her from all evil and chased away a mosquito-borne death.

It is not surprising that early Christians, as evinced by Joannia's beseeching inscription, blended faiths to suit their needs. In times of endemic malarial sickness and religious uncertainty, having a healthy variety of prayers and talismans to multiple gods, both pagan and Christian, increased the odds that one of them, presumably the one that is the authentic, bona fide savior, will take heed and heal. With its sacrament of tending to the ill, including the quaking malarial masses, the Christian god emerged as the top candidate to banish sickness, while offering salvation and an afterlife liberated from fevers, pain, and suffering. While the mosquito was forcefully nudging the momentum of Christianity forward, she received a boosting push from a couple of famous emperors along the way—Constantine and Theodosius.

During the tumultuous fourth century, Christianity gained traction in the waning Roman Empire and was reinforced by Emperor Constantine's conversion in 312 and his Edict of Milan the following year. In the aftermath of his predecessor Diocletian's "Great Persecution" of Christians, Constantine's legal decree did not make Christianity the official religion of the empire as commonly thought. It did, however, avow that all Roman subjects had the freedom to choose and practice their own faith without fear of persecution, thus satisfying both polytheists and Christians. In 325, Constantine went one step further at the ecumenical Council of Nicaea. To placate the adherents of the diverse and assorted polytheistic and Christian factions, and end religious purges, he blended their beliefs into one faith. Constantine ratified the Nicene Creed and the concept of the Holy Trinity, opening the doors for the compilation of the current Bible and modern Christian doctrine.

Following Constantine's codification of canon, between 381 and 392, Emperor Theodosius, the last sovereign to rule over both the eastern and western halves of the Roman Empire, forever fused Christianity and Europe together. He rescinded the religious tolerance of the Edict of Milan. He closed polytheistic temples, executed those worshipping Febris or wearing enchanted abracadabra charms, and officially proclaimed

Roman Catholicism as the singular state religion of the empire. The city of Rome would provide the pulsating heart of Christianity and house the earthly seat of God at the Vatican.

The full-scale arrival of Christianity in Rome itself, and the construction of the Vatican and other monuments of Christianity during the fourth century, were escorted in by entrenched malaria. "The first great Christian basilicas of the city, namely those of San Giovanni, St. Peter, San Paolo, San Sebastiano, Sant' Agnesi and San Lorenzo," as Cloudsley-Thompson points out, "were built in valleys that later became terrible centers of infection." We do know that malarious mosquitoes were present in the area of the Vatican prior to Christian construction of the original St. Peter's Basilica. As you may recall from the previous chapter, Tacitus tells us that following the eruption of Mount Vesuvius in 79 CE, large gatherings of refugees and displaced peoples "camped in the unhealthy districts of the Vatican, which resulted in many deaths" and with "the Tiber being close by . . . weakened their bodies, which were already an easy prey to disease."

While the early history of the Vatican is unclear, the name itself was already being used in the pre-Christian era of the republic for a marshy area on the west bank of the Tiber River, across from the city of Rome. The surrounding area was considered sacred; archeological evidence has uncovered polytheistic shrines, mausoleums, tombs, and altars to various gods, including Febris. Covering this sacred site, the sadistic emperor Caligula built a circus for chariot races in 40 CE (expanded by Nero), crowned with the Vatican Obelisk, which he stole from Egypt along with Alexander's breastplate. This towering needle is the only lasting relic of Caligula's debauched playground. Beginning in 64 CE, in the wake of the Great Fire of Rome—for which Christians were blamed—this eighty-four-foot-tall red-granite pillar became the site of state-sponsored martyrdom for many Christians, including Saint Peter, who was allegedly crucified upside down in the shadows of the obelisk.

On orders from Constantine, the old St. Peter's Basilica was completed around 360 CE on the grounds of the former circus and the purported site of Saint Peter's resting place. The Constantinian basilica quickly became the primary destination for pilgrimages, but also the epicenter for the concentric construction of the Vatican campus, which included a hospital that was often brimming to three times its capacity with malaria patients from Rome and the surrounding Pontine Marshes of the Campagna.

The legions of mosquitoes inhabiting the Pontine Marshes protected the headquarters of the Catholic Church from foreign invasion while they also killed those whom they sheltered. For most of this time period, popes did not reside at the Vatican. Fear of malaria drove them to live at the Lateran Palace on the opposite side of Rome for the next thousand years. It is not surprising that during malaria's reign in Rome, Catholics regarded their spiritual headquarters with more terror than respect, or perhaps respectful terror. Nevertheless, prior to the completion of the new St. Peter's Basilica in 1626 (designed by Michelangelo, Bernini, and others), at least seven popes, including the influential late-fifteenth-century libertine Alexander VI, known to Netflix as Rodrigo Borgia, and five rulers of the Holy Roman Empire died of the "Roman Fever." Acclaimed poet Dante died of malaria's inferno fevers in 1321, as he put it, "as one who has the shivering of the quartan."

The death trap that was Rome was not lost on outsiders, visitors, and historians. The sixth-century Byzantine administrator and historian John Lydus speculated that Rome was the site of a protracted battle between the spirits of the four elements of nature and the prevailing fever demon. Others believed a fever-puffing dragon lived in a subterranean cave, enveloping the city with its billowing, diseased breath, or a scorned and vengeful Febris was punishing the city for orphaning her in favor of Christianity. A medieval bishop on assignment to Rome remarked that when "the rising of the sparkling Dog Star at the morbid foot of Orion was imminent," malaria epidemics gripped the city, "and there were hardly any men left who were not debilitated by the seething heat and bad air." Hippocrates's miasmatic "dog days of summer" were still as relevant as ever and his catchy buzzword continued to ricochet across antiquity.

While the seat of Roman Catholicism might have been known for its healing, it could not shake its reputation for being the malarial capital of Europe. Even by 1740, in a letter penned from Rome, English politician and art historian Horace Walpole reported that "there is a horrid thing called malaria that comes to Rome every summer, and kills one," introducing the word "malaria" into the English language for the first time. The British, however, generally called the disease "ague." A century later, a fellow English art critic, John Ruskin, echoed his predecessor's words, exclaiming that there was "a strange horror lying over the whole city. It is a shadow of death, possessing and penetrating all things . . . but all mixed with fever fear." On a visit to the city in the mid-nineteenth century, Hans Christian Andersen, the Danish author of *The Little Mermaid*, was aghast at the "pale, yellow, sickly" inhabitants. The renowned English nurse Florence Nightingale described the silent, lifeless surroundings of Rome as "the Valley of the Shadow of Death." Romantic poet Percy Shelley commented on the disease that killed his close friend Lord Byron (despite rumors, they were not lovers), lamenting that he himself was also ailing from "a malaria fever caught in the Pontine Marshes." As late as the early twentieth century, travelers to these expanses were shocked by the squalor, feebleness, and skeletal complexion

La Mal'aria: This desolate and sullen 1850 painting by French artist Ernest Hébert depicting malaria-ridden Italian peasants fleeing the death trap Pontine Marshes of the Campagna was inspired by his personal travels and observations in Italy. *(Diomedia/ Wellcome Library)*

of the few pitiful locals trying to eke out an existence in the malaria-ridden Campagna. As we have seen and will continue to see, Rome, the Vatican, and the mosquito had a lengthy interdependent relationship and a capricious and lethal rapport.

While Rome certainly endured heavy malaria pressures, the rest of Europe was not immune, for the disease was marching steadily northward. Though the Romans had brought strains of malaria with them as they expanded into new lands, causing sporadic outbreaks such as those cases in Scotland and Germany referenced earlier, it was not until the seventh century that malaria became endemic in northern Europe. Although the deadly *falciparum* could not withstand the harsher climates of the frosty region, *malariae* and *vivax*, which can still be lethal, found it a suitable home, reproducing as far north as England, Denmark, and the Russian Arctic port of Archangel.

The mosquito's plodding grip on Europe was hastened by human interference. As always, mosquito pestilence followed the plow and the shifting and shuffling patterns of human movements, settlements, and trading passages. The expansion of the Roman Empire, and its later offspring of Christianity, activated the extension of mosquito-borne diseases into hitherto untapped human populations. Humankind's continual conquest of local environments, most notably the disturbed lands of cultivation and the unnatural undermining of ecosystems, produced sprawling mosquito habitats otherwise not organically possible. We reap what we sow. Or where we sow, the reaper appears.

The delicate balance between all life forces became increasingly subject to the impulses of human intervention. Introduced to Europe in the sixth century, the moldboard plow could be pulled by oxen through heavy loams. It allowed farmers to exploit the compact river-basin soils of central and northern Europe. Human and livestock population densities increased as towns and cities punctually emerged to support these agricultural colonies, generating a surge of traffic on vibrant waterways and at bustling trading ports. The webbed relationships of agriculture, increasing human population densities, and foreign trade allowed for the propagation of malarious mosquitoes.

With this transition to an agricultural surplus economy, northern

Europe joined the global market, and traders and merchants ventured farther for promising capitalist opportunities. "Human migrants," as historian James Webb explains, "had long been traveling bandwagons of infection." The misery of the Dark Ages was completed with new diseases and complicated by new approaches to faith. Escorting the mosquito was another foreign movement that would unveil a new global philosophy in the form of Islam.

Unlike the slow and labored spread of Christianity ministered by the mosquito, Islam sprang from the visions of the prophet Muhammad and quickly stormed the world. In 610, during one of his retreats for solace, a vision of the archangel Gabriel appeared, summoning Muhammad to worship Allah ("the god"), the same deity of the Jews and Christians. Muhammad continued to receive divine revelations and eventually began to relay these words of God to a small but growing assembly of Muslims ("those who submit to Islam") in Mecca and Medina. His sermons and messages eventually became part of the Qur'an ("recitation"). Islam ("submission to god") quickly won over the Arabian Peninsula.

During the seventh century, as mosquitoes and malaria insidiously crept northward in Europe, Islam rapidly expanded its territorial base across the Middle East. This new monotheistic faith patterned on the Christian god cascaded across North Africa and poured into the Byzantine and Persian worlds. When the Muslim Moors sailed the Strait of Gibraltar and invaded Spain in 711, they unleashed another surge of malaria, entrenching the parasite throughout the European Mediterranean. By 750, the Muslim Empire stretched from the Indus River in the east, across the entire Middle East, north to eastern Turkey and the Caucasus Mountains, across North Africa, before occupying Spain, Portugal, and southern France in the west. Islam and Christianity now squared off on two fronts—in Spain in the west and in Turkey and eventually the Balkans in the east. Europe was under siege from both mosquitoes and Muslims.

While darkness, disease, and death were descending on Europe, a Frankish king, Charles "The Hammer" Martel, and his unlikely bands of farmers and peasants staved off and reversed the remarkable Muslim general Abdul Rahman al-Ghafiqi's Moorish infiltration of Western

Europe in France at the Battle of Tours in 732. His grandson, the Christian Crusader Charlemagne, the first emperor of the newly minted Holy Roman Empire, would deal the Moors another setback in France and Spain and proceed to color Christianity across the map of Europe in bloodred. For the first time since the height of the classical Roman Empire, Charlemagne united most of Western Europe under one regime. Under his visionary yet brutal leadership, Europe began to emerge from the eclipse of the Dark Ages, prompting historians to anoint him the "Father of Europe."

The eloquent and brilliant Charlemagne was crowned king of the Franks in 768. He proceeded to launch over fifty military campaigns designed to expand his empire and save souls. A die-hard protector and promoter of Christianity, Charlemagne quickly blunted the Muslim expansion in Spain, before launching campaigns against the Saxons and Danes in the north and the Magyars of Hungary to the east, while also solidifying control of northern Italy. Charlemagne's military campaigns destroyed neighboring buffer states surrounding his Frankish kingdom, and unleashed a wave of invasions and new threats.

While not officially considered part of the Crusades, Charlemagne's zealous and fanatical Christianization of his conquered subjects was so extreme it could be defined as religious genocide. From a faith of conversion and devotion through healing and solace, Christianity under Charlemagne was now tendering another starkly opposite gateway to salvation. The conquered were given a simple choice: Embrace the Christian god or meet that god immediately at the point of a sword. At Verden in 782, for instance, Charlemagne ordered the massacre of over 4,500 Saxons who refused to prostrate themselves before his power and his Christian god. As Charlemagne consolidated his military, political, and spiritual clout, a distressed and scorned Pope Leo III appraised the Frankish king as a means to safeguard and strengthen his own authority and rule.

Pope Leo was quickly losing favor among Italian elites for his hush-money adultery, stormy affairs, political collusion, and economic scheming. Under Charlemagne's protection, Leo sought to preserve the legitimacy of the papacy and keep usurpers at bay. When Pope Leo crowned Charlemagne the first emperor of the Holy Roman Empire (or Carolingian Empire) on Christmas Day in 800, he was facing threats to his bastion on every front. While Charlemagne was the first emperor to rule a cohesive Western Europe since the collapse of the Western Roman Empire three centuries earlier, his policy of Christianization and military forays in all directions upset the balance of power and invited retaliation. When the seventy-one-year-old Charlemagne died of natural causes in 814, his heirs were tasked with defending the delicate and fragile Christian empire he had created.

His overstretched Holy Roman Empire was soon destabilized and deflated by invasions from the Magyars, a nomadic people originating between the Volga River and the Ural Mountains of eastern Russia. By 900, they drove a wedge into the established order by settling along the Danube River in modern-day Hungary. They continued to attack west into Germany and Italy, and even as far afield as southern France, over the next fifty years. Lastly, although in slow retreat in the west, Islam was still embedded in Spain, and was making headway in the east, knocking on the eastern door of the Byzantine Empire.

The Magyar design on Western Europe was halted by the German king Otto I in 955 at Lechfeld, earning him a fierce reputation as the savior of Christendom, propelling him to the throne of the decaying Holy Roman Empire in 962. Beginning with Otto, for our purposes, the king of Germany assumed the dual coronation as the ruler of the Holy Roman Empire, although not always with the blessing of the papacy. After defeat, the Magyars adopted Christianity under King Stephen (future Saint Stephen), and settled into a domestic farming culture in Hungary. The agricultural pursuits of the Magyars upset the ecological balance and once again provided the mosquito with new venues to host her malaria road show. For Europe, however, the malarial environment created by the Magyars along the Hungarian Danube was a blessing in disguise. During the merciless Mongol invasions of the thirteenth century, these malarious mosquitoes, farmed by Magyar husbandry, maintained a persuasive defensive perimeter and proved to be the saving grace for greater Europe.

The Muslim and Magyar offensives marked the final occurrence of major invasions of outsiders into the heart of European territory. The Holy Roman Empire was quickly portioned into various ethnically carved-out kingdoms. In many ways, they were the extension of the mosquito-thwarted raids of the Visigoths, Huns, and Vandals during the Era of Migrations, and of the warfare that had shaken the foundation of the Western Roman Empire in the fourth and fifth centuries. Like those marauding nomads before them, these outsiders stayed on in Europe and were absorbed into local societies or created new ethnic territories for themselves like the Hungarian Magyars, French, Germans, Croats, Poles, Czechs, and the Slavic Rus (Russians and Ukrainians). The ethnic makeup and map of modern Europe were beginning to take shape.

This marked the beginning of a period of relative European peace and homogeneous Christianity. This facade of unity spawned commercial diversification, guild specialization, intensified trade, and rising prosperity. In turn, the intensification of agronomy, market capitalism, and commercial traffic and trade spread the mosquito farther afield. This economic boom permitted the development and maintenance of local rule and the origins of feudal monarchy-based nations or princely states based on agricultural serfdom. These despotic rulers and their subordinate fiefdoms were protected by private mercenary armies of knights and tenant farmers conscripted as serfdom soldiers in times of need.

The new royal regions operated under the divine right of kings sanctioned by the always watching, always judging, wary eye of the papacy, which gradually became more concerned with the accumulation of wealth and power than with saving souls. The origins of the church as a remedial, antimalarial, therapeutic faith were now unrecognizable. The attainment of salvation was conveniently used as an intimidating, bribing weapon to reap the whirlwind of wealth from the ignorant huddled peasant masses. The papacy was eagerly carving out a profitable place within this lucrative commercial revolution that was engulfing Europe and beyond.

A successive line of Holy Roman emperors, beginning with Otto I, tried in vain to subdue an avaricious Rome and other rebellious Italian city-states, while also forcing an increasingly powerful and independent papacy to legitimize their supremacy. The mosquitoes of the Pontine

Marshes continued to protect Rome and the Vatican from foreign invasion during the conflicts of this era, as they had done in the past against swarms of Carthaginians, Visigoths, Huns, and Vandals. Like so many conquering suitors who previously courted Rome, including Hannibal, Alaric, Attila, and Geiseric, the armies of emperors Otto I, Otto II, Henry II (not to be confused with his later English counterpart), and Henry IV were also bested by the malarious mosquitoes.

The Germanic army of Otto I was plagued by malaria while suppressing an Italian revolt that was then inherited by his son Otto II, who died of malaria without victory in 983. Otto II's sudden death at the age of twenty-eight initiated a period of turmoil with numerous Germanic and foreign nobles vying for his vacant throne, which had been nominally filled by his three-year-old son, Otto III. Within this infighting, Germanic king Henry II loosely held the shrinking Holy Roman Empire together. By now this inheritance existed in name only. With ethnic states being carved out on its perimeters, the so-called Holy Roman Empire now consisted primarily of the Germanic kingdom in central Europe.

In his attempt to pacify Italy in 1022, Henry II was forced by a devastating sickness to abort his punitive campaign. Benedictine monk and cardinal Peter Damian (canonized in 1828), working in Rome at this time, summarized the life-sucking atmosphere of the city. "Rome, voracious of men, breaks down the strongest human nature," he wrote. "Rome, hotbed of fevers, is an ample giver of the fruits of death. The Roman fevers are faithful according to an imprescriptible right: Whom once they have touched, they do not abandon as long as he lives." Between 1081 and 1084, Henry IV, weakened by internal and external insurrections against his rule and five separate excommunications by three different popes, laid siege to Rome on four occasions. Rome and its papal rulers held out each time, as Henry was forced to withdraw the bulk of his mosquito-tormented army from the Campagna during the summer months. The shadow forces he left behind were invariably crushed by Rome's Anopheles allies, which feverishly patrolled the Pontine Marshes.

After a series of forgettable leaders, an impressive ruler finally took the reins of the forlorn Holy Roman Empire in 1155. Frederick I was so beloved by his contemporaries that they gave him the affectionate, everlasting nickname Barbarossa ("Red Beard"). He was a towering figure who combined all the essential talents and virtues of a strong leader. His name has echoed through time for his highly admirable résumé, but also for a more sinister association. A lionizing Adolf Hitler code-named his June 1941 invasion of the Soviet Union Operation Barbarossa to pay homage to the medieval German leader and visionary.*

Barbarossa was eager to restore the empire to its former glory, attained under Charlemagne. The mosquito, however, had other less than glorious designs in mind for the gathering armies of Barbarossa. His five campaigns against Italy and the papacy, beginning in 1154, were all consumed by swarms of malarious mosquitoes. One of Barbarossa's soldiers considered that Italy "is corrupted by poisonous mists rising from the neighborhood marshes, bringing scourge and death to all that breathe it." In his contemporary account of Barbarossa's invasions, Cardinal Boso, a member of the Papal Court, verifies that "suddenly such a deadly fever broke out in his army that, within seven days, almost all . . . were unexpectedly snatched away by a miserable death . . . and in August [he] began to withdraw his diminishing army. He was followed, however, by the deadly disease and, with every attempted step forward, he was forced to leave innumerable dead behind him." Stymied by the mosquito's staunch defense of Rome, Barbarossa withdrew to Germany and bowed to the social desire of his subjects, and that of his increasingly autonomous barons, to create "a greater Germany" and secure lebensraum or "living space" by conquering Slavic peoples to the east, a rallying cry resurrected by Hitler's Third Reich 750 years later.

After the malarial death of Pope Urban III, his successor, Gregory VIII, reversed the excommunication of Barbarossa and made peace with his old friend. When Gregory summoned Europe to reclaim the Holy Land during the Third Crusade, Barbarossa, now in the good graces of the papacy, responded with fervent Christian zeal. Concerned with Saladin's Muslim occupation of Egypt, the Levant, and the sanctified

* During the planning stages for the invasion, the original code name was *Otto*, after Otto I. It was renamed *Barbarossa* in December 1940.

city of Jerusalem, and unsettled by the erosion of Christian custody of the Holy Land, in 1187, Pope Gregory issued a papal bull calling for his Crusade.

Although he was struck down by malaria after only fifty-seven days in office, Pope Gregory's call to arms to reverse these setbacks, under the guise of "an opportunity for repentance and doing good," was answered by European Christendom. The Christian soldiers of Barbarossa were shepherded onward alongside the armies of Philip II of France, Leopold V of Austria, and a newly crowned Richard I "Lionheart" of England. These mustering Crusaders led by the greatest rulers of Europe marched headlong into a maelstrom of death driven by mosquitoes and by Muslims defending their homeland.

From its shaky start, the mosquito and her prodigious patrols of the Pontine Marshes shielding Rome and the papacy helped to transform Christianity from a small and scattered cult of healing to a corrupt spiritual, economic, and military enterprise of power. The mosquitoes of the Holy Land were not amused by this conversion from custodians of care to covetous Crusaders. She exacted her revenge on Christian trespassers to the Levant, halting their expansion into Islamic lands while slowly eating away at the fragile footholds of Christian Crusader states in the Middle East.

The term "Crusades" was not in use during the actual events. It became the catchall descriptor only around 1750, to represent nine separate Christian expeditions to the Middle East between 1096 and 1291 in a sustained attempt to wrest the Holy Land from Muslim hands. Coinciding wars in Europe ending with the *Reconquista* of Spain from the Muslims in 1492, the same year Columbus unwittingly changed the world, are often included or at least given as a footnote to the forays to the Holy Land. The First Crusade, launched in 1096, led to a series of ventures to the Holy Land spanning two hundred years to satisfy a compelling combination of greed and ideology and the lightly veiled religious catechism of invade to enrich trade.

While evangelists, movies, and children's books, including *Robin Hood*, would have us believe that the Crusades were championed to counter the infidel Islamic rule of the Holy Land, the religious element of the Crusades was far more sweeping, to include the suppression and extermination of all other non-Christian faiths. The Crusades were by no means as simplistic as some stirred-up crazy Christian jihad against Islamic rule of the Levant carried out by chivalrous European knights in shining armor atop their noble steeds storming Muslim castles. They were far more complicated than the symbolic fairy-tale imagery. As one leading Crusader casually explained, it was foolhardy to travel to attack Muslims, when other non-Christian heathens lived right next door. "That," he decreed, "is doing our work backward."

In truth, these faithful, cross-shielded knights, fulfilling the indulgences of their lordships or church leaders, were more the equivalent of Al Capone's or Pablo Escobar's mobsters and thugs than they were of the mythologized Arthurian saviors of damsels in distress and the guardians of greater Christendom. The routes through Europe to the Holy Land were specifically chosen for their high concentrations of Jews and pagans, who were subjected to a merciless orgy of ethnic and religious cleansing. As was customary, this was accompanied by the unbridled looting and pillaging of all local inhabitants, including fellow Christians. Another element of the Crusades was the resolution of conflict among rival Catholic factions. Monarchs and clergy looked the other way under the propaganda slogan "God wills it." After all, in the hopes of raising troops, popes offered mercenaries absolute forgiveness of sin, and the trials and tribulations of crusading would trump ordinary penance.

From the peasantry to the nobility, European men and women joined the movement to fight for God, as an opportunity for a military-escorted pilgrimage, as voluntary or conscripted soldiers, to excess in the debauched fleshpots of the Far East, to rape and plunder, or some personally motivated combination thereof. There was no consensus of individual inspirations for joining the crusading cause. Historian Alfred W. Crosby summarizes the Crusades as "a sort of banzai charge by hordes of the pious to rescue the Holy Sepulchre from the Muslims . . . a thought compounded of religious idealism, a desire for adventure, and, it turned out, rampant greed." The religious component was only one motivation for the architects of the Crusades and was generally used as a shroud to mask their real intention, which at the core was political, territorial, and economic advantage.

As the number of successive Crusades piled up, they became a lucrative commercial enterprise. The transport, maintenance, and supply of massive armies and hordes of pious pilgrims from Europe to the Eastern Mediterranean was no small feat, and no small financial undertaking. With the Levant in Christian hands, the entire Mediterranean economic sphere would be under the jurisdiction of the political monarchies of Europe and their religious masters. Over the next few centuries, avaricious rulers conveyed cloaked messages to their excited throngs, exhorting them to "wrest that land from the wicked race, and subject it to ourselves."

Driven by a Christian fervor, roughly 80,000 people from all walks of life abandoned Europe during the First Crusade (1096–1099) to brave the treacherous journey to Jerusalem, ravaging non-Christians along the way. As this motley crew advanced toward the Holy Land, their numbers thinned. When the diehards crossed into Asia at Constantinople, malaria set in, further diminishing their rank and file. Spring of 1098 was ushered in by monsoon rains that provided a summer season of unremitting mosquitoes and malaria. By early fall, thousands of Crusaders had died from the deadly parasite, including an entire German reinforcement of 1,500 men. Yet the remainder persisted, setting up fledgling Crusader states on the northern approaches to Jerusalem, which was eventually wrested from the Muslims in June 1099. "Now that our men had possession of the walls and towers," wrote the French warrior-priest Raymond d'Aguilers, "wonderful sights were to be seen. Some of our men cut off the heads of their enemies; others shot them with arrows, so that they fell from the towers; others tortured them longer by casting them into flames." However barbaric the manner of realization, Jerusalem was now in Christian hands.

By 1110, numerous tiny Crusader states, including Antioch and Jerusalem (and its primary port of Acre), had been assembled in the coastal Levant. Given its commercial importance, the region had long been a culturally diverse ethnic melting pot. Since most of the Crusaders returned to Europe with their spoils of war, these lordships and their diminutive European enclaves learned by necessity to coexist and cooperate with local populations, which included Muslims, Jews, Chaldeans, Persians, and Greeks. Trade from across the known world soon flowed in and out of these bustling, vibrant multiethnic ports, and the Eastern Mediterranean became the economic heart of global trade. While the Crusades were marked by violent conflict, they also produced a flurry of trade and a broader exchange of knowledge and innovation. Gaining a monopoly on this trade was worth fighting for, thereby extending this initial foray to the Levant into a string of Crusades.

The success of the First Crusade and the establishment of Christian states in the Levant were a mirage. Inevitably, even with the creation of the Knights Templar (charged by their vows of militant monasticism) in 1139, Christian traction in the Middle East would slowly slip away. Religious fanaticism and a blinding worship of God, conspiring with self-indulgent and lecherous greed, however, are compelling stimuli. Over the next two hundred years, they incited a series of Christian quests to secure Mediterranean trade and to unseat Islam from the Holy Sepulchre.

The Second Crusade (1147–1149), led by King Louis VII of France, accompanied by his brilliant, vivacious, and strong-willed warrior-wife Eleanor of Aquitaine—who, by the way, brought more troops than he did—and by Emperor Conrad III of Germany, was hastily designed to secure Damascus. Unleashing a wave of miasmatic biological warfare, the defenders of Damascus purposefully sabotaged all sources of water leading to and surrounding the city, creating a ripe malarial environment for the Crusaders' grand entrance. The five-day siege of Damascus in July 1148 during malaria season was a poorly planned and executed, parasite-peppered disaster.

The most important consequence of this mosquito-induced defeat was that a jilted Louis took out his disappointment on his wife, Eleanor, who had yet to bear him a son and whom he suspected of committing adultery with her uncle Raymond, the ruler of the Crusader state of Antioch. Upon their return to France, the pope "dissolved" their loveless marriage. Eleanor summarily wed her cousin Henry II, who was anointed king of England in 1154, just two years after their nuptials. The union of Henry and Eleanor (and her lands in France) would have eternal ramifications, as two of their eight offspring, Kings Richard and John, would lead directly to the ratification of the Magna Carta.

Following the botched Second Crusade, in 1187, Pope Gregory summoned Europe to reclaim Jerusalem from Saladin and his Muslim army. Newly minted King Richard the Lionheart raised the gauntlet of Christendom for England during the Third Crusade, alongside Leopold V of Austria, Philip II of France, and Barbarossa of Germany until his accidental death in transit to the Holy Land. Saladin blocked the Crusaders' path 100 miles north of Jerusalem at the coastal fortress city of Acre. A siege was initiated in August 1189 by a hodgepodge of local Crusaders led by the recently freed former king of Jerusalem, Guy of Lusignan, and the national contingents of Philip and Leopold. As malaria began to sap the strength of the siege, Saladin, in a brilliant and unexpected move, surrounded his enemies, allowing the mosquito ample opportunity to feed on the trapped Crusaders.

By the time Richard arrived with his army in June 1191, the Crusaders had suffered almost two years of nagging endemic malaria with frequent epidemic outbreaks. Malaria had already killed roughly 35% of the European Crusaders and drained the survivors of their once pulsating Christian ideology and fervor. Immediately upon landing, Richard contracted malaria, which his caretakers called "a severe illness to which the common people gave the name Arnoldia, which is produced by a change of climate working on the constitution." Battling malaria, scurvy, and Muslims, a feverish Richard broke the siege and captured Acre within a month. His European cohorts, however, no longer had the numbers nor the will to fight on to Jerusalem. The mosquito had effectively rendered them impotent. Both Philip, who was also incapacitated by malaria and scurvy, and Leopold felt cheated by the haughty Richard upon receiving their meager share of the spoils after the fall of Acre. Realizing their inferior military and economic position, the two sour and jaded kings gathered the wretched remnants of their national contingents and quit the Holy Land in August. They would, however, eventually exact their revenge upon Richard.

Undaunted by the desertion of his comrades, Richard vowed to push on to Jerusalem. When negotiations between Richard and Saladin foundered, the English king decapitated 2,700 prisoners in full view of the Muslim army. Saladin responded in kind. Richard proceeded south and was able to take and hold the city of Jaffa against fierce Muslim counterattacks. Richard's reputation for courage, military skill, and prowess, and for possessing a *coeur de lion*, was born (Richard spoke French, not English). His first push on Jerusalem faltered and stumbled in the heavy rains and mud of November, which is also often the worst month for malaria in the Levant. "Sickness and want," wrote an observer, "weakened many to such a degree that they could scarcely bear up." A second try for Jerusalem was also forced into a malarial retreat. Richard fell sick again with what his doctors whispered to be an "acute semi tertian" or a combination of *vivax* and *falciparum* malaria.

The straggling Crusaders were no better off than their commander. Richard's dream of Jerusalem, the Holy City, although in plain view, would not be realized. The mosquito ordained that Jerusalem remain in Muslim hands. Instead, a treaty was struck between the Lionheart and Saladin, the two mutually respected de facto leaders of the Christian and Muslim worlds. Jerusalem would remain under Islamic rule but was deemed to be an "international" city open and welcoming to Christian and Jewish pilgrims and traders.* In 1291, when the Muslims retook Acre, the last vestige of the malaria-addled Crusader states, the first large-scale Christian attempt at colonization outside of Europe sank into the desert sands.

The Holy Land remained in Islamic hands until the First World War and British general Sir Edmund Allenby's triumphant Christmas 1917 entrance into Jerusalem. Allenby of Armageddon, as he was nicknamed by his military and political superiors, was the thirty-fourth conqueror of Jerusalem and the first "Christian" (although he was an atheist) since the Crusades. The British Army medical services championed Allenby as "the first commander in that malarial region in which many armies have perished to understand the risk and to take measures accordingly." Also in 1917, Arthur Balfour, the foreign secretary and former prime

* The population of Jerusalem even in 1865, for example, was roughly 16,500, composed of 7,200 Jews, 5,800 Muslims, 3,400 Christians, and 100 "others."

minister of the United Kingdom, announced in his now notorious Balfour Declaration that "His Majesty's government view with favour the establishment in Palestine of a national home for the Jewish people, and will use their best endeavours to facilitate the achievement of this object." The Christian occupation of the Levant during the First World War, and the realization of Balfour's utopian statement, once again thrust the Holy Land into an antagonistic atmosphere and created the current hostility and acrimony engulfing the Middle East.

Allenby accomplished in 1917 what Richard could not do in 1192—outmaneuvering the mosquito. Both malaria and his own hubris during his Third Crusade were Richard's undoing. In October 1192, still throbbing with persistent malarial fevers, Richard quit the Levant for England. His journey was fraught with deceit and deception, and eventually led to his death. While Richard was crusading in the Holy Land, behind his back an aggrieved Philip of France and Richard's brother John conspired against him.

Upon his return to France, Philip secretly aided Prince John's revolt against his absent brother Richard. He also began a campaign to seize English kingdoms in France that had been transferred by the earlier marriage of Henry and Eleanor. Last, Philip denied Richard embarkation at French ports and forced him to take the dangerous overland route through central Europe, where he was captured shortly before Christmas by an awaiting Leopold. His ransom was set at an astonishing 100,000 pounds of silver. This amount, three times the annual tax revenue of the English Crown, was eventually raised by his mother, Eleanor. To muster this enormous bribe, Eleanor increased or demanded arbitrary taxes on property, livestock, and accumulated wealth, among other levies, from the peasantry, the barons, and the clergy. Upon receipt of this enormous cache, Richard was released. Philip sent an urgent message to John, proclaiming, "Look to yourself, the devil is loose."

Upon his release and his homeward-bound route to England, Richard began his reconquest of English provinces in France, consuming additional resources and revenues. During the siege of an insignificant castle in Aquitaine in 1199, a defender caught the attention of the king. Richard was amused by a man standing on the castle wall, armed with a crossbow in one hand and, in true Monty Python fashion, in the other hand clutching a frying pan, which he had been using as a shield. Distracted, Richard was struck by an arrow and later died from his gangrenous wounds. John assumed the throne of England. Over the next decade, to fund his repeated and fruitless campaigns in France to reverse the whittling away of English lands, John secured revenue by every means available, including increased taxation, supplemental dues, inheritance and marriage fees, and outright extortion and bribery. Sadly, and as much as I love the cartoon fox, Robin Hood was not a real person.

Robin Hood is a fictional representation and a symbol of hope and change during this dark and somber period of poverty and oppression in England at the hands of King John. While it is suspected that the story of Robin Hood had a longer oral tradition, he is first recorded on paper in William Langland's allegorical narrative poem *Piers Plowman* (c. 1370), which is considered, along with *Sir Gawain and the Green Knight*, to be among the greatest works of early English literature. Written during this same period, Geoffrey Chaucer's epic collection of twenty-four stories bound as *The Canterbury Tales* talks of "an ague that may be your bane," confirming that malaria was entrenched in the low-lying Fenland marshes of eastern England and found its way into English literature long before Shakespeare mentions malaria in eight of his plays.

The early stories of Robin Hood bore a distant resemblance to those rendered by Sean Connery, Kevin Costner, Cary Elwes, and Russell Crowe. The complete package of characters and complementary plotlines was not cemented until the swashbuckling 1938 film *The Adventures of Robin Hood*, starring Errol Flynn and Olivia de Havilland. One of the first movies ever made in Technicolor, this version of the renegade, jovial inhabitants of Sherwood Forest pitted against the greedy tyrants from Nottingham became the iconic story that won the hearts of audiences (and storytelling parents) the world over. The modern legend was perfected, and has yet to be eclipsed, in the 1973 Disney animated classic in which John is mockingly represented by a cowardly, thumb-sucking lion.

King John's resounding defeat by the French at Bouvines in 1214 ignited the confederation and revolt of his overburdened and discontented barons. At Runnymede on June 15, 1215, John was forced to concede to the demands of the rebellious barons and sign the Magna Carta Libertatum—"The Great Charter of Liberties." The revolutionary document outlined the rights and personal liberties of all free Englishmen (an extremely small category). For our purposes, I will overlook the mythological modern representations of the Magna Carta and its mangling by hindsight histories except one. The now universal attachment of the catchall slogan "No one is above the law" to the Magna Carta is a misconception. Nowhere among the sixty-three clauses of this groundbreaking charter does the phrase exist. The modern interpretation and construction of this expression can be loosely cobbled together from two articles: "*39. No free man shall be seized or imprisoned, or stripped of his rights or possessions, or outlawed or exiled, or deprived of his standing in any other way, nor will we proceed with force against him, or send others to do so, except by the lawful judgement of his equals or by the law of the land. 40. To no one will we sell, to no one deny or delay right or justice.*"

These concepts, regardless of their meaning in 1215, ushered in the age of modern democracy, common law, and the footing for the universal unalienable rights of the individual to life, liberty, and the protection of property. The Magna Carta was one of the most profound shifts in all the history of political and legal thought. Its influence echoes throughout the constitutions of modern democracies, including the Bill of Rights in the United States, the Canadian Charter of Rights and Freedoms, and internationally in the United Nations' 1948 Universal Declaration of Human Rights. If we climb the timeline and rabbit hole backward, the botched Third Crusade created the context and setting for the Magna Carta and its embryonic democratic platform.

While the Magna Carta might suffice as a consolation prize, the attempt of European Crusaders to claim the Holy Land was a resounding and unmitigated failure. The mosquito had ensnared Christianity in a crisis of faith. While she fostered the advancement of the healing foundations of Christianity during the Crisis of the Third Century, she also put a stark and abrupt finish to its commercial campaigns during the Crusades.

The Crusades were the first large-scale European attempts at permanent colonization and the projection of European power outside its continental borders. The mosquito helped ensure that these initial imperialist ventures ended in ruin. Alfred W. Crosby's assertions about the deadly meddling of the mosquito during the Crusades, in his work *Ecological Imperialism*, is worth repeating in full:

> With few exceptions, Westerners throughout history who have gone to the eastern Mediterranean to fight wars have believed their chief problems to be military, logistical, and diplomatic, and possibly theological, but the truth is that their primary and immediate difficulties usually have been medical. Westerners often have died soon after arrival, and more often have failed to have children who have lived to maturity in the East. . . . When the Crusaders arrived in the Levant, they had to undergo what British settlers in the North American colonies centuries later would call "seasoning"; . . . They had to survive the infections, work out *modi vivendi* with the Eastern microlife and parasites. Then they could fight the Saracens. This period of seasoning stole time, strength, and efficiency and ended in death for tens of thousands. It is likely that the disease that affected the Crusaders the most was malaria, endemic in the Levant's low, wet regions and along the coast, exactly where the bulk of the population of the Crusader states tended to concentrate. . . . The Levant and the Holy Land were and in some areas still are malarial. . . . Each new batch of Crusaders from France, Germany, and England must have been fuel shoveled into the furnace of the malarial East. The experience of Zionist immigrants to Palestine early in our own century may be pertinent: In 1921, 42 percent of them developed malaria in the first six months after their arrival, and 64.7 percent during the first year. . . . The Crusader states died like bowls of cut flowers.

In contrast to the Crusaders, the defending Muslims fought on their own turf. They had acquired immunity and were seasoned to local malaria strains. Many would have also possessed the previously mentioned genetic hereditary defenses of Duffy negativity, thalassemia, favism, and perhaps even sickle cell. Writing of his Muslim adversaries, Richard of Devizes, English monk and personal scribe to King Richard, recorded enviously during the Third Crusade that "the weather was natural to them; the place was their native country; their labour, health; their frugality, medicine." While defenders generally have the advantage in war as they decide the where, what, and how of a battle, in this instance, resistance to malaria proved to be the most advantageous defensive perimeter for Islam. It was also a war-winning weapon.

Although the Crusades were a miserable economic capitalist venture, they did lend themselves to future successful imperial ventures, if not directly to the European Age of Discovery and the ensuing Columbian Exchange. As mentioned, the Crusades included both invade and, more importantly, trade. The cross-cultural exchange between Muslims and Christians reintroduced the writings of ancient Greece and Rome into the academic abyss of Europe. Muslim innovations covering all academic fields were transmitted to Europe on the backs and in the packs of returning Crusaders and traders. The Muslim Renaissance or Golden Age spanning the warring centuries of the Crusades restored enlightening ideas and cultural illumination to the dark, recessed corners of Europe.

The Crusades spurred the quick dissemination of the Muslim contributions to navigation techniques, including the modern magnetic compass, and ship design, such as the sternpost rudder and triangular lateen three-mast sails allowing ships to tack against the wind. In 1218, an astonished, giddy French bishop at Acre relayed a message back to France exulting that "an iron needle, after it has made contact with the magnet stone, always turns toward the North Star, which stands motionless while the rest revolve, being as it were the axis of the firmament. Is therefore a necessity for those travelling by sea." The recipient of this letter must have thought the bishop had gone completely mad. This European enhancement of knowledge to climb out of the desolate caverns of the Dark Ages was afforded by a Muslim-anchored academic ladder. Aside from the gallant quests for the Holy Grail by Monty Python,

Indiana Jones, and Robert Langdon, among countless other romantic "knightfall" bedtime stories, movies, and television shows, this exchange of knowledge is perhaps the real legacy of the Crusades.

This cultural trade, and the global village at large, would be substantially broadened by another contender in the game of thrones during the crusading aftershocks of the thirteenth century. While Europe was climbing out of the Dark Ages with a boost from Muslim knowledge, a deadly threat was amassing, not only on the approaches to the Levant but on Europe's own eastern doorstep. Adroit horsemen from the steppes of Asia would unite east and west for the first time, spark the most lethal epidemic in human history, and threaten the very existence of Europe. With his mounted Mongol hordes, the brilliant, cunning strategist and warrior Genghis Khan would sweep west to the gates of Europe and secure the largest continuous land empire, and one of the largest empires, in history.

CHAPTER 6

Mosquito Hordes: Genghis Khan and the Mongol Empire

The inhospitable, remote high steppes and grassland of the austere and windswept northern Asian plateau were occupied by warring tribal clans and duplicitous factions. Alliances were capricious, changing course as swiftly as the whims of the blustery winds. Temujin was born into this unforgiving region in 1162 and reared in a clan-based society that revolved around tribal raids, plundering, revenge, corruption, and, of course, horses. After his father's capture by rival clans, Temujin and his family were reduced to dire poverty, scavenging for wild fruits and grasses, feeding on the carcasses of dead animals, and hunting small marmots and rodents. Then, with the death of his father, his clan had lost prestige and clout in the larger alliances and political arenas of Mongol tribal power. In this moment of desolation and despair, Temujin could not know that from these scraping, humble origins he would secure fame and fortune and a new name that would strike fear into the hearts of his enemies during his campaigns for world domination.

Vying to restore his family's honor, Temujin, now fifteen years old, was captured during a raid by his father's former allies. He successfully escaped from enslavement, and vowed revenge on his opponents, now a long list consisting of both traditional enemies and previous partners. Although Temujin was loath to share authority, he recognized that ultimate power and prestige, as he had been instructed by his mother as a boy, rested on numerous strong and stable alliances.

In his quest to unite the warring factions, Temujin broke from

Mongol tradition. Rather than killing or enslaving those he conquered, he promised them protection and the spoils of war from future conquests. Appointments to senior military and political positions were based on merit, loyalty, and acumen rather than clan affiliations or nepotism. These social ingenuities strengthened the cohesion of his confederacy, inspired loyalty from those he conquered, and augmented his military might as he continued to incorporate Mongol clans into his increasingly powerful alliance. As a result, by 1206, Temujin had united the warring tribes of the Asian steppes under his rule and created a formidable, cohesive military and political force that would eventually annex one of the largest empires in history. He ultimately brought Alexander's mosquito-deterred dream—the bridging of the "ends of the earth" from Asia to Europe—into reality. The mosquito, however, haunted his own visions of grandeur and glory just as she had haunted Alexander 1,500 years earlier.

By this time, his Mongol subjects had given Temujin a new name—Genghis Khan, or the "Universal Ruler." After completing his coalition of the competing and combative Mongol tribes, Genghis (or Chingiz) and his skillful mounted archers initiated a flurry of quick-striking outward military campaigns to secure living space . . . and then some.

Mongol expansion under Genghis Khan was in part the result of the mini ice age. This mercury-dipping climate change drastically reduced grasslands that sustained their horses and their mounted nomadic way of life. For the Mongols, it became expand or expire. The astonishing speed of the Mongol advance was due to Genghis Khan's military abilities and that of his generals, an impressively cohesive military command and control structure, wide-swath flanking techniques, specialized compound bows, and, most of all, their unparalleled skill and dexterity as horsemen. By 1220, the Mongol Empire stretched from the Pacific coasts of Korea and China, south to the Yangtze River and the Himalayan Mountains, reaching the Euphrates River in the west. The Mongols were true masters of what the Nazis later called *Blitzkrieg* or "lightning war." They encircled their hapless enemies with breathtaking, unrivaled speed and ferocity.

In 1220, Genghis divided his army into two prongs, and accomplished what Alexander could not—the binding together of the two halves of the known world. For the first time, the east officially met the west, albeit in cruel and hostile circumstances. Genghis led the main army back east through Afghanistan and northern India toward Mongolia. A second army of roughly 30,000 horsemen punched north through the Caucasus and into Russia, sacking the Italian trading port of Kaffa (Feodosia) on the Crimean Peninsula of the Ukraine. Throughout European Russia and the Baltic states, the Mongols routed the Rus, the Kievans, and the Bulgars. Local populations were ravaged, murdered, or sold into slavery and little quarter was given to opposing soldiers. When the dust settled and the Mongol hoofbeats drummed in the distance, upwards of 80% of the local populations had been killed or enslaved. The Mongols probed Poland and Hungary to gather intelligence before quickly retreating east in the summer of 1223 to join Genghis's Mongolia-bound column.

Why the Mongols decided to forsake Europe is subject to debate. It is widely held that the final strokes of this campaign were intended to be nothing more than reconnaissance missions for a future full-scale invasion of Europe. Historians have also suggested that the decision to postpone an invasion was based on the weakening of the Mongol army from malaria contracted in the Caucasus and along the river systems of the Black Sea, magnified by nearly twenty years of perpetual warfare. It is known that Genghis himself was suffering from habitual bouts of malaria at this time. The most generally accepted theory is that his death at sixty-five years old was the result of stubborn, festering wounds caused by the severe weakening of his immune system at the hands of chronic malarial infection.

The great warrior died in August 1227 and, in keeping with cultural norms, was buried without fanfare or marker. Legend has it that the small burial party killed anyone they met en route to conceal his final resting place, diverted a river over the grave, or alternatively, branded it into historical oblivion with stampeding horses. Like Alexander, the body of the Great Khan has been lost to legend and lore. All attempts and expeditions to locate his grave have ended in disappointment. The mosquito's thirst for Mongol blood, however, was not yet slaked, and she would continue to saddle his imposing empire.

Under Genghis's son and successor, Ogedei, the Mongols launched an unrestrained counterclockwise assault on Europe between 1236 and 1242. The Mongol hordes quickly smashed their way through eastern Russia, the Baltic states, the Ukraine, Romania, Czech and Slovak lands, Poland, and Hungary, reaching Budapest and the Danube River on Christmas Day 1241. From Budapest they continued their western drive across Austria, before heading south, and eventually back east, ransacking their way across the Balkans and Bulgaria. Continuing east, in 1242, the Mongols abandoned Europe, never to return. The invincible Mongols, as it turns out, could not defeat the mosquito and break her dogged defense of Europe.

Of this seemingly impulsive and surprising retreat Winston Churchill wrote, "At one moment it had seemed as if all Europe would succumb to a terrible menace looming up from the East. Heathen Mongol hordes from the heart of Asia, formidable horsemen armed with bows, had rapidly swept over Russia, Poland, Hungary, and in 1241 inflicted simultaneous crushing defeats upon the Germans near Breslau and upon European cavalry near Buda. Germany and Austria at least lay at their mercy. Providentially . . . the Mongol leaders hastened back the thousands of miles to Karakorum, their capital . . . and Western Europe escaped." During the summer and fall of 1241, the majority of the Mongol forces were resting on the Hungarian plains. Although the previous years had been unseasonably warm and dry, the spring and summer of 1241 were unusually damp, with higher amounts of precipitation than usual turning the formerly dry Magyar grasslands of eastern Europe into a marshy morass and a minefield of malarial mosquitoes.

For the Mongol military machine, the negative repercussions of this climate change created the perfect storm to shelter Europe. For starters, the quagmire and high water table robbed the Mongols of the essential grazing grounds and pasturelands for their innumerable horses, which were the crux of their military prowess.* The unusually high humidity also caused Mongol bows to falter. The stubborn glue refused to coagulate and dry in the moist air, and the diminished tautness of their

* Mongol warriors had a continuous supply of fresh horses, as each soldier usually possessed three to four of his own animals.

heat-expanding bow strings negated the Mongol advantage of increased velocity, accuracy, and distance. Compounding these military drawbacks was a bursting population of parched mosquitoes. The malaria parasite began its artful invasion of their virgin veins. The Mongol hordes, writes acclaimed historian John Keegan, "ferocious though they were, ultimately failed to translate their light cavalry power from the semi-temperate and desert regions where it flourished in to the high-rainfall zone of Western Europe. . . . They had to admit defeat." While the Mongols, and accompanying traders like Marco Polo, finally united the east and west, the mosquito helped prevent the west from being completely overrun. She harnessed her malarial might and held the reins of Mongol conquest, steering them away from Europe.

While the mosquito sucked dry their dreams of European subjugation, the Mongols, under Kublai Khan, the grandson of Genghis, launched their first campaign into the Holy Land in 1260, adding another contender to the ongoing, yet moribund, Crusades. Their entrance into this flagging competition occurred during the intermission between the Seventh (1248–1254) and Eighth (1270) Crusades. Indicative of the confusion engulfing the later Crusades, over the next fifty years, which witnessed four major Mongol invasions, alliances among the Muslims, Christians, and Mongol factions shifted and allegiances were regularly realigned and calibrated. Just like the mosquito, yesterday's friend colluded today to become tomorrow's foe. In fact, on numerous occasions, offshoots from each power lined up on opposite sides, as inner turmoil rankled and unraveled the cohesion of the three dominant groups.

Although the Mongols did have some limited success, including brief stopovers in Aleppo and Damascus, they were repeatedly forced to retreat in the face of malaria, additional disease, and powerful defensive coalitions. General Anopheles, the guardian of Christian Rome, also garrisoned the Holy Land for Islam. As she had done during earlier Christian campaigns, including Richard the Lionheart's mosquito-racked Third Crusade, she helped to stay the Levant's Mongol menace. The Holy Land, and its sanctified city of Jerusalem, remained in Muslim hands.

Rebuffed by the mosquito in both Europe and the Levant, Kublai sought to counter these setbacks by conquering the last independent vestiges of continental Asia east of the Himalayan Mountains. He set loose the weight of his might on southern China and Southeast Asia, including the powerful Khmer civilization, or Angkor Empire. From its origins around 800, Angkor culture quickly spread across Cambodia, Laos, and Thailand, reaching its zenith at the dawn of the thirteenth century. Agricultural expansion, poor water management, and climate change provided the mosquito a textbook opportunity to initiate a complete collapse. "Given the reliance on standing impounded water and the breeding of Anopheles," asserts Dr. R. S. Bray, "the seven deltaed Mekong River [was] the source of Khmer prosperity and the source of its malaria." The elaborate system of canals and reservoirs used for trade and rice and fish cultivation; extensive clear-cutting and deforestation to increase rice production to feed a growing population; and frequent violent monsoons and flooding created the perfect paradise for the proliferation of mosquito-borne dengue and malaria.

During his southern campaigns beginning in 1285, Kublai disregarded the customary tactic of withdrawing his forces to the nonmalarial north during the summer months. As a result, his marching columns totaling roughly 90,000 men were met by an entrenched mosquito defender. Malaria ravaged his armies throughout southern China and Vietnam, inflicting heavy losses and forcing a complete abandonment of his designs on the region by 1288. A straggling, sickly force of only 20,000 survivors staggered northward to Mongolia. This retreat from Southeast Asia and the corresponding collapse of the powerful Hindu-Buddhist Khmer civilization were both triggered by the mosquito. By 1400, the Khmer civilization was washed away, leaving only derelicts of awe-inspiring and majestic ruins, including Angkor Wat and Bayon, as reminders of the once flourishing Khmer sophistication and splendor.

Akin to the Khmer, following its misadventures in southern China and Southeast Asia, the vast Mongol realm corroded, fragmented, and collapsed over the next century, becoming politically and militarily irrelevant by 1400. By this time, political infighting, military losses, and malaria had drained the once invincible Mongol Empire. Remnants of

Mongol provinces lingered until 1500, with one in the backwaters of the Crimean Peninsula and the northern Caucasus limping on until the late eighteenth century. The legacy of the Mongols and of the largest contiguous land empire in history, however, still lives in today's global DNA. Geneticists believe that 8–10% of people living in the former Mongol Empire are a direct lineage of Genghis Khan.* To put this another way, roughly 40–45 million people currently on the planet are his direct descendants. If we collected all the descendants of Genghis Khan into one country, it would be the thirtieth most populous nation in the world today, ahead of countries like Canada, Iraq, Poland, Saudi Arabia, and Australia.

While the Mongols did not conquer Europe, thanks in part to the mosquito's indissoluble line of defense, their disease originating in China did. During the siege of the port city of Kaffa in 1346, the Mongols catapulted infected bubonic plague corpses over the city walls to contaminate the inhabitants and break the siege. More importantly, Kaffa was a bustling Italian trading center, so ships carrying rats with infected fleas, or the plague-ridden sailors themselves, soon made port in Sicily in October 1347, and then docking at Genoa and Venice in Italy and Marseilles in France in January 1348. The disease also traveled along the Silk Road on the backs of traders and Mongol warriors. The Black Death promptly "went viral," although *Yersinia pestis* is a bacterium transmitted by fleas that live and hitch a ride on numerous ground rodents, including, in this case, rats.

The plague peaked between 1347 and 1351 in Europe, with continuous outbreaks into the nineteenth century, including the Great Plague of London in 1665–1666, which killed 100,000 people, or 25% of the city's population, coinciding with the Great Fire of London in 1666. For the city of London, 1666 was not a great year. None of the frequent reappearances of bubonic plague matched the intensity and butcher's bill of the Black Death. While some scholars place the death toll of Europe as high as 60%, the modern consensus hovers around 50%. Philip

* The personal traveling brothel of Genghis Khan numbered in the thousands. He would discard and add women as he conquered new territories, circulating his DNA over a wide swath of the world.

Daileader, professor of medieval history at the College of William and Mary, is careful to point out, "There is a fair amount of geographic variation. In Mediterranean Europe, areas such as Italy, the south of France and Spain, where plague ran for about four years consecutively, it was probably close to 75–80% of the population. In Germany and England . . . it was closer to 20%." Across the Middle East, the death rate was roughly 40%, with Asia reaching 55%.

To make matters worse, the Black Death overlapped with the Great Famine, thought to be precipitated by the five-year eruption of Mount Tarawera in New Zealand. In northern Europe, the ensuing climate change caused a sudden spike in mosquito populations and malaria. Calculating a distinct death toll from this event is difficult, but it is generally believed to be in the ballpark of 10–15% of the affected populations. An anonymous eyewitness tells us that "the floods of rain have rotted almost all the seed . . . and in many places the hay lay so long under water that it could neither be mown nor gathered. Sheep generally died and other animals were killed in a sudden plague." Death dominated Europe.

In plain numbers, 40 million people in Europe died of the plague, with global fatalities estimated to be conservatively around 150 million and perhaps as high as 200 million. It took two hundred years for the global population to return to its previous level. These numbers are simply mind-boggling and difficult to rationally compute. The Black Death, in a league of its own, is the single most shattering individual Malthusian check in human history. As we have seen, the runner-up Justinian Plague in the sixth century killed *only* 30–50 million people.* Since the emergence of antibiotics in the 1880s and Alexander Fleming's penicillin breakthrough in 1928, the plague has mostly disappeared. According to the World Health Organization, plague currently kills 120 people per year.

Aside from the catastrophic loss of life wrought by the Black Death, the aftermath and implications for European survivors were actually remarkably positive. Large tracts of vacant and now unoccupied land

* I do not include the total body count of roughly 52 billion from mosquito-borne diseases across time, nor the 95 million indigenous peoples of the Americas who perished from European disease in the centuries after Columbus. These were not one-shot deals or true epidemics but rather long-term endemic infections featuring sporadic epidemics.

transferred to the living, equating to increased wealth. More land for fewer people meant less demand for the staple crop of wheat, leading to a diversification of agricultural produce and thus creating a much more robust and complete diet. Populations thrived as food was more abundant, cheaper, and more nutritionally balanced. Protein consumption also increased as previously cultivated marginal lands returned to their former natural state of livestock pastures or forests. This significantly reduced spawning haunts for malarious mosquitoes. Competition for jobs was reduced, which translated into higher wages for both skilled tradesmen and unskilled laborers. Birth rates continued to grow as couples could afford to marry at younger ages. Increased wealth, combined with less scholastic competition, allowed for a slow but steady growth of universities and higher education and the general advancement of academia, which eventually led to the Renaissance, the Age of Enlightenment, and a global projection of European power.

The Mongol invasions, which lasted roughly 300 years, changed the configuration of the world demographically, commercially, culturally, spiritually, and ethnically. The Mongols were willing to allow traders, missionaries, and travelers to navigate their entire empire, opening China and the rest of the east to Europeans, Arabs, Persians, and others for the first time. Small communities of Christian and Muslim converts soon appeared across these formerly unknown and untapped eastern lands, taking their place among the major eastern faiths of Buddhism, Confucianism, and Hinduism. These new land routes opened by Mongol military expansion created an immeasurably smaller global society by fusing two larger, previously distinct geographical worlds.

Spices, silk, and exotic imports beyond imagination became mainstays on the shelves and stalls of European markets. The Mongol Empire was a flexible, multifarious, and interconnected superhighway of foreign exchange. When a Flemish priest arrived at the Mongol capital of Karakorum in 1254 (hopefully not expecting a welcoming cup of tea), he was greeted in his native tongue by a woman from his neighboring village in his homeland. She had been captured as a child during a Mongol raid fourteen years earlier. Contemporary literature and archives reveal an incredibly safe and permeable Eurasian expanse for trekkers, moguls, and merchants. The travel stories of Marco Polo and others fed the trading frenzy and the economic machine of Europe.

The famous narrative of Marco Polo, however, was a publication of mere coincidence and chance. While imprisoned in Genoa in 1298–1299, to break the boredom and monotony of incarceration, Polo regaled a fellow inmate with stories spanning the years 1271 to 1295 of his travels across Asia and his tea-less stint in the court of Kublai Khan. The curious and amazed convict recorded these epic tales and eventually published them in 1300 as the *Book of the Marvels of the World*, now commonly read as *The Travels of Marco Polo*. Some experts question whether Polo ventured to China at all or was just repeating stories he had heard from other travelers. Researchers do agree that the stories, whether they are personal or plagiarized, are authentic and accurate depictions of contemporary events. A prized possession of Christopher Columbus was his well-worn and heavily marked-up copy of Polo's book.

The descriptions of the east and its limitless bounty depicted by Polo inspired Columbus's attempt to reach the riches of Asia by a westward seafaring route. In 1492, Columbus headed west to reach the east. "In a sense," articulates Loyola University historian Barbara Rosenwein, "the Mongols initiated the search for exotic goods and missionary opportunities that culminated in the European 'discovery' of a new world, the Americas." This unintended "discovery" unleashed a historically unmatched tidal wave of mosquitoes, disease, and death upon the isolated and nonimmune indigenous inhabitants of the Americas.

Prior to the Columbian Exchange, deadly Anopheles and Aedes mosquitoes had not yet penetrated the Americas. While pulsating vivacious mosquito populations thrived in the Americas, they were disease-free, and were nothing more than irksome, itchy pests. The Western Hemisphere remained quarantined and free from the forces of foreign occupation for the time being. Since their arrival in the Americas at least 20,000 years ago, at the onset of permanent European contact in 1492, the roughly 100 million indigenous residents had not yet been subjected to her scourge nor witnessed her wrath and so remained unseasoned and defenseless to her diseases. American mosquitoes did not shred human populations, at least not yet.

During the age of imperialism and biological interchange ushered in by Columbus, waves of fresh Europeans, African slaves, and imported stowaway mosquitoes clattered and rumbled upon the virgin rolling shores of this "New World." Their inadvertent biological warfare through stealthy foreign infections shuddered through the continents, killing indigenous populations at record rates. The mercantilist European powers of Spain, France, England, and, to a lesser extent, Portugal and the Netherlands clamored for imperial wealth and carried the cross of colonization and a cocktail of genocidal diseases, including malaria and yellow fever, beyond the gates of Europe and Africa to unsuspecting indigenous peoples across the globe. "Great was the stench of death," a Mayan survivor mourned. "After our fathers and grandfathers succumbed, half the people fled to the fields. The dogs and vultures devoured the bodies. The mortality was terrible. . . . All of us were thus. We were born to die!" As an accidental agent of the Columbian Exchange, the mosquito was one of the first and most prolific serial killers to stalk the Americas.

CHAPTER 7

The Columbian Exchange: Mosquitoes and the Global Village

Sailing in the shadows of Columbus's fourth and final voyage, the Spanish-born priest Bartolome de las Casas arrived at Hispaniola (now the Dominican Republic and Haiti) in 1502 and proceeded to pen his famous scathing eyewitness history *A Brief Account of the Destruction of the Indies*. King Ferdinand and Queen Isabella were horrified by his original reports of Spanish brutality and he was quickly anointed with the official title and role of Protector of the Indians in 1516. Las Casas chronicles the first decade of colonization with an intense, raw, and unfiltered spotlight on the numerous atrocities committed by his fellow Spaniards against the Taino people. His firsthand account is a lengthy indictment of Spanish colonization and of the immediate human harvest reaped by malaria, smallpox, and other diseases.

Las Casas reports that the Spanish treatment of the indigenous peoples of Hispaniola was "the climax of injustice and violence and tyranny. . . . The Indians were totally deprived of their freedom and were put in the harshest, fiercest, most horrible servitude and captivity which no one who has not seen it can understand. . . . When they fell ill, which was very frequently . . . the Spaniards did not believe them and pitilessly called them lazy dogs and kicked and beat them. . . . The multitude of people who originally lived on the island . . . was consumed at such a rate that in these eight years 90 per cent had perished. From here this sweeping plague went to San Juan, Jamaica, Cuba and the continent, spreading destruction over the whole hemisphere." Swarms of malaria-vectoring mosquitoes made up a large portion of his "sweeping plague."

When visiting the Darien settlement in Panama in 1534, Las Casas was shocked to see the open-pit mass graves of mosquito-bitten Spaniards. "So many died daily," he recounted, "they did not want to close it, because they knew for certain that within a few hours another might die." He concluded that the Spanish residents at Darien were mercilessly molested by "the large numbers of mosquitoes that attacked them . . . they began to fall ill and die." While cruising this northern shoreline of Central America during his final voyage, Columbus and his crews were so assailed and ravaged by mosquitoes and malaria that they duly christened the region "the Mosquito Coast." Founded in 1510 in the wake of this voyage, the Spanish settlement at Darien on the Panama isthmus of the now infamous Mosquito Coast was the first European colony on the mainland of the Americas. The mosquitoes of Darien, as we will see, would also put an end to Scottish sovereignty.

Darien was a hell on earth ruled by bloodthirsty mosquitoes. The Mosquito Coast was, as one early chronicler asserted, "corrupted by miasmatic emanations," and quickly established a reputation as "death's door." The low-lying settlement of Darien was surrounded by swamps and, to one recent arrival, was a cesspool where "dense and sickly vapors rise, the men began to die and there died two-thirds of them." The initial 1,200 Spanish adventurers "began to sicken to such an extent that they were unable to care for each other," wrote another participant, "and thus in one month seven hundred died." Las Casas, and other contemporary reporters, surmise that between 1510 and 1540, over 40,000 Spaniards had perished in the wilds of the Mosquito Coast alone. As shocking as this may be, the suffering and death of the indigenous peoples was disproportionately worse. Fifteen years after the establishment of Darien, it is estimated that disease, most notably malaria, had already killed roughly two million indigenous people in Panama.

In 1545, Las Casas reached Campeche on the western Yucatan Peninsula of Mexico shortly after the establishment of a slave-labor Spanish sugar colony. The indigenous Mayans were long gone, having perished, fled, or been flogged into slavery. Las Casas lamented that his comrades soon "began to find themselves ill because the village is unhealthy," and quickly became "feverish and indisposed." One of his tormented malarious companions lamented the "many long-beaked mosquitoes . . . that it was a pitiful thing to see, because this type of mosquito is very poisonous." On his travels throughout the burgeoning Spanish Empire, Las Casas was appalled and sorrowed by the death of Spanish and Indians alike.

What Las Casas did not know was that his dying compatriots had brought the diseases and their vectoring mosquito reservoirs with them, directly from Spain and their African pit stops en route to the Caribbean. For the fugitive mosquitoes from Africa and Europe, the journey across the middle passages of the Atlantic Ocean was an all-inclusive, two-to-three-month cruise vacation offering an all-you-can-eat buffet and an orgy of breeding in the plentiful and readily available cisterns and casks of welcoming water. They arrived at an untarnished virgin environment in the Americas on board the first European ships, steered by one of the most celebrated *and* vilified characters in history—Christopher Columbus.

From its epicenter in Turkey, the Islamic Ottoman Empire expanded across the Middle East, the Balkans, and eastern Europe during the fourteenth and fifteenth centuries, and closed the Silk Road to Christian traders and European access to the Asian market. With an economic recession at hand, the great powers of Europe sought to reopen this crucial commercial lifeline by circumventing the increasingly vast and combative Ottoman Empire. After six years of pestering the monarchies of Europe for funding, King Ferdinand and Queen Isabella of Spain finally relented and agreed to back the first voyage of a mystic crackpot named Cristóbal Colon (as Columbus was known in 1492) to reestablish trade with the Far East. Columbus was willing to be the vanguard of such an enterprise to, as he put it, "reach the lands of the Great Khan." He set sail with a satchel of royal letters of introduction and a stack of fill-in-the-blank trade agreements for tendering to Asian rulers.

The reluctance of Europe's monarchies to invest in such an audacious and risky scheme is understandable, for oceanic voyages were extremely expensive. The Spanish Crown's nominal token investment in Columbus, one-thirtieth of what was spent on their daughter's wedding, illustrates not only their concern over finances but also their lack of faith in his abilities. He sailed with only three small ships manned by a total crew of ninety. Columbus himself also had to front 25% of the budget, and was made to borrow from his Italian merchant brethren. By all logical assessment, his was a reckless and financially ruinous enterprise.

Columbus set sail into the great unknown in August 1492 determined to reopen access to the riches of the Asian east by sailing west. He believed the world was undersize and that it was composed predominantly—six-sevenths, to be exact—of land. "Columbus changed the world not because he was right," comments author and Pulitzer Prize–winning journalist Tony Horwitz, "but because he was so stubbornly wrong. Convinced the globe was small, he began the process of making it so, by bringing a new world into the orbit of the old." Despite being nearly 8,000 miles off course, and believing he had reached the East Indies (referring to all of Asia east of Alexander's threshold, the Indus River), his first small step onto the island of Hispaniola in December was indeed a giant leap for mankind.

This first voyage of Columbus marked the beginning of a new world order, including the introduction and enduring establishment of deadly mosquitoes and their diseases in the Americas, courtesy of the Columbian Exchange. Coining this term with the title of his seminal 1972 work, *The Columbian Exchange: Biological and Cultural Consequences of 1492*, historian Alfred W. Crosby proposed that, whether by accident or by design, global ecosystems were forever rearranged in the largest interchange in natural and human history.

The trek to the Americas roughly 20,000 years ago (possibly earlier) by the small band of original hunter-gatherers from Siberia put a freeze on any cycles of parasite transmission.* Their passage over the Bering Strait land bridge by foot, or more likely by seaworthy vessels hugging the northwest coast of the Americas, was too frigid for the animals or insects (and their reproduction) needed to complete the sequence of infection. Moreover, the population densities of these early migrants were too low and they weren't mobile enough to support the life cycle of zoonotic

* The First Peoples of the Americas, like all cultures the world over, have their own creation stories and oral histories, which I do not presume to disparage or dishonor.

diseases. The chains of infection were broken. These reasons also explain why there was apparently no, or at best fleeting, transference of disease to indigenous peoples during the brief Norse visits to Newfoundland initiated around 1000 CE. Although the Anopheles mosquitoes of the Americas were certainly capable and not unwilling to house the malaria parasite, climate conditions on the routes traversed by both the original inhabitants of the Americas and their Scandinavian visitors froze out this possibility for the time being. This, however, would not be the case when Europeans stormed the southerly climes and beaches of the New World.

At the commencement of his Columbian Exchange, both New World Anopheles mosquitoes and those Anopheles and Aedes breeds imported from Africa and Europe were part of the larger mosquito-borne disease cycle in the Americas. The formerly benign Anopheles species native to the Americas promptly became a vector for malaria. Given that they had been following their own evolutionary line for 95 million years, and had never known the parasite, this is an amazing adaptive feature of both the mosquito and malaria. As Harvard entomologist Andrew Spielman relayed to acclaimed author Charles Mann, "In theory, one person could have established the parasite in the entire continent. It's a bit like throwing darts. Bring in enough sick people in contact with enough mosquitoes in suitable conditions, and sooner or later you'll hit the bull's-eye—you'll establish malaria." Spielman's assertion was a reality across the Western Hemisphere from South America through the Caribbean and the United States to Canada's northerly capital city of Ottawa. Person zero, that one human malarial conduit, was a member of Columbus's initial voyage.

On Christmas Day 1492, Columbus's first voyage came to an abrupt end when his flagship, the *Santa Maria*, ran aground on the northern shoals of Hispaniola. The remaining vessels, the *Nina* and *Pinta*, could not accommodate the spillover crew, forcing Columbus to leave behind a crude palisade-garrison of thirty-nine men when he returned to Spain. Eleven months later, in November 1493, his second voyage, to create a permanent Spanish colonial bastion (supposedly in Asia) for further economic penetration, found the island in ruin. His marooned Spaniards were dead and the indigenous Taino people were in the thralls of a dual outbreak of malaria and influenza. The virgin blood of the Taino, whom Columbus nonchalantly described as "innumerable, for I believe there to be millions upon millions of them," was a welcoming red carpet for the famished parasite. Columbus also attested that during his second visit to Hispaniola, "all my people went ashore to settle, and everyone realized it rained a lot. They became gravely ill from tertian fever." One such sufferer recorded that "there are plenty of mosquitoes in those countries which are extremely annoying." Another penned, "There are many mosquitoes, and very vexing, and of many types." Given its utter lack of prejudice for the nonimmune, the mosquito and its malaria took a heavy toll on Spaniards and Taino alike. Foreign mosquitoes and their diseases were immediately embraced by the New World.

During his fourth and final voyage, of 1502–1504, Columbus also discloses, "I had become ill, and many times approached death with strong fever, and so fatigued that the only hope of escape was death." At the same time as Columbus and his sailors were exhibiting malarial "delirium and ravings" while cruising the Mosquito Coast and the Caribbean, across the Atlantic in Spain a bitter and resentful Hernan Cortes thought he had missed his opportunity for adventure, treasure, and adoration. He was sidelined from joining an auxiliary fleet to Columbus's last voyage by a nasty bout of domestic Spanish malaria. Cortes, as it turned out, would soon gain fame, glory, and unimaginable wealth by bringing down and sacking a vast and mighty empire—or so the story goes.

All the original zoonotic pathogens that ran amuck in the Americas were of European or African origin. Smallpox, tuberculosis, measles, influenza, and, of course, mosquito-borne disease reigned supreme during the so-called Age of Exploration or Age of Imperialism, kick-started by Columbus in 1492. These diseases to which many Europeans, but by no means all, were immune allowed the invaders to conquer and colonize much of the world, including the Americas. Time and again, European triumphs, including that of Cortes, rode the coattails of infection, not the other way around. Conquistadors and colonizers simply mopped up after the conquest by disease. Europeans began their global push with the advantage of their contagions. This is the explanation and the sole reason why Europeans conquered the world. The "germs" in Jared

Diamond's title trifecta Guns, Germs, and Steel were far and away the most effective tool of colonization and the subjugation and extermination of indigenous peoples. In numerous (I hesitate to say all) European colonial outposts, indigenous peoples suffered genocide by germs.

Peoples of European heritage now generally inhabit the temperate zones of the world or "Middle Earth." These biological environments, from the United States and Canada to New Zealand and Australia, were relatively comparable to that of their European homelands, allowing settlers to adapt more easily to their new surroundings. Even today, we are protected by our acclimatization or seasoning to our immediate surroundings and our local germs. Our homes and where we live for extended periods are natural safe zones. Our immunological defenses become accustomed to the different bacteria and viruses that cohabitate in our local ecological spheres, bringing a balance to the force. We strike this equilibrium with these germs so that, for the most part, we can all procreate and live without causing undue harm to the other. In short, we carefully coexist. If new, foreign germs are introduced into our safe little bubble, and upset this delicate balance, we get sick. If we travel to foreign environments with alien germs, we get sick, until we are resident long enough to meld into and become part of that ecosystem, which then becomes our own.

Upon my arrival at Oxford to pursue my doctorate, I remember being sick for a month. My unsympathetic teammates on the university hockey team told me that it happens to every "newbie." I soon found out that this biological "seasoning period" was legendary and was touted as "the Oxford flu." Inoculations and medications can ease the illnesses and diminish the dangers associated with these transitions. During the Columbian Exchange, many Europeans had the benefit of acquired immunity, having long been exposed to their own infections. They simply carried their germs with them.

These diseases, including malaria and yellow fever, introduced by Columbus and the successive hordes of colonizers laid waste to nonimmune indigenous peoples who teetered on the precipice of extermination. He personally oversaw and participated in brutal acts of barbarity and sexual transgressions by his Spaniards against indigenous peoples. The United States celebrates Columbus Day as a federal holiday on the second Monday in October (honoring his arrival in the Americas on October 12, 1492), even though he was 8,000 miles removed (or disoriented and lost) from his intended destination; his résumé is the stuff of Neverland nightmares; and he was nowhere near the actual United States. In 1992, on this work-free day of celebration, indigenous Sioux activist Russell Means poured blood on a statue of Columbus, declaring that the "discoverer" of the New World "makes Hitler look like a juvenile delinquent." Although the Norse preceded Columbus by 500 years with their colonial outpost erected at L'Anse aux Meadows on the island of Newfoundland, Canada, Columbus's name is still synonymous with the "discovery" of the New World. Disdain aside, Christopher Columbus's impact, including his unintentional introduction of mosquito-borne disease to the Americas, is unshakable.

Acclaimed historian Daniel Boorstin argues that, unlike Columbus, the Norse visit to "America did not change their own or anybody else's view of the world. Was there ever before so long a voyage (L'Anse aux Meadows is a full forty-five hundred miles as the crow flies from Bergen!) that made so little difference? . . . What is most remarkable is not that the Vikings actually reached America, but that they reached America and even settled there for a while, without *discovering* America." Certainly, Columbus did not discover the Americas, as indigenous peoples breathed in this world for millennia before his blundering arrival. Columbus was not even the first foreigner to discover the Americas. Columbus was, however, the first to open the doors permanently to the prevailing presence of Europeans, African slaves, and their diseases in their new world.

There are numerous well-known reasons why zoonotic diseases were absent from the pre-Columbian Americas. Indigenous peoples did not domesticate many livestock, making the disease jump from animals to humans highly improbable, if not impossible. This is a point I brought up earlier, but given the weight of its importance, it deserves another mention. By the end of the last great ice age around 13,000 years ago, 80% of the big mammals of the Americas were extinct. The few domesticated animals that were kept, such as turkeys, iguanas, and ducks, did not live in large clusters, did not require hovering "helicopter-parent" supervision, and were generally left to their own devices. And while I suppose it depends on personal preference, fur is more alluring to our senses than feathers or scales. Cuddling an infant turkey poult or iguana hatchling does not sound as appealing as snuggling a newborn lamb, foal, or calf.

Along with this lack of domesticated zoonotic animals, indigenous peoples had not practiced industrial agriculture to the extent of upending the ecological balance, as was seen throughout much of the Old World. Resource and climatic limitations generally allowed only for subsistence farming. Unlike their European counterparts, indigenous peoples of the Americas lacked any large beasts of burden, limiting crop sizes and any significant commercial or tradable agricultural surplus. In fact, the dog was the only animal of labor employed in the Americas, and its use was limited to the northern plains of the United States and Canada. In South and Central America, it was semidomesticated (essentially taming itself by loitering for scraps) and was eaten. Yes, indigenous peoples purposefully cleared land, usually by controlled burning, to control the migration of animal herds, and to farm the Three Sisters of corn, beans, and squash, and other crops, but the relative equilibrium of local ecosystems remained uninterrupted.

It would, however, be folly to romanticize the noble, loincloth-modeling, ecological, tree-hugging "Indian Environmentalist" and to misrepresent the precontact Americas as some organically utopian Garden of Eden. Indigenous peoples' interaction and manipulation of their local environments was far from a perfect harmony. This is not realistic or attainable by the very nature of our existence and our intrinsic survival instincts. Their land usage was simply not intrusive enough to alter the natural rhythm and status quo. "Indigenous peoples produced goods not for a distant marketplace," writes James E. McWilliams, "but mainly for themselves and their communities. Trade was local rather than foreign and overtly capitalistic, and the ecosystem reflected the effect of this difference. . . . The distinction between local and market production was critical." On the eve of the Columbian Exchange and the imminent

European onslaught, only 0.5% of the land east of the Mississippi River in the United States and Canada was under cultivation. For European countries, this figure ranged from 10 to 50%! When Europeans arrived on the East Coast of the United States in the early seventeenth century, they were clearing 0.5% of the old-growth forests per year.

With the introduction of commercial agriculture and dam building, European settlers unwittingly created a toxic environment for themselves by establishing ideal mosquito-breeding habitats. Entomologists have suggested that within a century of colonization, indigenous and imported mosquito populations increased by fifteen times, prompting Thomas Jefferson to ominously declare that the ravages of mosquitoes were immutable and "not within human control." Malaria and yellow fever were soon rooted along the Atlantic seaboard of North America.

These colonies of European lust, while teeming with mosquitoes, were not yet tainted by the disease-carrying Anopheles and Aedes breeds. These angels of death were stowaways on board European ships. Foreign migrant mosquito populations thrived in the sanguine climates of their new homes, pushing out or destroying several local mosquito species. Their human counterparts played out this same scenario, as Europeans drove out or destroyed indigenous populations. The blood of settlers was boiling with mosquito-borne disease. With each new and distinct colonial footprint, malaria was introduced by Europeans, consuming outposts from Spanish and Portuguese South America, through the multinational haunts of the Caribbean, to the northerly British settlements at Jamestown, Virginia, and the Puritan haven of Plymouth, Massachusetts.

Cavalcades of disease marched across the Americas through indigenous trading channels immediately after Columbus's first voyage and were given a timely reinvigorating push by Juan Ponce de Leon's exploratory and slave-raiding expedition to Florida in 1513.* Researchers have theorized that by the 1520s and 1530s, smallpox, malaria, and other epidemics ravaged indigenous populations from the Great Lakes region of Canada south to Cape Horn.

* Ponce de Leon's alleged quest for the fountain of youth in Florida is a vibrant and genuine fairy tale and has no credibility whatsoever.

Well-established, intersecting indigenous trade routes stretched across the entire Western Hemisphere. Peoples of the interior plains adorned their clothes with seashells although they had never tasted the salty breeze of an ocean. Coastal peoples who frolicked in those waves wore bison hides, yet they had never laid eyes on the magnificent creature. Indigenous nations smoked ceremonial tobacco, only imagining what the uncured plant might look like. Canadian Great Lakes copper was fashioned into jewelry in South America. Colonizing diseases, including malaria and smallpox, were also traded along these extensive economic corridors, ravaging indigenous peoples long before they ever set eyes on a European. During both the past and present, commerce is one of the most efficient carriers of communicable disease. William H. McNeill confirms that "malaria appears to have completed the destruction of Amerindians . . . so as to empty formerly well-populated regions almost completely."

When the first European expeditions of Hernando de Soto and Francisco Vazquez de Coronado trekked across the southern United States in the 1540s in search of great golden cities, according to chroniclers they found the lifeless ruins of countless villages occupied only by grazing bison. Galloping from Mexico City to Arizona's Grand Canyon and northeast to Kansas, Coronado was traveling through the remnant survivors of once thriving communities. Likewise, de Soto's climb from Florida to the Appalachians through the Gulf states and Arkansas, rafting the Mississippi River, traversed the graveyards and ghosts of already decimated indigenous populations. Clues to the cause of the collapse of these indigenous communities and the derelict ghost towns surveyed by these Spanish conquistadors can be found in a firsthand account from a decade earlier.

Four marooned Spanish sailors had traversed the de Soto-Coronado corridor from Florida, west across the Gulf of Mexico, before straggling into Mexico City in 1536. Reporting to the governor of New Spain, they regaled a captivated crowd with the events of this implausible and incredible eight-year journey. One noteworthy detail was their description of indigenous peoples who were already infected with malaria. According to the Spaniards' testimony, "In that land we encountered a very large number of mosquitoes of three different kinds, which are very bad and annoying, and during the rest of the summer they gave us great trouble." The "Indians," they reported, "are so bitten by mosquitoes that you would think they had the disease of Saint Lazarus the Leper . . . many others were lying in a stupor. We found these very ill and skinny and swollen-bellied, so much so that we were astonished. . . . I can affirm that no other affliction suffered in the world can equal this. It made us extremely sad to see how fertile the land was, and very beautiful, and very full of springs and rivers, and to see every place deserted and burned villages, and the people so thin and ill." The introduction of malaria across the southern United States preceded Europeans, killing indigenous populations and paving the way for European settlement. Following in de Soto's footsteps, a seventeenth-century French explorer traversing the abandoned shells of Natchez settlements on the lower Mississippi River wrote that with "these savages, there is a thing that I cannot omit to remark to you, it is that it appears visibly that God wishes that they yield their place to new peoples." European diseases, including malaria, had penetrated the interior of North America long before the arrival of Europeans themselves.

The Caribbean Arawak, the Inca and the Aztec of Mesoamerica, the Beothuk of Newfoundland, and a staggering number of indigenous cultures across the globe would suffer the same fate as the Taino—extinction. Hernan Cortes did not conquer six million Aztecs, just as Francisco Pizarro did not subjugate ten million Inca. Following crippling epidemics of smallpox and endemic malarial fever, these two conquistadors simply rounded up the few ailing survivors and sold them into slavery. When Pizarro arrived on the coast of Peru in 1531, the devastation wrought by smallpox (having been introduced five years earlier), allowed his whopping 168 men to conquer an Inca civilization that only a decade prior numbered in the millions. Crosby recognizes that "the miraculous triumphs of that *conquistador*, and of Cortes, whom he so successfully emulated, are in large part the triumphs of the virus of smallpox." Repeatedly across the Americas, disease made the European attainment of "victory" over indigenous peoples a leisurely and undemanding undertaking. It must have also been utterly demoralizing for indigenous peoples to observe that these illnesses tore at their own peoples while sparing and passing over many Europeans.

One of the few surviving Aztecs lamented that before the Spanish arrival, "there was . . . no sickness; they had no aching bones; they had then no high fever; they had then no abdominal pain; they had then no headache. . . . The foreigners made it otherwise when they arrived here." Cortes had no more than 600 men and a few hundred local allies in 1521 during his successful seventy-five-day siege of Tenochtitlan (present-day Mexico City). Once home to over 250,000 people, the Aztec capital was far more populated than any European city of the time. Tenochtitlan was a magnificent metropolis possessing, among other engineering marvels, an elaborate system of interconnected lakes, canals, and aqueducts allowing mosquitoes and malaria to blossom during the Spanish siege. Following this annihilation of the Aztec civilization, a malaria epidemic tore through Mexico during the 1550s. By 1620, only 1.5 million (or 7.5%) of Mexico's original indigenous population of 20 million endured.

The military achievements of the European armies, like those of Cortes and Pizarro, are seemingly easily explained. Repeatedly, the history books tell us that the use of steel weapons and guns versus those fashioned of stone or wood safeguarded European victories. The real reason that European colonizers displaced or destroyed indigenous peoples, however, was largely a matter of disease and differing immunities. It was the dissemination of exotic European germs and foreign mosquitoes and their diseases unconsciously acting as biological weapons that sounded the death knell for indigenous peoples.

With disease and the mosquito having set their hooks, European settlers and successive colonial and national governments used an assortment of strategies to subjugate indigenous populations. These approaches included, but were not limited to: waging decisive military campaigns; destabilizing political organizations; inhibiting identifiable cultural traits; creating economic dependency; drastically shifting demographics in Europeans' favor, which disease and the mosquito made certain; and expropriating and limiting the land base of indigenous nations. Indigenous peoples attempted to promote and protect their own interests and agendas in the face of a cultural upheaval and genocidal epidemics of European disease, including malaria and yellow fever.

In the wake of this tsunami of change unleashed by Columbus, and at the onset of intensified European colonization, Sir Thomas More's 1516 political satire *Utopia* foreshadowed the pervasive themes that dominated global European-Indigenous relations:

> If the natives wish to live with Utopians, they are taken in. Since they join the colony willingly, they quickly adopt the same institutions and customs. This is advantageous for both peoples. For by their policies and practices the Utopians make the land yield an abundance for all, which before seemed too small and barren for the natives alone. If the natives will not conform to their laws, they drive them out of the area they claim for themselves, waging war if they meet resistance. Indeed they account it a very just cause of war if a people possess land that they leave idle and uncultivated and refuse the use and occupancy of it to others who according to the law of nature ought to be supported from it.

In his highly readable 2011 narrative, *1493: Uncovering the New World Columbus Created*, Charles Mann argues that of all the people to have walked this earth, Columbus "alone inaugurated a new era in the history of life." While this is perhaps a touch overstated, there can be no questioning that his voyages set in motion a chain of sweeping events, as prophesied by Thomas More, arranging the current symphony of global power.*

In the centuries following Columbus, infection cut a contagious swath through indigenous populations. European diseases to which indigenous peoples had no immunity exterminated local populations to

* Sir Thomas More (1478–1535) was an English Renaissance philosopher, humanist, author, politician, and civil servant. As a Catholic, he was opposed to the Protestant Reformation. Although serving as lord high chancellor of England, and as a top aide and counselor to King Henry VIII, More refused to endorse Henry as the head of the new Church of England or support the 1534 Act of Supremacy. After refusing to take the oath of fealty to Henry, believing it to be an infringement of the Magna Carta, More was charged with high treason and beheaded at the Tower of London in 1535. Four hundred years later, in 1935 he was canonized by the Catholic Church.

the point of near extinction. As Charles Darwin observed in 1846, "Wherever the European has trod, death seems to pursue the aboriginal. We may look to the wide extent of the Americas, Polynesia, the Cape of Good Hope and Australia, and we find the same result."* Of the estimated 100 million indigenous inhabitants of the Western Hemisphere in 1492, a population of roughly 5 million remained by 1700. Over 20% of the world's population had been erased. The mosquito, along with other diseases such as smallpox, was culpable of genocidal extermination.† The small bewildered surviving populations then faced an unrelenting merry-go-round of wars, massacres, forced relocations, and enslavement.

Until recently, academics across various fields underestimated the potency of disease in reducing indigenous peoples in the Americas, thereby miscalculating the actual population prior to contact. Extremely low estimates eased the burden and guilt of colonization for the descendants of European settlers. Until the 1970s, schoolchildren were taught that most of the United States was vacant and summoning European settlement. After all, the alleged one million "Indians" did not need all this land that was yearning for American manifest destiny. It was prophesied that expansion was inevitable, justified, and ordained by divine providence. But it is now believed that Florida *alone* was home to almost one million indigenous inhabitants. Current estimates for the

* Aboriginal Australians and New Zealand Maori also suffered from the influx of European disease during the Columbian Exchange. From an estimated precontact population of roughly 500,000, by 1920 the Aboriginal population of Australia was counted at 75,000. Similarly, when James Cook landed at New Zealand in 1769, the Maori population is thought to have been around 100,000 to 120,000, reaching its nadir at 44,000 in 1891. Malaria and dengue were introduced to Australia by Malaysian traders in the 1840s. Australia has been malaria-free since the last outbreak in the Northern Territory in 1962. Dengue, which globally infects 400 million people a year, has made a troublesome resurgence in Australia over the last decade. Australia and Papua New Guinea also host unique, although rare and generally non-lethal, mosquito-borne viruses called Murray Valley Encephalitis and Ross River Virus.

† The exchange of disease was a one-way street—Old World to New World—with perhaps one exception. Syphilis, although nonvenereal in the original American bacterial strains of Yaws and Pinta, may have been brought back to Europe with Columbus. The first European outbreak of the disease appears to have occurred in Naples, Italy, in 1494 shortly after the return of Columbus from his first voyage. Whether this is a connection, or a coincidence, is still hotly debated and is the subject of ongoing academic research. Within five years, the disease had slept its way across Europe, with each nation blaming its neighbor. In 1826, Pope Leo XII banned the condom because it prevented debauched people from acquiring syphilis, which he viewed as their necessary and divine punishment for their immorality and sexual transgressions.

total indigenous population of the pre-Columbian United States hover around 12–15 million accompanied by 60 million bison.*

As Jared Diamond explains, low numbers were "useful in justifying the white conquest of what could be viewed as an almost empty continent. . . . For the New World as a whole, the Indian population decline in the century or two following Columbus's arrival is estimated to have been as large as 95 percent." Conservatively in plain numbers, that is 95 million dead across the Americas—the largest single population catastrophe in recorded human history, nearing an extinction-level event. It far exceeded even the Black Death. On the other hand, over the same time period, the immigration of Europeans and their shipments of African slaves to the Americas marks the greatest human population transfer and relocation in history. As always, the mosquito was one of the stars of this touring Columbian Exchange horror show.

The Columbian Exchange was truly universal and involved peoples, products, plants, and disease from every corner of the globe. In addition to mosquitoes, in 1494 during his second voyage, Columbus introduced the zoonotic animal hosts horses, cattle, pigs, chickens, goats, and sheep to their new world. Tobacco, corn, tomatoes, cotton, cocoa, and the potato were uprooted from the Americas to fertile fields across the planet, while apples, wheat, sugarcane, coffee, and various greens found an awaiting home in the Americas. The potato, for example, was lovingly transplanted to pastures across Europe, half a world away from its indigenous roots. It entered the waves of the Columbian Exchange for a second time during the Irish Potato Famine. Potato crops were ravaged by a blight from 1845 to 1850, leading to mass starvation that killed over one million Irish. Over this five-year period, the island's total population decreased by an astounding 30%, as an additional 1.5 million Irish fled the famine and emigrated predominantly to the United States, but also to Canada, England, and Australia.

During the Columbian Exchange, the planet was forever rearranged demographically, culturally, economically, and biologically. The natural

* By 1890, the total bison population in North America had been purposefully reduced to 1,100. American governmental policy authorized the systematic eradication of the bison to starve out indigenous peoples of the Plains, specifically the Sioux, to force them onto reservations.

order of Mother Nature and the balance of the force was turned on its head and thrown to the wind like a deck of cards. In a sense, the human international village became a singular, wholly united body for the first time, and immeasurably smaller. Globalization, including mosquito-borne diseases, became the new reality.

American tobacco, for instance, became a household drug. It was also frequently used to ward off bugs. Smoke has been used all over the planet as an insect deterrent, presumably since fire was first harnessed and domesticated. "Some human species may have made occasional use of fire as early as 800,000 years ago," explains Yuval Noah Harari. "By about 300,000 years ago, *Homo erectus*, Neanderthals, and the forefathers of *Homo sapiens* were using fire on a daily basis." Perhaps tobacco's allure was also tied to its mosquito-repellent properties. In any event, the addiction spread so quickly that by the early seventeenth century, the Vatican was receiving complaints that priests were conducting Mass with a Bible in one hand and a cigar in the other. At the same time, the Chinese emperor was fuming upon discovering that his soldiers had been selling their weapons to purchase tobacco. Little did he know that this was just a "gateway drug," as it quickly became common to mix tobacco with opium.

By the mid-nineteenth century the British trade in opium was a late addition to the Columbian Exchange and a clandestine instrument in the toolbox of British imperialism. Manipulating the endemic presence of malaria, the British government creatively argued that for Indians and Asians, opium was a highly effective antimalarial drug. The 1895 report of the Royal Commission on Opium, "compelling because of the terror and suffering it addressed, portrayed opium as being able to prevent and cure malaria," writes Paul Winther in his study on malaria and the British opium trade. "By 1890 the opium and 'malaria' correlation appeared periodically. . . . By 1892 it was commonplace. The severity of malaria in South Asia permitted the Commission to phrase its opposition to substantial cuts in production . . . as a refusal to contribute to human suffering. The people who did not want Great Britain to stop being involved in the cultivation, processing, and distribution of opium had interpreted the Commission's findings as a moral imperative."

Spuriously, the mosquito was scapegoated and was now a drug dealer and a trafficker of narcotics. Both opium and tobacco set their hooks into Asia, particularly China. By 1900, 135 million Chinese, an astonishing 34% of the total population of 400 million, were smoking opium at least once a day, initially as a malarial suppressant, and then, once hooked, to feed their addiction.

By 1612, when John Rolfe shipped the first crop of Virginia-grown tobacco to England, London already boasted more than 7,000 "tobacco houses." These cafés offered nicotine junkies a place to sit and converse while drinking (as smoking was originally labeled) tobacco. Coffee, a newcomer to the Columbian Exchange, soon joined the smoke-filled dialogue. From their Oxford origin as an intellectual meeting place, coffeehouses soon appeared on street corners across England, as ubiquitous as today's Starbucks where people pose over laptops pondering as they sip $6 spiced lattes. In fact, by 1700, coffeehouses in London occupied more properties and paid more rent than any other retail trade. Within the walls of these "penny universities," you could pay that sum for a "dish of coffee" and sit endlessly listening to and engaging in academic and highbrow conversation and exchanges, as was the expectation whether you knew your tablemates or not. "The results could be shared, debated, and refined in the society of like-minded men in the coffee house," explains Antony Wild in his book *Coffee: A Dark History*. "The Enlightenment in England was born and nurtured there." Of course, as coffee went viral in England and Europe, it was still linked to its origin as a malarial cure championed in the mid-eighth century by our Ethiopian goatherd Kaldi.

In addition to curing malaria, or "ague," as the English knew it, coffee was also marketed as a panacea for plague, smallpox, measles, gout, scurvy, constipation, hangovers, impotence, and general melancholy. As with anything new and trendy, there was the inevitable backlash. In 1674, a women's social organization in London published a pamphlet, "The Women's Petition Against Coffee," carping that after spending all day in coffeehouses, "never did Men wear *greater Breeches*, or carry *less* in them of any *Mettle* whatsoever. . . . They come from it with nothing *moist* but their snotty Noses, nothing *stiffe* but their Joints, nor *standing* but

M

their Ears." The equally sexually explicit and graphic rebuttal pamphlet, "The Men's Answer to the Women's Petition Against Coffee," countered that the drink "makes the erection more Vigorous, the Ejaculation more full, adds a spiritual essence to the Sperme." I will let modern medicine resolve this lovers' quarrel.

Even into the early twentieth century, it was still alleged that Kaldi's "coffee is a valuable remedial agent, or rather a preventative, when there are epidemics of . . . the various types of malarial fever." More importantly, as William Ukers advocated in his 1922 book, *All about Coffee*, "Wherever it has been introduced it has spelled revolution. It has been the world's most radical drink in that its function has always been to make people think. And when the people began to think, they became dangerous to tyrants." Tea or coffee? This was but one question asked during the political parties prior to the American Revolution. Both could be sweetened with the choice of sugar or honey, however. Just two more items on the menu of the Columbian Exchange.

Along with mosquitoes, English settlers also introduced honeybees to the Americas. Feral hordes quickly began the mass pollination of indigenous plants and also aided the bounty of European farms and orchards.* Although insect pollination was not discovered until the mid-eighteenth century, the bees assisted European agricultural pursuits so much that indigenous peoples quickly recognized that the sight of these foreign "English flies" was accompanied by aggressive European expansion. Given that the Mongols had previously and forever bound Asia and Europe, as evidenced by the Black Death, the Columbian Exchange was a worldwide yard sale. It not only included poisonous mosquitoes but also their antidote.

Quinine, the first effective prophylactic and treatment for malaria, rode the later swells of colonization and washed up on the global shores of the Columbian Exchange. In the mid-seventeenth century, the gossip

* Currently, 35% of foods consumed in the United States are derived from honeybee pollination. A mysterious sweeping occurrence known as Colony Collapse Disorder has been wiping out bees by geographic-dependent margins between 30% and 70% and threatening their survival. Recently, a noticeable marketing campaign has been directed at saving honeybees and fostering bee-friendly local environments. I recently bought a box of Honey Nut Cheerios, which was promoting the giveaway "Free Seed Packet Inside to Help 'Bring Back the Bees!'" My insect-loving son urged his mother and me, and helped, to make all our gardens bee-friendly.

corridors of the Old World were abuzz with a miraculous tale from a mysterious place called Peru. Within a few decades, advertisements extolling the enchanted power and curative properties of "Jesuit's Bark," the "Countess's Powder," and "Cinchona" were plastered across Europe. According to the rumor mill, in 1638, the beautiful Dona Francisca Henriquez de Ribera, the fourth countess of Chinchon, a Spanish province of Peru, was inexplicably cured of malarial fevers.

The countess, or so the story goes, contracted a virulent strain of malaria. Although attending physicians performed one bleeding perforation after another, she continued to deteriorate, and death seemed imminent. Her loving husband, the count of Chinchon, determined to save his spouse, remembered an old wives' tale he had heard a few years back. The story, as he remembered, was of a Spanish Jesuit missionary curing the governor of Ecuador of malarial fevers through local Indian black magic called *ayac cara* or *quinquina*. This was not some sorcerer's stone amulet, "expecto patronum" incantation, or recited abracadabra dirge. It was the "bitter bark" or "bark of barks" from a rare and fickle tree growing at high altitude in the Andes Mountains. Intrigued by what he had passed up as a folktale, the count was willing to give it a shot to save his ailing wife. He hurriedly acquired a small sample of the mysterious bark from what remained of the once thriving native Quechua people.

Sure enough, the countess was delivered from death, and upon her triumphant return to Spain, word spread of this miracle "fever bark." This was the equivalent of someone today instantaneously conjuring up a cure for cancer or AIDS. Not only was malaria a huge obstacle to imperialism in the colonial tropics, its peak in Europe during the mid-seventeenth century corresponded with this lifesaving discovery of quinine, which is toxic to the malaria parasite by inhibiting its ability to metabolize hemoglobin.

With the widespread uprooting, transference, and acceleration of global agriculture, commerce, and human populations during the Columbian Exchange, the period between 1600 and 1750 was the pinnacle of malarial misery in Europe, and the parasite was infecting the masses with reckless abandon. Keep in mind that this same period also witnessed a mass influx of European settlers and their malaria parasites to the Americas, adding potency to an already spiked punch bowl of colonial pathogens. Certain areas of Europe acquired strong malarial reputations, such as the littoral lowlands of the Scheldt in Belgium and the Netherlands, the Loire River Valley and the Mediterranean coasts of France, the salty marshes of the Fenlands or Fens in the counties east of London, England, the Don River delta in the Ukraine, certain regions lining the Danube River in eastern Europe, and as always the mosquito playgrounds of the Pontine Marshes and Po River in Italy. At last, a cure had been found for Roman Fever, English ague, Dante's infernos, and Europe's prevailing hellfire fevers.

In the end, although the countess certainly had malarial bouts, she died of yellow fever and never made it back to Spain. The story connecting the countess to quinine seems to be a refashioned fairy tale. Cinchona, the common name of this "Miraculous Fever Tree," nevertheless clings to the romance of the count and countess of Chinchon. This Jesuit's Bark, however, quickly became an economic colonial cash crop for Spain, and was a later addition to the lengthy and booming list of products, foods, peoples, and diseases crisscrossing the oceans during the Columbian Exchange. Quinine and malaria are a perfect example of this unprecedented union and cross-pollination of extremely different, previously isolated, and evolutionarily distinct worlds kick-started by the voyages of Columbus. Quinine was a New World treatment for an Old World disease. The disease itself, and its vectoring mosquitoes, were born of Africa and the Old World and were transported to the New World, where they flourished.

By the mid-nineteenth century, European powers armed with quinine even secured fragile footholds in more tropical outposts such as India, the East Indies, and Africa. In much of this lush zone between the Tropics of Cancer and Capricorn, peoples of European ancestry are still transient backpackers in terms of natural selection and evolutionary history. They lack those lifesaving inherited genetic immunities to malaria of some African and Mediterranean peoples. Although at the time, malaria remained a mystery, quinine has been used as a malarial suppressant since its discovery in the mid-seventeenth century and the

Curing the Countess of Chinchón with Quinine, 1638: This painting circa 1850 recounts the legend of the beautiful Dona Francisca Henriquez de Ribera, the fourth Countess of Chinchon, a Spanish province of Peru, being inexplicably cured of malarial fevers through local Quechua "Indian black magic" called *ayac cara* or *quinquina*. Quinine derived from the Cinchona tree became the first effective medicine to combat malaria. As part of the Columbian Exchange, it was a New World treatment for an Old World disease. *(Diomedia/Wellcome Library)*

fabled story of the countess of Chinchon who finally defanged the beastly fever.

The British imperialist adventure in India is the succinct narrative I use when teaching the ripple effects of the Columbian Exchange. This scenario, however, can also be applied to European colonies in Africa or the East Indies. British control of colonial India required the ability to combat malaria, so Brits in India consumed powdered rations of quinine in the form of "Indian tonic water." By the 1840s, British citizens and soldiers in India were using 700 tons of cinchona bark annually for their protective doses of quinine. They added gin to the liquid to cut its bitter taste and, most certainly, for its intoxicating effect. And the gin and tonic cocktail was born. It became the drink of choice for Anglo-Indians and is now of course a universal staple on bar tabs worldwide.

Quinine powder kept British troops alive, allowed officials to survive in low-lying and wet regions of India, and ultimately permitted a stable (though surprisingly small) British population to prosper in tropical colonies. By 1914, roughly 1,200 British Indian Civil Service members and a garrison of only 77,000 British troops ruled over 300 million Indian subjects. The scramble for empire was allied to epidemiology. A competitive scramble for scientific knowledge, including the discovery of quinine, was one small but historically weighty brick of the Columbian Exchange. The intermingling thematic ingredients of the exchange, including European colonization, the conveyance of diseases, the destruction of indigenous peoples, and the attainment of overseas imperial wealth, were all interwoven and bound by blood to the mosquito.

Columbus himself never realized his influence, believing until his death at fifty-five years of age that he had discovered outlying bits of Asia. He died in 1506 of "reactive arthritis," heart failure usually associated with syphilis. As his geographical miscalculations and personal failings emerged, he was defamed by the higher echelons of society and viewed as a pariah by the Spanish court, who rescinded his privileges and honors. Although he was a wealthy man, his later years were marked by humiliation, anger, and an omnipotent messiah complex outlined in his manuscript *The Book of Prophecies*. Due to severe isolation and depression, or perhaps from the last syphilitic symptom, insanity, he believed that he was a prophet of God destined to reveal to the world "the new heaven and earth of which Our Lord spoke through Saint John in the Apocalypse." Shortly before his death, Columbus wrote to the unamused king of Spain that only he, the stalwart Columbus, could convert the Chinese emperor and his subjects to Catholicism.

Progressively, over the last few decades, his legacy has fared no better. Columbus did open a new world for European economic expansion and enterprise, but at a terrible price—the near extermination of indigenous peoples and the ensuing establishment of the exploitive transatlantic African slave trade.

African slavery was a central element of the Columbian Exchange and the prosperity of a plantation economy. As the captive indigenous labor force was destroyed by infection, African slaves, and their complementary free-of-charge diseases, were shipped directly to any destination in the Americas, or globally for that matter. The mosquito played its part by ensuring the selective genetic immunity to mosquito-borne diseases of the millions of Africans being delivered to the shores of the Americas as replacement for a dwindling pool of indigenous slaves. Questions of morality aside, "Why trade when you can invade?" was now chained to "Why pay when you can enslave?" At its core, the Columbian Exchange was always predicated upon the European accumulation of wealth derived from African slave labor in plantation and mining colonies in the Americas. The New World was a vast and biologically diverse landmass with boundless economic potential initially breached and opened for business by Columbus, Spanish conquistadors, and conquering mosquitoes.

CHAPTER 8

Accidental Conquerors: African Slavery and the Mosquito's Annexation of the Americas

In 1514, only twenty-two years after Columbus's fateful first steps on Hispaniola, the Spanish colonial regime conducted a census with the intention of divvying up the surviving Taino among the colonists as slave labor. I imagine they were sorely disappointed to count only 26,000 among the living from what was once a thriving population of 5 to 8 million. By 1535, malaria, influenza, and smallpox, which made its New World debut in 1518, in combination with Spanish brutality, brought the Taino to extinction. For the sake of comparison, an equivalent level of killing in Europe would have wiped out the entire British Isles and then some. While I do not want to trivialize Spanish cruelty, known as the Black Legend, it did not play the main role in the cataclysmic demise of local populations. Across the Spanish dominion, malaria, smallpox, tuberculosis, and eventually yellow fever were the paramount killers. As a result, however, the mosquito, and the Spanish colonists to a much lesser extent, had wiped out the prospect of a substantial, self-reproducing Taino labor force. As both Europeans and indigenous peoples succumbed to malaria and other diseases, alternative labor was needed to fuel the lucrative production of tobacco, sugar, coffee, and cocoa. The African slave trade was caught up in the whirlwinds of the Columbian Exchange.

The first African slaves to the Americas arrived at Hispaniola in 1502, along with our Spanish priest Bartolome de las Casas, piggybacking on Columbus's fourth and final voyage. These initial Africans joined a dwindling number of Taino slaves in the search for imaginary gold seams and laboring on the newly minted tobacco and sugar plantations of Hispaniola. In the opinion of Las Casas, however, not all slaves were created equal. Shortly after his arrival in the Americas in 1502, Las Casas asserted that Indians, including the Taino, were "truly men" and must not "be treated as dumb beasts," and he petitioned the Spanish Crown for their humane management. "The entire human race is one," he proclaimed, while entreating that Indians receive "all guarantees of liberty and justice. Nothing is certainly more precious in human affairs, nothing more esteemed than freedom."

Long before 1776, Las Casas was extolling the virtues of the American and French Revolutions and the philosophical ideals of John Locke, Jean-Jacques Rousseau, Voltaire, Thomas Jefferson, and Benjamin Franklin: "that all men are created equal, that they are endowed by their Creator with certain unalienable Rights, that among these are Life, Liberty and the Pursuit of Happiness" and, per Locke's template version, "the protection of property." Like the American Founding Fathers, Las Casas also included a fine-print disclaimer as to the definition of men. Within the principles and moral clauses of both Las Casas and the Declaration of Independence, it turns out that not all men are created equal after all, for African slaves were considered chattel and property, not persons, even by this Spanish priest who at the same time was passionately endorsing the virtue of personhood for the enslaved indigenous populations of the Americas.

At the same time that Las Casas was demanding a gentle hand for the Taino, he was also championing the importation of African slaves, arguing that they were more constitutionally fit for tropical labor, in part due to their "thick skin" and "offensive odors from their persons." He boasted that in the Spanish colonies checkering the Caribbean, "the only way a black would die would be if they hanged him." The fate of Spanish fortune in the Americas, he surmised, hinged on the importation of African slave labor.

In his 1776 masterpiece, *The Wealth of Nations*, economist and philosopher Adam Smith proclaimed, "The discovery of America, and that of a passage to the East Indies by the Cape of Good Hope, are the two greatest and most important events recorded in the history of mankind. . . . To the natives however, both of the East and West Indies, all the commercial benefits which can have resulted from those events have been sunk and lost in the dreadful misfortunes which they have occasioned. . . . One of the principal effects of those discoveries has been to raise the mercantile system to a degree of splendor and glory which it could never otherwise have attained to. It is the object of that system to enrich a great nation." European imperialism was coupled to the wealth of resources offered by the colonies. The backbone of reaping this capital and the economic system of mercantilism, to which Smith referred, was the African slave trade, which included the introduction of African Aedes and Anopheles mosquitoes and their diseases to the Americas.*

African transport slavery only became a profitable replacement after local indigenous servitude was no longer an option. An early observer noted "the Indians die so easily that the bare look and smell of a Spaniard causes them to give up the ghost." As malaria, and eventually yellow fever, helped to eliminate the feasibility of indigenous slave labor in the hotbed mosquito climates of the Spanish and other European empires, the transatlantic African slave trade flourished. Duffy negativity, thalassemia, and sickle cell provided the Africans hereditary shields against malaria. Many had also been previously seasoned by yellow fever in Africa, rendering them immune to reinfection. While these factors were unknown at the time, what was easily observable to European owners of mining operations and plantations was that African slaves were relatively unafflicted by malaria and yellow fever, and simply did not die at the same rate as non-Africans. Their genetic immunities and prior seasoning made Africans an important ingredient of the Columbian

* Mercantilism, or the Atlantic triangular trade, was an economic system practiced by the modernized countries of Europe between the sixteenth and eighteenth centuries. It was designed to maximize profits for the imperialist European mother country. Overseas colonies were exploited for their natural resources, such as sugar, tobacco, gold, and silver, by way of African slave labor. These raw materials were shipped back to the home country to be turned into manufactured goods, which were traded for more African slaves, and also sold back at inflated prices to the colonial populations. A greater collection of colonies meant not only increased and more diverse resources but, given the monopoly of the European power on import/export, also a larger market/population for homespun manufactured goods. The unequal balance of mercantilism between country and colony was one of the causes for the revolutions and independence movements that engulfed the Americas, including the United States, in the late eighteenth and nineteenth centuries.

Exchange and indispensable in the development of New World mercantilist economic markets.

Yes, Europeans came, but they did not conquer indigenous peoples and the Americas by themselves. The Anopheles and Aedes mosquitoes came and conquered. As involuntary entries in the Columbian Exchange, they were, Jared Diamond proclaims, "Accidental Conquerors." In the immediate centuries following Columbus, Europeans were generally the beneficiaries of this lopsided global traffic and its transactions.* "Events four centuries ago set a template for events we are living through today," explains Charles Mann. "The creation of this ecological system helped Europe seize, for several vital centuries, the political initiative, which in turn shaped the contours of today's world-spanning economic system, in its interlaced, omnipresent, barely comprehended splendor." Mann is also mindful to point out "the introduced species that shaped, more than any others, societies from Baltimore to Buenos Aires: the microscopic creatures that cause malaria and yellow fever." The introduction of these toxic twins, and other mosquito-borne diseases, to the Americas by infected Europeans, their African slaves, and stowaway mosquitoes changed the course of history. "Had the slave trade not brought yellow fever and malaria to the Americas," notes J. R. McNeill, "none of the story offered here would have happened." Yellow fever was one of the most important historical influences defining the political, geographic, and demographic arrangements of the Western Hemisphere.

The deadly yellow fever virus disembarked in the Americas with African slaves and an imported Aedes breed of mosquito that easily survived the journey on the slave ships, reproducing in the plentiful barrels and pools of water. European slave traders and their human cargo provided ample opportunity for a continuous cycle of viral infection during the voyage until fresh blood could be claimed upon arrival at a foreign

* Given the devastation caused by Europeans and their diseases to the indigenous peoples of the Americas, New Zealand, Australia, and Africa through their colonial settler societies, it is hard to argue that the Columbian Exchange was favorable to indigenous peoples at all. One example I can give, with little solace or consolation, is the adoption of a thoroughly transformative horse culture by the peoples of the North American plains. Those First Nations of Canada and the United States quickly adopted a mounted way of life and society after the introduction of the horse by the Spanish.

port. The Aedes mosquito quickly found its niche and a suitable home in the cheerful climate of its new world and thrived both in its superiority to domestic species and in its role as a deliverer of suffering and death.

A Dutch slaving vessel from West Africa anchoring at Barbados in 1647 introduced yellow fever to the Americas. In less than two years, this first definitive outbreak of the disease killed over 6,000 in Barbados. The following year an outbreak killed 35% of the populations on the islands of Cuba, St. Kitts, and Guadeloupe in six months, before slashing its way through Spanish Florida. At Campeche, a struggling Spanish garrison on Mexico's Yucatan Peninsula, a traumatized tenant recorded the telltale signs of yellow fever, noting that the region was "totally laid waste." To the scattered Mayan remnants, the contagion was "a great mortality of people in the land, and for our sins." Within fifty years of its arrival, the dreaded "Black Vomit," "Yellow Jack," or "Saffron Scourge" had gone viral, gnawing through Caribbean expanses and the coastal regions of the Americas as far north as Halifax and Quebec City, Canada.

The deadly virus first surfaced in British North America courtesy of the Royal Navy in transit from the Caribbean to attack Quebec. Mooring with the flotilla at the port of Boston in 1693, yellow fever sparingly killed only 10% of the 7,000 townsfolk. Predictably, Philadelphia and Charleston were hit later that year, and New York surrendered to yellow fever for the first time in 1702. Prior to the American Revolution, there were at least thirty major yellow fever epidemics in the British North American colonies, striking every major urban center and port on the 1,000-mile stretch of seaboard from Nova Scotia to Georgia.

Throughout the Americas, yellow fever became the topic of fear, loathing, and legend, most notably at port cities that operated as the choke points for slaving and trading vessels of all nations. These ships of death ferried mosquito-borne disease across the Western Hemisphere and beyond. New Orleans, Charleston, Philadelphia, Boston, New York, and Memphis head a lengthy list of American cities that would experience deadly yellow fever epidemics. In fact, these were the most lethal epidemics of *any* disease in American history. The epidemics, coupled with chronic malaria, helped mold the current configuration of the United States. Yellow fever, 3,000 miles removed from its 3,000-year-old ancestral home in West Central Africa, would significantly shape the density of the Americas. Without the African slave trade, however, the transformative influence of this deadly virus in the Americas would have followed an entirely different historical script.

Since its origin, slavery has been chained to economic imperialism and a territorial projection of power. This bond has been a common theme in our story as evidenced by the Greeks, Romans, Mongols, and others. In antiquity, however, slavery was indiscriminate—race, creed, or color was irrelevant. The slaves within the Roman Empire, for example, came from all walks of life and a broad geographic radius, making up roughly 35% of the entire population. Slaves were often criminals, debtors, and prisoners of war. Among peoples across the planet, from the indigenous nations of the Americas to the Maori in New Zealand to the Bantu of Africa, slaves were often a primary motivation for hostility and also one of the leading spoils of war. This form of slavery, while perpetuating a chronic state of small raids, was localized and strictly controlled by codes of conflict and social mores. After a period of servitude, slaves were either killed or, more commonly, fully adopted and integrated into their new tribal family. In western Asia, impoverished parents often sold their children into servitude. When the Ottomans invaded the Balkans in the late fourteenth century and closed off the Silk Road to Asian trade, many locals became slaves, toiling on the land they formerly owned. Within the Ottoman army, however, slaves formed elite contingents with rank, privilege, and authority.

For the most part, the majority of slaves were often treated as part of the extended family. They were often emancipated; they could not be subjected to corporal punishment; their offspring could not be enslaved or sold; and they were generally not constrained socially or physically by the bonds of slavery as they were in American plantation slavery. Many slave laws and the social conventions and customs of the ancient world were compassionate, sympathetic, and surprisingly concerned with the well-being and equitable treatment of slaves. In other cultures, slavery was localized and relatively small-scale and exhibited none of the tormenting and cruel traits of African chattel slavery.

By the twelfth century, most of northern Europe had abandoned the practice of slavery, opting instead for a more refined and complex system of serfdom. With colder climates and shorter growing and toiling seasons, serfs were responsible for their own upkeep, thus saving the landowner money and labor overhead. In simple terms, prior to Columbus, slavery did not resemble the beast that it came to be after the colonization of the Americas. The Africa-to-America transatlantic slave-trading corridor tapped into, extended, and enlarged a preexisting African slave market, creating a uniquely American industrialized form of transport stock slavery.

The Islamic conquest of northern Africa in the eighth century first opened West Africa to an overland slave-trading system. Muslim caravan routes crisscrossed the Sahara Desert, transporting slaves from West Africa to southern Europe, the Middle East, and beyond. African eunuchs became a favorite prized possession of the Chinese imperial court. By 1300, as many as 20,000 West Africans a year were being shuttled northward by both Muslim and Christian traffickers often working in unison. With the arrival of true European colonialism between 1418 and 1452, under the Portuguese prince Henry the Navigator, this region would became the hub of origin for the transatlantic slave trade. Prince Henry kicked off the Age of Exploration with his voyages to the archipelagos of the Azores, Madeira, and the Canary Islands and his ventures along the Atlantic shoreline of northwestern Africa. The Portuguese continued to creep southward along this coast until Bartolomeu Dias rounded the Cape of Good Hope, at the tip of Africa, reaching the Indian Ocean in 1488.

By the time Vasco da Gama finally reached India in 1498, the Portuguese African slave trade was in full swing, as was the corresponding dissemination of mosquitoes and malaria. Both mosquitoes and their diseases accompanied the slave-trading voyages or were transported within the blood of the Africans slaves themselves to their final destinations. When Columbus finally pushed the western limits of the known world, 100,000 African slaves had been snatched from their homelands and accounted for 3% of Portugal's entire population.

The first Portuguese slave port in West Africa was active by 1442. Sugar and slaves were imported from Africa to the plantation colonies on Madeira, which became the harbinger and model for the prototypical colonial slave economy and plantation system in the New World. During this time, Columbus himself had lived on the island of Madeira and married the daughter of the governor, a beneficiary of this newfound plantation wealth. Columbus also worked as a sugar runner for an Italian shipping company and frequented the slave forts of West Africa. Columbus had an appreciation for the European model of African mining and plantation slavery. He exported this system to the Americas as part of his own personal Columbian Exchange. His initial voyages prompted Spain to officially establish slave forts in West Africa in 1501. The English began competing at the grisly slave game by 1593. As Antony Wild illuminates in his book on the history of coffee, Columbus was "at the crest of the black slave wave that was to crash onto the shores of the New World, bringing first sugar, then coffee in its wake." The grim reaper also rode on this tidal wave, masquerading as African mosquitoes, malaria, dengue, and yellow fever.

By and large, until the eventual painstaking mass export production of Indonesian-grown cinchona quinine by the Dutch, beginning in the 1850s, the mosquito kept Europeans out of Africa. The cinchona tree is persnickety about altitude, temperature, and soil type. It will grow only in very strict and specific environments. This limited, expensive supply opened the door for numerous quinine shams and impostors to flood the market, feigning to meet the massive demand. William H. McNeill reiterates that "the penetration of the interior of Africa that became a prominent feature of Europe's expansion in the second half of the nineteenth century would have been impossible without quinine from the Dutch plantations." Armed with this transplanted quinine, the imperial European scramble for Africa began in 1880 and straddled the decades of the First World War. Quinine was not a panacea, however, as yellow fever continued to stalk Europeans who dared enter the wilds of Africa.

Such was the fate of Belgian king Leopold II's mad enterprise to exploit the Congo between 1885 and 1908. Convincing the international community that his main objectives were humanitarian and

Grafting Cinchona Trees in the Dutch East Indies, c.1900: The Cinchona tree is finicky when it comes to altitude, temperature, and soil type. It will grow only in very specific environments, which made the quinine-producing bark extremely rare and expensive. In the 1850s on the colony of Indonesia, the Dutch initiated the first successful Cinchona plantations outside of small isolated pockets in the South American Andes Mountains. Britain and America quickly became the primary importers of the valuable and lifesaving Cinchona quinine grown across the Dutch East Indies. *(Diomedia/Wellcome Library)*

philanthropic, Leopold was given absolute title and rule over the Congo Free State. He made a personal fortune in ivory, rubber, and gold while subjecting local populations to unspeakable and widespread atrocities. Polish-British author Joseph Conrad served as captain on a Belgian steamer shuttling valuable cargo on the Congo River. His 1899 novella, *Heart of Darkness*, is a semifictional account of his adventures, including his near-death experiences from malaria and yellow fever.* His book raised questions about imperial racism while also igniting international outcry over Belgian cruelty and carnage. Roughly 10 million Africans died as a direct result of Leopold's policies and rule. His European traders and mercenaries fared no better, with reports from his Congo

* The script for Francis Ford Coppola's 1979 film *Apocalypse Now* was a direct adaptation of Conrad's book. Leopold's Congo was substituted with Vietnam and Cambodia during the American Vietnam War.

indicating that "there are only seven per cent who can do their three year service."

Prior to the intensification of Dutch Indonesian cinchona plantations permitting the "African Scramble" of the 1880s, however, mosquito-borne diseases firewalled European meddling and intrusion in Africa. Any attempt by Europeans to penetrate the interior of the continent to capture slaves, construct gold mines, exploit economic resources, or spread the word of their god was met by an impenetrable perimeter of lethal mosquito defenders. These expeditions ended in failure, with European death rates consistently between 80% and 90%. For Europeans, Africa was nothing short of a death sentence. During the sixteenth century, for example, the Portuguese monarchy was accused by the Vatican of violating the ban on the execution of immoral Catholic priests by banishing the criminal clergymen to Africa, "knowing that within a short time they would be dead." Sir Patrick Manson, a pioneer of malariology and often recognized as the "father of tropical medicine," saluted the mosquito in 1907 and confirmed that "the Cerberus that guards the African Continent, its secrets, its mystery, and its treasure is disease, which I would liken to an insect!" For the indigenous peoples of the Americas, mosquito-borne disease functioned as an offensive European biological weapon; for Africans, however, it was a defensive European biological deterrent.

For the initial three centuries of global European expansion, Africa remained "the dark continent." For the British, the mosquito's reign of terror earned Africa the title the "White Man's Grave." Europeans could sparsely occupy little more than crude slave forts, called "barracoons." Even these were boneyards.* It is estimated that annual European mortality rates in these West African shoreline slave centers hovered around 50%. "When civilized nations come into contact with barbarians," wrote Charles Darwin in 1871, "the struggle is short, except where a deadly climate gives its aid to the native race." Substitute "climate" with "mosquito-borne disease." The mosquito safeguarded Africa and was both a killer and a savior. An early king of Madagascar rightly boasted

* The derogatory racial slur "coon" is derived from the word *barracoon*.

that no foreign power could defeat the dense forests and crushing malarial fever of his country. The mosquito, he said, had saved not only his motherland but Africa as a whole. This statement would have held true if not for the collusion of Africans with European goals and objectives.

The willingness of Africans to participate in the slave trade in Africa allowed it to flourish. Africans delivered fellow Africans into the clutches of European subjugation and servitude, something the mosquito made impossible for Europeans to do themselves. The mosquito would not allow Europeans to pluck Africans from their homelands. Without African slavery, New World mercantilist plantation economics would have failed, quinine would not have been discovered, and Africa would have remained African. The entire Columbian Exchange would have been vastly different, or perhaps not have occurred at all.

As it was, however, the Portuguese, and eventually the Spanish, English, French, Dutch, and other Europeans, were able to tap into the existing internal African slave culture that revolved around captives of war. Africans initially sold their captives to the Portuguese, and a small, localized slave trade emerged. Originally, it generally operated under the cultural umbrella of customary and conventional African slavery. By exploiting this traditional feuding among African nations and social networks, Europeans were able to introduce a vastly different form of captive slavery, one of bulk commercial export. African leaders and monarchs began raiding traditional enemies and allies alike, solely for the purpose of capturing slaves to sell at a growing number of slave forts on the coast, operated by an increasingly broad range of European nationalities. The European demand was met by an African supply of African slaves. The cycle of coastal African violence and slave raids continued to intensify and ultimately penetrated the interior of what became known by its primary exports as the Slave Coast, the Gold Coast, or the Ivory Coast.

With the European discovery of the Americas, the near annihilation of its indigenous people by disease, and the desire to export and expand the Portuguese sugar plantation system of Madeira to other cash crops, the African transatlantic slave trade was fully charged. The floodgates were opened, and the mosquito was swept up in these history-making currents, thanks to the trade winds stretching from Africa to the

Americas. Columbus secured for Spain the prestigious honor of being the first to transport African slaves, foreign mosquitoes, and malaria to the New World. Although starting out as a trickle, as indigenous manpower declined, the importation of African slaves became a steady and ever-rising stream of human trafficking.

As Spanish "extraction" colonies proved increasingly profitable, thriving manpower meant more raw materials, which equated to more money. African genetic immunities and seasoning resistance to malaria, yellow fever, dengue, and other mosquito-borne diseases simply made them more productive. Where others died on the mosquito-infested plantations, they survived. Africans lived to produce profit, thereby becoming profitable themselves.

For early European settlers, however, it was essentially playing Russian roulette with mosquitoes loaded with malaria and yellow fever. It was a personal gamble at the game of life. Nevertheless, despite the danger and high death rates from mosquito-borne diseases to the European owners and overseers themselves, these profits fueled the extraordinary growth of the plantation-slave economy in the Americas. At the height of the slave trade in the mid-eighteenth century, the French and English were each importing over 40,000 slaves a year. This uptick in tempo of African slavery in the late seventeenth and early eighteenth centuries was directly tied to the mosquito.

African slaves withstood her wrath and became a hot commodity because of their genetic defenses to mosquito-borne disease. The extensive hereditary evolution of Africans was shaped by their homeland and their local environments *in Africa*. Mother Nature never intended for, nor factored in, the Columbian Exchange of Africans, mosquitoes, and their diseases. In this sense, Africans and these elements of their natural environment were imported to the Americas as one cohesive, interdependent unit. In an unforeseen genetic, but nevertheless cruel, biting twist of mosquito-driven irony, these African traits of natural selection against mosquito-borne diseases ensured their survival, which ensured their enslavement.

On a far more lethal scale, during the Columbian Exchange, Africans brought their complex and highly evolved man-mosquito-disease relationship with them. When sugar, cocoa, and coffee arrived from Africa as the staple plantation cash crops in the New World, the cycle of this imported African ecosystem to the Americas was complete. "Only after a significant African slave trade was established did the British American New World disease environment begin to resemble that of tropical West Africa," assert professors of disease economics Robert McGuire and Philip Coelho. "The changed environment made the American South a pest house, and the New World's tropics a graveyard for Europeans." For African mosquitoes, their new home, despite being half a world away, seemed indistinguishable from the one they had left, and native mosquitoes quickly adapted to their new surroundings. Africa was transplanted to the Americas complete with the appendages of year-round malaria, dengue, and yellow fever.

Karl Marx chastised this early displaced colonial capitalism in 1848 with the admonition, "You believe perhaps, gentlemen, that the production of coffee and sugar is the natural destiny of the West Indies. Two centuries ago, nature, which does not trouble herself about commerce, had planted neither sugarcane nor coffee trees there." Notwithstanding Marx's observations of the natural world order and his disdain for the bourgeoisie, the basis for this wholesale forced relocation and capitalist system was still African slaves. As the demand for coffee and sugar (and its waste product molasses, used to distill rum) grew, so, too, did the importation of Africans. Coffee cultivation was complementary to sugar, not in competition with it.

By 1820, the Portuguese colony of Brazil was importing 45,000 slaves a year, where coffee and sugar profits hovered between 400% and 500% on up-front investments. During this same period, sugar and coffee accounted for 70% of Brazil's total economy. It is not surprising that Brazil was the leading destination for African slaves, accounting for an astonishing 40% (or 5 to 6 million people) of the entire transatlantic slave trade. By the end of the eighteenth century, coffee was being grown in suitable locations across the Western Hemisphere from Portuguese Brazil to English Jamaica and Spanish Cuba, Costa Rica, and Venezuela to French Martinique and Haiti.

To fuel the European mercantilist economies, including the coffee, sugar, tobacco, and cocoa plantation colonies in the Americas, over 15 million Africans were transported across the middle passages of the Atlantic and arrived *alive* at plantation and mining destinations in the Western Hemisphere. Another 10 million died between their abduction and the port of terminus in the New World, while an additional 5 million Africans were marched across the Sahara Desert to be sold in the slave bazaars of Cairo, Damascus, Baghdad, and Istanbul. In total, roughly 30 million people were stolen from West Central Africa during the slave trade to produce profit for their masters. In colonies across the Americas, these African slaves, the accumulation of plantation wealth, and the preservation of imperial authority were inseparable from the mosquito. With the voyages of Columbus and his swashbuckling conquistadors, Spain got in on the ground floor of this capitalist opportunity in the Americas.

Seeing as Spain arrived first, disease quickly carved out a mighty Spanish overseas empire. By 1600, Spanish mining settlements and plantation colonies stretched across South and Central America, the Caribbean islands, to the southern United States. Spanish imperialism had two advantages over other contending European nations. First, some Spaniards, especially those from the southern coast, had genetic immunity to *vivax* malaria through G6PDD (favism) and thalassemia. Second, the fact that the Spanish were the first also meant they were the first to be seasoned to New World malaria and yellow fever.

Partial immunity to malaria is the result of repeated infections. This curse and blessing, however, takes time. Of the 2,100 Spaniards who accompanied Columbus to colonial stations, for example, by the end of his last voyage, only 300 remained alive. For thirsty mosquitoes and her malaria parasites, the blood of the initial Spanish explorers and that of freshly arrived pioneers were open for business. Early Spanish conquistadors bushwhacked their way through unmapped tropical landscapes, clutching a sword in one hand and swatting mosquitoes with the other. Europeans in the New World tropics, and the southern United States, were marked with a mosquito-mobilizing bull's-eye.

Prior to 1600, Spain dominated the New World, reaped the economic benefits of its sugar and tobacco plantation colonies, and controlled the profits of the African slave trade. Eventually, Spanish settlers, traders, soldiers, and their slaves who permanently settled in the Americas built up an acquired immunity to malaria and yellow fever. The envious nations of England and France jealously coveted Spain's preeminent place in colonial commerce. By the early seventeenth century after a rocky start and a period of trial and error, England and France, with luck and pluck, doggedly forged their own exploitive economic empires in the New World. European susceptibility to malaria and yellow fever in the Caribbean was observed by a traveling French missionary who noted that "of ten men that go to the islands [from each nationality], four English die, three French, three Dutch, three Danes and one Spaniard." This observation reaffirms the lengthier Spanish colonial occupation, their genetic immunities, and their more robust disease seasoning in the New World when contrasted with other, more recent European arrivals. This early ethnic mapping of the Americas by mosquito cartographers can still be seen today.

The introduction of mosquito-borne diseases, according to McGuire and Coelho, "served to eliminate substantial numbers of Europeans from the sugar-producing regions of the New World tropics, resulting in present-day populations in the former Caribbean colonies of Britain, France, and Holland that are primarily of African origins. The former colonies of Spain (Cuba, Puerto Rico and Santo Domingo) are exceptions. These islands have retained a substantial European contingent."

During the seventeenth and eighteenth centuries, nearly half of all Europeans who ventured into Caribbean waters were killed by a mosquito-borne disease. The need and demand for African slaves became strikingly clear. During the first two centuries of industrial slavery in the Americas, slaves imported directly from Africa fetched top dollar. Direct African imports cost three times more than a European indentured servant, and double an indigenous slave. Africans who had proved themselves locally immune and seasoned to New World mosquito-borne disease were of the highest value, twice that of an imported, as yet untried African. Over time, however, with local home-grown reproduction and the banning of the slave trade, genetic immunities decreased among country-born slave populations.

Britain banned the slave trade in 1807, the United States capitulated the following year, and Spain relented in 1811. The import of new slaves to these countries or their colonies directly from Africa was outlawed. And yet, slave populations continued to grow. One repulsively common feature of slavery was the rampant sexual abuse of women at the hands of their masters. After all, the legal definition coded that any offspring born to a slave was automatically and legally born into slavery. Given the perversely high up-front cost of purchasing a slave, rape was a surefire as well as sadistically satisfying way to acquire slaves free of charge. These sexual transgressions, emotionally and physically torturous for the victims, also had severe biological consequences. The interracial sex and genetic exchange resulted in the gradual loss of Duffy negativity and sickle cell immunities, especially in the southern United States. The result was a much larger percentage, and ever-creeping ratio, of nonimmune American-born slaves. Malaria was now attacking country-born slaves in greater number, altering the place of Africans within the bogus racial constructs of Social Darwinism. Ignorant of the debilitating indicators of malaria, Americans now deemed Africans to be listless and lazy.

The loss of hereditary immunity had unforeseen and lasting consequences. This increasing susceptibility to mosquito-borne diseases, as we will encounter during the American Civil War, also equated to higher death rates, which fueled the demand for more and increasingly expensive slaves. Given that the slave trade was illegal and the British Royal Navy was diligently patrolling the West African coast, forced breeding and plantation rape became not only extremely lucrative but also exceedingly common. The standard of slavery, the growing number of those chained to servitude, and the callous means to produce this swelling population, however, invited insurrection.

Attempting to keep one step ahead of slave revolts and domestic racial conflict, beginning in the mid-nineteenth century the United States and Britain shipped freed Africans to the colonies of Sierra Leone and Liberia in West Africa. Having been born outside of Africa and lacking genetic immunities, within the first year of residence, four out of every ten of these relocated former slaves died of mosquito-borne disease, with half of their non-African overseers suffering the same fate. The mosquito provoked history to unfold in mysterious and macabre ways. Her insurance of the African slave trade is certainly one of her more sinister historical influences and cruel manipulations during the Columbian Exchange.

African resistance to many mosquito-borne diseases helped fashion the hierarchy of races, with long and far-reaching implications—slavery and its legacy of racism. This immunity was used to "scientifically" and legally justify African slavery in the southern United States, factoring into the multiple causes of the American Civil War, during which time the mosquito went on a feeding frenzy. Historian Andrew McIlwaine Bell points out that prior to the Civil War, abolitionists believed that southerners were smote by ominous yellow fever epidemics as "divine punishment for the sin of slavery and argued (correctly as it turns out) that the malady was a consequence of the slave trade." Undeniably, the slave trade was the direct cause of yellow fever and its towering influence in the Americas.

Historically, despite the presence of suitable mosquitoes, Asia and the Pacific Rim, for example, have been completely pardoned from yellow fever. Given that the Far East did not deal in the African slave trade, the renowned killer of yellow fever never materialized as it did across the intersected circles of the Columbian Exchange. While other mosquito-borne diseases, such as malaria, dengue, and filariasis, were endemic, this absence of yellow fever diminished the mosquito's historical influence across the Asian Pacific expanse.

In the Americas, however, these same diseases were leading agents of history. Malaria and yellow fever had evicted and emptied indigenous peoples from large swaths of land. European settlers clamored to occupy these same, vacant mosquito-infested and compromised regions. Charles Mann notes that "after malaria and yellow fever, these previously salubrious areas became inhospitable. Their former inhabitants fled to safer lands; Europeans who moved into the emptied real estate often did not survive one year. . . . Even today, the places where European colonists couldn't survive are much poorer than places Europeans found more healthful."

The southern British American colonies, for example, "[were] no country for old men, or rather for men who wished to become old," writes Peter McCandless in his study of disease in low-country America. "Observers often noted how quickly people aged and died. . . . Along with the human migrants came their microbes, funneled through the tiny Charleston peninsula into the continent like an injection from a hypodermic needle." Colonists in the South were ruined, as one resident noted, by "the numerous fevers which every summer and autumn so generally prevail." Much to the chagrin of investors, the southern colonies and eventually the southern United States quickly gained an unwelcoming reputation as realms of mosquito-borne disease. Countless diaries, letters, and journals echo the observation of a German missionary who noted that these regions are "in the spring a paradise, in the summer a hell, and in the autumn a hospital." While the American colonies offered early European settlers a new life and financial opportunities in the form of land, it also offered them the opportunity for an early grave, courtesy of the mosquito.

The British colony of South Carolina, for instance, was shredded by yellow fever and malaria. Prior to 1750, in its hardest-hit regions of rice and indigo plantations, an astonishing 86% of European American babies died before they reached the age of twenty, with 35% dying before the age of five. A typical youthful South Carolina couple married in 1750 represents the norm. Of their sixteen children, only six survived into adulthood. In the southern colonies, wealth was spent quickly on lavish lifestyles. You can't take money to the grave, and theirs was a "live fast, die young" existence. Alternatively, those who could afford it retreated to their northern abodes during the sickly season. A ship captain recounted to his passengers headed for Charleston, South Carolina, that on a previous voyage to the city in 1684, of the thirty-two "vigorous Puritans" he transported from Plymouth Colony, within a year only two remained alive. His alarmed audience ordered him to turn the ship around. Such was the fate of a Franco-Spanish invasion fleet that was beaten back by a yellow fever epidemic in the late summer of 1706 during Queen Anne's War. Charleston's reputation as a center of malaria and yellow fever is not surprising. It is estimated that 40% of the current African American population are descendants of slaves who entered through the port of Charleston with their imported mosquito-borne diseases.*

Although English privateer-turned-full-pirate Edward Teach, better known as Blackbeard, blockaded the port of Charleston in 1718, he kept his fleet anchored at a distance for fear of Yellow Jack. He did stop all vessels leaving or entering the port, holding the passengers, including a group of prominent residents, for ransom aboard their own ships. The dreaded pirate Blackbeard, however, was not after valuables or treasure. His instructions were simple. He would release the hostages and depart peacefully when all the medicine in Charleston was safely aboard his ship *Queen Anne's Revenge*. His rotten swashbuckling crew was festering with mosquito-borne disease. Within a few days, his demands were met by the frightened citizens of Charleston. When the chests of drugs were furnished, Blackbeard honored his word. He released all ships and captives without harm, albeit only after relieving them of their valuables and fine festoons and frocks.

While Charleston was a buzzing hive of mosquito-borne disease, thanks in part to its trading in slaves, it was not flying solo in the Columbian Exchange of colonial British America. Stepping back, Charleston's preeminent status as a slave port, a den of malaria and yellow fever, and a lair of death was the direct result of the sprawling British settlement, plantation, and slavery patterns on the Atlantic coast, stemming from the first successful colony at Jamestown. The 1607 British settlement at Jamestown, Virginia, as we will discover, was awash with mosquitoes, disease, misery, and death. Its sister colony raised at Plymouth by the Puritans in 1620 fared no better.†

These inaugural British satellites set the precedent for and initiated the sequence of mosquito-influenced historical events that spawned the Thirteen Colonies and the United States. British settler societies in the Americas were also colonized by mosquitoes and their malaria and

* Charleston was also the leading port for exporting indigenous slaves. Between 1670 and 1720, over 50,000 indigenous slaves left Charleston bound for Caribbean plantations.

† Plymouth was not the first English settlement in New England. That honor belonged to Fort St. George in Popham, Maine, founded in 1607 a few months after Jamestown. Prior to this, a small English outpost was established in 1602 on Cuttyhunk Island, Massachusetts, to harvest sassafras. Although it is the main ingredient in traditional root beer, at this time it was believed

yellow fever. Daring settlers, powerless slaves, and instinct-driven mosquitoes were all lead actors in their own tragedy they helped write. For the Americas, the rabbit hole dug by the connection between the mosquito and slavery is deep and dark. As the accidental conquerors of the Columbian Exchange, mosquitoes and slavery transformed every aspect of the United States from Pocahontas and Jamestown to the politics and prejudice of the present day.

to be a cure for gonorrhea and syphilis. Following the voyages of Columbus, there was a growing, and profitable, demand for sassafras in Europe. Both of these colonies, however, were abandoned within a year.

CHAPTER 9

The Seasoning: Mosquito Landscapes, Mythology, and the Seeds of America

Poor Matoaka. The eleven-year-old daughter of Chief Powhatan would hardly recognize herself in the fictional plot of her star-crossed romance with John Smith unfolding on the screen in the 1995 Walt Disney animated movie. Her cinematic caricature looks more like a voluptuous Kim Kardashian look-alike than a prepubescent indigenous girl. The well-preserved and prevailing mythology that surrounds the English colony of Jamestown, John Smith, and the youthful Matoaka, known to history and Hollywood as Pocahontas, allows for these fabricated narratives to persist.

The name John Smith is synonymous with the lore of the founding of Jamestown and the misrepresented frontier glamour of America. As it turns out, he was really just a shameless self-promoter. Smith was the architect of so much disinformation, personal propaganda, and outright deceit that it is hard to take his five autobiographies, published in less than eighteen years, seriously. According to his own testimony of wild tales, Smith's fanciful adventures began when he was orphaned at thirteen. By the time he was a mere twenty-six years old, he had fought the Spanish in the Netherlands, spent months living in a lean-to immersing himself in Machiavelli, Plato, and the classics, before becoming a pirate on the Mediterranean and Adriatic Seas. He went on to act as a spy in Hungary, lighting torches on mountaintops to signal the approach of the Ottoman enemy, and continued to battle the Turks in Transylvania, Romania, where he was captured and sold into slavery. He escaped this bondage when he cunningly murdered his tormentor by, as he claims, "beating out his braines." Wearing the dead man's clothes, Smith wandered across Russia, France, and Morocco, where he returned to piracy, raiding Spanish ships off West Africa. Eventually, in 1604 he drifted home to England. Two years later, Smith enlisted for the Jamestown expedition that set sail for Virginia in December 1606. That, my friends, is the epitome of "youth gone wild" and one hell of a way to spend thirteen years! Most experts agree that John Smith was a con man and a fraud. None, however, doubts that he was fleetingly familiar with Pocahontas during his two-year tarriance at the miserable, mosquito-infested colony of Jamestown.

It is true that Smith made peace with the Powhatan upon the establishment of Jamestown in May 1607, to secure much-needed provisions and to keep the vastly outnumbered colonists from being annihilated in this extremely lopsided balance of power. In December, Smith was captured while foraging for food and brought before Chief Powhatan. What happened next remains the stuff of legend. Smith claims that after running the gauntlet of club-wielding warriors, he was to be put to death in the central longhouse but only *after* a great feast was held in his honor. An eleven-year-old Pocahontas intervened; "at the minute of my execution," boasted Smith, "she hazarded the beating out of her own brains to save mine; and not only that, but so prevailed with her father, that I was safely conducted to Jamestown: where I found about eight and thirty miserable poor and sick creatures." The allegedly smitten Pocahontas then "brought him so much provision, that saved many of their lives, that els[e] for all this had starved with hunger." Since its first publication in 1624, Smith's account has also been put through a rigorous academic gauntlet and has buckled under the immense weight of research.

There are numerous problems with his story. The first is timing. Smith's earliest report in 1608, written a few months after his abduction, contains no trace or hint of his later story of rescue by a lovesick Indian princess. In fact, he claims that they first became acquainted some months after his capture. He does, however, mention the great feast followed by a long conversation with Chief Powhatan, or "good wordes, and great Platters of sundrie Victuals," as he put it. This testimony was written for a private audience and, therefore, unlike in his ego- and profit-driven autobiographies, there was no obvious need to embellish or exaggerate what actually happened. We later find out through his memoirs that the undersize and homely Smith relished the story line of being rescued by a besotted maiden, for this scenario plays out on four separate occasions.

Second, culturally, the Powhatan did not hold feasts for prisoners of war prior to execution, nor were children like Pocahontas allowed to be present at official banquets. Trapped in his own lies, Smith got the traditional practices of the Powhatan completely backward. Anthropologist Helen Rountree, who has published a dozen books on the topic, argues, "None of the story fits the culture. Big meals are for honored guests, not criminals to be executed. It's hard to see them killing an intelligence asset." Smith was run through the gauntlet and honored with a feast not because he was going to be killed by Chief Powhatan but because, as the leader of Jamestown, he was being initiated and adopted by the Powhatan as a medium for trade and peace with the English settlers. Pocahontas was absent and irrelevant. Smith would rewrite this history with her inclusion only after she became a household name. Not to be bested in a contest for fame with John Rolfe, who was the true English husband of Pocahontas, John Smith put the finishing touches on his romantic tale as an early American idol only *after* she had attained celebrity status in England in 1616. He creatively exploited her newfound notoriety to increase his own.

Disney would have us believe that Jamestown, though a fledgling settlement, was a peaceful and promising one. In its vision, Pocahontas and Smith run barefoot through the utopian natural splendor of the New World, frolicking in its idyllic waterfalls. In truth, the situation at Jamestown was a cannibalistic, mosquito-ravaged mess. The early, improvident colonists were devoured by malaria. It was reported that a first-wave settler was burned at the stake for murdering and cooking his pregnant wife during the winter of 1609–1610, known as the "Starving Time." Although Jamestown teetered on the precipice of disaster, unlike previous English attempts at colonization, including the legendary Lost Colony of Roanoke, it managed to survive, thanks to tobacco and, eventually, African slavery. It was not John Smith, but rather John Rolfe, who in 1610 planted the seeds for the United States of America. Tobacco seeds, that is.

The English, who would eventually dominate the North American continent, were a late arrival to the Columbian Exchange and its mercantilist enterprises. When John Smith purportedly met the innocent, cartwheeling Pocahontas at Jamestown in 1607, other Europeans had already left footprints on half of what are now the forty-eight states of the continental United States. By the time the English and French finally entered the cutthroat colonial land grab in the Americas in the early seventeenth century, the Spanish had been playing solitaire for a century and had fleshed out a mighty southern empire, laying waste to thriving indigenous civilizations in the process.

Left with limited territorial options, the first English and French colonies in Canada and the northeast corner of the United States offered little in the way of economic potential. Although spirited mobs of hungry mosquitoes plagued these early settlements in Newfoundland and Quebec, they were too northerly for disease-carrying species. These initial English and French outposts were also too inhospitable for the cash crops of tobacco, sugar, coffee, and cocoa that filled the Spanish coffers. Once these two European contenders secured a fragile foothold, they craved expansion and extractive colonies to reap the benefits of the rich resources and the lands of plenty afforded by the Americas. The economic mercantilist system was beckoning and inroads needed to be made into the lower tropics of the Western Hemisphere, through colonization or conquest, to secure profitable slave-labor plantations.

Following a shaky start, the French and British eventually challenged Spain's monopoly of the Caribbean in a steady stream of colonial wars that reshuffled the territorial spoils of the Americas. These imperialistic forays, fought against the backdrop of the maturing Columbian Exchange, were decided by waves of mosquitoes and their imported reapers of malaria and yellow fever. The early experimental settlements of both the French and English were consumed by desolation and disease, including their own imported and smuggled malaria, with many settlements disappearing or abandoned in the face of attacks from indigenous peoples, an absence of resupply, and a relentless parade of death.

The mosquito actively dictated European imperial designs and settlement patterns in the Americas.

The French had been mucking around the northeastern coast and penetrated the St. Lawrence River region of "Kanata" beginning with Jacques Cartier's three expeditions between 1534 and 1542.* Nothing permanent came of it until 1608, when Samuel de Champlain set up his fur-trading headquarters at Quebec City. New France was not an attractive destination for settlers. The French presence in North America was kindled by a handful of young French adventurers who sought out peaceful relations with the indigenous Algonquian and Huron peoples to trade in furs. The French fur trade quickly expanded and soon monopolized the St. Lawrence River Valley and the Great Lakes region. The number of assimilated French traders, however, remained small. By the beginning of the eighteenth century, the French had established a series of isolated but interconnected military garrisons and fur-trading outposts arching from the Atlantic maritime shores of Canada and the United States, west down the St. Lawrence River across the Great Lakes corridor, and then south through the Mississippi River delta to the Gulf of Mexico at New Orleans.

The French population of this vast horseshoe belt of New France, consisting of immigrants, those born in country, and Métis (the offspring of French men and indigenous women), was meager, counting only 20,000 by the year 1700. Young men with no prospects, and other forgotten members of French society, made up the bulk of French immigrants. Natural colonial population growth was minimal as French women were in short supply. It became common practice for French fur traders to take an indigenous wife and assimilate into indigenous societies. In time, this petite French population was at an economic and military disadvantage when competing with more robust British and Spanish colonial populations. As a remedy, the French Crown coerced 800 single women between the ages of 15 and 30, called "the King's Daughters," to make the journey to Quebec City and New Orleans. The Crown paid

* *Kanata* is an Iroquoian word meaning "settlement" or "village" as told to Jacques Cartier. He took the word to mean the entire region, which he dubbed "le pays des Canadas" (the country of Canadas).

their passage and gave them supplies and money as a dowry. Given the dearth of females in New France, this wedding gift to their new husbands might have been an unnecessary, complimentary bonus.

The initial French Empire was restricted to North America. The fur trade did not require large numbers of Frenchmen, or any African slaves for that matter. Indigenous peoples furnished the manual labor, trapped and harvested the animals (primarily beaver), and delivered the furs in exchange for guns, metal goods, and glass beads. Given the French fancy for furs and the diminutive and assimilated French population, the local indigenous peoples held the balance of power. Farther south, in French Louisiana, however, the mosquito and the trickle of French immigration kept settler populations relatively small and scattered.

When the city of New Orleans gained official title in 1718, yellow fever and malaria were already permanent residents in the region, and the French population of the entire Louisiana Territory numbered a mere 700. The French colony at New Orleans was the epicenter for yellow fever and malaria epidemics that raced up and down the Gulf Coast and the Mississippi River, wiping out numerous fledgling French settlements. New Orleans, with its cavalcade of endemic malaria and epidemics of vampiric yellow fever, was also doomed by the mosquito to fail. As a vital port, New Orleans was crucial to French economic designs. But as a place to live, New Orleans was a sinking, hurricane-pounded coastal swamp, drowning in mosquito-borne disease.

Needing the French settlement at New Orleans to survive, the Mississippi Company arranged for French male prisoners to be set free on the conditions that they marry prostitutes and embark for New Orleans. These newly married couples were chained together until their vessels reached open waters. Between 1719 and 1721, three shipments of these altogether strange bedfellows were transplanted to New Orleans, where it was anticipated they would breed a new country-born, seasoned population. Despite the mosquito's best efforts, New Orleans and its handful of disease-seasoned settlers survived and the port city became the entry point and epicenter for numerous catastrophic epidemics of mosquito-borne disease, chiefly yellow fever that surged up and down the Mississippi River, with historic consequences.

Aside from the subsistence farming encircling New Orleans, mosquito-borne disease restricted any sizable sugar or tobacco plantation colonies. Small-scale indigenous slavery began in 1706 and was quickly replaced by African slavery, at first by raiding Spanish ships, and subsequently by direct import from Africa. The number of African slaves in New Orleans was small, as subjugation proved difficult. Slaves frequently escaped, revolted, fled to the swamps, or were adopted by local indigenous nations. By 1720, the Louisiana Territory had 2,000 African slaves, and twice that number of free Africans. Sugar found a home in Louisiana only as a consequence of the 1791 mosquito-sponsored slave revolt and independence movement led by Toussaint Louverture on the French colony of Haiti, which was then the largest sugar producer in the world. Importing the Haitian model, the first sugar plantation was finally established in Louisiana Territory in 1795, shortly before its purchase in 1803 by United States president Thomas Jefferson.

While the early northern colonial schemes of France purposefully tiptoed around the mighty Spanish Empire to the south, England had other strategic designs. The inner circle and financiers surrounding Queen Elizabeth I, who reigned from 1558 to 1603, were clamoring for a taste of the overseas wealth being gobbled up by Spain. In addition, newly Protestant England, as ordained by Elizabeth's father, King Henry VIII and his 1534 Act of Supremacy, had a pious philanthropic duty to save "those wretched people. The people of America crye out unto us [to] bringe unto them the glad tidings of the gospell."* Catholic Spain, they argued, had already converted "many millions of infidels," and in reward, their god had opened "the bottomless treasures of the riches." Spain was basking in the opulent waters of the Americas, while England was confined to "outrageous, common, and daily piracies." As an antidote to this unequal balance of world power and profit, Elizabeth let loose, to be legal "privateers" in her service, two of the most famous

* The common portrayal of Henry as an overweight, slovenly, crazed monarch is not entirely accurate. In his younger days, Henry was extremely attractive, tall and well-built, intelligent, multilingual, and a hopeless romantic. He was also an accomplished athlete and musician. He was a true Renaissance man. Like Alexander, it is thought that the sudden change and rapid decline in Henry's appearance and mental health beginning in 1536 was due to CTE sustained by repeated concussions from his avid love of jousting. He died morbidly obese in 1547 at 55 years old.

pirates and merchants of terror—Sir Francis Drake and Sir Walter Raleigh. During their swashbuckling adventures in the Americas, both buccaneers and soldiers of fortune would square off against and be repeatedly bested by the greatest and most gifted menace the world has ever known—the mosquito.

Following in the wake of Ferdinand Magellan's global circumnavigation from 1519 to 1522, Drake embarked on his own world tour between 1577 and 1580. He pillaged Spanish treasure ships and colonies along his merry way, seizing today's equivalent of $115 million in plunder. Drake's booty makes him the second-richest pirate of all time, trailing Samuel "Black Sam" Bellamy by roughly $5 million. He rounded South America and headed north along the Pacific shores of the Americas. After a respite at Drakes Bay/Point Reyes, thirty miles north of San Francisco's Golden Gate Bridge, Drake spun west across the Pacific. At the expense of the Spanish Crown, the extremely wealthy privateer eventually found his way home to Plymouth, England. Spain was becoming increasingly angered by English and Dutch high-seas piracy on both sides of the Atlantic, and by English Protestant interference in the Spanish Netherlands.

When war between Catholic Spain and Protestant England (and her Dutch Reformed allies) finally erupted in 1585, the recently knighted Drake would not be denied the spoils of war. Always the shrewd and cunning opportunist, he convinced Queen Elizabeth to appoint him head of a grand expedition to launch a preemptive strike on the money-spinning Spanish Caribbean colonies. For *El Draque*, as he was known in Spain, fame, glory, and riches awaited, steered by an immense pirate fleet legally authorized by his "Virgin Queen," Elizabeth. Prior to crossing the Atlantic to "impeach the Spanish King in the Indies," Drake made a brief stop to plunder the Portuguese Cape Verde islands off the coast of West Africa, unsuspectingly taking on an uninvited and fatal fugitive.

As he launched his fleet toward the Caribbean, *falciparum* malaria soon began to atrophy his crews. "Wee were not many dayes at sea," Drake recorded in the ship log, "but there beganne among our people such mortalities, as in a fewe dayes there were dead above two and three hundred men." He also mentions that the deathly fever did not begin "until some seven or eight days after our coming from St Iago [Santiago, Cape Verde] . . . and then seazed our people with extreme hot burning and continual agues whereof very few escaped with life." Drake's fleet was shrouded with malaria prior to its arrival in the Caribbean, and the mosquito captained his fruitless six-week campaign. The Caribbean, wrote English trader Henry Hawks, "is inclined to many kinde of diseases, by reason of the great heat, and a certeine gnat or flie which they call a mosquito, which biteth both men and women . . . with some venimous worme. And this mosquito or gnat doth most follow such as are newly come into the country. Many there are that die of this annoyance." Indeed, Hawks's "mosquito" and malarial "worme" forced Drake and his newcomers back to England.

The mosquito having coerced Drake and his pirates of the Caribbean to abort their mission, Drake quickly realized "who so is then abroad in the open ayre, shall certainly be infected with death." Seeking redress and reluctant to head home empty-handed, in the spring of 1586 he ransacked the vulnerable Spanish colony at St. Augustine, Florida, transplanting another malaria epidemic to the local indigenous Timucua people for good measure. Drake mentions that the Timucua, "at first coming to our men died very fast, and said amongst themselves, it was the English god that made them die so fast." Only twenty-one years after the Spanish founded St. Augustine in 1565, in the oldest continuously inhabited European settlement in the United States, a mere 20% of the precontact Timucua population survived.

After raiding St. Augustine, Drake charted north toward Roanoke (South Carolina), where his fellow pirating privateer, Sir Walter Raleigh, had financed a now floundering colony. Drake had ample space to accommodate all the surviving first-wave colonists of Roanoke for passage back to England. Of Drake's original crew of 2,300 only 800 were fit for service—950 had already perished from the ague and another 550 lay sick or dying. The mosquito repulsed Drake's first attempt to plant the English flag in the Americas. For Queen Elizabeth, colonization of the Caribbean or the hijacking of Spanish settlements would have to wait for the time being.

After receiving a conqueror's welcome at home, Drake was promoted to vice admiral of the English fleet, which convincingly defeated the invading Spanish Armada in 1588. This resounding victory propelled him to national hero status. He used the notoriety to obtain official license to resurrect his mosquito-bitten piracy and his forays against Spanish Caribbean colonies that he had started a decade earlier. Although war with Spain was still ongoing, England held the advantage after their defeat of the Armada. A weakened Spain meant that her valuable Caribbean colonies were compromised. Who better to undertake this marauding mission than the dreaded pirate El Draque?

In 1595, he set his sights on San Juan, Puerto Rico, to establish the first permanent English settlement in the Caribbean. General Anopheles and her resilient Spanish allies quickly ended this imperialist dream, and Drake's life. Within a few weeks of Drake's arrival, malaria had reduced his crew by 25%, which was magnified by a disastrous round of dysentery. After the unsuccessful siege of San Juan, and with Drake and his men in the throes of this combined epidemic, he anchored in Mosquito Gulf (aptly named in October 1502 by Columbus during his fourth and final voyage), not far from the present-day northern entrance to the Panama Canal.* In January 1596, Drake succumbed to this lethal blend of malaria and dysentery; he was buried at sea. Responsible for Drake's defeat and death, the mosquito again dashed English colonial hopes in the Caribbean, for the time being, forcing English imperial eyes further afield. While Drake was being bested by the mosquito, England struck its first overseas colony 2,200 miles north of the sun, rum, and mosquito-patrolled warm waters of the Caribbean.

In 1583, the first successful English overseas colony was established on the island of Newfoundland. As a repellent against the eclipsing hordes of mosquitoes and blackflies, the resident indigenous Beothuk people covered themselves in a red ocher/animal fat paste, dying their skin a deep maroon-red color. Numbering no more than 2,000, the Beothuk

* The Mosquito Coast, also christened during Columbus's fourth voyage, starts farther north, encompassing the coastline of Nicaragua and Honduras and continuing south to Panama. The Mosquito Gulf is specific to a body of water on the Panamanian coast.

quickly became known to Europeans as "Redskins."* A series of unfortunate events led to the Beothuk demise. While some historians hint at a possible genocide, no such thing happened. Smallpox and tuberculosis were the biggest stalkers, followed by starvation caused by a lack of access to traditional coastal fishing, tailed by "sport hunting" by murderous settlers. The combined outcome was the inability to reproduce and sustain an already small population. As a result, the Beothuk became extinct in 1829 when the last, a young woman named Shanawdithit, died of tuberculosis.

While St. John's, Newfoundland, is one of the preeminent natural harbors, and the island's Grand Banks was the most bountiful fishery in the world, the Newfoundland Colony was too far north to produce plantation profits.† It was also too remote to be used as a port from which to raid the galleons charted for Spain, weighed down with the riches coursing out of her colonial mines. With Newfoundland economically barren and the Caribbean stonewalled by seasoned Spanish defenders and stubborn mosquito fevers, Drake's contemporary Sir Walter Raleigh sought to reverse this situation and status with the founding of his colony at Roanoke.

The Roanoke venture was originally financed and organized by Sir Humphrey Gilbert. A fellow privateer, Gilbert drowned (quoting Thomas More's *Utopia* with his last words) on his return voyage after founding the Newfoundland Colony. The Roanoke mission passed to his younger half brother, Sir Walter Raleigh. As a favorite of Elizabeth, "the Pirate Queen," Raleigh inherited the seven-year royal charter and blank check to colonize any "remote, heathen, and barbarous lands, countries and territories, not actually possessed of any Christian Prince or inhabited by Christian people." In other words, any available and obtainable land not already occupied by Spain. In return, the Crown laid claim to 20% of the ill-gotten gains. Privately, Elizabeth instructed Raleigh to set up a base north of the Caribbean from which privateers could raid

* Other common indigenous insect repellents, aside from smoke, were animal fat lotions, ideally "bear grease." Ocher also acted as a natural sunscreen.

† Newfoundland gained independence from Britain in 1907 and became the last territorial addition to Canada, joining the Confederation in 1949.

Spanish treasure fleets bound for Europe. History knows this pirate cove as the Lost Colony of Roanoke. Consumed by "gold fever" and possessed with his pursuit of a gilded El Dorado in South America, Raleigh never actually stepped foot on North American soil. He simply funded the original Roanoke colonists to carry out his bidding.

The first set of 108 colonists arrived at Roanoke Island in August 1585. The ships departed for Newfoundland with the hollow promise of resupply by April the following year. By June 1586, with no relief fleet forthcoming, the withered survivors were starving and fending off retaliatory strikes by the local Croatan and Secotan peoples. You will recall that, in mid-June, as luck would have it, Drake checked in on the colony after his malaria-addled adventures in the Caribbean. The straggling Roanoke survivors clambered aboard his ships, which were in need of the helping hands since two-thirds of Drake's crew was either dead or rotting of malaria. Roanoke, round one, was abandoned. When the resupply finally came, and found the colony deserted, a small detachment of fifteen forsaken men was left behind, sacrificed to maintain an English stamp on the region.

In 1587, Raleigh dispatched a second group of 115 colonists to establish a colony north of Roanoke at the Chesapeake Bay. These settlers were likely malaria-free since they came from Devon, opposite England's malarial expanse known as the Fenlands or simply the Fens, marshlands that interlaced the southeast counties radiating from the mosquito-assailed nucleus of Kent and Essex. Stopping at Roanoke to collect the small, forlorn English garrison, the new settlers found nothing but a single skeleton. The captain of the fleet ordered the colonists to debark and establish the colony at Roanoke and not at Chesapeake Bay as planned. Only the leader of the expedition, John White, a friend of Raleigh's and also one of the original colonists rescued by Drake, returned to England to ensure a resupply for Roanoke that, again, never came.

War between Spain and England outweighed White's concerns and the needs of Roanoke. All ships were sequestered to meet the threat posed by the mighty Spanish Armada. Roanoke was a lost cause. When White finally returned three years later, he found nothing but the word *CROATOAN* carved into the sole remaining fence post, and the letters

C-R-O carved into a nearby tree. There were no signs of struggle, or of burning, and it looked as though everything had been systematically dismantled and removed. Rumors immediately began to swirl around England, some furtively planted by conniving financiers of mercantilist imperialism. No one would be willing to volunteer to pioneer future settlements if it meant certain death. For the English Crown and its commercial backers, colonization could not have the stigma of guaranteed suicide by starvation, disease, and torture at the hands of savage Indians. The truth would be bad for business.

Theories abound as to what happened to these lost colonists. While flamboyant documentaries litter TV channels and Netflix, only one explanation based on supporting archeological evidence passes the "Ancient Aliens" fiction test. Most died of starvation and disease, and the remainder, most likely only women and children, were adopted and absorbed by the local Croatan and Secotan peoples. This cultural practice of integration and assimilation was customary among indigenous peoples of eastern North America as we have already seen with French fur traders and their Métis offspring. Until the Lost Colony of Roanoke DNA Project, founded in 2007, unearths scientific genealogical proof, however, conspiracy theorists will still get airtime to poison the historical record with alleged Dare Stones, alien abductions, and fraudulent maps.

Although Raleigh never visited North America, between 1595 and 1617, he did lead military ventures against colonial Spain during the Anglo-Spanish War, piggybacking on his pirating expeditions, including his quest for the elusive golden temples of El Dorado in modern-day Venezuela and Guyana. All of his New World adventures were met with mosquito-borne failure. When Queen Elizabeth died in 1603, Raleigh was found guilty of orchestrating a coup against her successor, James I, who begrudgingly commuted his death sentence. Raleigh was imprisoned at the Tower of London until his pardon in 1616. Upon his release, he immediately gained approval to embark on his second attempt to find El Dorado, which turned out to be his last expedition.

In the process of treasure hunting in Guyana, Raleigh was sidelined by recurrent bouts of malaria. In his absence, a handful of Raleigh's men raided a Spanish settlement against his direct orders. Not only was his son killed in the exchange, it was also in direct violation of his parole agreement and the larger 1604 Treaty of London ending the nineteen-year Anglo-Spanish War. With Spain furious and demanding Raleigh's head, King James had no choice but to reinstate his death sentence. Raleigh's last words before he was beheaded in London in 1618 were inspired not by pride in his exploits, nor anger at their end, but by the mosquito and his recurrent malarial fevers: "Let us dispatch," he told the ax-wielding headsman. "At this hour my ague comes upon me. I would not have my enemies think I quaked from fear. Strike, man, strike!"

During his colorful life, perhaps most significant among his other "achievements" is that Sir Walter Raleigh popularized tobacco in England, acquired during one of his many swashbuckling raids against Spain. The rescued colonists of Roanoke also returned to England with tobacco-lined pockets and "with insatiable desire and greediness sucked in the stinking smoak." Roanoke survivor and famed English mathematician and astronomer Thomas Harriot came home extolling the medicinal benefits of smoking tobacco, declaring that it "openeth all the pores and passages of the body . . . bodies are notably preserved in health, and know not many grievous diseases, wherewithal we in England are often times afflicted." While the chain-smoking Harriot was eventually, and quite ironically, proven dead wrong (he succumbed to mouth and nose cancer caused by his smoking, chewing, and snuffing addiction), the Spanish monopoly on tobacco was so lucrative that selling tobacco seeds to a foreigner was punishable by death.

This Spanish tobacco cartel was soon undermined by one hardworking Englishman blending a taste for adventure and an entrepreneurial American spirit. Where Roanoke had failed, a young English tobacco farmer named John Rolfe and his Powhatan bride Pocahontas would ensure the survival of Jamestown and plant the seeds for the creation of English America and ultimately the United States. Tobacco was the lucrative cash crop and commercial currency that would breathe life into British America, originally filtered through Jamestown. Unwittingly, by cultivating tobacco, the British colonists also summoned mosquito-borne death.

After the initial shock and gossip associated with the failure of

Roanoke subsided, plans for another English mercantilist colony surfaced. Following layovers in the Canary Islands and Puerto Rico, on May 14, 1607, with the combined financial backing of the London Company and the Plymouth Company (known collectively as the Virginia Company), three ships carrying 104 ill-equipped and undersupplied males, including John Smith, limped into the Chesapeake Bay. In keeping with the time-honored miasma theory of mosquito-borne disease, the written instruction of the London Company for choosing a settlement site was simple and straightforward. The colonists were ordered not to establish the English outpost "in a low or moist place, because it will prove unhealthfull. You shall judge of the good air by the people; for some part of that coast where the lands are low, have their people blear eyed, and with swollen bellies and legs." The transports proceeded gingerly up the James River, its banks lined with freshly planted corn interspersed with stands of towering trees.

As the fleet's manifest and cargo attest, they did not come to explore or to farm or even to erect an enduring settlement. There were no women, a dearth of provisions, few livestock, and no seeds, farming equipment, or construction materials. There was, however, a haughty group of predominantly upper-class men unaccustomed to manual labor but armed with tackle for the extraction of gold and the goal of exploiting the mineral wealth of Virginia. On an uninhabited swampy peninsula in the James River, these hundred-odd foolhardy Englishmen would, quite accidentally, give birth to English America.

It soon became apparent why no indigenous Powhatan lived near the crude English colony. Thanks to a beaver population forty times larger than it is today, much of eastern North America was smeared with boggy swamps, double the present-day coverage. For mosquitoes, these wetlands must have been a nirvana-like playground.* The near extinction of beaver populations during the aptly dubbed Beaver Wars of the

* Weighing up to ninety pounds, beavers (which are giant rodents) reside in dome-shaped lodges made by blocking waterways with trees, mud, and stones and creating a checkerboard of smaller channels and wetlands. There can be as many as twenty dams per mile of stream or river. The largest beaver dam on record, almost a kilometer long (0.62 miles), is in northern Alberta, Canada. When the English colonists arrived at Jamestown, there were more than 220 million acres of wetlands in the United States, more than double the current total of roughly 110 million acres, including Alaska!

seventeenth and eighteenth centuries caused these marshes and floodplains to revert into fertile landscapes beckoning for English plows. These fur-trading wars, which pitted the Iroquois Confederacy and their British cohorts against various Algonquian nations and their French benefactors fractured long-standing indigenous relations. The Seven Years' War (1756–1763), known to Americans as the French and Indian War, was the culmination of this intermittent warfare in North America. It was also truly the first *world war* with far-reaching implications. The British and French finally came to decisive blows for supremacy in North America, and as we will see, mosquitoes stalked the encampments and battlefields as wanton warriors. English hunger for New France, however, was not immediate, as the survival of the original colonies of Jamestown and Plymouth was by no means a sure thing.

Jamestown, thanks to a busy beaver population, was not an ideal location to set up shop. The directive of the London Company was blithely ignored, and the consequences of this decision proved deadly. "No Indians lived on the peninsula because it was not a good place to live," Mann wryly acknowledges. "The English were like the last people moving into a subdivision—they ended up with the least desirable property. The site was boggy and mosquito-ridden." The brackish, salty water "full of slime and filth," as one colonist griped, was not potable, and also rendered the soil unserviceable.* Tidewater swamps offered no forage for wild game and only seasonal fish habitats.

Malarious mosquitoes, on the other hand, thrived in these conditions. Both imported foreign and receptive local Anopheles mosquitoes vectored malaria to the recently landed colonists, many of whom also arrived with the parasite roosting in their veins or hibernating in their livers. Nathaniel Powell, an early Jamestown settler, reported in a letter that "I have not yet lost my quartane Ague. But as I had him yesterday so I expect him on Thursday next." Jamestown was situated on one of the worst pieces of real estate for farming, hunting, and health you can imagine, and, to make matters worse, the gold, silver, and precious gems the languishing colonists clamored for were nowhere to be found.

* The staggering inertia of the original colonists is exemplified by the fact that it took two years to solve this problem with the most obvious solution—digging a well.

Instead, there was starvation, disease, and stealthy attacks from indigenous peoples who awed the English with their physical stature and prowess. They were also armed with bows and arrows that were nine times faster to fire and reload than an English musket. Unlike the small numbers of assimilated sojourner French who came to trade in furs, the English came for land and to set up expansionist colonies spreading from beachhead fringes to inland frontiers. Conflict with indigenous peoples was inevitable. The sickly English settlers, however, were both outgunned and outmanned. The sprawling Powhatan Confederacy surrounding Jamestown was made up of over thirty smaller allied nations and boasted a total population of 20,000. Within eight months, only 38 miserable Englishmen were left at Jamestown, roasting in the fires of malarial fevers, their own private hell on earth.

Although two separate resupplies in 1608 brought batches of settlers, including a handful of women, the colonists were dying faster than they could be replaced. "Our men were destroyed with cruell diseases, as Swellings, Fluxes, Burning Fevers," wrote demoralized colonist George Percy. "In the morning their bodies trailed out of their Cabines like Dogges to be buried." The initial lack of females also hampered any in-house population growth. A message was relayed to England to prepare new arrivals for "fevers and agues, which is the country distemper, a severe fit of which (called a *Seasoning*) most expect, some time after their arrival." The colony of Jamestown moldered within its mosquito-besieged surroundings. By the winter of 1609–1610, the Starving Time, only 59 of the original 500 colonists remained. It was summarily dispatched that "the Seasoning here, as in other parts of America, is a Fever or Ague, which the Change in Climate and Diet generally throws new Comers into." The first clumsy steps and initial swampy footing of Jamestown were jolted by unshakable malarious mosquitoes and gut-wrenching famine.

In his book *Bacteria and Bayonets*, tracking the impact of disease in American military history, David Petriello is careful to point out, "The problems that buffeted the small settlement could have easily sent Jamestown the way of Roanoke and delayed if not doomed further English exploration. The tale of the colony is a well-known one. How the settlers battled the Natives, food shortages, greed, and each other to eventually emerge as a sustainable settlement. The troubles that beset the colony during its first few years in which the majority of the population died has historically been termed the Starving Time. Yet once again this is an oversimplification if not an outright misnomer. What almost doomed Jamestown and Virginia was not a lack of food, but disease." Throughout the literary record, the original settlers to Jamestown have been pigeonholed as lazy and apathetic by historians and commentators. They probably were; they had chronic malaria. Jamestown starved because the occupants were too sick, and perhaps unwilling, to perform manual labor to farm, forage, or even steal food. The Starving Time should be rechristened the Mosquito Time. Malaria, typhoid, and dysentery came first and proceeded to shadow the subsequent period of starvation.

Early arrivals expected to trade for food with the local Powhatan and not grow it for themselves. After trading everything they owned for sustenance, and with nothing left to barter, they began stealing scarce Powhatan crops. The year 1609 had been a drought harvest, and food and game were in short supply. This precipitated larger indigenous raids and punitive expeditions, forcing the skeletal, malaria-trembling survivors to hole up in the stewed muck of Jamestown, cloistered by a wooden palisade. As true starvation set in, their gourmet meals consisted of tree bark, mice, leather boots and belts, engorged rats, and each other. It was later reported that ravenous colonists clawed at the earth to "dig up dead corpse out of graves and to eat them." One starving settler, as we've seen, killed his pregnant wife and, as an onlooker recorded, "salted her for his food." To make matters worse, John Smith, the skillful English leader who had brokered a tenuous peace and reciprocal trade with the Powhatan, returned to England in October 1609, shortly before the Starving Time and the ensuing conflict with the Powhatan. Smith was seriously injured after accidentally and quite clumsily igniting a bag of gunpowder dangling from his breeches. Badly burned, he left for England, never to return to Virginia.

Shortly after Smith's departure, another John arrived at Jamestown with a pocketful of tobacco seeds, determined to start a new life in Virginia. In the process, he would also unknowingly plow the future for a new nation—the United States of America. While John Smith has been glorified by Hollywood and history, the genuine celebrity of Jamestown is John Rolfe, the authentic English husband of our Disney darling, Pocahontas.

Rolfe sailed from England with his wife, Sarah, and 500 to 600 other passengers on board nine ships of the third supply fleet to Jamestown in June 1609. Seven of the nine transports reached Jamestown that summer, unloaded their supplies and settlers, and in October returned to England with news of the Starving Time, a few unwanted criminal colonists, and an injured and seared John Smith. The two Johns never met, at least not in Virginia.

Rolfe's ship, the *Sea Venture*, was thrashed by a hurricane on the crossing and eventually foundered on the northern shoals of Bermuda. Marooned on the island for nine months, the survivors—which group did not include Rolfe's wife and their newborn daughter, Bermuda, who were buried on the island—constructed two small vessels from local timbers and the wreckage of their derelict ship. The two hand-fashioned ships limped into Jamestown in May 1610, seven months after the departure of Smith and the other convoy.

For all of you Shakespeare lovers, the unlikely and intrepid voyage of the *Sea Venture* was the source and provided the setting for *The Tempest* (written in 1610–1611), which is loaded with references to slavery and agues. Shakespeare was conversant with malaria since the Fenland marshes of eastern England were already infamous for their pale, sallow, ague-stricken populations during the bard's lifetime. In *The Tempest,* the slave Caliban curses his master, Prospero, with malaria: "All the infections that the sun sucks up / From bogs, fens, flats, on Prosper fall and make him / By inch-meal a disease!" Later in the play, a drunk Stephano stumbles across Caliban and Trinculo shivering under a cloak while sheltering from a storm and mistakes them for "some monster . . . with four legs, who / hath got, as I take it, an ague." There was, however, another spin-off of the improbable passage of the *Sea Venture* in addition to what is thought by many critics and historians to be the last play fully penned by Shakespeare himself.

The misfortune of the *Sea Venture* was England's gain. Although no one from Rolfe's party stayed behind in Bermuda save the dead, the English flag was now planted on this strategic subtropical island in the North Atlantic. Located 1,000 miles north of Cuba and 650 miles east of the Carolinas, Bermuda was officially incorporated into the charter of the Virginia Company in 1612. It served as a rest stop for English ships of war and imperialism in transit to their final objectives. As one contemporary commentator wrote, Bermuda could serve as a springboard for England's larger colonial concerns, "as for the present they bee even as a new life and a seminarie to Virginia. The planting of them 'our countrimen' must needs adde much to the strength, prosperitie, and glorie of this kingdome, would proove a singular benefit to the native inhabitants of Virginia, and also to such our countrimen as should go over." By 1625, as the Puritans were converting Massachusetts, the colonial population of Bermuda far outnumbered that of Virginia. While other plantation crops such as sugar and coffee were still a pipe dream, tobacco fueled the English economies of both colonies. Colonists from Bermuda, however, fanned out to settle both the Bahamas and Barbados by 1630, and English sugar production found a home. Barbados became the leading edge of English Caribbean sugar commerce, and the population quickly soared, reaching 70,000, including 45,000 slaves, by 1700.

Interestingly, although Barbados witnessed the first conclusive epidemic of yellow fever (spread by the Aedes mosquito) in the Americas in 1647, it remained free of the malaria-causing Anopheles species. Despite epidemics of yellow fever and other diseases, the absence of malaria quickly gained Barbados a reputation as a "salubrious" and hygienic colony, and was even prescribed as a sanatorium for malaria patients. I can imagine the colonial advertisements for settlers and all-inclusive beach vacations in Barbados: BARBADOS: FUN, RUM, AND EVERYTHING UNDER THE SUN—*EXCEPT MALARIA!* or simply BARBADOS: THE BEST PLACE TO BE, WE ARE MALARIA-FREE! The apparent wholesome and healthy atmosphere of the island and anticipated economic opportunity enticed boatloads of immigrants. Indeed, prior to 1680, Barbados attracted more settlers than any other English New World colony. England finally made its long-desired entry into the profitable Caribbean market of sugar and tobacco. With the harrowing voyage of John Rolfe and the *Sea Venture*, England made economic inroads in the Caribbean but also entered deeper into the mosquito den and the tumult of her disease and death.

Following their nine-month shipwreck respite in Bermuda, when Rolfe and his 140 resourceful companions (and one resilient and loyal dog) finally made it to Jamestown in May 1610, they were confronted with a colony in ruins. The sixty starving and malaria-depleted residents pleaded for evacuation. There were no supplies left, and these new arrivals meant more mouths for the already starving colony to feed. The colonists had run out of options and Chief Powhatan was forcing their hand. For the first few years, he had permitted the colony to endure on worthless land if trade goods such as guns, axes, mirrors, and glass beads continued to flow. As long as these foreigners had popular products to offer, Powhatan kept them alive by funneling food their way. Given their low numbers and sickly state, the English were not a threat and could have easily been wiped out at a moment's notice. Superior numbers and food were the deadliest weapons in Powhatan's arsenal.

Following John Smith's departure in October 1609, the English had worn out their welcome with the Powhatan, who tired of their thieving and boorish behavior. The colonists had also spent their value as they had nothing left to trade. Their usefulness sailed with John Smith. Both for the hardened veterans of Jamestown's nightmare and for Rolfe's exhausted new arrivals, it was time to abandon ship. Jamestown was sinking in its own stinking malarial cesspool. In June 1610, the two makeshift boats Rolfe's party had sailed in on, and the only other two shoddy ships at Jamestown, were readied to sail to Newfoundland, where the fleeing settlers would beg Grand Banks fishermen for passage home. Like Roanoke, the colony at Jamestown would be forsaken.

As the ships solemnly weighed anchor and began their retreat down the James River, Lord De La Warr and his fortuitous relief fleet arrived with 250 colonists, military equipment, a doctor, and, most importantly, over a year's worth of supplies. Jamestown was given a timely injection of hope and England's ambitious economic aspirations of enduring settlement on the eastern Atlantic seaboard were whisked from the brink of abandonment and malarial ruin. As a token of appreciation,

Lord De La Warr, the redeemer of Jamestown, was, as he put it, "welcomed by a hot and violent Ague" followed by "a relapse into the former disease, which with much more violence held me more than a moneth, and brought me to great weakenesse." As settlers flooded into the resuscitated agricultural colony, De La Warr ensured that the mosquito, like John Rolfe and his starving expatriates, would never go hungry again.

Rolfe planted his first tiny tobacco crop inland of the dead marshes, and when it was exported to England in 1612, it fetched the current equivalent of $1.5 million. Rolfe named his sweeter strain of Trinidad tobacco "Orinoco" in honor of Sir Walter Raleigh's introduction of tobacco to England and to commemorate his trekking expeditions along the Orinoco River in Guyana in search of El Dorado. For Jamestown and its offspring of English America, El Dorado was not some towering, jewel-encrusted golden city, it was the herbaceous nightshade plant, *Nicotiana tabacum*. Here, I will defer to Charles Mann's concise commentary on the rapid maturity and vital importance of Virginia's commercial tobacco industry: "Much as crack cocaine is an inferior, cheaper version of powdered cocaine, Virginia tobacco was of lesser quality than Caribbean tobacco but also not nearly as expensive. Like crack, it was a wild commercial success; within a year of its arrival, Jamestown colonists were paying off debts in London with little bags of the drug. . . . By 1620 Jamestown was shipping as much as fifty thousand pounds a year; three years later the figure had almost tripled. Within forty years Chesapeake Bay—the Tobacco Coast, as it later became known—was exporting 25 million pounds a year." John Rolfe's tobacco venture paid dividends in spades—and in farming settlers, indentured servants, and field slaves. Jamestown went from bust to boom.

The unseasoned colony, however, still required investments of capital, a self-reproducing population and labor force, and, most agnostically, land that belonged to others. Recognizing the profits in tobacco, the Virginia Company poured in resources and supplies to ensure the survival of Jamestown. The company also sponsored the passage of both male and female convicts as indentured servants to toil in the tobacco fields and reproduce a country-born, locally disease-seasoned, population. After fulfilling their seven-year obligation and, hopefully, spawning a bounty of seasoned offspring, these indentured workers or convicts were given fifty acres of land in Virginia. Although Jamestown was not established primarily as a penal colony like Australia, over 60,000 British prisoners were shipped to colonial America. The company also sent over nonindentured "Tobacco Brides," for arranged marriages to independent men. As a result, the early 5-to-1 ratio of men to women in Virginia Colony slowly began to equalize. The investment was forthcoming, the labor force was trickling in, and a self-reproducing, seasoned population was emerging. All that was needed was precious land removed from the brackish mosquito-crawling bogs encircling Jamestown. Amplified conflict with the Powhatan was now, or perhaps had always been, inevitable.

Given his wealth, John Rolfe quickly became a de facto leader of Jamestown. As the balance of power was tilting toward the foreign settlers, Powhatan sensed an opportunity to rebuild peace and restore trade. His young, inquisitive daughter, Matoaka, was a frequent visitor to Jamestown. She played with the local children, learned English and Christianity, asked way too many questions for the colonists' liking, and was generally getting into mischievous but good-natured trouble. Her nickname, Pocahontas, "annoying brat" or "little hellion," was a no-brainer. As raids between the two camps intensified, Pocahontas was kidnapped in 1613 and used as leverage by the English. Rolfe was on the negotiating committee, and a deal was struck with Chief Powhatan. It was also agreed that Pocahontas, now seventeen, would remain with the English. More specifically, she would marry John Rolfe. This union certainly served as a pragmatic political tool to promote peace, similar to marriages among the monarchies of Europe. From all accounts, however, it appears that in the course of their three-year friendship, the two had genuinely fallen in love.

While he recognized their relationship served an economic and diplomatic contract, Rolfe's personal correspondences do not shy away from their emotional bond. In a letter to the governor requesting permission to wed, he expressed that he was "motivated not by the unbridled carnal affection, but for the good of this plantation, for the honor of our country . . . Pocahontas, to whom my hearty and best thoughts are, and have a long time been so entangled, and enthralled in so intricate a labyrinth that I was even a-wearied to unwind myself thereout." Apparently, John Rolfe was a hopeless romantic. They were married in April 1614, and their only child, Thomas, arrived ten months later. A colonial wedding crasher remarked about the union, "Ever since we have had friendly commerce and trade . . . so as now I see no reason why the colony should not thrive apace." The marriage between John and Rebecca, as she was now known, created an unofficial eight-year period of peace often nicknamed the "Peace of Pocahontas."

The Rolfes returned to England with their son in June 1616. Pocahontas, "Princess of the Powhatan," was received and entertained as a celebrity, with pomp and parade, although perhaps more out of curiosity than respect. A surprised Pocahontas and her husband even ran into John Smith at a dinner party (she having thought him dead), creating what I assume to be an awkward exchange of requisite courtesies between the two Johns. Pocahontas sat for an engraving, her only genuine likeness, which was sold as a "postcard" curio souvenir throughout the country. In March 1617, prior to embarking for their Virginia tobacco plantation, Pocahontas became deathly ill and died a few days later, at the age of twenty-one. The definitive cause remains a mystery although tuberculosis is most often blamed. According to Rolfe, she died uttering "all must die, but tis enough that her child liveth."* Within a year, Chief Powhatan, too, was dead, and the Peace of Pocahontas was broken. The English claimed ascendancy in the balance of power. The tide had turned in their favor, propelling boatloads of settlers, adventurers, investors, and African slaves across the Atlantic.

As settlers fanned out to farm tobacco along the more fertile lands of the James and York Rivers, the cycle of punitive raids dramatically increased, as did the spread of disease to indigenous peoples. In 1646, a boundary was established demarcating the lands belonging to the

* Matoaka was buried at the Parish of St. George in Gravesend. The exact location has been lost to time, as the church was destroyed by fire in 1727 and rebuilt. A life-size statue in the church garden honors her memory and unknown final resting place. Today, there are hundreds of direct descendants of Pocahontas through her son, Thomas, and this continued lineage.

Powhatan, signaling the inauguration of the Indian Reservation system in America. Following Bacon's Rebellion, the Treaty of Middle Plantation established an official Indian Reservation in 1677.* The colonists simply ignored the treaties that guaranteed indigenous peoples their homeland, hunting and fishing rights, and other territorial protections, signaling the inauguration of the treaty-making and treaty-breaking system in America.

In the end, disease, war, and starvation defeated the Powhatan Confederacy. The remnants drifted west, joined other nations, or were captured and sold into slavery. Disease, including malaria, writes Petriello, "brought about the final conflict between the English and the Native which cleared the way for the further development of Virginia. The defeat of the coastal Chesapeake tribes allowed for generations of Englishmen to push further west, deeper into the New World." The original "American Dream" was the ownership of land. Property equaled opportunity and prosperity.

Land, or wealth accrued from land in the form of tobacco, was the central issue of the 1676 rebellion of heavily taxed, smallholding tobacco farmers, newly arrived settlers, and indentured servants, led by Nathaniel Bacon. The rebels scoffed at the corrupt colonial regime's protection of Powhatan land and the restrictive limitations placed on western expansion at the expense of land-hungry settlers, a contentious issue that would also fan the embers of revolutionary fire a century later.

A handful of large plantation owners had carved out a monopoly on the production and transportation of tobacco through the use of indentured servants and by lining the pockets of the long-standing governor, William Berkeley, to restrict the doling out of new land grants. For their cartel owners, these sprawling tobacco plantations located in the fertile lowlands brought wealth and political power to Berkeley's inner circle. They also caused a staggering malarial death toll for indentured servant field hands. In the end, the rebellion itself failed and Bacon

* The treaty required indigenous people to wear an identification tag when leaving the reservation, very similar to the late-nineteenth-century "Pass Laws" in the United States, Canada, and apartheid South Africa.

died of a combination of malaria and dysentery after weeks of rain-soaked fighting.

This uprising, however, did have two grimly important consequences. The first, as mentioned, was the failed reservation system and the final removal of the Powhatan Confederacy, opening up land for unbridled tobacco production. The second was the dramatic increase of African slavery in Virginia. Africans were introduced to Jamestown in 1619 by English pirates sailing on the *White Lion* under the Dutch flag. The ship was carrying a cargo of Africans stolen from a Portuguese slaving vessel bound for Mexico. As reported by John Rolfe, the *White Lion*, a former decrepit pirate ship of Drake's fleet, "brought not anything but 20. and odd Negroes." A few days later, a damaged second ship requiring patchwork and restoration traded its cargo of thirty African slaves for much-needed repairs. The slave trade between Africa and the English colonies had not been formally established, and early colonists had no model for chattel slavery. Although the status of these Africans remains unclear, it is likely that they were purchased and put to work on tobacco plantations, first as indentured servants and later rebranded as slaves.

At the outbreak of Bacon's Rebellion in 1676, there were roughly 2,000 African slaves in Virginia. Bacon's rebellion revealed the limitations of an expanding labor force made up of indentured servants. For starters, on the expansive mosquito-plagued large plantations, they died too easily from malaria. It was also rightly assessed after the rebellion that they were too hard to control and subjugate. As their numbers increased so, too, did the threat of larger rebellions. Moreover, many simply ran away, squatted on a piece of vacant land, and planted tobacco of their own. Lastly, as mercantilism improved the economy of England, increased job opportunities, and decreased unemployment, fewer people were willing to indenture themselves. Thirty years after Bacon's Rebellion, the African slave population of Virginia topped 20,000. In short, as indentured servitude decreased, the labor ranks were filled with African slaves, signaling the inauguration of African chattel slavery, and its broader dissemination of mosquito-borne disease, into the American economic, political, and cultural landscape. English America, with its settlers, tobacco, slaves, and mosquitoes, was open for business. The triumph of John Rolfe's Jamestown tobacco experiment ignited a rush of commercial and territorial mercantilist expansion, the proliferation of mosquito-borne disease, and eventually a seasoned country-born colonial population.

Wrapped up in the chaos of the Columbian Exchange and the clamor of colonization, Drake, Raleigh, Smith, Pocahontas, and Rolfe all played their own part in establishing an English presence in the New World, and ultimately acted as the vanguard for the eventual creation of a mighty English mercantilist empire. These memorable but often misrepresented and mythologized historical characters were supported in the creation of English America by an ensemble cast of mosquitoes, settlers, and African slaves, all tied to the lucrative and addictive enterprises of tobacco and sugar. With each new English footprint from Plymouth to Philadelphia, mosquito-borne disease was stamped on an ever-transforming map of the Americas. The mosquito and her diseases were caught up in these winds of change blowing from Europe through Africa to the Americas by way of the Columbian Exchange.

Global English dominion and the escalating imperial domination of Pax Britannica would be both encouraged and, at times, discouraged by the mosquito. She carved out the union of a greater Britain itself by crafting the English annexations of Northern Ireland and Scotland. English tenancy over Northern Ireland was arranged by mosquitoes from the Fenland peat bogs of England, while mosquitoes basking in the jungle canopy of Panama dashed Scottish dreams of sovereignty and self-determination. Conversely, while she helped Britain attain control of French Canada, she also expelled the British from her American colonies, poking and prodding the United States down its path to independence.

While Pocahontas would certainly not recognize her mythical Disney adaptation, the New World as it stood a century after her death would also have been unrecognizable to her. "Jamestown was the opening salvo, for English America, of the Columbian Exchange," reiterates Charles Mann. "In biological terms, it marked the point when *before* turns into *after*." Yet Pocahontas, along with her husband, John Rolfe, her cartoon lover, John Smith, and boatloads of other conquistadors, convicts, pirates, and colonists, including many from England's malarial mosquito-infested Fenland marshes, planted the seeds for the creation of this "after" and its future.

CHAPTER 10

Rogues in a Nation: The Mosquito and the Creation of Greater Britain

The malarial epicenter of England, called the Fens or Fenlands, stretched for three hundred miles along the east coast from Hull in the north to Hastings in the south. Radiating from the nucleus of Essex and Kent, marshlands awash with malarious mosquitoes consumed the seven southeastern counties of the country. During the late sixteenth and seventeenth centuries, England began to recover from the devastation wrought by the Black Death. Its population more than doubled during the seventeenth century, reaching 5.7 million by its close. London's population grew from 75,000 in 1550 to 400,000 a century later. Migrant drifters, smugglers, and the land-hungry poor flooded into the Fenlands unclaimed by humans but fully utilized by mosquitoes.

The inhabitants of the Fens, often called "marsh dwellers" or "lookers" due to their malaria-modeled jaundice and drawn appearance, braved malarial death rates upwards of 20%. The survivors eked out a living and suffered through their miserable malarial existence. Novelist Daniel Defoe, famous for his shipwreck castaway tale, *Robinson Crusoe*, wrote a shocking exposé, *Tour through the Eastern Counties of England,* in 1722. Defoe informally chatted with numerous marshmen and discovered that "it was very frequent to meet with men that had had from five or six to fourteen or fifteen wives . . . there was a farmer who was then living with the five-and-twentieth wife, and that his son, who was but about thirty-five years old, had already had about fourteen." Since pregnant women possess a magnetism for both the mosquito and the malaria

Ague and Fever: A frenzied fever beast stands racked in the center of a room, while a blue monster representing ague (malaria) ensnares its victim by the fireside. To the right, a doctor writes a prescription for quinine. Colored etching by Thomas Rowlandson, London, 1788. *(Wellcome Images/Science Source)*

parasite, one "merry fellow" nonchalantly explained to Defoe that when young women "came out of their native air into the marshes among the fogs and damps, there they presently changed their complexion, got an ague or two, and seldom held [survived] it above half a year, or a year at most; 'And then,' said he, 'we go to the uplands again and fetch another.'" Children also died disproportionately.

In Charles Dickens's *Great Expectations*, the seven-year-old protagonist, Pip, is orphaned after his parents and "five little brothers of mine—who gave up trying to get a living, exceedingly early in that universal struggle," succumbed to malaria in the Fenlands. The story begins with Pip mourning his dead kin in the local graveyard, while narrating the earthly contours of his home: "Ours was the marsh country . . . intersected with dykes and mounds and gates, with scattered cattle feeding on it, was the marshes; and that the low leaden line beyond was the river; and that the distant savage lair from which the wind was rushing, was the sea; and that small bundle of shivers growing afraid of it all and beginning to cry, was Pip." Later, Pip tells a quaking man who escaped the convict hulks moored in the Thames River, "I think you have got the ague. It's bad about here. You've been lying out on the marshes, and they're dreadful aguish."

As the miasmic, ill-natured reputation of the marsh country was realized, during the latter half of the seventeenth century, many "lookers" moved farther afield to the American colonies. In fact, embarkation nominal rolls and ship manifests reveal that 60% of these first-wave settlers and indentured servants came from England's malaria belt. They left England to escape malaria and inadvertently acted as malarial agents for the Columbian Exchange. In their new world they suffered not only from their old-world malaria but also from a host of other varieties, including the more lethal *falciparum*. The tragic reality, as we will see, was that their new malarial landscape was worse than the one they had purposefully left.

In addition to seeking malaria sanctuary in the American colonies, large numbers of marsh dwellers also fled the Fenlands to Ireland, giving rise to a popular proverb, "From Farm to the Fen, from the Fen to Ireland." The current partition of the Republic of Ireland and Northern Ireland is directly tied to the settlement patterns of these malaria-fleeing English Fenland farmers of the seventeenth century. The mosquito prepared the foundations for, and the underpinnings of, the twentieth-century ethnonationalist conflicts called "The Troubles." This protracted violence between the Irish Republican Army and the Ulster Volunteer Force, in addition to the British Army, in Northern Ireland (with tremors across the British Isles), has only recently subsided.

The mosquito forced over 180,000 Protestant English farmers to Catholic Ireland, where they settled among the landed English gentry and Protestant Scots who had fled the English Civil War that raged from 1642 to 1651. This motley crew of Protestants created what came to be known as the Early, Munster, Ulster, and Later Plantations during the sixteenth and seventeenth centuries. Their immigration, presence, and territorial expansion ignited a nationalist racial and religious war and the Troubles between English Protestants and Irish Catholics. These plantations have had obvious and profoundly violent effects on the history of Ireland ever since. And while the mosquito was busy carving up the "Emerald Isle," she also bit directly into the territorial integrity of Ireland's Scottish neighbor.

During the religiously fueled English Civil War, the fanatically devout Protestant Oliver Cromwell led the Parliamentarians in the overthrow of King Charles I and the monarchy. The controversial Cromwell ruled for almost a decade as lord protector over the Commonwealth of England, Scotland, and Ireland, having conducted near-genocidal campaigns against both the Scottish and the Catholic Irish.

During his short reign, Cromwell expanded English holdings in the Caribbean to include Jamaica. Fresh off a war with the Dutch over colonial trade and rival piracy, Cromwell was uneasy with the vast English Army and Navy sitting idle. With England, Ireland, and Scotland in a religious uproar, an underemployed military was an invitation for a potential, and not all that unlikely, rebellion against his zealous Protestant rule. Utilizing this force for far-flung imperial purposes might serve to unite the embittered factions, providing his military with an amphibious mission and Spanish plunder while distancing himself from possible revolution. Although Cromwell refused their quinine to treat his recurring bouts of malaria, a good old-fashioned war might be just what the doctor ordered.

Cromwell's "Western Campaign" was launched in 1655. At this point in time, it was the largest combined fleet (thirty-eight ships) ever dispatched to the Americas. Over half of the 9,000 troops came from England, with the majority described as "knights of the blade, with common cheats, thieves, cutpurses, and such like lewd persons who had long time lived by sleight of hand, and dexterity of wit, and were now making a fair progress unto Newgate [the notorious prison in London]." The remainder, some 3,000 to 4,000 broken men, pirates, and used-up indentured servants, were recruited from the malaria-free, unseasoned island of Barbados. To one senior officer of the expedition, these men were like "the most profane debauch'd person that I ever saw." This ragtag force was put through a trial run in April 1655 during a quick sortie against the Spanish fort at Santo Domingo, Hispaniola. The English quickly abandoned their siege after losing 1,000 men, including 700 to mosquito-borne disease.

Undaunted, a month later, the English initiated the invasion of their primary target, Jamaica, home to 2,500 vastly outnumbered Spaniards and slaves. Within a week, the English had overrun the island with minor losses, and the Spanish fled to Cuba. The mosquito, however, did not abandon her post. She was flourishing on the island since an El Niño season had provided her with extra warm and wet weather—perfect conditions for stalking over 9,000 newly arrived, unseasoned, and enticing Englishmen, as one witness explained, "at such time that these insects collect in swarms, and make war on every daring intruder." Within three weeks, malaria and yellow fever were killing 140 men per week. Six months after landing in Jamaica, of the 9,000 original troops, only one-third remained standing. Robert Sedgwick, a crafty veteran, left an eyewitness testimony describing this massacre by mosquito: "Strange to see young lusty men, in appearance well, and in three or four days in the grave, snatch'd away in the moment with fevers, agues, fluxes." Sedgwick died of yellow fever seven months after his arrival in Jamaica.

Eventually, by 1750, enough soldiers and settlers were sacrificed on the altar of mosquito-borne disease to secure the island and to establish a seasoned, sugar-producing population of 135,000 African slaves and 15,000 English planters. A burgeoning British slave-plantation mercantilist economy began to thrive. The English commandeering of Jamaica from Spain also marked the last time a large Caribbean island permanently shifted between European imperialist hands by force of arms.*

Jamaica joined the growing list of English possessions in the Caribbean, including Bermuda, Barbados, Bahamas, and half a dozen smaller islands of the Lesser Antilles. To reap the profits of this expanding English empire, and to promote domestic prosperity, Cromwell passed the first of a series of Navigation Acts designed to strengthen England's mercantilist economy. Cromwell's initial act required all English freights

* Between 1651 and 1814, for example, St. Lucia went back and forth fourteen times between the British and French as a result of conquest. Smaller, less valuable, and lightly defended islands like St. Lucia and St. Kitts were easier targets and teeter-tottered between imperial powers.

of trade—raw resources from the colonies and manufactured goods from England—to enter and exit through English ports. To appease English traders and secure investment for overseas enterprise, Scotland was barred from this covenant and was forbidden to trade with English colonies. Cromwell, however, did not live long enough to collect the personal economic kickbacks of his arrangements.

His reign of tyranny—or liberty, depending on which side of the historical debate you're on—and his life were ended by a malarious mosquito. His doctors begged him to take cinchona quinine powder. He flat-out refused. Given its discovery by Catholic Jesuits, Cromwell insisted that he did not want the "Pope-ish remedy" or to be "Jesuited to Death" or poisoned by the "Jesuit's Powder." In 1658, twenty years after quinine first voyaged to Europe on the later winds of the Columbian Exchange, Cromwell died of malaria. Two years after his death, the monarchy, under Charles II, was restored. Unlike Cromwell, Charles was begrudgingly saved from malarial death by sacramental cinchona bark.

The exclusionist economic policies and sadistic campaigns of Cromwell during the English Civil War had left Scotland in a shambles. To make matters worse, a decade of drought had scorched the countryside, ravaged crops, instigated catastrophic famine, and otherwise crushed an already fragile Scottish economy. During the Great Famine that devastated Scotland and Scandinavia between 1693 and 1700, the Scottish oat harvest failed every year but one. It is estimated that as many as 1.25 million Scots, nearly 25% of the population, died as a result of this drought. As food shortages and starvation gripped the nation, thousands of Protestant Scots established themselves in Northern Ireland, as mentioned, forming the smoking tinder for a firestorm of cultural and religious violence that endures to this day. Others became mercenaries for the monarchies of Europe. In England, throngs of Scottish refugees begged for work, money, and food. During this time of hunger and hardship, the English contemptuously scoffed that their northern neighbors needed only eight of the ten commandments because in Scotland there was nothing to steal or covet.

There was an increasing demand for indentured servants in the

American colonies, and these Scottish transients were obvious applicants, and in generous supply. "English farmers had employed indigent Scots for centuries," notes Charles Mann. "Yet at the very time the supply of desperate Scots was increasing the colonists turned to captive Africans. . . . Why?" The answer lies half a world away, cloaked by mosquitoes in the jungle wilds of Panama.

To alleviate the economic recession in Scotland and boost financial prospects, in 1698, Scottish investors launched a daring colonial undertaking. Scotland's financial woes were aggravated by her lack of access to the English mercantilist system. The obvious solution, at least according to Scottish nationalist, entrepreneur, and a founder of the Bank of England, William Paterson, was for Scotland to take up the sword of imperialism and create a mercantilist realm of its own. Panama, he reckoned, would be the commercial heart of a money-pumping Scottish empire, or as he put it, "the key to the universe . . . arbitrator of the commercial world." Paterson had visited the area as a young man and was enthralled by the spicy, rum-soaked stories of pirates such as Francis Drake, Walter Raleigh, and Henry "Captain" Morgan.

Carving a trade route through the jungle isthmus of Panama at Darien was not a novel idea. As you may recall, the Spanish erected a settlement at Darien in 1510 that was visited by the priest Bartolome de las Casas, who recorded the open-pit mass graves demanded by the unrelenting deaths from malarious mosquitoes. The Spanish attempted to blaze a trail across Panama as early as 1534 and were rebuffed by the mosquito. Subsequent attempts were also mosquito-afflicted fiascos. An estimated 40,000 Spanish died, mostly of malaria and yellow fever, during these fruitless attempts to unlock the passage to commerce. Where the Spanish had failed, Paterson was sure his hardy highland Scots would succeed.

He envisioned a road, and eventually a canal, spanning the Panama isthmus at Darien, "seated between the two vast oceans of the universe. . . . The time and expense of navigation to China, Japan, and the Spice Islands, and the far greatest part of the East Indies will be lessened by more than half. . . . Trade will increase trade, and money will beget money." Such was Paterson's pitch to potential wealthy English investors who rejected his solicitations, fearing for their tight-knit English monopoly on trade. A dejected Paterson left London to float his business proposition on the damp winds of his independent home country, Scotland. He rallied 1,400 Scottish investors, including the Scottish Parliament, to his cause with a total pledge of 400,000 pounds, estimated between 25% and 50% of the total liquid capital of the already smarting, cash-strapped country. Desperate times call for desperate measures, and the spectrum of adventure capitalists spanned the classes of Scottish society from the Edinburgh elite to the poor and landless.

Paterson's vision became a reality in July 1698 when five ships ferrying Paterson and 1,200 Scottish settlers weighed anchor to create the colony of New Caledonia and its commercial capital, New Edinburgh, at Darien, Panama. Envisioned as a trading settlement at the crossroads of global commerce, the ships destined for this providential Scottish station were stuffed with exchangeable goods that included the finest wigs, pewter buttons, doily frocks, combs inlaid with mother-of-pearl, warm woolen blankets and socks, 14,000 sewing needles, 25,000 pairs of stylish leather shoes, and thousands of Bibles. Lastly, a Gutenberg-style printing press made the voyage to record Indian treaties and to compile financial ledgers tracking the immense volume of trade and wealth accumulated by dealing in a foreign god and woolen Scottish winter-wear in the sweltering tropics. To make room for these impractical items, food and farming rations were cut in half.

Paterson's outbound Scottish armada of fortune stopped at Madeira and then paused for a week at the Danish Caribbean island of St. Thomas before tracking along the Mosquito Coast to Darien. By this time, yellow fever, which first arrived in the Americas in 1647 aboard a slave ship docking at Barbados, as detailed earlier, was already firmly established across the Caribbean expanse. And yet, during the voyage of three months, even as epidemics rippled north through major port cities, including Charleston, New York, Philadelphia, Boston, and even as far north as Quebec City, only forty-four passengers bound for Darien died of malaria and yellow fever, stowaways picked up at the two previous ports of call. I say "only" because, as we have seen with other voyages, like Drake's for example, the body count could have been much worse.

It was actually less than average for a seventeenth-century transatlantic voyage, which usually consumed about 15% to 20% of the commuters and crew. It was also probably far less than the number that would have died had they remained in famine- and recession-stricken Scotland. Their luck, however, would not hold.

What unfolded when they arrived at Darien was nothing short of the script for an apocalyptic horror movie. The words that are repeated to the point of nausea in the diaries, letters, and accounts of the Scottish settlers are mosquitoes, fever, ague, and death. Within six months of arrival, nearly half of the 1,200 colonists were dead of malaria and yellow fever (and possibly also from a first appearance of dengue in the Americas), with as many as a dozen dying each day.* As word of Darien's desperation reached England, King William III forbade any relief for fear of offending Spain and France, and his wealthy English subjects. And so the Scots at Darien continued to die of mosquito-borne disease, decaying among their stores of woolen blankets, wigs, warm socks, Bibles, and, of course, their idle printing press.

With rumors of a looming Spanish attack, the 700 survivors loaded three ships after six months of hell. Those too sick to walk the boarding plank were left on the beach to die. One ship found Jamaica, losing 140 passengers on the short trip. The other hobbled into Massachusetts after witnessing a fever "so universal," wrote the ship's captain, "mortality so great that I have hove overboard 105 Corps." Observing the king's orders and paranoid about the "spread of the Scottish fever," the English authorities in the Caribbean and North America gave no quarter to the sick Scots. Eventually, one ship shuttled the entire lot of fewer than 300 survivors, including Paterson, back to a tattered Scotland. Darien, round one, was abandoned.

Ironically, or tragically as it turned out, just days before Paterson's pitiful party arrived home, a second fleet of four ships carrying 1,300 Scottish reinforcements, including 100 women, sailed for Darien.

* There is some evidence to suggest that dengue first landed in the Americas with imported African slaves and/or mosquitoes in Martinique and Guadeloupe in 1635, twelve years before the first recorded case of yellow fever in the Americas. There are also clues and hints pointing to a dengue epidemic ravaging Panama in 1699.

Losing 160 people during the voyage, this second serving of Scots for the mosquitoes of Darien landed exactly one year after their mosquito-doomed predecessors. Like the second arrivals at Roanoke, they found next to nothing. The Spanish and local indigenous Guna had torched the makeshift tiki huts and looted everything, except the printing press, standing memorial-like on the beach, surrounded by fragmentary sand-blasted gravestones. The script for the first horror movie was recycled for the showing of "Darien: The Sequel."

By March 1700, four months after the party landed, malaria and yellow fever were killing Scots at a rate of 100 per week, with Spanish raids filling any unused graves. In mid-April, the surviving Scots surrendered to the Spanish. As a parting gift, the mosquito's toxic twins continued to ravage the fleeing Scots, killing an additional 450 on the Atlantic crossing. Of the 1,200 settlers that made up the second colonization attempt at Darien, less than 100 returned to Scotland. Darien was abandoned. This time for good. The mosquitoes of Darien remained undefeated against unseasoned Europeans.

When consolidating the numbers, of the 2,500 Scottish settlers who sailed for Darien, the mosquito made a death-row last meal of 80%.* As Mann is quick to point out, "Lost with the dead was every penny invested in the venture." Panamanian mosquitoes bit at the heart of Scottish independence, mocking William Wallace's bloodcurdling cries of freedom.

Already fiscally floundering, Scotland was bankrupted by the mosquito-liquidated Darien venture. In the jungle wilderness of Panama, the mosquito had quite literally eaten away the Scottish treasury. Thousands of Scots lost their savings, riots filled the streets, unemployment rates hit the ceiling, and the country was in financial chaos. At this time, although England and Scotland shared a monarch, they were two independent countries with distinct parliamentary legislatures. England was wealthier, more populous, and generally much better off, and had been badgering its poorer northern neighbor for unification for centuries.

The Scots, including a claymore-wielding William Wallace in the late thirteenth century, had fiercely resisted every English entreaty until

* As ludicrous as this sounds, upon his return home from Panama, Paterson tried to persuade investors to finance a third Darien expedition in 1701.

now. "When England offered to pay off the entire debt of the Scottish Parliament and reimburse the shareholders," explains J. R. McNeill, "many Scots found this offer irresistible. Even some committed Scottish patriots such as Paterson endorsed the Act of Union of 1707. Thus, Great Britain was born, with assistance from the fevers of Darien." Lamenting the loss of Scottish independence, Robert Burns, lionized as the national poet of Scotland, chastised the corrupt politicians and wealthy merchants for selling out the Scottish people by endorsing the Acts of Union. "We're bought and sold for English gold," Burns chided. "Such a parcel of rogues in a nation." While the Acts of Union and the forfeiture of Scottish independence were not popular among the Scottish masses, the economy began to rebound, riding on the coattails of England's booming mercantilist and extractive colonies in the Americas.

The disaster at Darien also signaled to English colonial plantation owners the danger of using Scots as indentured servants. There was no purpose and, more importantly, no profit in hiring a Scottish workforce if four of every five died within six months. Darien had made it all too clear that Scots, and other Europeans, died too fast of mosquito-borne disease to be of any use. "Individual Britons and their families continued to make their way to the Americas," recaps Mann, "but businesspeople increasingly resisted sending over large groups of Europeans. Instead they looked for alternative sources of labor. Alas, they found them." The English Civil War also cut the population of both Scotland and England by 10%, reducing the number of domestic workers, opening the job market, and driving up wages. As a result, the pool of prospective indentured servants was significantly drained. European indentured servitude as a form of mass labor was doomed by the mosquito. The replacement was found in African slaves, many of whom were immune to these very same mosquito-borne diseases. The demand that was fueling chattel slavery across the Americas was injected with a turbo-boost and was punched into hyperdrive.

The English American colonies narrowly avoided abandonment, failure, and a Scottish Darien-like disaster. They barely scratched through their trials by mosquitoes, starvation, and war, and their settlement was by no means easy. I do not want to give the impression that simply because of tobacco and African slavery (which were inseparable), the eventual Thirteen Colonies grew and thrived instantaneously. Settlers plodded slowly down a treacherous and uncharted road. The diary entry of Mary Cooper sums up life in the early colonies. "I am dirty and distressed, almost wearied to death," she bemoaned. "This day is forty years since I left my father's house and come here, and here have seen little else but hard labor and sorrow." With hard labor, eager capitalistic settlers cleared land for tobacco and created new habitats for mosquitoes with a summons to spread malaria, yellow fever, and misery.

The colonies grew because settlers, including women, were continuously injected in such large numbers that a handful survived malaria, eventually yellow fever, and other diseases to spawn a seasoned, country-born population. This broke the stalemate and prevented Jamestown, Plymouth, and others from vanishing like Roanoke, while also sparing us from more misleading documentaries on other "lost colonies." Colonial-born generations eventually survived, having become accustomed to, and a part of, their communal ecosystems. American-born generations and their local germs eventually reached a biological balance after an unremitting parade of death. This seasoning, however, took time. Initially, aside from clearing land and stirring up mosquito populations, the waves of English settlers, predominantly fleeing the mosquito-swamped Fenlands, were also their own worst malarial enemies.

The problem for these colonists was they now faced an entirely new mosquito and malarial environment. Theirs was both an endemic and epidemic malarial stew with multiple gruesome seasonings. The English imported their own *vivax* and, to a much lesser extent, *malariae* parasites. In the malarial cauldron of the colonies, they morphed into new, expatriate-specific strains, while African slaves injected *falciparum* into this increasingly diverse American malarial landscape. In a repeated cycle of contagion, new arrivals from the Fenlands and West Central Africa continued to introduce foreign malarial varieties, while the colonists cultivated their own domestic breeds. The mosquito and her multiple, unique malarial offspring never went hungry.

In his volume *The Making of a Tropical Disease: A Short History of*

Malaria, Randall Packard, director of the Institute of the History of Medicine at Johns Hopkins University, confirms that malaria "reached its peak in England around the middle of the seventeenth century. . . . One of the consequences of this outward movement may have been the transplantation of malaria infections to the emerging American English colonies, where many men and women from the southeast counties [Fenlands] traveled in order to find a new life." James Webb adds to Packard's observation by affirming, in his book on the global history of malaria, that the "establishment of denser settlements allowed infections to increase in the late seventeenth century and early eighteenth century when malaria emerged as the most important killer in the North American colonies."

For Virginia Colony, the numbers are staggering. In its first two decades of existence from 1607 to 1627, over 80% of new arrivals to Jamestown and Virginia died within a year! Most perished within weeks or months. Over this time period, of the roughly 7,000 immigrants to Virginia Colony, only 1,200 survived their first year. Tobacco planter and governor of Virginia George Yeardley counseled his London stakeholders in 1620 that they "must be content to have littell service done by new men in the ffirst yeare till they be seasoned." Tobacco was so profitable, however, that the Virginia Company was willing to shell out enormous sums to send settlers, criminals, prostitutes, indentured servants, and eventually African slaves, to the colony to ensure its survival and its own accumulation of wealth. Tobacco farmers and plantation owners were making a mind-boggling 1,000% margin and taxable return on their initial investments. In Virginia, both profits and population continued to grow. A century after the death of Pocahontas, 80,000 Europeans called Virginia home, where they enslaved a further 30,000 Africans. The colony continued to prosper, so much so that for the British, it was a moneymaker worth fighting for. On the eve of the American Revolution, the population of Virginia touched 700,000, including almost 200,000 slaves.

The second colony, the Puritan settlement at Plymouth, Massachusetts, fared no better at its outset than its older Virginian sister. Eventually, like its twelve other siblings, a country-born, seasoned population crested the wave of malaria and other diseases. Having been persecuted in both England and the Netherlands for their extreme Protestant beliefs, a group of English Puritans, later known as Pilgrims, sought to start a religious commune in the New World. Even after Martin Luther and his *Ninety-Five Theses* kindled the Protestant Reformation in 1517, the Puritans still believed that the Church of England retained too many elements and dogmatic compounds of Catholicism. Busting the common mythology, this group of 102 people who sailed on the *Mayflower* in 1620 were a portion of an exceptionally small minority of settlers who came to the Americas for religious freedom. The lion's share came for land, or alternatively, were cajoled into passage as indentured servants, convicts, or slaves.

A rough sea voyage diverted the *Mayflower* 200 miles north of their intended target, the Hudson River. Just in time for a nasty New England winter, on November 11, 1620, the damaged *Mayflower* hobbled into a small cove roughly two miles north of the four-ton granite boulder known as Plymouth Rock. This tourist attraction of mythology is viewed by more than one million sightseers each year.* Bestselling author Bill Bryson scoffs at the idea, noting, "The one thing the Pilgrims certainly did not do was step ashore on Plymouth Rock." During this first winter, the Puritans split their time between their ship and a few crudely constructed buildings. When the *Mayflower* sailed for England in April 1621, only 53 of the original 102 Pilgrims were still alive. Of the 18 adult women, only 3 survived this five-month freeze.

Malaria soon found a home in the settlement, and as entomologist Andrew Spielman confirms, "Given that hundreds or thousands of people from malaria zones [Fenlands] came into the area, I wouldn't have trouble believing that. Once malaria has a chance to get into a place, it usually gets in fast." The governor of Plymouth Colony, William Bradford, penned a short note following the sickly mosquito season of 1623: "The question which has been brought up against the Colony was that the people are much annoyed by mosquitoes." Bradford recognized the benefits of seasoning, deducing that new arrivals "are too delicate and

* The first recorded instance of this random rock as the landing site of the *Mayflower* was in 1741 (121 years after the Puritans arrived). The two most trusted firsthand accounts of the founding of Plymouth Colony, from Edward Winslow and William Bradford, do not mention any rocks.

unfit to begin new plantations and colonies that cannot endure the biting of the mosquito. We wish such to keep at home until at least they be mosquito proof." Although it is widely reasoned that malaria became endemic immediately in the Massachusetts colonies, epidemics ravaged the region every five years from 1634 to 1670.

Their god had instructed the Puritans to "be fruitful and increase in number; multiply on the earth and increase upon it." The Puritans, never ones to shirk responsibility or to sidestep the proverb of an honest day's work, diligently set forth to follow this command. And they did just that, at a prolific, indefatigable rate. It is estimated that 10–12% of Americans today are direct descendants of this small group of Puritans. Like Jamestown, after their initial malarial seasoning, the Puritan population began to stabilize and eventually grow. By 1690, their population reached 7,000, when their expansive colony was annexed into Massachusetts Colony with a total population nearing 60,000 people. Again, like Jamestown, expansion off the beachhead settlements of Massachusetts into the westward frontiers resulted in conflict with local indigenous populations, who died of disease, war, and starvation. The survivors straggled farther west or were rounded up and sold into slavery.

This native-newcomer cycle of malarial and yellow fever seasoning, country-born population growth combined with a continual influx of immigrants, westward expansion, war with indigenous peoples, and their eventual defeat, exodus, forced removal, or captivity played itself out across the evolution of all Thirteen Colonies. Beginning in 1700, each new country-born seasoned generation doubled the population of the colonies. For example, the combined colonial population, excluding slaves and indigenes, was roughly 260,000 in 1700. It reached 500,000 by 1720 and topped 1.2 million by 1750. Six years later, on the eve of the Seven Years' War, this English colonial population had increased by 300,000, while New France housed a measly *total* of 65,000 who by this time viewed themselves as distinct peoples rather than "French." When the "shot heard 'round the world" ignited the American Revolution at Lexington in April 1775 the colonial population was nearing 2.5 million, set against a British homeland population of 8 million.

Mosquito landscapes were an integral part of this colonial progression and framework. Across the Western Hemisphere, however, not all environments of mosquito-borne disease were created equal. They differed by regions, coupled to their unique blends of mosquito species. These distinct mosquito-borne disease landscapes were shaped by multiple factors that included climate, geography, farming habits and crop selections, and population densities, including that of African slaves. These differences would be decisive in the upcoming imperial hostilities and wars of independence that rocked the Americas during the seventeenth and eighteenth centuries. The fates and fortunes of these conflicts would largely be decided by the mosquito and her marching columns of malaria and yellow fever.

For our purposes, and to identify the areas of operation for the upcoming mosquito-prejudiced hostilities and happenings, we can carve the Americas into three distinct geographic zones of mosquito-borne disease or zones of infection. We will start with the first and worst, in the southern colonies, then progress through the middle colonies, and on to the last and best (only relative to the suffering farther south) in the northern colonies.

The first geographic area extended from central South America along the Amazon River basin to the southern United States, or as J. R. McNeill succinctly states, "the Atlantic coastal regions of South, Central, and North America, as well as the Caribbean islands themselves, that in the course of the seventeenth and eighteenth centuries became plantation zones: from Surinam to the Chesapeake . . . the establishment of a plantation economy improved breeding and feeding conditions for both [Aedes and Anopheles] mosquito species, helping them become key actors in the geopolitical struggles of the early modern Atlantic world." This zone was a mosquito sanctuary and was ravaged by both endemic and epidemic *vivax* and *falciparum* malaria. It was also simultaneously swamped by yellow fever and dengue. Infection (and seasoning) and mortality rates across this zone, such as those witnessed on our earlier visit to South Carolina and its slave trader haven, Charleston, were extremely high, convincing insurance companies to charge higher life insurance premiums to clients in the mosquito-addled South. Unlike the northerly tobacco colonies, in South Carolina, given its high volume of

Safety Net: A woodcut print from 1797 depicting a typical scene of Japanese women dressing under mosquito netting with the aid of servants. *(Library of Congress)*

slave trafficking and its main industry of rice cultivation, mosquito-borne diseases hit especially hard. *Falciparum* became the overriding killer. Georgia became a miniature version of South Carolina's "rice kingdom." In fact, around the planet, from Japan to Cambodia to South Carolina, rice husbandry was chaperoned by malarious mosquitoes.

In North America, we have a handy, well-known cultural symbol to mark the northern limit of this first deadly zone of infection. The Pennsylvania-Maryland border, surveyed in 1768 by Charles Mason and Jeremiah Dixon to resolve a boundary dispute among these two colonies and Delaware and Virginia (now West Virginia), serves as the northerly border of this lethal mosquito landscape. While *vivax* malaria blighted both sides of the Mason-Dixon Line, as the boundary is commonly known, this frontier was the northern endemic threshold for both *falciparum* malaria and yellow fever. Infrequent and sporadic epidemics of both diseases did occur north of the line, but they came, killed, and left. In Maryland, for example, during a malaria epidemic in 1690, a visitor commented on "the washed countenances of the people standing at their doors . . . like so many standing ghosts . . . every house was an infirmary."

The Mason-Dixon Line has come to represent the division between slave states and free states, although this is not entirely accurate. Maryland lies north and east of the line, and although opting not to join the Confederacy during the Civil War, Maryland did not abolish slavery until the passage of the Thirteenth Amendment to the Constitution.* Its ratification in 1865, following the Union victory in the Civil War, legally certified, "Neither slavery nor involuntary servitude, except as a punishment for crime whereof the party shall have been duly convicted, shall exist within the United States, or any place subject to their jurisdiction." The Mason-Dixon Line runs like a scar across the cultural landscape of the United States. It snakes through American history like a main circuit cable plugging straight into the differences and enduring divisions between Dixie South and Yankee North.

The association of the Mason-Dixon Line with chattel slavery, plantations, and mosquito-borne disease is not a coincidence. Tobacco and cotton did not grow in the northern states; therefore, the plantation-slave system was nonexistent. These crops grew in the warmer climes of the South, where mosquitoes thrived. These plantations also needed slave labor to produce profit. The imported slaves added to the robust mosquito landscape by introducing *falciparum* and yellow fever, and perhaps *vivax*. The endemic and epidemic mosquito-borne disease environments south of the Mason-Dixon Line flourished. Plantation colonies, African slavery, and deadly mosquito-borne diseases were intertwined, and as it turned out, so was the seemingly arbitrary Mason-Dixon Line.

Traversing north along the Atlantic shore from our southern colonies and crossing the Mason-Dixon Line, we enter the second zone of mixed mosquito-borne infection, the middle colonies. This region stretched from Delaware and Pennsylvania to New Jersey and New York. Here, *vivax* was generally entrenched, and, from time to time, some of America's worst epidemics of *falciparum* and yellow fever would materialize. These epidemics cut a swath through the unseasoned populations. In then US capital Philadelphia in 1793, as we will see, yellow fever killed

* Although Maryland was a slave state, it opted not to join the Confederacy. In fact, five slave states refused to secede, and generally fought on the side of the Union during the Civil War: Missouri, Kentucky, West Virginia, Delaware, and Maryland.

over 5,000 people in three months. An additional 20,000 fled the city in terror, including President George Washington. The government ceased to function. Whispers of moving the nation's capital to a safer location quietly entered political dialogue and casual conversation.

The third and final zone of infection is the northern colonies, including the Canadian portion of New France which, as a result of the Seven Years' War, became the British colony of Canada in 1763. This region was too cold for yellow fever or endemic malaria of any form. With suitable summer climates, however, merchant and naval vessels, as well as soldiers and transients, introduced sporadic outbreaks of mosquito-borne disease. The American colonies, stretching from Connecticut to Maine, witnessed periodic outbreaks of *vivax* and yellow fever. Mosquito-borne disease popped up in Toronto and the Great Lakes region of southern Ontario, in Quebec, as evidenced by a nasty yellow fever outbreak in 1711, and was a relatively common visitor to the bustling Atlantic port of Halifax, Nova Scotia.

While researching this book, I was surprised to learn that malaria went on a rampage in Canada's northerly capital of Ottawa during the construction of the 125-mile Rideau Canal between 1826 and 1832. Each year, from July through September, known to the builders as "the sickly season," roughly 60% of the workforce contracted malaria. Following the malaria season of 1831, chief contractor and engineer John Redpath wrote that "the exceeding unhealthiness of the place from which cause all engaged in it suffered much from lake fever and fever & ague, and it has also retarded the work for about three months each year." Redpath himself "caught the disease both the first and second year missed the third but this year had a severe attack of Lake Fever—which kept me to bed for two months and nearly two months more before I was fit for active service." Not to worry. Redpath survived his malarial fits to create Canada's largest sugar company in 1854. Still in existence today, the headquarters of Redpath Sugar is a landmark of Toronto's harbor front and bustling port.

During the construction of the Rideau Canal, approximately 1,000 workers died of disease, including 500 to 600 from malaria. The canal malaria also spread to local communities, where it is believed to have killed 250 civilians. At the Old Presbyterian Cemetery in Newboro, a commemorative marker honors their sacrifice: "Buried in this cemetery are the bodies of sappers and miners who took part in the construction of the Rideau Canal at this isthmus during the years 1826–1832. These men laboured under appalling conditions and succumbed to malaria. Their graves remain unmarked to this day." Prior to the work of Dr. Walter Reed in Cuba and Dr. William Gorgas in Panama at the close of the nineteenth century, canal building was a perilous enterprise. Large groups of close-quartered workers clearing land, digging trenches, and adding water is nothing short of a cordial invitation to mosquito-borne disease, even in the northern climes of Canada.

It is thought that seasonal malaria was introduced to Canada in the wake of the American Revolution when over 60,000 Empire Loyalists flooded across the border into British Canada. Historically, as we have seen and will continue to see, human migration, quick-stepping foreign armies, travel, and trade are prime conduits for the spread of contagion. In the 1790s, as the worst pandemics of yellow fever and malaria ripped through the American Atlantic states, another 30,000 "Late Loyalists" and refugees sought asylum from disease in Canada, inadvertently expanding the range of malaria into Ontario, Quebec, and the Atlantic maritime provinces.

In 1793, for example, the wife of John Graves Simcoe, the governor of Upper Canada and a prominent British officer during the revolution, contracted malaria in the provincial capital of Kingston. Located on the shores of Lake Ontario, the city also operated as the southern terminus for the Rideau Canal with its point of origin in Ottawa. Simcoe briefly led British troops during the Haitian Revolution ignited by Toussaint Louverture in 1791, which was eventually decided by the mosquito. In the recent television drama series *Turn: Washington's Spies*, Simcoe is cast as the primary antagonist, much to my irritation with historical inaccuracy. Despite historical evidence to the contrary, Simcoe is portrayed as the sadistic and psychopathic commander of a murderous group of irregular British Rangers.*

The authentic and actual Simcoe, however, stood at the crossroads of

* Simcoe was the first governor of Upper Canada, from 1791 to 1796. He founded the city of York (Toronto), instituted standing courts and common law, trial by jury, freehold land ownership, opposed racial discrimination, and abolished slavery. He is celebrated and revered by many Canadians as a founding father and his name adorns streets, cities, parks, buildings, lakes, and schools across the country. The irregular British Ranger regiment he commanded during the American Revolution is still operational as the Queen's York Rangers, an armored reconnaissance regiment of the Canadian Armed Forces.

colonialism. He was caught up in the winds of mosquito-swept historic change and the drift from European clamor and contest for colonies in the Americas to mosquito-sponsored independence movements forged in the crucible of the yellow fever and malarial fires of these same colonies. The unwavering prize worth fighting for was the wealth amassed through mercantilism and the plantation crops of sugar, tobacco, and coffee, among others, courtesy of the Columbian Exchange.

During the first two centuries of colonization, Spain, France, and England/Britain (and the Netherlands, Denmark, and Portugal to a lesser extent) initially squabbled and scrapped among themselves. Rich in natural resources, the Americas lured imperialist European nations to her shores. Colonists and slaves were dispatched to the wilds of the Western Hemisphere to secure territory and create economic empire. As part of this global transfer, early settlers were sacrificed to mosquito-borne disease until they, and their country-born descendants, became seasoned to their local environments and sicknesses.

This seasoning would initially help shield the established Spanish Empire from its two burgeoning predatory overseas rivals, France and Britain, as they tried in vain to seize mosquito-defended Spanish bastions during two centuries of economic competition and colonial warfare. Throughout the seventeenth and eighteenth centuries, yellow fever, dengue, and malaria attacked newcomers to these regions, which helped shelter the senior Spanish Empire from its plundering and covetous European challengers. During the colonial wars of the late eighteenth and early nineteenth centuries, however, these same diseases helped revolutions against European rule succeed.

A new breed of seasoned, country-born populations eventually jumped ship from their mother countries, yearning to sail into uncharted independent waters. After the colonists had bestowed enough blood sacrifice on the mosquito and paid their dues in death, she proffered the seasoned, independent-minded populations protection from the European armies of their colonial masters. Resident militias, even those of European descent, had been seasoned to local diseases. The armies of the various imperial powers sent directly from Europe to quell these rebellions were more prone to mosquito-borne disease. With the aid of ravenous mosquitoes, revolutionaries shrugged off the yoke of European subordination. The countries of South and Central America, the Caribbean, Canada, and the United States all owe a debt of gratitude to the mosquito for facilitating their ascent to self-governing nationhood. For the original English forebears and their offspring, they eventually completed the malarial crossing from Fenlands to freedom.

The heroes of the wars of liberation in the Americas, such as Simon Bolivar and Antonio Lopez de Santa Anna, and the legendary enemies that are forever paired in history, such as James Wolfe and Louis-Joseph de Montcalm, Chief Pontiac and Jeffery Amherst, George Washington and Charles Cornwallis, and Napoleon and Toussaint Louverture, were all born into Simcoe's world of flux. Their destinies, played out on the chessboard battlefields of the Americas, would all be decided by mercenary mosquitoes.

CHAPTER 11

The Crucible of Disease: Colonial Wars and a New World Order

"They are devils," General Jeffery Amherst muttered under his breath. "They must be punished, not bribed. . . . Punish the delinquents with Entire Destruction." Although the British had just won the Seven Years' War and expelled the French from North America, the commander of British forces was in no mood to celebrate. He had a rebellion on his hands and was desperately short of troops and funding. Amherst was furious. Odawa chief Pontiac, and the 3,500 warriors of his pan-Indian coalition of over a dozen nations, was ruining his reputation. Anticipating a deluge of British settlers into these recently vacated French lands, Pontiac leaped on the opportunity to create a unified indigenous homeland. "Englishmen, although you have conquered the French, you have not yet conquered us!" Pontiac declared. "As for these English—these dogs dressed in red," he exhorted his people, "you must lift the hatchet against them. Wipe them from the face of the earth." By June 1763, only a month into the rebellion, Amherst was desperate. Pontiac's warriors had already overrun eight British forts in the Ohio River Valley and Great Lakes region. Fort Pitt in the western wilds of Pennsylvania was under siege. Reports from inside were grim: "We are so crowded in the fort that I fear disease. . . . The Smallpox is among us." Starved of men and resources, Amherst deployed an innovative weapon to turn the tide of Pontiac's Rebellion in his favor.

Amherst questioned Colonel Henry Bouquet, commander of a relief expedition to Fort Pitt, "Could it not be contrived to send the small pox among the disaffected tribes of Indians? We must on this occasion Use

Every Stratagem in our Power to Reduce them." Bouquet responded, "I will try to inocculate [*sic*] [infect] them with some blankets that may fall in their hands and take care not to get the disease myself." Amherst officially endorsed the scheme. "You will Do well to try to Innoculate [*sic*] the Indians by means of Blankets," he replied, "as well as to try Every other method that can serve to Extirpate this Execrable Race." Both men were obviously unaware that five days earlier, Simeon Ecuyer and William Trent, militia officers holed up in Fort Pitt, had already utilized just such a weapon. "Out of our regard to them," they recorded identically in their diaries, "we gave them two blankets and a handkerchief out of the Small pox Hospital. I hope it will have the desired effect." Although it is generally believed that nothing came of these biological smallpox-blanket weapons, their use reveals the grave deficiency of men, materials, and money at Amherst's disposal on the heels of the Seven Years' War.

In 1756, while war clouds were gathering over the Americas, British secretary of state Philip Stanhope warned the king, "In my opinion, our greatest danger arises from our *expense*, considering the present immense National Debt." As Stanhope anticipated, when the chaotic dust of war settled in 1763, Britain was economically crippled, militarily bankrupt, and could not afford protracted Indian campaigns on its newly defined North American borders. Spiraling debt and Pontiac's initial success forced the British hand.

While the passing of the 1763 Royal Proclamation placated Pontiac, creating an Indian Territory by barring colonial expansion west of the Appalachian Mountains, it also sowed the seeds of discontent among American colonists and ignited the slow-burning fuse of rebellion. Britain's bankruptcy and military woes, and these revolutionary historical events, were created by nearly a century of mosquito-ravaged colonial conflicts in the Americas, crowned by the Seven Years' War.

These military campaigns in the Americas prior to the Seven Years' War were sparked by a series of imported European confrontations and mercantilist rivalries. For a century, France and Spain teamed up to turn back rising British power. Minor possessions in the Caribbean changed hands and British designs on Quebec were thwarted. A British force of

4,500 sent to take both Martinique and Canada in 1693, for example, was broken by yellow fever. After 3,200 deaths, the skeletal force docked at Boston in June at the onset of mosquito season. An observer recorded that "there was an English fleet of our good friends with a direful plague aboard 'em." Resultant yellow fever epidemics, the first to definitively visit the American colonies, killed 10% of the populations of Boston, Charleston, and Philadelphia.

During these forays, American colonial troops received their trial by fire and mosquitoes in the Caribbean. These deployments of colonial troops outside of North America shaped future opinion about raising American colonial forces for use in the Caribbean. The most notable was the British campaign in April 1741 to capture Cartagena, Colombia. A hub of Spanish trade, this port city was the release point for the full menu of the Columbian Exchange, including precious metals and gems, tobacco, sugar, cocoa, exotic timbers, coffee, and quinine, collected from across Spain's southern empire. A prior attempt to capture Cartagena in 1727 was aborted without firing a shot after 4,000 of the 4,750 men, a staggering 84% of the British invasion party, died of yellow fever while cruising off the mosquito-laced coast. The expedition of 1741, however, dwarfed that of its predecessor. A total of 29,000 men were readied to invade Cartagena under Admiral Edward "Old Grog" Vernon, including 3,500 American colonists described as "all the Banditry the colonies afforded."* For the mosquito, this massive unseasoned force was fodder for yellow fever.

Within three days of the soldiers' landing, the mosquito had slaughtered almost 3,500 British troops. The operation was a lost cause as "the sickness amongst the Troops increased to so great a Degree, that any longer Continuance in that unhealthy Situation, seemed to threaten no less than their total ruin . . . the whole Fleet set sail for Jamaica." Vernon decided to cut and run after only a month: "Thus ended the fatiguing part of the Campaign & it certainly was the most disagreeable one that has been known . . . universal Sickness & Death. . . . Everybody was

* The slang term for alcoholic spirits, "grog," is attributed to Vernon. Originally, it was rum diluted with water and citrus juice to help prevent scurvy. Vernon soon acquired the loving nickname "Old Grog."

taken alike; they call this distemper a bilious fever, it kills in 5 days; if the patient lives longer it's only to die of greater agonies of what they then call Black Vomit." The mosquito killed 22,000 of Vernon's total force of 29,000, an astounding 76%. The majority of the seasoned Spanish defenders, who had been stationed at Cartagena for five years, survived the onslaught.

One of Vernon's colonial survivors was Lawrence Washington, the older and admired half brother of George. Upon his return to Virginia, Lawrence carved out a plantation on a piece of the family's extensive property holdings. In honor of his commander, he named it Mount Vernon. Upon Lawrence's death in 1752, twenty-year-old George inherited the sprawling estate. During the Cartagena campaign, Lawrence's colonial cohort fared no better than their British comrades. The disaster was widely covered in colonial newspapers and left bitter scars across the collective consciousness of the American colonies. When the British tried to raise troops for another Caribbean adventure during the Seven Years' War, this time to take Havana, colonial volunteers were not as forthcoming. The mental images of Cartagena hung harshly in the hallways of colonial legislatures.

Given these isolated, intermittent, but comparatively diminutive imperial campaigns in the Caribbean, including the British succubus mosquito nightmare at Cartagena, it was inevitable that European empires and mercantilist economies would collide in a global conflict. Fought in Europe, across the Americas, India, the Philippines, and West Africa, the Seven Years' War was this first world war. Although mosquito-borne diseases ripped through British, French, and Spanish troops battling for colonial possessions in India, the Philippines, and West Africa, they did not tip the battlefields to aid the British victories. All European soldiers were relative newcomers to these foreign theaters of war, sent directly from their temperate homelands. Without local seasoning, the soldiers of these competing imperial powers were visited fairly equally by mosquito-borne disease. The mosquito's military and historical manipulation was generally confined to the multiple campaigns, and the corresponding manpower determinations and troop deployments, in North America and the contested Caribbean colonies.

In the Americas, the team player benches had been selected during the preceding wars. Team Britain included the American colonies and the aggressive Iroquois Confederacy. The rival underdog, Team France, was joined by relatively small numbers of uninterested Canadiens and a handful of Algonquian allies. Eventually, in 1761, Spain decided to get into the game on the side of France. The British bench, however, had more depth. Manpower and available substitutions favored Team Britain.

While the professional European armies were relatively even, the number of American colonists dwarfed that of French colonists by a ratio of 23 to 1. The British also fielded stronger indigenous allies. During the Beaver Wars of the late seventeenth century, the Iroquois Confederacy went on a sequence-repeating military campaign to reap trapping grounds and secure fur to trade for British guns for exacting revenge on traditional enemies. These conquests gained more trapping lands to secure more fur to acquire more guns to extend these reprisals. Up to this point, within this long-standing traditional warfare, the Algonquian and Huron nations, having gained access to French firearms almost a century earlier, had been getting the better of the Iroquois. Now, having acquired British weapons for furs, the Iroquois launched retaliatory campaigns across eastern North America before turning their wrath across the wide swath of the Great Lakes. The Beaver Wars marked the last of the Mahican, Erie, Neutral, Tobacco, and Huron nations or confederacies. Others, like the Shawnee, Kickapoo, and Odawa, simply fled the fierce Iroquois onslaught. Although promoting their own punitive agenda, not only did the Iroquois inadvertently clear out land for future British/American settlement, they wiped out most of France's indigenous allies, some to the point of extinction.

The Seven Years' War was truly a global conflict. Strategy, manpower considerations, and territorial priorities were intertwined, and troop allocations were prioritized and packaged accordingly. For France, the war in Europe and the defense of her lucrative Caribbean plantation colonies far outweighed the security of Quebec's commercial contributions of fish, timber, and fur. France's concerns for her Caribbean sugar and tobacco colonies, however, were costly. Within the first six months, yellow fever and malaria killed half of newly arrived unseasoned French defenders. Mosquito-borne disease ravaged French garrisons in Haiti, Guadeloupe, Martinique, and other smaller islands. French troops were siphoned and reinforcements were redirected from Quebec to these besieged outposts. As a result, Caribbean mosquitoes starved Canada of men and munitions and all payments on Canadian invoices were shelved. These indispensable necessities of war—soldiers, weapons, and money—were diverted to Europe and the Caribbean. The ability of French commander Marquis de Montcalm to coordinate any meaningful defense of Canada was stymied by Caribbean mosquitoes.

At the same time, a smallpox epidemic ripped through Quebec, killing Frenchmen, Canadiens, and their residual indigenous allies with reckless abandon. By 1757, 3,000 were hospitalized at any given time, with 25 dying daily. Within a year, 1,700 French soldiers had perished. This epidemic drained precious manpower from an already undersize French coalition force in Canada. With this smallpox outbreak in Quebec, and with mosquito-borne disease in the Caribbean consuming all available French reinforcements, Canada was left vulnerable.

Conversely, wanting to secure the northern flank for their precious and profitable Thirteen Colonies, the British afforded a greater number of soldiers and resources to the Canadian theater of war. British and colonial commanders and soldiers petitioned to be sent to North America for fear of mosquito-borne illness in the Caribbean. Stories of ordinary soldiers and sailors taking 1,000 lashes from a cat-o'-nine-tails rather than accept a Caribbean cruise were common. Others mutinied, officers bought their way out or resigned their commission, and naval convoys got "lost" in transit. Casualty rates inflicted by mosquito-borne disease could not be ignored, and the British high command refrained from sending elite units to the tropics. Instead, Caribbean assignments were detailed as a punishment.

American colonial assemblies dithered when summoned to raise regiments for expeditionary forces. Voluntary enlistments all but dried up when recruiters pitched Caribbean campaigns. Until the final conquest of Canada in 1760, most colonial troops, including militia colonel George Washington, were employed in North America strengthening the British position in this theater. "Raising troops in America for service elsewhere was uncommon," points out Erica Charters in her detailed work on disease during the Seven Years' War. "The last expedition in which this had occurred was the disastrous expedition to Cartagena in 1741. . . . The experience at Cartagena encouraged the development of a 'self-conscious Americanism.'" Given the death rates from mosquito-borne disease during this botched mission, British officer William Blakeney ominously warned that the American colonists "seem to set a great value on themselves, and think a regard is due to them, especially in the assistance they are able to give to the mother country on such occasions; and, as they are a growing Power, should they be disappointed in what is promised them and which they expect, future Occasions of the like Nature may suffer for it." Blakeney astutely recognized the gradual shift in American self-confidence and that revolution flickered on the horizon.

In the Americas, Britain launched two geographically distinct but strategically welded campaigns against French holdings—Canada and the Caribbean. By 1758, the British under General Amherst had captured French maritime holdings along the Atlantic coast, called Acadia. Roughly 12,000 Acadians were rounded up and deported. We will pick up the shockingly grizzly story of the expelled Acadians and their mosquito death sentence on Devil's Island off Guyana at the end of the war. In January 1759, the British launched an unsuccessful invasion of the French Caribbean island fortress of Martinique. This task force was redirected to Guadeloupe, which was captured in May 1759. The mosquito, however, made them pay for their hard-earned victory, killing 46% of the 6,800-man British force. Of the tiny garrison of 1,000 men left behind, 800 died of yellow fever and malaria by the end of 1759. The British threat to the lucrative French sugar islands set off alarm bells. At this point, France's war against Britain was being buoyed by enormous loans from neutral Spain. The loss of these moneymaking plantation colonies would doom the French war effort, not only in the Americas, but also in the main European theater. At the expense of Canadian defense, unseasoned French reinforcements were continuously shoveled into and burned in the mosquito-stoked furnace of the tropics, leaving Canada exposed.

The fragile dominion of the French over Canada came undone in September 1759. Major General James Wolfe, the young, talented, and arrogant British commander, was determined to take Quebec by any means necessary. "If, by accident in the river, by the enemy's resistance, by sickness, or slaughter in the army, or, from any other cause, we find that Quebec is not likely to fall into our hands (persevering however to the last moment)," a feverishly ill Wolfe submitted to his superior, General Jeffery Amherst, "I propose to set the town on fire with shells, to destroy the harvest, houses and cattle, both above and below, to send off as many Canadians as possible to Europe and to leave famine and desolation behind me; belle résolution & très chrétienne! but we must teach these scoundrels to make war in a more gentleman like manner." Such militant and uncompromising tactics were not necessary. Wolfe's swift victory over the Marquis de Montcalm's beleaguered and outnumbered French forces on the Plains of Abraham at Quebec City paved the way for an influx of British settlers and the creation of modern Canada. Although Wolfe was killed (as was Montcalm) on those nation-defining plains, Amherst took up the gauntlet, forcing the surrender of Montreal the following year. With backing from Caribbean mosquitoes, Canada was now officially British.

Following the conquest of Canada, British resources were funneled to the Caribbean. Spain officially entered the war in 1761 to protect prized colonial property and to back her militarily and economically exhausted French ally. Britain now had additional targets, chiefly Havana, the linchpin of Spanish enterprise in the Americas. A second attempt at French Martinique, however, came first. Following its capitulation in February 1762, the British went on to take the French islands of St. Lucia, Grenada, and St. Vincent. British planners reckoned these smaller colonies could serve as diplomatic leverage and brokering chips during the anticipated peace negotiations. These strategists now set their sights directly on Havana, "the key to the Indies."

The massive British force assembled at Barbados counted roughly 11,000 soldiers. Amherst also expected an additional 4,000 "Provincials" from the colonies. While he had been urged to specifically recruit from the American colonies on the recommendation that "they would be very acceptable and necessary, to shorten and ease our Work, as the season of the Year is not favorable to the health of Europeans," these numbers failed to materialize. The mosquito-borne disease awaiting colonial conscripts in the Caribbean was a bone-chilling visual, a distressing probability or at least expectation, which intimidated volunteers. The governor of New Hampshire reported he would not be able to meet his quota unless, he wrote, "I could assure the men that they were to serve in regiments at Halifax, Quebec, or Montreal, but the people in general entertain terrible thoughts of serving in the West Indies." Representatives from New York also stressed that volunteers demanded "to be Employed on the Continent of North America only, & that they shall be Returned to the Province, as soon as Service is over." Eventually, after threats from General Amherst, 1,900 unseasoned colonial provincials, mainly from the northern colonies, and 1,800 British regulars sailed for Cuba.

The British armada reached Havana in June 1762 and laid siege to the city of 55,000 people. The roughly 11,000 guardians were aware that a successful defense hinged on mosquito-borne disease, as "fevers and agues [were] enough to destroy a European army division." Cuba had a long, brutal history with its mosquitoes. Outside of Africa, the island's ecosystem was one of the finest for the proliferation of Aedes and Anopheles mosquitoes. Malaria had been rife since the arrival of Columbus. After its first appearance in 1648, yellow fever was also an annual event, although certainly some years were worse than others. Distinctly worse than the typical yearly staining of yellow fever were twelve savage epidemics that had hunted the island, with the worst outbreaks killing upwards of 35% of the total population.

During early British operations in June and July 1762, however, Havana's mercenary mosquito defenders were absent without leave. They simply did not show up. The rainy season that usually began in early May and peaked in June had been deferred by an El Niño effect. This delay meant that mosquitoes took a rain check for breeding, so the usual epidemic season was postponed. For the British, this abnormally dry spring allowed relatively healthy forces to secure a beachhead and capture Havana's suburbs. Nevertheless, a British victory would still require a race with death. At the end of July, "the arrival of the American reinforcements," wrote a participant of the siege, "has with very great reason cheered our drooping spirits." The arrival of colonial reinforcements awoke the hungry mosquito from her hibernation. She immediately went on a feeding frenzy.

Havana's governor, however, had already evacuated the city, and without the usual defensive perimeter manned by mosquito-borne disease, he knew the game was up. "Timing—even of rains, mosquitoes, and viruses—is everything. . . . Had he known that the late rainy season, finally underway in August, ensured an abundant and active mosquito population and a yellow fever epidemic, he might have held out longer than he did," asserts J. R. McNeill in his brilliantly thorough depiction of the events. "But he did not know . . . he chose to seek terms and on August 14th, 1762, he surrendered the city." Two days after the capitulation of Havana, only 39% of British soldiers were fit for duty. "Our sickness instead of diminishing increases daily," reported a senior officer at the beginning of October. "We have buried upwards of 3,000 men since the capitulation, and I am sorry to say there are many Men in Hospitals." Still not satiated, by mid-October, the mosquito had achieved a body count bordering on the absurd. From a total force of 15,000, only 880 men, a measly 6%, were alive or healthy enough to stand to post. In total, she consumed two-thirds of the entire force, killing 10,000 men in less than three months. Combat claimed fewer than 700 British/colonial lives. Although doctors did their best to fight this contagion, medical knowledge was not really knowledge at all; it was more guesswork and superstition.

The altogether strange, and at times barbaric, medical treatments reflect the complete ignorance of the causes for mosquito-borne diseases, or most diseases for that matter. Knowing what so-called remedies awaited them, most sufferers steered clear of the crude hospitals and their attending physicians. When ordered to go to the hospital by his superior, one soldier who was drenched in Havana's yellow fever replied, "Indeed I am not bad, and if I was, I would rather stab myself at once, than go where so many are dying." His knife remained sheathed, for he was dead before the day was out. Common treatments included ingesting animal fats, snake venom, mercury, or pulverized insects. The ancient Egyptian practice of bathing in fresh human urine was still practiced. Drinking one's own urine was now also widespread. Bleeding, blistering, leeches, and cupping glasses were also staples in the medicine chest. Although no more effective than the popular remedy of using poultices and dressings of freshly killed pigeons or chipmunk brains, copious amounts of alcohol, coffee, opium, and cannabis at least offered some numbness and pain relief from the ghastly symptoms. Quinine was also used, but it was expensive. As a result, it was consistently understocked, administered at low, ineffective doses, or reserved for officers. It was often cut with other substances, much like cocaine and other street drugs are today, downgrading its active ingredient and effectiveness.

If the disease didn't kill them, often the cure would. Thomas Jefferson jested, "The patient, treated on the fashionable theory, sometimes gets well in spite of the medicine." Most sufferers just took their chances with the sickness rather than seek treatment. Given the medical inaccuracy and the miasmic miscalculations of the causes of mosquito-borne disease, European campaigns in the Americas during the Seven Years' War were swallowed by sickness. Areas with high rates of malaria, yellow fever, and dengue, including the Caribbean and the southern United States, remained mosquito-infested sinkholes of humanity.

Although the British now controlled Cuba, manpower and resources were so taxed that any further designs on the Spanish domain or the envisaged campaign against French Louisiana were abandoned. Benjamin Franklin remarked that the victory at Havana was "the dearest conquest by far that we have purchas'd this war when we consider the terrible Havock made by the sickness in that brave Army of Veterans, now almost totally ruined." English poet, writer, and lexicologist Samuel Johnson mourned, "May my country never be cursed with another such conquest!" From a military and monetary standpoint, Britain, like her enemies, was drained. British politician Isaac Barré voiced the opinion that the "war dragg'd thro' the Streets more like a funeral than a triumph. We are drain'd of money & our resources are mostly stopp'd." Unseasoned soldiers and replacements continued their rotations through the Caribbean colonies of all nations. They continued to die of mosquito-borne disease at rates exceeding 50% or even 60%. The mosquito had seized the initiative from the warring nations of Europe. Although the British were victorious on paper, they were just as depleted as their rivals by war's end and could not press their advantage. Posturing and bravado were hollow threats when backed by mosquito-bitten soldiers and empty bank accounts. The only way out of this mess was negotiation and compromise.

In the end, the mind-boggling suffering and the mountain of lives lost at Havana, Martinique, Guadeloupe, and other islands were all in vain. I suppose the only real winners were the gluttonous Caribbean mosquitoes, who pulled up their own chairs to the catchall "Taste of Europe" dinner-party buffet and extravaganza. In February 1763, the Treaty of Paris was signed, sorting out the spoils of war. Europe maintained its prewar boundaries. Throughout empires, the antebellum status quo ruled the day and little prewar territory changed hands.

The real deliberation among British negotiators was what to do with France. It was quickly realized that Britain did not hold the leverage cards to keep both Canada and the conquered French Caribbean islands. They were gambling with a weak hand, and they knew it. France knew it as well. In the end, the British cut deals in the Caribbean to retain Canada. Protecting the northern flank of the American colonies took priority over Caribbean and overseas possessions. The islands of Martinique and Guadeloupe, on which the British had fed the mosquito so many lives, as well as tiny St. Lucia, were returned to France. Britain acquired three small islands of the Lesser Antilles in the southern Caribbean and Spanish Florida. Havana was given back to Spain. Spain also acquired the Louisiana Territory from France, although it would be secretly returned to Napoleon's France shortly before its purchase by the United States in 1803. France forfeited to Britain all colonial rights in India in exchange for custody of two minuscule islands sixteen miles south of Newfoundland, to retain fishing rights to the Grand Banks. St. Pierre and Miquelon, 95 square miles combined, were the last vestiges of French territory in North America. Currently, these islands, which by all territorial and economic logic should be Canadian, officially remain a self-governing overseas possession of France.

Canada, however, became a British colony in name only. Following the Seven Years' War, the diminutive and colonially distinct Canadien population, who had not taken up arms with any prodigious patriotic zeal and felt no unwavering affinity for France anyway, retained the rights to their seigneurial land system, civil law, language, Catholic faith, and culture. Aside from swearing allegiance to the British Crown, for the Canadiens, or "Quebecois," life remained relatively unaffected and the status quo prevailed. Canada's small population remained predominantly French until the mass influx of British Loyalists that would occur after the American Revolution.

The French maritime Acadians, however, faced an entirely different and markedly divergent strategic situation. They had fought in larger numbers, refused the oath of fidelity to their new overlords, and in the immediate peace were viewed by the British as likely insurgents. Deemed a disloyal threat, the undesirable Acadians were forcibly removed during the "Great Expulsion," leading to one of the most altogether strange and scandalous side stories of colonialism, courtesy of the mosquitoes basking in the infernos of Guyana.

After bouncing around the Americas from Charleston to the inhospitable Falkland Islands in the South Atlantic, a sizable contingent of refugee Acadians were permitted by Spain to settle in Louisiana, where they remain today. With time and isolation, these Acadians evolved and fostered the modern-day Cajun culture. The word itself morphed from "Acadian" into "Cajun." A smaller group of Acadians, however, was sent to colonize a new French settlement in Guyana on the northern coast of South America in 1763. This colony is commonly known as Devil's Island.

France was disheartened with the territorial results of the Seven Years' War. Of tangible flags on the global map, Britain gained, Spain remained, and France was drained. It was recognized after the war that France's inferior position in the Americas was the result of so few, if any, loyal colonial populations. British American colonists fought in relatively large numbers, as did Spain's Caribbean defenders. With the loss of Canada, France's remaining Caribbean populations consisted largely of slaves that were rightly presumed to be politically unreliable at best, and at worst spitefully rebellious. These colonies, largely devoid of

French nationals, were also easy prey for the British in the next hand of colonial warfare just as they had been during the Seven Years' War. They needed to be protected by a local source of robustly seasoned French settlers. Guyana was projected to be this bastion, a tropical reincarnation of Quebec or, even better, a rebirth of Canada's Acadia itself.

Although France established a small outpost in Guyana in 1664, the colony had, it was reported, "made little progress since its inception and, consisting of an inert group of derelict colonists, has generally been a curse to the King." At the end of the Seven Years' War, the population consisted of 575 French and roughly 7,000 free and enslaved Africans, all living at the settlement of Cayenne. The wallowing colony was a mosquito utopia consisting of brackish tidal marshes and manatee-hosting mangroves. A preliminary French survey in 1763 candidly testified that for the current inhabitants, "their primary business is to find pleasures, and if they have any disquietude it is for the lack of them." In its current state, Guyana was deemed an orphaned backwater colony. Comically, the only colonists outside of Cayenne—a handful of Jesuit priests and a few indigenous and African converts—were cloistered thirty-five miles away in a church mission at Kourou.

With promises of land, bountiful harvests of sugar and tobacco procured by slaves, and the riches of El Dorado, 12,500 settlers set out for Kourou. These dreamers mostly came from the war-torn regions of France and Belgium, with smaller numbers of Acadians, Canadiens, and Irish. Half were under the age of twenty, and single male and female settlers were shrewdly urged to marry local indigenous peoples to get the population up and running as quickly as possible. On Christmas Day 1763, the first settlers disembarked with their utopian visions of paradise. They were to be the vanguard of a mighty, seasoned French colonial population that could tackle the British and avenge the French humiliation of the Seven Years' War.

Boatloads of settlers poured into Kourou along with the first shipment of supplies. While this delivery did not include a printing press, its contents were just as bizarre as those at Darien. Given that Canada was now in British hands, French authorities saw an opportunity to unload crates of ice skates, woolen toque hats, and other essential, everyday

Canadian-closet winter items on the unsuspecting tropical settlers at Kourou. Classic colonial bumbling. To accommodate the influx of new arrivals, and their ice hockey gear, they were settled on an offshore island already bearing the name Devil's Island. Kourou quickly descended into a hellish paradise lost. In June 1764, the island lived up to its name and to the evil gods of the ancients, as the mosquito conjured up one of history's deadliest three-headed Cerberus epidemics—yellow fever, dengue, and malaria—killing 11,000 settlers (90%) within a year.

Despite this nightmare, the colony remained a French "curse to the King," as no one else wanted it or would dare take it. Lingering on as an orphan of imperialism, it was put to good use as a fleeting penal colony during the French Revolution, caging political dissenters and other radical troublemakers. A full-scale, multisite penal colony opened in 1852. Devil's Island was converted into a brutal French version of Alcatraz. Convict mortality rates from barbaric treatment, starvation, and insidious mosquito-borne disease reached upwards of 75%. Devil's Island did not close its doors until 1953.* Kourou, and much of the former penal colony, is now home to the European Space Agency's spaceport and launch site. This original French, Darien-like disaster in the aftermath of the Seven Years' War, however, further crippled an already bankrupt French economy. The silver lining, perhaps, was that Britain's economy was even more unhealthy.

The Seven Years' War and the mosquito had consumed the British fighting spirit and the treasury. At the onset of Pontiac's Rebellion in the shadows of European peace, General Jeffery Amherst summed up his military position: "A vast diminution for a regiment . . . since the regiment came from the Havana, and some of the officers as well as the men have yet frequent relapses of their disorder." Havana's guerrilla mosquitoes

* One of the most famous prisoners was Alfred Dreyfus, who during the infamous Dreyfus Affair was convicted of treason in 1895 for passing military secrets to the Germans. Another was Henri Charrière, who served time at Devil's Island for murder in the 1930s. His book, *Papillon*, detailing his experiences and the horrific, inhumane treatment at the penal colony was published in 1969. It was turned into a blockbuster movie of the same name in 1973, starring Steve McQueen and Dustin Hoffman. A 2017 Hollywood remake of the same name stars Charlie Hunnam and Rami Malek. Historical analysis of Charrière's "memoir" debunked almost all of what he wrote. His work is now deemed to be mostly fictional or, at best, highly embellished and based on the experiences and accounts of others, much like *The Travels of Marco Polo*.

influenced events far beyond their own tropical dining halls. They helped chart a world-altering collision course between Britain and her colonies, headed straight for revolution. "As Amherst well knew," acknowledges Fred Anderson in his 900-page tour-de-force account of the conflict, *Crucible of War*, "the measures he could take—appealing to the provinces for militiamen or drafting invalids from the Havana Regiments to replace soldiers in garrisons, freeing what healthy men he could find to aid in the relief of Fort Pitt or Detroit—were only stopgaps, and at most they could buy time." The British could not afford time.

Caribbean mosquitoes had helped suck the British dry of both money and manpower, and what Anderson refers to as "gruesome losses to disease at the end of the war." Of the 185,000 men deployed to the Caribbean during the Seven Years War, 134,000, or 72%, were, according to government records, "lost to disease and desertion." The war had also doubled the British debt from 70 million to 140 million pounds (today's equivalent of over $20 trillion). The interest alone consumed half the annual government tax revenue. The British response to the rebellion was as much a penny-pinching strategy as it was a reactionary solution to appease Pontiac and his warring parties after smallpox blankets failed in their macabre mission.

In October 1763, with Pontiac's coalition dominating the battlefield, the Royal Proclamation took effect, prohibiting colonial settlement west of the Appalachian Mountains. This middle ground, the lands west of the Proclamation Line, to the Mississippi River and Spanish-held Louisiana Territory, was legally and exclusively reserved for "the occupancy and use of the Indians." The entrenched hatred the colonists had for indigenous peoples would surely drag Britain into a parade of never-ending, futile, and expensive conflicts on the borderlands, wars that the British could ill afford. The Proclamation Line, which was as much a cost-saving measure as anything else, cleaved a divide between colonists and indigenes with the intention of restoring peace on the western frontier. Only Americans styled (and still do) the Seven Years' War by a distinguishing name, the French and Indian War, that reflects their hostility toward the perceived indigenous obstruction to their own heaven-ordained westward expansion, recloaked in the mid-nineteenth century as Manifest Destiny. Given this American colonial rancor, with the ratification of the financially pressured Royal Proclamation, Pontiac was appeased and the colonists were punished.

Many American colonists were outraged by this tyrannical betrayal. The country-born population was booming, with eyes trained west, and immigrants were still sailing for land, but the only avenues for expansion were now legally restricted. Colonial militiamen, or provincials, had fought alongside the British Redcoats in the Caribbean and North American campaigns of the Seven Years' War, with many lives frittered away or fed to the mosquito by British arrogance and hubris. The colonies aided in a British victory yet were denied these former French lands on their western frontier as a spoil of war. To add insult to injury, they were expected to pay for the patrolling and protection of the Proclamation Line. The annual cost of colonial security was roughly 220,000 pounds, and Britain expected the colonists to shoulder some of the financial burden for their own defense. They recouped these expenditures through a series of now famous taxes and tariffs from the Sugar Act of 1764 to the Intolerable Acts a decade later. In hard currency, however, the taxes themselves were not really an issue.

The American colonists paid the least amount of tax of anyone in the British Empire, ten times less than the average Englishman.* When combined, the supplementary tolls and tariffs imposed on the colonies in the decade prior to the revolution raised taxes by an average of only 2%. Taxation without democratic representation in British Parliament, however, was an issue. William Pitt, the influential leader of the House of Commons, was aware of the dangers of this mounting debt: "And when we consider that such immense issues of money, out measuring any experiment of past time, are to be supplied by new loans, heaped upon a debt of eighty millions, who will answer for the consequence, or insure us from the fate of the decayed states of antiquity?" The British themselves would have to answer for the consequence—the loss of their lucrative American colonies.

* Individual colony tax rates varied. Taxes in Massachusetts for example, were 5.4 times less than those levied in England, while those in Pennsylvania were an astounding 35.8 times less than the taxes assessed in the mother country.

For many colonists, the Seven Years' War and its immediate aftermath, including Pontiac and the Royal Proclamation, was a turning point, marking the beginning of a new era of America. Colonists, along with their political assemblies, began to reevaluate their position *within* the empire and their connection to the mother country. If anything, these contributions fostered increased expectations for a more equal and balanced relationship *with* Britain. The opposite turned out to be true. As Anderson so pertinently states, "American leaders—men like Washington and Franklin, who otherwise would have liked nothing better than to pursue honor, wealth, and power within the British imperial framework—were compelled to confront these issues of sovereignty in ways that imparted new, universalistic meaning to an inherited language of rights and liberties. . . . Americans who would have been imperialists in any case became Revolutionaries." Britain's increasing political and financial interference in the colonies without colonial consent dominated American discourse in the decade following the passage of the Royal Proclamation. American disenchantment about their status and citizenship eventually ignited open rebellion against the authoritarian British administration of their colonies. Although neither party wanted war, revolution came anyway.

Unexpectedly, in the words of Richard Middleton, "the umbilical cord of maternal union was threatening to become a noose." Successive and uninterrupted generations had been country-born and seasoned, not just in America but also in Cuba, Haiti, and a host of other colonies. For these populations, their lifeline no longer stretched to the mother country. Their umbilical cord was attached to their home and native land, whether that be Boston, Port-au-Prince, Philadelphia, or Havana. Many, perhaps without even realizing it, had become Americans, Cubans, and Haitians. When seasoned, this nationalism was a powerful instrument of revolution.

James Lind, physician in chief to the British Royal Navy, warned his superiors in his groundbreaking 1768 *Essay on Diseases Incidental to Europeans in Hot Climates*, "The recent examples of the great mortality in hot climates, ought to draw the attention of all the commercial nations of Europe. . . . Unhealthy settlements require a constant supply of people, and of course drain their mother country of an incredible number." To this he added an ominous revolutionary disclaimer: "Merchant, farmer, or soldier, thus constitutionally naturalized to the country, becomes more useful, and his services may be more depended upon there, than ten new arrived unseasoned Europeans."*

The evolution to revolution in the American colonies was born during and in the immediate aftermath of the Seven Years' War. "Overall, disease helped to both conquer and secure North America for the English," contends David Petriello. "At the same time though, the British victory was achieved at a dreadful cost, both in treasure and lives . . . animosity began to fill the void. Disease was both to win and lose a continent for England." During the Seven Years' War, Caribbean mosquitoes helped secure British hegemony in North America. Their northern cousins breeding in the backwaters of the Carolinas and Virginia, however, would soon assure victory for the rebellious Americans.

In the wake of the Seven Years' War, and its rearrangement of the colonial checkerboard, revolutions swept across the Americas, beginning in 1775 with George Washington and his ragtag crew of colonial civilian soldiers. J. R. McNeill's brushstroke summary of his 2010 masterpiece book, *Mosquito Empires: Ecology and War in the Greater Caribbean, 1620–1914*, paints the scene for what follows. Mosquitoes, he proves, "underpinned the geopolitical order in the Americas until the 1770s, after which they undermined it, ushering in a new era of independent states." McNeill strengthens this reasoning by emphasizing that "European domination came to an end between 1776 and 1825 when some of the populations of the Americas successfully rose up. . . . Revolutions in British North America, Haiti, and Spanish America each created new states, trimmed back European empires, and together ushered in a new era in Atlantic American geopolitics and world history. They all owed their success in part to yellow fever or malaria." Seasoned American, Haitian, and South American revolutionaries fought for independence with courage and bravery. It was feverish mosquitoes, however, that granted them their freedom.

* Lind was the first to conclusively demonstrate, using clinical trials, that citrus fruit prevented and cured scurvy. He was also the first to propose that potable water could be obtained by distilling seawater. His research drastically improved the overall health and quality of life for British sailors.

CHAPTER 12

Unalienable Bites: The American Revolution

A month after the opening salvos of the American Revolution at Lexington and Concord in April 1775, the newly appointed commander in chief of the Continental Army, George Washington, had a request for his political masters in the Continental Congress. He urged them to buy up as much cinchona bark and quinine powder as possible. Given the dire financial pressures of the squabbling colonial government, and the dearth of pretty much everything needed to fight a war, his total allotment was a paltry 300 pounds. General Washington was a frequent visitor to the quinine chest as he suffered from recurrent bouts (and reinfection) of malaria since first contracting the disease in 1749 at the age of seventeen.*

Luckily for the Americans, the British were also drastically short of Peruvian Spanish-supplied quinine throughout the war. In 1778, shortly before they entered the fray in support of the American cause, the Spanish cut off this supply completely. Any available stores were sent to British troops in India and the Caribbean. At the same time, the mosquito's merciless, unrelenting strikes on unseasoned British troops lacking quinine during the final British southern campaign—launched in 1780 with the capture of Charleston, the strategic port city and mosquito sanctuary—determined the fate of the United States of America.

* It is known that eight presidents suffered from malaria: Washington, Lincoln, Monroe, Jackson, Grant, Garfield, T. Roosevelt, and Kennedy.

As J. R. McNeill colorfully contours, "The argument here is straightforward: In the American Revolution the British southern campaigns ultimately led to defeat at Yorktown in October 1781 in part because their forces were much more susceptible to malaria than were the American. . . . [T]he balance tipped because Britain's grand strategy committed a larger proportion of the army to malarial (and yellow fever) zones." A full 70% of the British Army that marched into this southern mosquito maelstrom in 1780 was recruited from the poorer, famished regions of Scotland and the northern counties of England, *outside* the malaria belt of Pip's Fenland marshes. Those who had already served some time in the colonies had done so in the northern zone of infection and had not yet been seasoned to American malaria.

General Washington and the Continental Congress, on the other hand, had the advantage of commanding acclimated, malaria-seasoned colonial troops. American militiamen had been hardened to their surroundings during the Seven Years' War and the turbulent decades heading toward open hostilities against their king. Washington personally recognized, albeit short of scientific affirmation or medical endorsement, that with his recurrent malarial seasonings, "I have been protected beyond all human probability or expectation." While they did not know it at the time, this might well have been the Americans' only advantage over the British when, after twelve years of seething resentment and discontent since the passing of the Royal Proclamation, war suddenly and unexpectedly came. The opening clash at Lexington and Concord was not sanctioned by the newly confirmed Continental Congress. Colonial politicians did not want and were not prepared for war. The Congress, the colonists it represented, and the consequent Continental Army had next to nothing and they knew it. Introducing Washington's ill-equipped, rag-wrapped amateur militia as the underdog is an arrant understatement.

The Continental Congress was first convened in Philadelphia in the fall of 1774, prior to the outbreak of war, in response to the Boston Tea Party and the taxing Intolerable Acts. Fifty-six delegates from twelve of the thirteen colonies assembled to negotiate a unified stance of solidarity in relation to the mother country.* Essentially, it was the "All for one and one for all, united we stand, divided we fall" motto of the Three Musketeers, or Article 5, "an attack against one ally is an attack against all allies," of the North Atlantic Treaty Organization (NATO).† The central question surrounding this inaugural caucus was confrontation or compromise.

This issue was not new to 1774, for it had been discussed at length by the Sons of Liberty, a secret, loosely organized group of radicals led by Samuel Adams, John Hancock, Paul Revere, Benedict Arnold, and Patrick Henry. In the wake of the Stamp Act of 1765, these future insurgents met in the dank basement of Boston's Green Dragon Tavern and Coffee House, which gained the historical reputation as the "Headquarters of the Revolution." I like to envisage the Green Dragon as something akin to the Prancing Pony tavern from J. R. R. Tolkien's *The Lord of the Rings*, where scheming, shifty-eyed, cloaked and hooded colonists sip on bitter tea or coffee while sneeringly conspiring to plot revolution.

By the late seventeenth century, tea had become the preferred British and colonial beverage. Following the Townshend Acts of 1767, which imposed tariffs on numerous items, including tea, and the subsequent Tea Act sanctioned six years later, it became a patriotic American duty to shun the drink. In December 1773, shortly after the ratification of the Tea Act, a strategic yet spiteful band of the Sons of Liberty disguised only in blankets and lampblack (*not* in the mythical Mohawk Indian regalia commonly portrayed) heaved 342 chests containing 90,000 pounds of tea into Boston Harbor during their Tea Party. The Continental Congress legitimized this hostile act by passing a resolution "to oppose the vending of any tea sent . . . with our lives and fortunes" the

---

* Georgia, the last of the Thirteen Colonies to be established, did not send representatives for fear of alienating the British. Georgians needed the support of British soldiers who were trying to quell the fierce Cherokee and Creek resistance to colonial expansion.

† The origin of this concept dates back to Aesop's fables around 600 BCE. The Gospel of Mark also alludes to it: "And if a house be divided against itself, that house cannot stand." Lincoln paraphrased this passage in the 1858 Lincoln-Douglas debates. Cultures around the planet have similar creeds, from the Iroquois Confederacy to the Mongols to the "Little Red Hen" children's fable of Russian origin.

following year. "Tea must be universally renounced," barked the cantankerous John Adams to his brilliant wife, Abigail, "and I must be weaned, and the sooner the better." The American switch to coffee, argues Antony Wild, "now became a patriotic imperative." When Americans forswore tea, "they made up the loss with one of the principal products of the slave colonial system in the hemisphere—coffee."

Not only was it cheaper due to its plantation proximity, coffee was also highly touted as a cure for malaria, which at the time, as we have seen, was percolating throughout the colonies, specifically in the southern zone of infection. Peddled as a wonder drug against "agues and fevers" by legitimate doctors and snake-oil salesmen alike, coffee seeped into American colonial culture, and its consumption increased dramatically. "Physicians long suspected that coffee-drinking had antimalarial properties," confirms malaria researcher Sonia Shah in *The Fever*, "which seemed to explain why coffee-drinking French colonists suffered less malaria than tea-drinking English ones, and may have helped inspire a nation of American tea drinkers to switch allegiances." Given that Americans currently consume 25% of the world's coffee, Starbucks ought to raise a toasting glass to the tiny mosquito. "Malaria even explains how the nation of the 1773 Boston Tea Party," affirms Alex Perry in *Lifeblood*, "became today's land of the latte."

With the debate over confrontation or compromise moving from the coffee-stimulated conversations of the Green Dragon to Carpenters' Hall in Philadelphia, the speeches favoring compromise carried the day. Any foolhardy notions of revolution (there were not many, nor were these taken seriously) were dismissed. The prominent opinion and guiding political principle was the attainment of equal rights as Englishmen *within* the British imperial framework through negotiation, including the right to send elected colonial officials to Parliament in London. When Congress was reconvened in May of 1775, this question of confrontation or compromise had already been settled by musket shot at Lexington and Concord a month earlier. Now the fundamental issues were the actual objectives and strategic aim of this armed rebellion. An unassuming British-born troublemaker who had failed at everything from rope making to tax collecting to teaching answered this question. He had immigrated to Philadelphia in 1774 under the sponsorship of Benjamin Franklin only a few months before the opening volleys of the war.

Thomas Paine published his short pamphlet "Common Sense; Addressed to the Inhabitants of America" in January 1776, and it sold 500,000 copies in its first year. It remains in print and is the all-time bestselling American-authored title. Paine, offering "nothing more than simple facts, plain arguments, and common sense," made a persuasive argument for independence and the creation of a democratic republic as "an asylum for mankind." His short appeal not only caught the attention of France, it fueled colonial support for the war and ultimately ended the deliberations of the Second Continental Congress. Having prodded and provoked the lion this far, there was no turning back.

A letter to King George III proclaiming the colonies' sovereignty, and a groundbreaking philosophical and political statement, was drafted by Jefferson, Franklin, and John Adams—the stirring words of the Declaration of Independence. A constitution, the Articles of Confederation, was ratified in 1777, officially uniting the colonies and retaining the Continental Congress as the governing body. All that was left to do was win the war, with collaboration and military service from the mosquito of course.

Her convincing role and performance as a war-winning battlefield weapon, steering surrender by terrorizing and subverting unseasoned British soldiers across the southern colonies, has been largely and speciously snubbed or overlooked. She was not a sideline spectator to the rumbling volleys of revolution that sounded across the swamps, valleys, river basins, and pitches of her own backyard. The mosquito, perhaps more than anything else, provided the Americans with a game-changing home-field advantage and would help to forge a nation. General Anopheles has been denied her praiseworthy and rightful place in the annals of American history.

In his detailed investigation *Slavery, Disease, and Suffering in the Southern Lowcountry*, Peter McCandless dissects the role of mosquitoes in attaining American independence, in a meticulous chapter titled "Revolutionary Fever." He argues that "reading the evidence in contemporary accounts, it is hard to escape the conclusion that the biggest winners in the Southern campaigns were the microbes and the mosquitoes that transported so many of them. . . . In terms of the outcome of the war, mosquito bites may have done more than partisan bullets to ensure an American victory." The mosquito consumed British forces and ultimately decided the fate of the revolution and, by extension, the world as we now know it.

At the onset of hostilities, the British dominated every portfolio of war. While they were certainly struggling financially in the cash-strapped aftermath of the Seven Years' War, the British were still in a far superior economic position to the hapless colonies. The British Navy could attack anywhere along the eastern seaboard at will, while simultaneously blockading the colonies' shipments of resources, starving out their war effort and will to fight. The British captured the major colonial ports of Boston at the Battle of Bunker Hill in 1775 and New York in 1776, tightening the noose of the naval blockade. The British military was battle-hardened, trained, and equipped with modern weaponry and military kit, and it was the most proven and potent fighting force on the planet. They complemented their formidable national contingent by contracting 30,000 German Hessians as mercenaries, including Sleepy Hollow's legendary Headless Horseman, a practice demonized in the Declaration of Independence. "He is at this time transporting large Armies of foreign Mercenaries," decried Jefferson, "to complete the works of death, desolation, and tyranny, already begun with circumstances of cruelty & perfidy scarcely paralleled in the most barbarous ages, and totally unworthy the Head of a civilized nation." The Americans had few, if any, of these benefits.

On the short list, they lacked a trained professional army, modern weaponry, artillery, industry to make these weapons of war or anything else for that matter, long-term financial backing, allies, and, most importantly, a blue-water navy to break the British blockade and begin importing these and other indispensable requirements of war. Although unaware at the outbreak of hostilities, they eventually acquired a war-winning mercenary army of their own, led by General Anopheles. Her battlefield appearance and influence, however, was not immediate. She doesn't deserve a proper slap on the back until she starts biting into British blood. The mosquito finally took her rightful place on center stage only after the British shifted their supreme strategy to the mosquito-teeming southern colonies in 1780—a full five years into the conflict.

At the outset of the war, given these severe military shortcomings and impediments, the best Washington could do was run. If he could keep his Continental Army afloat and avoid decisive pitched battles, the revolution would survive until help, either increased American participation or French assistance—or as it turned out, both—arrived. Two and a half years into the war, in October 1777 at Saratoga, the Americans, using French-supplied weapons, scored their first decisive victory. The setting for the battlegrounds at Saratoga, astride the Hudson River in the interior of New York, neutralized British naval supremacy, arming the Americans with a significant tactical advantage. Denied reinforcements, outnumbered nearly three-to-one, and surrounded, General John Burgoyne understood the futility of his position and surrendered. The Americans, led by General Horatio Gates and a fired-up, heroic Benedict Arnold, captured or killed 7,500 British troops against only 100 losses of their own. This show of force was enough to convince the French that the Americans had a fighting chance.

France officially joined the American cause in 1778, with Spain aligning the following year, followed by the Netherlands a year later. It is doubtful that the Americans would have won the war without this timely French intervention. The French Navy broke the blockade, and 12,000 professional French soldiers and 32,000 sailors participated in the final campaigns of the war. The shockingly young, dazzlingly brilliant, and bilingual French general Marquis de Lafayette, a close friend and confidant of Washington, coordinated the combined Franco-American forces along with his comrade Count Rochambeau. Lafayette had joined the Continental Army independently prior to official French involvement. He was commissioned as a major general by the Continental Congress in 1777 at the age of nineteen. By 1780, the battlefields were resonating with both the buzzing of mosquitoes and the vernacular of his French comrades.

The decision of France (and Spain and the Netherlands) to enter the conflict, however, turned the revolution into a second global serving of the Seven Years' War as engagements spread to Europe, the Caribbean, and India. This benefited the Franco-American alliance, as Britain was drawn into a larger war with more complex strategic imperial considerations. Troop commitments were now required elsewhere, and Britain could not replace losses as easily or as quickly as the Americans. British forces were spread thinly across the empire from Bournemouth and Bengal to Barbados and the Bahamas to Boston. The British fielded no more than 60,000 army personnel during the entire revolution, making the losses sustained at Saratoga, and the ensuing casualties inflicted by mosquitoes in the southern colonies and Nicaragua, even more impactful.

As the war went viral across the globe, British forces in the Caribbean were, as usual, cut to pieces by mosquito-borne disease. The mosquito-tutored lessons so callously taught and horrifically learned at Cartagena in 1741 and Havana in 1762 apparently were all but forgotten or blithely ignored. In 1780, a British fleet under twenty-two-year-old Captain Horatio Nelson sailed to upend the Spanish domain on the Mosquito Coast, and to establish naval bases on a slice of Nicaragua with access to both the Caribbean and the Pacific. Nelson's 3,000-man contingent opened a gift-wrapped disaster: yellow fever, malaria, and dengue. When the retreat was finally sounded after six miserable months, only 500 survivors stumbled out of the jungle. In manpower, this was the single costliest military action of the entire Revolutionary War. "Nicaragua's mosquitoes killed more British soldiers," stresses J. R. McNeill, "than the Continental Army did at the battles of Bunker Hill, Long Island, White Plains, Trenton, Princeton, Brandywine, Germantown, Monmouth, King's Mountain, Cowpens, and Guilford Courthouse combined. In political terms, however, the siege at Yorktown fifteen months later cost far more."

Mosquito-borne disease, though, was nothing new to Horatio Nelson. He had first contracted malaria on service in India in 1776. While Nelson cheated malarial death again four years later during his mosquito-directed nightmare in Nicaragua, he never fully recovered and was haunted by countless serious relapses and reinfections for the remainder of his life. He lived long enough, however, to gain immortality on his flagship, HMS *Victory*, at the Battle of Trafalgar in 1805 when his outnumbered fleet annihilated a combined Franco-Spanish flotilla during the Napoleonic Wars. Nelson was killed in the engagement, but his unconventional tactics and unexpected victory reconfirmed and elevated Britain's command of the seas.

As the final British mosquito-bitten southern campaign commenced in the colonies in 1780, Nelson and his crew were being devoured by a mosquito-sprung trap in the wilds of Nicaragua. They were quite literally shredded to pieces. While the historical spotlight was focused north on the events transpiring in the American colonies, in Nicaragua the British suffered the single worst loss of any belligerent or nation during the revolution, which by now was a global war. During Nelson's Nicaraguan fiasco, nearly 85% of his force succumbed to dengue, yellow fever, and malaria, dwarfing all other casualty figures for the entire conflict, fettering available British manpower.

Britain's siphoning of troops to her Caribbean commitments, including Nelson's fateful and costly campaign in Nicaragua, came at the expense of the American theater. By 1780, when the British placed their largest force yet of 9,000 men into South Carolina (which annually spawned twelve generations of mosquitoes), over 12,000 British troops had already perished of mosquito-borne disease during His Majesty's Caribbean adventures to secure economic cash-crop colonies. Ships bound for the West Indies lost upwards of 25% of their human cargo before docking at their destination. British replacements could not be recruited or trained fast enough to replenish these losses. Mercenary mosquitoes continuously punched death tickets for unseasoned British reinforcements in both the Caribbean and during the final southern campaign in America.

By 1779, both sides had achieved victories in the American colonies, and so the war marched on. Britain controlled the major ports and key cities. The Americans roamed the countryside, and the newly appointed British commander in chief, General Henry Clinton, could not lure Washington into major engagements. Frustrated by the lack of success in the northern campaigns and by Washington's refusal to commit to a final all-or-nothing showdown, Clinton endorsed a new southern strategy to end the war, which for fiscal reasons was becoming increasingly unpopular in Britain. The war for America was supplementing an already staggering and suffocating debt accrued before and during the Seven Years' War.

A change from northern to southern scenery to silence these demurring British voices by finally crushing the rebellion in one swift stroke was just what Clinton ordered. It was also believed, based upon spurious reports from American exiles or spies in London, that the rice plantation slave colonies of Georgia and the Carolinas, being the youngest colonies with more recent British arrivals, housed a large population of Loyalists who at the sight of British liberators would flock to the Union Jack and take up arms in aid of the mother country. Clinton hoped this would alleviate British manpower concerns.

The British captured the port of Savannah in 1778. The annual wastage rate from mosquito-borne disease at Savannah's defensive garrison was 30%. Reports indicate sickness "beyond anything you can conceive . . . our suffering from sickness in this vile climate is terrible and continuous in a very great degree." Savannah's suffering was soon replicated at Charleston, the linchpin of Clinton's southern strategy. A previous attempt to take this "key to the south" in 1776 was aborted by Clinton, who reasoned, "I had the mortification to see the sultry, unhealthy season approaching us with hasty strides, when all thoughts of military operations in the Carolinas must be given up." In May 1780, however, as the first documented outbreak of dengue in the colonies unfurled in Philadelphia, the British stayed the course and quickly captured the mosquito bastion, Charleston.*

Expecting an attack on New York from General Washington, Clinton returned to the prized port city, leaving his second-in-command, General Charles Cornwallis, to direct the 9,000 troops of the southern regiments. Prior to the revolution, the devastating disease environment of the southern colonies was no secret. Cornwallis immediately recognized this danger, reporting to Clinton in August that "the climate is so bad within one hundred miles of the coast, from the end of June to the middle of October, that troops could not be stationed during the period

* Dr. Benjamin Rush was the attending physician in Philadelphia. He recorded the symptoms of the disease as "break-bone fever," now a common nickname or synonym for dengue.

without a certainty of their being rendered useless for some time for military service, if not entirely lost." Cornwallis shrewdly moved his army into the interior to show a strong British presence to rally Loyalists, to secure British forward operating bases and outposts, and, of course, to abstain from the deathly hallows of Charleston during peak mosquito season. Cornwallis was fully aware of Charleston's reputation as a wretched hive of mosquito scum and villainy.

His movements inland from Charleston initiated a series of battles with American forces under Generals Gates and Greene, which for the most part favored the British. As Greene put it, "We fight, get beat, rise, and fight again." Greene received an intelligence report painting British forces as "the emaciated picture of disease." Fighting the American rebels was one thing, fighting the marauding armies of mercenary mosquitoes was quite another. A frustrated Cornwallis repeatedly, and quite fruitlessly, relocated his forces to avoid "miasmic diseases" during his southern campaign.

Subverted and thwarted by General Anopheles at every turn, Cornwallis continued to move his forces, fleeing not from the Americans but from mosquito-borne disease. He zigzagged across the Carolinas in hopes of finding respite at locations that were promised by resident Loyalists to be healthy. "And if that will not keep us from falling sick," reported Cornwallis, "I shall despair." These bivouacs, reasoned the British commander, had "the appearance of being healthy, but it proved so much the contrary and sickness came on so rapidly." Establishing his ailing army at Camden, Cornwallis noted that 40% of his troops were crippled by "fevers and agues and rendered unfit for service." After scattering Gates's army at Camden in mid-August, Cornwallis appealed to Clinton, "Our sickness is very great, and truly alarming." Malaria, yellow fever, and dengue gnawed at British manpower and morale and would continue to erode Cornwallis's ability to fight. Thomas Paine portrayed the revolution as "the times that try men's souls." In this case, the mosquito devoured and collected British souls.

The exhaustive research of McCandless reveals, "The most commonly used terms in the British correspondence relating to the soldiers' sickness are 'intermittents,' 'agues and fevers,' 'malignant fevers,' 'putrid fevers,' and 'bilious fevers,' all of which point to malaria and possibly yellow fever and dengue." Frequent references were also made to "break-bone fever," a nickname for dengue, and to the telltale signs of yellow fever. British reports from 1778 noted, "The French have brought the Yellow Fever." Given the high mortality rates, it is doubtful that *vivax* and even *falciparum* malaria, both of which made the rounds, could have gone it alone. It is worth mentioning here that American soldiers also suffered from these same mosquito-borne diseases during the southern campaign. The same phrases are echoed in the American correspondences as well. But, *and this is the big but*, seeing as the Americans were seasoned and somewhat shielded, they did not contract, or die from, mosquito-borne diseases at the same rate as their unseasoned British counterparts. As a result, the Americans retained their punching power and combat effectiveness.

By the fall of 1780, Cornwallis, who was himself fighting a nasty bout of "the ague," reported that his army was "nearly ruined" by malaria, and numerous units were "so totally demolished by sickness [and] will not be fit for actual service for some months." Following his pyrrhic victory over Greene's larger American force at Guilford Court House in the spring of 1781, Cornwallis moved his shrinking army to Wilmington on the coast of North Carolina. Despite advice from seasoned locals to the contrary, he soon realized no location was safe from the clutches of mosquito-borne disease. "They say go 40 or 50 miles farther and you will be healthy," complained Cornwallis. "It was the same language before Camden. There is no trusting to such experiments." It was time to flee the strangling grip of mosquito-borne disease and head north to shelter from her impending swarm.

With mosquito season approaching, Cornwallis realized that he did not have enough men to hold the interior and, much to his dismay, the anticipated recruitment of throngs of Loyalists never materialized. Many southerners may well have internally harbored pro-British political views, but they simply refused to outwardly commit to any side so long as the outcome of the war hung in the balance. They, like nearly 40% of all colonists, sat on the fence or remained neutral, wanting simply to be left alone. At its peak, roughly 40% of colonists supported the revolution, while 20% rallied to their British king. In this instance, however, General Anopheles was a staunch revolutionary.

Having been denied his decisive victory in the Carolinas, and with malaria season bearing down, Cornwallis staffed a few vital garrisons, including Charleston, then marched the bulk of his army north toward Jamestown "to preserve the troops, from the fatal sickness, which so nearly ruined the army last autumn." Although not satisfied, he was prepared to consolidate with other British columns, sit out the mosquito season in the supposed safety of Virginia, and resume campaigning in the late fall. Lafayette, however, had different plans.

In Virginia, the French general played a productive and crafty game of Tom and Jerry–style cat and mouse with Cornwallis, by continuously harassing British forces without committing to pitched confrontations. Luring the British into brief skirmishes, Lafayette denied them the rest they desperately sought. During this war game of hide-and-seek, like Amherst before him, Cornwallis tried his hand at biological warfare, substituting slaves for blankets. He raided the home of Thomas Jefferson at Monticello, nabbing thirty slaves to infect with smallpox and use as biological weapons. Jefferson commended the plan, as it "would have done right, but it was done to consign them to the inevitable death from smallpox and putrid fever." Like Amherst, Cornwallis also failed to deliver his anticipated plague of pestilence. British attempts at biological warfare were now an unconvincing 0 and 2.

Despite Cornwallis's objections and trepidations concerning the health of his troops, Clinton ordered him to find a suitable encampment on the Chesapeake Bay, from where his army could be summoned quickly to New York. Clinton still clung to the idea of an inevitable Franco-American assault on the strategic port city and was willing to risk Cornwallis's soldiers to ensure its defense. Cornwallis repeatedly questioned the judgment of his superior officer. "I submit to your Excellency's consideration whether it is worth while to hold a sickly defensive post in this bay." He reported to Clinton that his current position "only gives us some acres of an unhealthy swamp" and that he already had "many sick." Cornwallis nevertheless followed his orders, knowing full well that, as McCandless calculates, "Clinton's southern strategy seriously undermined the health of his forces and may have cost the British the war."

On August 1, 1781, Cornwallis encamped his army among the rice fields and tidewater estuaries between the James and York Rivers at an insignificant hamlet called Yorktown. Home to no more than 2,000 people, Yorktown was only fifteen miles from Jamestown, as the mosquito flies. The creation of America started by settler mosquitoes at Jamestown would be completed by their more lethal country-born heirs at Yorktown. As the British, Americans, and French mustered their troops, armies of salivating mercenary mosquitoes collected in a gathering swarm in the verdant marshes surrounding Yorktown. It was both prime mosquito country and the right time of year for Washington's Anopheles ally to attack. And attack she did, unleashing a storm of malaria upon her British guests and changing the course of history.

General Clinton was stunned when the French fleet arrived at Yorktown in early September and not New York as expected. Learning of this French decision, Washington, in consultation with Rochambeau, was forced "to give up all idea of attacking New York" and hurried his combined Franco-American force south to Yorktown. Washington's column arrived in late September, joining Lafayette's blocking force for over 17,000 men positioned on the high ground surrounding Yorktown. "Cornwallis now had the worst of both worlds," comments McNeill. "His army was entrenched on the coast, at maximum risk to malaria, yet the Royal Navy could not get through to relieve him." Needing a British surrender before the end of the mosquito season and the onset of winter, on September 28, Generals Washington, Rochambeau, Lafayette, and Anopheles orchestrated a skilled and hasty siege by land and sea (and air).

Realizing his inferior position, and with his men cowering before malaria, a desperate Cornwallis again tried his hand at biological warfare. He fruitlessly released smallpox-infected slaves into the Franco-American lines. Although Edward Jenner would not perfect smallpox vaccination until 1796, risky immunization techniques had been practiced since the 1720s. Beginning in 1777, Washington insisted that his soldiers receive the perilous inoculation. Some certainly died, but the rest of his army acquired herd immunity against smallpox. Cornwallis's second failed effort to culture a premeditated smallpox epidemic brought British attempts at biological weaponry to a perfect 0 and 3.

A desperate Cornwallis pleaded to Clinton for reinforcements, relief, and quinine. "This place is in no state of defense . . . if relief does not come soon you must prepare to hear the worst . . . medicines are wanted." While the Franco-American force tightened its siege, the mosquito continued its unrelenting attack on the trapped British at Yorktown. David Petriello's clinching remarks on Clinton's ill-fated southern strategy sealed by the mosquito-fenced and malaria-fetid position of Cornwallis at Yorktown determine that "the English had been chased from the South not by the guns of the Patriots but by the proboscis of the Anopheles mosquito."

At the outset of the siege of Yorktown on September 28, Cornwallis commanded 8,700 men. By the time of his official surrender on October 19, he had 3,200 men (37%) fit for duty. Given that British casualties from combat were no more than 200 killed and 400 wounded, over half of his total force was too sick to fight. The British Army at Yorktown had been eaten alive by malarious mosquitoes. Reporting to Clinton the day after his surrender, Cornwallis credited his defeat and final capitulation not to the enemy but to malaria: "I have the mortification to inform your Excellency that I have been forced to give up the post. . . . The troops being much weakened by sickness. . . . Our numbers had been diminished by the Enemy's fire, but particularly by Sickness. . . . Our force diminished daily by sickness . . . to little more than 3,200 rank & file fit for duty." The commander of the Hessian mercenaries, holed up in Yorktown with Cornwallis, reported two days before the surrender that the British were "nearly all plagued with fever. The army melted away . . . among whom not a thousand men could be called healthy." The mosquito had chased the British from the southern battlefields of revolution and won the long and bloody struggle for American liberty.

J. R. McNeill emphasizes that "Yorktown and its mosquitoes ended British hopes and decided the American war." He closes his chapter "Revolutionary Mosquitoes" saluting the tiny female General Anopheles, who "stands tall among the founding mothers of the United States."

Her American victory not only redirected the flight path of history and the heart of Western civilization away from Britain toward the United States; it also generated immediate shock waves with global reverberations.

The British outpost of Australia, for example, was a by-product of both Yorktown and the mosquito. In the decades preceding the revolution, the American colonies received an annual import of 2,000 British convicts. In total, approximately 60,000 British convicts were dumped in the colonies. With American independence, British Parliament was forced to consider an alternative station to unload a swelling number of domestic felons. The fledgling colony of the Gambia was originally considered, but it was deemed that exile to Africa amounted to nothing more than a death sentence. Within one year of arrival, 80% of the British diaspora perished from mosquito-borne disease. This defeated the dual purpose of a penal colony: to punish and rid the mother country of criminals, while using these banished British subjects as the vanguard of colonization. If convicts could not survive, how could these colonies eventually thrive? The first 1,336 British convicts arrived at the substitute destination of Botany Bay (Sydney) in January 1788, and British Australia was born.

Like its Commonwealth cousin of Australia, British Canada was also conceived by the mosquito-manipulated outcome of the American Revolution. While Canada remained a British colony after the revolution, it was the influx of postrevolutionary American Loyalists that swung the demographic profile and prevailing culture from French to British. By 1800, over 90,000 Loyalists landed in Canada, fleeing the United States to uphold personal political loyalties, to escape persecution, or as asylum seekers from yellow fever epidemics that consumed the coastal states between 1793 and 1805. Twenty-five years after the mosquito helped secure American autonomy, British Canadians outnumbered French Canadians by a ratio of ten-to-one.

Retaining Canada, however, was the only solace for the British at the signing of the Treaty of Paris in September 1783, which officially ended what had become not just America's war of independence but also a global conflict. British Florida was handed over to Spain, and France acquired Senegal and Tobago. All British lands east of the Mississippi River between Florida and the Great Lakes–St. Lawrence River were surrendered, marking the national boundaries of the new, and internationally recognized, country of the United States of America. With the Proclamation Line now null and void, America more than doubled in size. Triggered by the American Revolution, a wave of rebellions against European rule swept the Americas. Decided by the mosquito's dealings in yellow fever and malaria, these colonial insurrections and conflicts, while determining the fate of freedom for numerous nations, also inadvertently augmented the westward-tilting landmass of the United States.

While the mosquito had helped Generals George Washington and the Marquis de Lafayette secure American independence, she had not yet completed the finishing touches on her masterpiece designs of American Manifest Destiny and territorial annexation. General Anopheles and her compatriot General Aedes, as we have seen, are fickle friends and allies. The birth of the United States came at the expense of the mosquito-bitten British. American westward expansion into Louisiana Territory, and the subsequent escapades of Lewis and Clark, resulted from the mosquito's merciless attacks on Napoleon's unseasoned French troops struggling to quell their own insurgency in Haiti within the larger French Revolution and Napoleonic Wars.

Just as American mosquitoes had aligned with and respected Washington's mutineers, Haitian freedom-fighting mosquitoes reinforced the slave revolt and protracted rebellion led by Toussaint Louverture against draconian French rule. She also buttressed seasoned revolutionaries during the budding wars of liberation against Spanish authority across South and Central America driven by the dazzling Simon Bolivar. "The separation of America from the Spanish Monarchy resembles the state of the Roman Empire," Bolivar proclaimed in 1819, "when that enormous structure fell to pieces in the midst of the ancient world." Mirroring her ruin of the Roman Empire 1,500 years earlier, the mosquito also gnawed the mighty Spanish-American Empire into autonomous, independent pieces. "Historians for generations have brilliantly illuminated this age of revolution. . . . These were stirring events, the stuff of political history, replete with heroism and drama, providing stages for characters such as George Washington, Toussaint Louverture, and Simon Bolivar," acknowledges J. R. McNeill. "One thing that has escaped their spotlight is the role of mosquitoes in making the revolutions victorious." Beginning with the American Revolution, across crumbling European colonial empires the mosquito apportioned and dispensed liberty and death. Both consummations delivered a new birth of freedom.

CHAPTER 13

Mercenary Mosquitoes: Wars of Liberation and the Making of the Americas

In the spring of 1803, President Thomas Jefferson commissioned Meriwether Lewis and William Clark to lead the Corps of Discovery Expedition to explore and map the newly acquired Louisiana Territory. It was imperative that the thirty-four resourceful trailblazers of this cross-country excursion travel light—only indispensable gear and equipment suited for survival in the exotic, undiscovered wilderness of the American West. While carefully choosing and bundling the bare necessities, the voyagers made sure to pack 3,500 doses of quinine bark, a half pound of opium, over 600 mercury pills they nicknamed "Thunder Clappers," liquid mercury, and penile syringes, among other essential supplies. Swallowing mercury or injecting it into the urethra did not cure their dysentery, gonorrhea, or syphilis, or fend off Smokey Bear. The mercury-laden feces and mercury dribbles they left behind, however, have enabled modern researchers to meticulously pinpoint the locations and track the exact route of the Sacagawea-led expedition. "Despite dysentery, sexually transmitted diseases, snake bites, and the occasional bear attack," writes Petriello, "the expedition returned relatively unscathed" after a successful trek of more than two years.

The main goal of the Lewis and Clark Expedition, as ordered by Jefferson, was to find "the most direct and practicable water communication across this continent, for the purpose of commerce." Among the secondary objectives was the establishment of trade relations with indigenous peoples and an examination of the flora and fauna to price economic potential. In short, its purpose was to generally figure out what the hell Jefferson had just bought from Napoleon, who needed a quick injection of capital to help fund and front his unfinished European campaign.

The American mosquito-brokered purchase of the Louisiana Territory was a by-product of both the larger international affairs surrounding the tumultuous and confused French Revolution and Napoleon's subsequent quest to restore the French Empire in the Americas, tarnished by the Seven Years' War, to its former glory. Within this upheaval, the fledgling American nation suffered through one of the worst outbreaks of disease in its history. French colonial refugees fleeing a vicious slave revolt against French rule in Haiti swamped Philadelphia in yellow fever. As we will see, in the wake of the American Revolution, the mosquito connected four seemingly unrelated events over the span of fourteen years: the outbreak of the French Revolution in 1789, the rebellion launched in Haiti in 1791 led by Toussaint Louverture, followed by the appalling 1793 yellow fever epidemic in Philadelphia, and, finally, the completion of the Louisiana Purchase of 1803.

Throughout this period, from France to the far reaches of the Americas, the mosquito spliced and plaited a tangled web of infamous and influential historical episodes. She tore at the heart of colonial empires by encouraging revolution, pressed US Manifest Destiny west, and otherwise toppled the balance of power in the Americas. The mosquito turned the darker and more sinister sides of the Columbian Exchange against its own European creators and custodians by unleashing a torrent of yellow fever and malaria against unseasoned imperial soldiers attempting to subdue slave revolts and country-born independence movements in their American colonies. They were the inadvertent biological architects of their own imperial demise. In the process, the mosquito reconfigured the map of what was by now a not-so-new or small world after all. The economic, political, and philosophical foundations of revolution fermented in colonial America, advocated by General Anopheles, roused the miserable and bedraggled subjects of France to shrug off the yoke of subordination fastened by an oppressive and supercilious monarchy.

Stirred by the statutes of liberty carved by their American compatriots, the French steered their own revolution against the tyranny of King Louis XVI and his bride, Marie Antoinette, initiated by the celebrated Storming of the Bastille on July 14, 1789. Although the French monarchs were put to the guillotine in 1793, the revolution gained momentum and spread to French colonies. In 1799, the genius thirty-year-old general Napoleon Bonaparte executed a bloodless coup against the leaders of his own republican revolutionary government. Napoleon established himself as the head of a more authoritarian regime, effectively ending the French Revolution. Craving absolute rule, in 1804 he colluded for his election as emperor of France in an imperial system based on the Roman Empire. His lust for power and war ignited the Napoleonic Wars, the largest European and international conflict yet witnessed. Napoleon's bid for global domination and a resurrected French Empire in the Americas, including frontier interests and stakes in the United States, would be devoured by Haitian mosquitoes.

France had acquired Haiti, the western portion of the island of Hispaniola, in 1697 during the colonial wars preceding the Seven Years' War. At the onset of the slave revolt in 1791, Haiti (called Saint-Domingue until the expulsion of the French) had 8,000 plantations and produced half of the world's coffee. It was also a leading exporter of sugar, cotton, tobacco, cocoa, and indigo, which was used as a posh purple-blue fabric dye. The petite island colony accounted for an astounding 35% of France's total mercantilist economic empire. Predictably, it was also the leading destination for African slaves (and imported mosquitoes), with 30,000 arriving annually. By 1790, Haiti's half a million slaves, two-thirds of which were born and seasoned in Africa, made up 90% of the total population. Most African-born Haitian slaves arrived preseasoned to malaria and yellow fever.

In August 1791, over 100,000 slaves revolted against a handful of brutally repressive and harsh French plantation owners. A former slave turned revolutionary summed up the horrors underpinning the causes of the rebellion:

> Have they not hung up men with heads downwards, drowned them in sacks, crucified them on planks, buried

> them alive, crushed them in mortars? Have they not forced them to eat shit? And, having flayed them with the lash, have they not cast them alive to be devoured by worms, or onto anthills, or lashed them to stakes in the swamp to be devoured by mosquitoes? Have they not thrown them into boiling cauldrons of cane syrup? Have they not put men and women inside barrels studded with spikes and rolled them down mountainsides into the abyss? Have they not consigned these miserable blacks to man-eating dogs until the latter, sated by human flesh, left the mangled victims to be finished off with bayonet and poniard?

Mark Twain cynically remarked, "There are many humorous things in the world; among them, the white man's notion that he is less savage than the other savages." The same ideals championed by the coffee-fueled enlightenment of life, liberty, and the pursuit of happiness that had sparked the American and French Revolutions also triggered the Haitian War of Independence against their French masters. Initially, the violence was sporadic, confused, and incoherent. Coalitions were vague and continuously reshuffled, and alliances shifted across battlefields. Widespread atrocities, however, were committed by all factions.

While this chaotic and muddled uprising in Haiti gained momentum, the widening of a general European war united a coalition against Napoleon's France that included (at various times) Russia, Austria, Prussia, Portugal, the Dutch Republic, and Britain, among other, smaller nations or princely states. The French Revolution went global and spread to the Caribbean. Britain viewed the slave rebellion in Haiti as a dangerous inspiration for slaves in its own Caribbean colonies. Fearing a domino effect of slave revolts, the British intervened in 1793. Already at war with France, the British aimed to both quell the insurrection and capture the undersize but exceedingly lucrative French colony.

Unseasoned British troops sent to Haiti, relates J. R. McNeill, "died with astonishing quickness, seemingly disembarking from ships straight to their graves." The disease-bitten British stayed on in Haiti for five years, accomplishing very little aside from feeding mosquitoes and dying in droves. "The symptoms as they appeared," wrote a British army surgeon in 1796, "were prostration of strength; heavy, sometimes acute pain of the forehead; a severe pain of the loins, joints, and extremities; a glazy appearance of, with a bloody suffusion of the eye; nausea or vomiting of bilious, sometimes offensive black matter, not unlike coffee grounds." Of the roughly 23,000 British troops deployed to Haiti, 15,000, or 65%, died of yellow fever and malaria. A British survivor later recalled that "death presented itself under every form an unlimited imagination could invent, some died raving Mad. The putridity of the disorder at last arose to such a height that hundreds almost were absolutely drowned in their own Blood, bursting from them at every pore." In 1798, the mosquito chased the once mighty and now aching British Army from Haiti.

Haiti, however, was only one operation in Britain's larger Caribbean campaign. The British tried in vain to capture other French, Spanish, and Dutch holdings. Every expedition was met by stalwart flights of mercenary mosquitoes, ending in heaping ruins of British dead. By the time the British finally gave up in 1804 to concentrate their forces against Napoleon in continental Europe, the mosquito had killed 60,000 to 70,000 British servicemen (roughly 72%) in the Caribbean. The British were "fighting to conquer a cemetery," says McNeill. "St. Domingue was the biggest part, but only a part, of this graveyard of the British army." The potential of economic bounty and enterprise seemed to outshine, even eclipse, all logic of vainly funneling a persistent parade of unseasoned soldiers into the mosquito's suffocating chamber of horrors recounted by Royal Navy lieutenant Bartholomew James. "The dreadful sickness that now prevailed in the West Indies is beyond the power of the tongue or pen to describe," James recorded from Martinique in 1794. "The constant affecting scenes of sudden death [were] in fact dreadful to behold, and nothing was scarcely to be met but funeral processions."

In the Caribbean, the British and their imperialist European counterparts certainly clung to philosopher and poet George Santayana's original, and often misquoted, maxim: "Those who cannot remember the past are condemned to repeat it." During the first wave of the British Caribbean campaign in 1793, for example, an initial dispatch from Guadeloupe affirmed, "That dreadful malady the yellow fever, which, though it had subsided when we first came to the West Indies, was now, as it were, awakened by the arrival of fresh victims." Gluttonous tropical mosquitoes gorged on a smorgasbord of unseasoned European fodder continuously fed into her jungle furnace of disease across the Caribbean, most notably in war-ravaged Haiti. These localized epidemics, however, soon found an amenable international host audience. They spread from the Caribbean like a deathly shadow, skulking and stalking across the Americas and beyond.

The revolution in Haiti and imperial conflicts across the Caribbean expedited the movement of troops, refugees, and yellow fever across the Atlantic world. Troops and refugees fleeing these tropic thunders to Europe were escorted by mosquito-borne disease. Yellow fever stormed through the coastal Mediterranean, including southern France, before making guest appearances as far north as the Netherlands, Hungary, Austria, and the Germanic principalities of Saxony and Prussia. In Spain, 100,000 people died of the dreaded yellow fever or *vómito negro* between 1801 and 1804, adding to the 80,000 who had already perished from the disease during previous outbreaks. In Barcelona alone, yellow fever took the lives of 20,000 people in three months, representing 20% of the city's population.

Having amassed enormous wealth at the expense of African plantation slaves, European imperialist powers were now reaping a transatlantic whirlwind of disease and death imported directly from their mercantilist American empires and the mosquito ecologies they themselves created. In an ironic twist of fate, or perhaps even karma if you prefer, the mosquito was now biting back at the mother countries of Europe for their reshuffling of global ecosystems during the Columbian Exchange. Their colonies in the Americas, however, were by no means passed over or pardoned from the bloodcurdling terrors of yellow fever.

Between 1793 and 1805, the disease ricocheted through the entire Western Hemisphere like a poison dart, gaining strength during one of the most intense El Niño oscillations of the millennium. Outside of the Haitian horror show, the hardest hit were Havana, Guyana, Veracruz, New Orleans, New York, and Philadelphia, which was home to an epidemic every year of this twelve-year run of yellow fever.

Vómito Negro: An epidemic of the dreaded "Black Vomit," or yellow fever, rearing its ugly head in the streets of Barcelona, Spain, 1819. *(Diomedia/Wellcome Library)*

Prior to the historic epidemic of 1793, Philadelphia had not seen yellow fever for thirty years. The population, therefore, was relatively unseasoned and ripe for infection. In July 1793, the *Hankey*, dubbed the "Ship of Death," docked at the nation's capital, carrying roughly 1,000 French colonial refugees fleeing Haiti. A few days later, in a brothel next to the pier in a seedy area known as Hell Town, a prowling scourge of yellow fever was let loose on Philadelphia's unsuspecting population of 55,000. In total, 20,000 people fled the city, including most politicians and civil servants who were not already dead.

Yellow fever shut down the federal government of the United States (and the Pennsylvania state government, both of which resided in Philadelphia). President Washington endeavored to govern from his perch in Mount Vernon but, in his hurried flight, remarked, "I brought no public papers of any sort (not even the rules which have been established in these cases), along with me. Consequently, am not prepared at this place to decide points which may require a reference to papers not within my reach." He was advised that he did not have the power to relocate the capital and convene Congress at an alternate location because that "would clearly be unconstitutional." By late October, as mosquitoes succumbed to the onset of winter chills, the city was described by First Lady Martha Washington as having "suffered so much that it can not be got over soon by those that was in the city—almost every family has lost some of their friends—and black seems to be the general dress of the city." The 1793 yellow fever epidemic killed 5,000 people in roughly three months, nearing 10% of the capital city's population. To match this mortality rate, two million metropolitan New Yorkers would have to perish in a horrific modern-day equivalent outbreak, like a mutated virulent strain of West Nile. This certainly puts into perspective the cataclysmic death caused by the mosquito.

Yellow fever continued to stalk the city. During the epidemic of 1798, for example, the virus killed 3,500 in Philadelphia and another 2,500 in New York. "Yellow fever," whispered a disheartened Thomas Jefferson, "will discourage the growth . . . of our nation. The yellow fever epidemics spelled the doom of large cities." Although the Residence Act of 1790 endorsed the relocation of the capital to a purposefully constructed centerpiece of the country, Philadelphia had been lobbying to be that showpiece. The yellow fever epidemics beginning in 1793 ended any deliberation about the final location and hastened the construction and completion of the new capital. In 1800, Washington, DC, opened for business. Ironically, seeing as it was built at the confluence of the Anacostia and Potomac Rivers, it was an actual mosquito-toured swamp before it became a so-called political swamp. Washington, however, did not live long enough to see the architectural marvel named in his honor.

In December 1799, as 1,200 more yellow fever victims were being mourned in Philadelphia, sixty-seven-year-old George Washington died. That autumn he had suffered another bout of his reoccurring malaria, leading to a string of other complications.* By December, with his health failing, the catchall cure of bloodletting was administered. More than half of his total blood volume was drained in less than three hours! He died the following day. Napoleon ordered a ten-day period of mourning throughout France, as he circulated battle orders to crush the Haitian slave revolt and threaten the United States, the very nation that George and his own French countrymen helped to create.

Where the British had failed, Napoleon was determined to succeed in preserving the slave-produced wealth of Haiti for France. He unknowingly thrust unseasoned soldiers headlong into a maelstrom of mosquito death and into the clutches of the brilliant strategist Toussaint Louverture, who effectively used yellow fever and malaria as a potent ally. Louverture had been fighting with various factions since the early part of the revolution. When the British evacuated in 1798, he quickly became the undisputed leader of the revolution through shrewd diplomacy and military acumen. His nickname "Black Napoleon," used by both his adversaries and his allies, was a tribute to his reputation. He confiscated coffee plantations and used the black-market coffee trade to finance his revolution.† Upon learning of this bootlegging, a furious Napoleon burst out, "Damn Coffee! Damn Colonies!" This particular colony, however, was too valuable to French economic designs to simply walk away.

Napoleon had a lofty vision of resurrecting the former French glory in the Americas. Haiti was critical, not only for its capital but also as a staging area for establishing Napoleon's envisaged North American empire. Given Napoleon's thirst for war and power, rumors swirled as to his

* Malaria was a mainstay in the Washington household. In July 1783, shortly before the Treaty of Paris was ratified solidifying international recognition of American independence, Martha Washington came down with a serious case of malaria. George reported to his nephew, "Mrs. Washington has had three of the Ague & fever & is much with it—the better, having prevented the fit yesterday by a plentiful application of the Bark—she is too indisposed to write to you."

† There is still a strong connection between revolution and the illicit smuggling of narcotics and other goods, including the opium poppy production in Afghanistan and the Taliban/Al-Qaeda, cocaine and Maoist revolutionaries in South America, and pirated petroleum in the case of ISIS, Boko Haram in Nigeria, and Al-Shabaab in Somalia.

intentions in the Americas, ranging from an assault on British Caribbean possessions, to a march on Canada, and even to an invasion of the United States from his recently obtained Louisiana Territory.

During the American Revolution, colonial products flowed, unencumbered by Spanish taxes or tariffs, up and down the Mississippi River. To fund the rebellion, Spain had allowed the Continental Congress to store and export goods at the port of New Orleans duty-free. In 1800, in a backroom deal, an economically depleted and globally distressed Spain ceded the Louisiana Territory to Napoleon's France. American shipping and export privileges at New Orleans were immediately suspended. Spain was also on the verge of handing over Florida as well. President Jefferson rightly understood that American access to the Gulf of Mexico would be cut off, and American trade would be dealt a severe blow, one that the financially fledgling republic could ill afford. At the time, roughly 35% of American exports were dispatched from New Orleans. Purposeful leaks circulated that America was prepared to send 50,000 troops to take New Orleans, when in fact the entire United States military numbered just 7,100. The Americans, not wanting to be sucked into war with France, nervously watched as events unfolded in Europe and the Caribbean.

In December 1801, Napoleon finally launched his looming and ambitious campaign in the Americas. Under the command of his brother-in-law, General Charles Leclerc, an initial French detachment of 40,000 soldiers was dispatched to discipline the insubordinate and defiant slaves of Haiti. Standing to post with Toussaint Louverture, the mosquito had other ideas in mind. Using guerrilla tactics and a policy of scorched earth, Louverture lured the French into an unwinnable insurgent quagmire of mosquito-imposed death. He practiced hit-and-run tactics from the hills during the peak mosquito months, confining the French to the mosquito-plagued coast and low-lying miasmic marshes.

Louverture's forces whittled away at the French while his mosquito allies attacked with fury. Following the sickly season, with French forces weakened and thinned by yellow fever and malaria, Louverture launched fierce counterattacks. He explained his brilliantly simple strategy to his followers: "Do not forget that while waiting for the rainy season, which will rid us of our enemies, we have only destruction and fire as our weapons. The whites from France cannot hold out against us here in St. Domingue. They will fight well at first, but soon they will fall sick and die like flies. When the French are reduced to small, small numbers, we will harass them and beat them." Not only was Louverture aware of the impact of seasoning and the divergent immunities between his men and his enemies, he used it as a war-winning strategy.

Louverture allowed his mercenary mosquito allies to win the war for him. "If my position has changed from very good to very bad, what is to blame is only the sickness that has destroyed my army," Leclerc reported to Napoleon in the fall of 1802. "If you wish to become master of Saint-Domingue, you must send me twelve thousand men without wasting a single day. If you cannot send me the troops that I have asked for, and by the time I have requested, Saint-Domingue will be forever lost to France. . . . My soul has withered, and no joyful idea can ever make me forget these hideous scenes." A month after penning this dark vision and morose premonition, Leclerc died of yellow fever. More than twenty other French generals who were deployed to Haiti followed him to a mosquito-hollowed grave. The French invasion, like so many other ambitious would-be conquerors with delusions of grandeur, also fell to the succubus mosquito mistress of the Caribbean.

Napoleon was one of the most brilliant military minds in history, but even he could not defeat Generals Aedes and Anopheles. While his French forces were dominating the battlefields of Europe, in the Caribbean, Napoleon yielded and conceded to the mighty mosquito in November 1803. "Happy were the French soldiers who died quickly," wrote a victorious revolutionary. "Others suffered from cramps, aching heads that seemed about to blow up, and insatiable thirst. They would vomit blood, as well as a substance dubbed 'Black Soup,' then their faces turned yellow, and bodies were encased in malodorous phlegm, before death happily intervened." With French soldiers drowning in a bloodbath of yellow fever and malaria, Napoleon's Haitian campaign was abandoned after less than two years. The fate and future of Haiti and its independent-minded slaves was dictated by the mosquito.

In total, of the roughly 65,000 French soldiers sent to Haiti, 55,000 died of mosquito-borne disease, a jarring and mind-blowing death rate of 85%. Generals Aedes and Anopheles unveiled Haiti's official independence two months later. "Haiti's slave revolution was the only such rebellion to lead to a free and independent nation," acknowledges Billy G. Smith in his book *Ship of Death*. "Born out of one of the most brutal slave regimes in history, midwifed by yellow fever, it was a spectacular achievement. The slaves of Saint-Domingue had defeated the best troops that European nations could send against them." Freedom, however, came at a terrible price. Roughly 150,000 Haitians, including a considerable number of noncombatant civilians, were killed by British and French forces. Louverture, who was captured under confusing and suspect circumstances in the spring of 1802, died in martyr-like fashion of tuberculosis in a French prison a year later. Toussaint Louverture and his freedom fighters, like George Washington and his American civilian soldiers, undeniably deserve credit. Smith, however, is careful to affix the disclaimer that "it was the fever that enabled them to do it." Altogether the British, French, and Spanish lost a staggering 180,000 men to Haiti's mosquitoes.

Finally, after three centuries of mind-boggling losses to mosquito-borne disease, European powers also lost the desire to contest Caribbean mosquitoes. They were forced to reconsider and retool their larger imperial ambitions and strategies in the face of relentless and murderous mosquito-borne disease. With her blood-tipped proboscis, the mosquito was writing the unforgiving finale, and forever closing the book on the era of European colonialism in the Americas. The vanquished, however, still had a few economic cards up their sleeves. They vowed to commercially cripple the former slaves of Haiti for their insubordination and hijack of imperial wealth.

The slaveholding nations of Europe and the United States spitefully punished the renegade Haitians to discourage similar revolts. A blanketing economic embargo was placed on Haiti for decades, sending the nation into an economic tailspin, delivering the Haitian people into abysmal poverty. Once the wealthiest economy in the Caribbean, Haiti is now the poorest nation in the Western Hemisphere and the seventeenth poorest nation in the world. Although yellow fever no longer stalks the country, Haiti currently hosts the full gamut of mosquito-borne diseases, including endemic *falciparum* malaria (and *malariae*), dengue, Zika, chikungunya, and its recently evolved cousin the Mayaro virus.

Following their horrific experiences, not just in Haiti but across the Caribbean over two centuries of mosquito ridicule, the British never again mounted a large-scale campaign in the Caribbean. Britain's imperial eye shifted east to Africa, India, and central Asia. More importantly, the successful Haitian Revolution ignited the abolitionist movement in Britain, and domestic public opinion soured on the institution of imperial African slavery. This outcry convinced Parliament to ban the slave trade in 1807. In 1833, slavery itself was abolished across the British Empire.

The French also gave up their futile struggle with Caribbean mosquitoes following their embarrassment in Haiti. With his hopes for a New World empire shattered by mosquito-borne disease, Napoleon turned his back on the whole bloody mess in 1803. Without Haiti (and its vast resources), New Orleans served no purpose and was defenseless against attacks by the powerful British Royal Navy or even by the weaker but aggrieved United States. Napoleon also feared that without economic concessions in Louisiana the United States would, in Jefferson's words, "marry ourselves to the British fleet and nation." Haitian mosquitoes had emptied the economic veins of France. With finances and resources increasingly needed for his war in Europe, Napoleon understood the futility of pursuing his crippled North American strategy. The stinging success of Haiti's mosquito-succored slaves had unintended historical implications that would eventually broker the Louisiana Purchase and quickly scatter and steer Lewis and Clark, and Sacagawea, across the United States.

Napoleon's dream of rekindling the French Empire in the Americas had been bitten in the cradle by Haiti's mosquitoes. By default, he enacted what he called the Continental System. "In former days, if we desired to be rich, we had to own colonies, to establish ourselves in India and the Antilles, in Central America, in San Domingo. These times are over and done with," Napoleon decreed to his chamber of commerce.

"Today we must become manufacturers. We shall make everything ourselves." Kicked out of the Caribbean by mercenary mosquitoes, the French initiated modern innovations in industry and agriculture. French botanists, for example, replaced the loss of Caribbean cane sugar by extracting sweetener from European sugar beets.

Following the loss of Haiti, Napoleon had no use for New Orleans or his vast, relatively barren Louisiana estate. Seeing as France was at war with both Spain and Britain, the sale of not just New Orleans but the entire 828,000 square miles of Louisiana Territory to the United States was the only option. Jefferson had given his negotiators permission to spend up to $10 million on New Orleans alone, and they were dumbfounded by, and immediately accepted, Napoleon's offer of $15 million ($300 million today) for the entire French property holdings. The vast territory stretching from the Gulf of Mexico in the south to southern Canada in the north, from the Mississippi River in the east to the Rocky Mountains in the west, included land from fifteen current US states and two Canadian provinces. The 1803 Louisiana Purchase, brokered with the pressure of Haiti's mosquitoes, doubled the size of the United States overnight at less than three cents an acre. Given her immeasurable impact in shaping the United States, including the addition of the Louisiana Territory, the mosquito deserves a place on Mount Rushmore with her protuberant face tucked in between the grateful glances of the indebted Washington and Jefferson.

Following this sale of his North American assets, and with his navy in tatters after its resounding defeat by Admiral Lord Nelson at the Battle of Trafalgar in 1805, Napoleon's continental campaign in Europe was ended in 1812 by Generals Winter and Typhus and the methodical Russian scorched-earth retreat during his futile invasion of Russia. Of the 685,000 men of his Grande Armée who marched to war in June, only 27,000 were fit for duty upon his retreat in December. He left behind some 380,000 dead, 100,000 prisoners of war, and 80,000 deserters. His doomed Russian campaign was the turning point of the war and led to his eventual defeat at the Battle of Waterloo in 1815 by a British-led allied army under the command of the Duke of Wellington. Prior to this final defeat and exile, however, Napoleon is credited with having crafted the only purposeful and successful deployment of biological warfare in the nineteenth century.* The mosquito was his delivery system of choice to launch aerial malaria missiles against a colossal British invasion force.

Encouraged by victories over the French in Portugal and Austria, in 1809 the British had decided to mount a raid against Napoleon in northern Europe to open a second front and relieve their beleaguered Austrian allies. The site chosen was Walcheren, a low-lying marsh in the Scheldt Estuary of the Netherlands and Belgium, where it was believed the French fleet had taken harbor. In July, the potent British expeditionary force consisted of 40,000 men and 700 ships—the largest force yet assembled by Britain. An undaunted Napoleon was aware of the impending invasion, as a fleet this size could not go unnoticed, and more importantly, he was also cognizant of the recurrent summer-fall fevers that annually besieged the Walcheren region. "We must oppose the English with nothing but fever, which will soon devour them all," he told his commanders. "In a month the English will be obliged to take to their ships." Taking a page from his Haitian adversary Toussaint Louverture's playbook, Napoleon ushered in the worst epidemic of malaria that Europe had ever seen.

Breaching the dikes to flood the entire area with brackish water, he created the perfect storm for mosquito breeding and malaria transmission. Eschewing the frustrated failures of Amherst and Cornwallis at premeditated biological warfare, Napoleon's perverse effort was a feverish success. The word "Walcheren" has since become a synonym and byword for military blundering. By the time the British called off the expedition in October, after a cost of 8 million pounds, 40% of the British force had been rendered impotent by malaria. The "Walcheren Fever," as it was dubbed, had killed 4,000 men, while another 13,000 were sweating it out in makeshift hospitals. Napoleon's use of malaria as a biological weapon would be emulated by the Nazis against the American landings at Anzio, Italy, in 1944 during the Second World War.

Where Britain and France bowed to the harsh retribution of the mosquito, the Spanish would stubbornly fight on for their imperiled and

* Ironically, during Napoleon's final exile, his prison island of St. Helena in the South Atlantic, where he died in 1821, was patrolled by the British cruiser *HMS Musquito*.

evaporating imperial possessions in the Americas, fruitlessly sacrificing thousands of lives to mosquito-borne disease. Like the British and French showdowns with Washington, Lafayette, and Louverture, the Spanish also faced a brilliant revolutionary leader in Simon Bolivar. Like the British and French, they also suffered the wrath of rebellious mercenary mosquitoes. Between 1811 and 1826, every Spanish American colony attained independence save Cuba and Puerto Rico. As J. R. McNeill states, the mosquito ensured that "Spanish America came untethered from Spain."

During the first forays of the Napoleonic Wars, Spain had been a French ally. The Spanish Navy was also irrevocably shattered by Nelson at Trafalgar, and Spanish maritime influence steadily eroded. After a successful Franco-Spanish occupation of Portugal in 1807, Napoleon turned on his ally and invaded Spain the following year. The British, now in command of the high seas, redirected Spanish colonial trade toward its own empire. This benefited the Spanish colonies, for it loosened restrictions on trade and allowed for relative access to a free market economy. Local revolutionary councils, or *juntas,* made up of Spanish or Casta/Mestizo "mixed race" elites sprang up across Spanish America. The privately motivated leaders of these quasi-freedom fighters understood the economic benefits of operating outside Spain's mercantilist system.

In 1814, Spain sent over 14,000 troops, its largest force ever engaged in the Americas, to restore order and trade with the colonies of Venezuela, Colombia, Ecuador, and Panama (collectively called New Grenada). Mercenary mosquitoes quickly displayed a "decided preference," as one Spanish combatant noticed, "for Europeans and new-comers." By 1819, as Colombia rolled out its red carpet of independence, less than a quarter of the Spanish Army remained alive. With surprising accuracy, the Spanish minister of war was notified that across the embattled Spanish colonies, "the mere bite of a mosquito often deprives a man of his life . . . this contributes to our destruction, and to the annihilation of the troops." Undaunted, a financially floundering Spain, in possession of nothing more than a bathtub navy, dispatched another 20,000 soldiers on rented Russian transports to crush Bolivar and preserve its American empire.

Bolivar, who had visited Haiti in 1815 and 1816 and discussed tactics with veterans of the revolution, incorporated mosquito-borne disease into his strategy just as his predecessor Louverture had done. It was a proven war-winning strategy, and it worked for Bolivar as well. The Spanish, the first to import African slaves, mosquitoes, and their maladies to the Americas, were eaten alive, undermined, and ultimately destroyed by their own former dark deeds, repaying in disease and death for the unatoned sins of their fathers. The mosquito assailed, infected, and killed unseasoned soldiers delivered directly from Spain without any measure or quality of mercy. Like Napoleon's French troops in Haiti, Spanish soldiers also suffered the wrath of their own Columbian Exchange environmental constructions. Yellow fever and malaria killed between 90% and 95% of all Spanish forces sent to the Americas to defend economy and empire.

Like Louverture, Bolivar died of tuberculosis in 1830. Unlike Louverture, he witnessed the realization of his dreams. By this time, Bolivar and his mercenary mosquitoes had gnawed the Spanish Empire in the Americas into numerous independent nations. All that remained of this once glorious and vast domain was Cuba, Puerto Rico, and the Philippines, all of which would eventually be gobbled up by rough-riding mosquitoes and by the inaugural volleys of American imperialism in 1898.

The seasoned slave and colonial rebellions against imperial European rule, which rumbled across the Americas, shattered the old order and ushered in a new age of independence. Unforgiving mosquitoes rallied in support of their seasoned country-born comrades, exacting hellfire retribution on their former European masters. With a fierce loyalty to the struggles of freedom unfolding in their midst, mosquitoes violated and killed unseasoned British, French, and Spanish soldiers, forcing the last clumsy, feverish retreat of European imperialism in the Americas. She severed the main economic and territorial arteries connecting Europe to colonial America. The biological consequences of the Columbian Exchange struck directly at the hearts of their European creators, who now reaped the disease and death they themselves had sown.

Imported mosquitoes and disease once benefited Europeans by killing indigenous peoples at unrivaled rates, enabling and expediting territorial expansion and a European labyrinth of lucrative slave-powered extractive mercantilist colonies. During these revolutions, ruthless mosquitoes steeped unseasoned European soldiers in yellow fever and malaria and destroyed their institutions. European dominion over the Americas, empowered by African mosquitoes and slaves, was also doomed by these same elements of the Columbian Exchange. Although the United States was the first to be born of revolutionary mosquitoes, her battlefield prowess in support of the slave rebellion in Haiti forced Napoleon to sell his North American lands.

With the mosquito acting as the real estate agent for Jefferson's purchase of the Louisiana Territory, and with Lewis and Clark's subsequent cartographic and economic mission to the Pacific Ocean, the young country was one step closer to its ocean-to-ocean-and-everything-in-between dream of Manifest Destiny. The United States continued its westward expansionist drive, battling, slaughtering, and forcefully removing indigenous peoples and the bison, their livelihood, and solidified its continental landmass and global status by declaring war on British Canada, Mexico, and, eventually, Spain. Opportunist mosquitoes roamed and reaped the bloody harvest of these conflicts of American nation building.

CHAPTER 14

Mosquitoes of Manifest Destiny: Cotton, Slavery, Mexico, and the American South

There was trouble brewing in the heart of the fledgling United States. Indigenous peoples west of the former Proclamation Line skirting the Appalachian Mountains were violently resisting American expansion and the aggressive encroachment of hostile settlers onto their lands. William Henry Harrison, the governor of Indian Territory, warned President James Madison in October 1811 of the grave threat posed by Shawnee chief Tecumseh and his mounting, British-backed pan-Indian coalition. "The implicit obedience and respect which the followers of Tecumseh pay him, is really astonishing, and more than any other circumstance bespeaks him one of those uncommon geniuses which spring up occasionally to produce revolutions, and overturn the established order of things. If it were not for the vicinity of the United States, he would, perhaps, be the founder of an empire that would rival in glory Mexico or Peru [Maya, Aztec, and Inca civilizations]. No difficulties deter him . . . and wherever he goes he makes an impression favorable to his purposes. He is now upon the last round to put a finishing stroke on his work."* The call to action boisterously chirped by the "War Hawks" in Congress was answered by a declaration of war on Britain, which was signed into effect by Madison in June 1812 to uphold the notions of sovereignty outlined in the 1783 Treaty of Paris and to seize the Canadian Great Lakes transportation routes to stimulate trade.

The economic expansionist convictions of many immigrants and

* Elected president in 1840, Harrison died, likely of typhoid, thirty-two days after taking office.

settlers seeped into American political and military policy under the cultural ideology and media-driven ruse of the preordained right destined by the Almighty itself to spread American refinement and democratic governance from the Atlantic to the Pacific Oceans. This vision of Manifest Destiny was epitomized by the painting *American Progress* by John Gast. It depicts the angelic figure of Columbia, personifying both the United States and the "Spirit of the Frontier," cloaked in a streaming white gown as she virtuously floats from the east to deliver civilization and its modern trappings to the untamed wilds of the west.

Beginning with the War of 1812, this fulfillment of American Manifest Destiny was anything but benevolent or altruistic. Aggressive and combative American territorial expansion stood in sharp contrast to the benign and serene image of the innocently drifting Columbia. Manifest Destiny, and its driving force of plantation cotton production, thrust the United States headlong into a series of wars against its northern neighbor, British Canada; internally against indigenous peoples in America; and, eventually, against Mexico to the southwest to secure the coveted Pacific ports of California. The mosquito was an active participant in these American wars of conquest and helped consolidate the landmass of the continental United States.

The Mexican-American War represents a departure from the historical norm of mosquitoes devouring foreign invaders and deciding the outcome of wars. During this imperialist conflict, American military planners and commanders deliberately dodged Mexican mosquitoes. By purposefully sidestepping her swampy miasmatic death traps, they circumvented her deadly diseases and secured the rest of the west. With California statehood established in 1850, the American flag, born of the blood of revolution seventy years earlier, was hoisted from shore to shore across the vast continent and stretching domain of the United States.

Following American independence, a vanquished Britain realized the threat a growing American economy posed to her self-interest. Britain used its war with Napoleon's France to undermine American trade. Beginning in 1806, the British not only placed a trade embargo on American exports to starve Napoleon's war effort, they blockaded the middle passages of the Atlantic and boarded American merchant ships, hunting for British deserters. By 1807, the British had stolen or "impressed" roughly 6,000 American seamen into service in the Royal Navy. To keep America preoccupied in its own backyard, the British also funneled weapons and supplies from Canada to a powerful and surging indigenous coalition, led by the esteemed Shawnee warrior Tecumseh, that stretched from southern Canada to the southern United States. Like Pontiac before him, Tecumseh envisioned a sprawling pan-indigenous homeland.

Seeing as the United States was in no military or financial position to directly invade the island fortress of Britain (something that had not happened since William the Conqueror's Norman invasion of 1066), Canada was the closest and most valuable target of opportunity. During the War of 1812, often referred to as the Second American Revolution, numerous American invasions of Canada were repulsed by indigenous coalitions, British regulars, and Canadian militias, although both Tecumseh and British commander Sir Isaac Brock were killed.

In 1813, American forces looted and burned York (Toronto), the capital of Upper Canada, before evacuating the smoldering city. In retaliation, battle-hardened British regulars who arrived from Europe after defeating Napoleon in Spain, landed at Washington, DC, in August 1814. They proceeded to put the White House, Capitol, and other administrative buildings to the torch. First Lady Dolley Madison, who incidentally had lost her first husband and young son in Philadelphia's crushing yellow fever epidemic in 1793, is heroically credited with saving numerous priceless artifacts from the blazing White House.

Following the assault on Washington, the British commander, Admiral Alexander Cochrane, requested to take leave, fearing the onset of malaria and yellow fever season sponsored by the congress of mosquitoes basking in the American capital's vast labyrinth of rivers and swamps. "Cochrane had wanted to remove the entire fleet from Chesapeake Bay in late August to avoid the onset of yellow fever and malaria," reports David Petriello, "preferring instead the pestilence-free harbors of Rhode Island." Although he pleaded with his superiors that mosquito season would repulse further offensive actions, he was overruled. Mosquitoes or not, Cochrane was persuaded to assault Baltimore. His initial strike directed at its harbor bastion, Fort McHenry, inspired a defining cultural moment for the United States. In the dawn's early light of September 14, after a perilous twenty-seven-hour British naval bombardment of Fort McHenry, Francis Scott Key was still able to see the oversize American flag gallantly streaming over the wreckage of the fort. He scribbled down a poem, "Defence of Fort M'Henry," to be better known with musical accompaniment as "The Star-Spangled Banner."

By the close of 1814, neither side wanted to prolong a costly war that had devolved into stalemate. With Napoleon defeated and exiled to Elba, the causes of the war disintegrated. America now had open access to foreign markets, including Britain, and sailors were no longer being kidnapped. As President Madison lay bedridden with malaria, the Treaty of Ghent was signed on Christmas Eve 1814, ending the small war with no decisive winner. Of the 35,000 total deaths during the War of 1812, including indigenous allies and civilians, 80% were caused by disease, predominantly malaria, typhoid, and dysentery. No territory changed hands, and as a result, for all intents and purposes, Canada and America became lifelong best friends.

After the Rush-Bagot Treaty of 1817, and the subsequent Treaty of 1818, demilitarized the border and its waterways (among other cordial covenants), Canada would never again pose a so-called national security threat to the United States. The two countries remain close military allies, and they partner and reciprocate in fair and free trade. Today, within this mutually beneficial marriage, 70% of Canadian exports head south across the longest international border in the world, spanning an astounding 5,525 miles (with 350,000 people crossing daily), while 65% of Canadian imports arrive from its southern neighbor. For 2017, commerce between the two nations totaled roughly $675 billion, with an American take-home surplus of $8 billion.

Ironically, the largest battle of the War of 1812 occurred after the official peace. It was at the Battle of New Orleans that General Andrew Jackson, commanding a motley crew of militiamen, pirates, outlaws, slaves, Spaniards, newly liberated Haitians, and anyone else that he could threaten or groom into service, became a household name. In January 1815, as news of the peace was sailing across the Atlantic, Jackson and his ragtag army of 4,500 men staved off a British force three times its size. Jackson, a poor backwoods kid who had been taken prisoner at age thirteen during the American Revolution, rode his fame to the presidency.

To his supporters, Jackson was the defender of the "common man." He was touted as a war hero, a self-made man, and a champion of the underdog. To his adversaries, he was uncouth, volatile, and mentally unhinged. He was an uneducated barroom brawler prone to volcanic outbursts.* He frequently caned men in the street for, in his opinion, being dishonorable or insulting him or his wife, and challenged men to duels at the drop of a hat after dueling had become passé. As a result, for most of his life, he permanently carried two bullets lodged in his body, along with recurrent infections of malaria. His detractors commonly referred to him as "Jackass" or "Jackass Jackson." In true Jacksonian spirit, he embraced the name and the ass/donkey became the symbol for the Democratic Party. Jackson, whom Jefferson described as "a dangerous man," was elected president in 1828. The first order of business for General Jackson, as he demanded to be called rather than Mr. President, was the removal of all indigenous peoples east of the Mississippi River to Indian Territory (present-day Oklahoma). Their homelands were needed for the establishment of slave-labor cotton plantations to energize a flagging American economy.

During the 1820s, the economy of the expansionist and westward-craving country needed an overhaul. Its commercial mainstay of tobacco, which had been kick-started by John Rolfe in Jamestown, was no longer producing the profits of the past. The tobacco market was flooded, demand had leveled out, and cheaper and higher-quality tobacco was being pumped out closer to Europe by Turkey and other foreign markets. With acquisitive American eyes sharply focused on the southwest, a complete plantation renovation from tobacco to cotton would jump-start the economy and drive it forward. Cotton, which was in high demand as a replacement for wool, could be grown only in the American south. This cotton country, sweeping westward from northern Florida, Georgia, and

* Jackson's pet parrot Poll had to be removed from his state funeral to end its persistent tirade of obscenities, no doubt learned from its former master.

the Carolinas along the Gulf Coast and the interior Mississippi River delta to eastern Texas, was inhabited by populous indigenous nations, specifically the Cherokee, Creek, Chickasaw, Choctaw, and Seminole, referred to as the Five Civilized Tribes. These indigenous occupants were viewed as an obstruction to American cotton-based capitalist expansion. President Jackson, who prided himself on being a passionate "Indian fighter," fastened his personal opinions to federal policy with the passage of the 1830 Indian Removal Act.

The choice for indigenous peoples was simple: Voluntarily pack a bag and start walking to a predetermined allotment in Indian Territory or be forcefully and brutally removed and relocated to a predetermined allotment in Indian Territory. "You have but one remedy within your reach; and that is, to remove to the West," the firebrand Jackson demanded of the Cherokee in 1835. "The fate of your women and children, the fate of your people, to the remotest generation, depend on the issue. Deceive yourselves no longer." Throughout Jackson's evil but successful wars of ethnic cleansing against the Creek, Cherokee, and Seminole in Florida, Georgia, and Alabama, roughly 15% of American soldiers died of mosquito-borne disease.

During the Seminole Wars fought intermittently between 1816 and 1858 in Florida's austere, unforgiving alligator alley and mosquito-crawling sawgrass Everglades, roughly 48,000 US soldiers squared off against no more than 1,600 Seminole and Creek warriors. This conflict was the longest and most expensive "Indian War," in both money and lives, in American history.* The notorious punitive campaigns of the US Cavalry against Geronimo and his Apache, and the Sioux led by Red Cloud, Sitting Bull, and Crazy Horse in the lingering shadows of the Civil War pale in comparison.

For the average American soldier, the futile and resoundingly unpopular Seminole campaigns were a miserable, rotten, mosquito-ruled hell on earth. "The vegetation was so dense in most parts that the sun's rays seldom penetrated the earth's surface," a malaria-ridden soldier stated. "Water stood year round with little movement, and a thick layer

* The Second Seminole War (1835–1842) alone cost American taxpayers a staggering $40 million, an enormous expenditure for that time period.

of green slime covered most of the area. When the surface was disturbed, foul toxic vapors arose which caused the men to retch." Endemic malaria and yellow fever added to the psychological trauma and the combat fatigue of already edgy, brittle-nerved American troops. "The war against the Seminole Indians is one of unmitigated privation and suffering," conceded campaign commander General Winfield Scott, "without the least possible expectation of fame or glory to individuals." The Seminoles' methodical and successful use of innovative guerrilla warfare and sporadic ambush strikes, the relentless pursuit of mosquitoes and alligators, and the toxic mixture of malaria, yellow fever, and dysentery created a constant state of fear.

With quinine stores stretched thin, medical records reveal soldiers dying of "a fit of insanity produced by brain fever," "great distress in his head," or "in a fit of derangement," "mania," or "raving madness." Medical officer Jacob Motte was both bewildered and horrified that priggish, arrogant politicians were willing to sacrifice American soldiers for worthless, squalid Indian swampland, or in his estimation "the poorest country two people ever quarreled over. It is a most hideous region to live in, a perfect paradise for Indians, alligators, serpents, frogs, and every other kind of loathsome reptile." And, of course, mosquitoes. The journals and letters of combatants and military medical records portray a grizzly, fevered, paranoid, and frightened sketch of the conflict. With the straggling Seminole survivors confined to their swampy settlements in Florida (deemed valueless by American authorities) and the renegade Chief Osceola dying of malaria, however, Jackson accomplished his strategic goal of Indian Removal east of the Mississippi River.

In one of the darkest chapters in American history, as many as 100,000 indigenous peoples were force-marched to Indian Territory along what was dubbed the "Trails of Tears." It is estimated that 25,000 died during the wars of removal and on the somber journey, from starvation, disease, hypothermia, murder, and general neglect. Their former homelands, however, were now open for the businesses of cotton, slavery, and mosquito-borne disease.

Cotton production and slavery were inseparable in the South. The global demand for American cotton was literally infinite. Northern

American and British textile mills, and other foreign markets, would take as much raw cotton as slave labor could produce, which fostered a skyrocketing demand for slaves. In 1793, the US produced 5 million pounds of cotton. Thirty years later, thanks to Eli Whitney's cotton gin and the proliferation of slave labor, this output rose to 180 million pounds. On the eve of the Civil War, the South produced 85% of the world's raw cotton, and "King Cotton" in some form accounted for 50% of the total American economy. A full 80% of the southern economy was cotton driven, while the North manufactured 90% of all American goods. The two halves of the country, sundered by the Mason-Dixon Line, were so different that they were masquerading as one nation in name only.

Over this same thirty-year period between 1793 and 1823, the total number of slaves increased from 700,000 to 1.7 million. Over the next forty years, 2.5 million slaves would be bought and sold in the South. Given that many were relocated from defunct tobacco plantations in the east, the term "sold down the river" became common vernacular, as it literally meant that slaves were sold and shipped down the Mississippi River to the Deep South. For these American country-born slaves, their seasoning and hereditary genetic shields against malaria and yellow fever born and bequeathed in Africa, including sickle cell, were being diluted through interracial reproduction or "miscegenation" following the prohibition of the slave trade by Congress in 1808. These captive peoples were aware of the increased threat of mosquito-borne disease that awaited them on southern cotton plantations and adapted abolitionist John Greenleaf Whittier's 1838 poem "The Farewell" into a work song: "Gone, gone, sold and gone. . . . Where the slave-whip ceaseless swings,/ Where the noisome insect stings,/ Where the fever-demon strews/ Poison with the falling dews,/ Where the sickly sunbeams glare/Through the hot and misty air."

This territorial push and the realignment of the American economy in the South from tobacco to cotton during the first half of the nineteenth century breathed new life into the waning institution of slavery. Southern cotton fed a northern industry-fueled economic rejuvenation. This newfound export wealth in southern cotton and northern manufactured goods required additional trading ports.

America continued its Pacific push, declaring war on Mexico in 1846 to seize the western third of the United States, chiefly California. During the mosquito-sponsored revolutions that chiseled the Spanish-American Empire into self-governing states, Mexico had gained independence in 1821. America had long coveted California for its ports, to gain access to Asian markets. Numerous offers to purchase the territory were snubbed by Mexico. President James K. Polk declared war on Mexico in May 1846 to seize California and the rest of the west by gunboat diplomacy amid a substantial public antiwar outcry. As the US military readied its mighty expeditionary force, Mexican mosquitoes swarmed in wait for fresh American blood.

An American force of 75,000 marched on the halls of Montezuma against an equal number of Mexicans under the command of General Antonio Lopez de Santa Anna, a veteran of the Mexican War of Independence. An American column under General (and future president) Zachary Taylor advanced from the north, while the US Navy captured key ports in California, including San Francisco, San Diego, and Los Angeles. Simultaneously, General Winfield Scott, commander of the US Army during the Seminole campaigns, landed the main body of troops at the port of Veracruz, taking the shortest route to the capital, Mexico City.

With forty years of military service, Scott was a painstaking planner and an avid and accomplished student of military history. He was acutely aware of the death and defeat unleashed by mosquito-borne disease on unseasoned British, French, and Spanish soldiers across the Caribbean and South and Central America, including Mexico. His adversary, Santa Anna, was also aware of the damage and impairment his deadly mosquito ally could inflict on the invading Americans. As he had done during the Mexican revolution against Spain, Santa Anna intended to pin the American troop landings on the coast, biding time until the mosquito could roll out her bloodred carpet and deliver her infectious welcome. "The summer season will fall upon them unexpectedly, with its numerous diseases and epidemics," he told his senior officers, "as perilous to the unecolimated [unseasoned]; and thus, without a single shot from the Mexican ranks, they will perish daily by hundreds . . . and in a short time their regiments will be decimated."

Determined to escape the appalling, disastrous losses (and eventual defeat) exacted by eager and thirsty mosquitoes, Scott was adamant that Veracruz needed to be taken quickly to advance inland onto higher dry ground as soon as possible, to avoid yellow fever and malaria. The landing zone possessed an enemy, as he put it, "more formidable than the defences of other countries: I allude to the vomito [yellow fever]." Upon alighting at Veracruz in March 1847, a young junior officer, Lieutenant Ulysses S. Grant, shared the concern of his commander: "We will all have to get out of this part of Mexico soon or we will be caught by the yellow fever which I am ten to one more afraid of than the Mexicans." While the true nature of mosquito-borne disease had yet to be uncovered, Scott fully understood the prevailing miasma theory of illness and planned his tactical campaign to counter this disease and death toll on his troops. By purposefully sidestepping the coastal swampy lowlands, he also inadvertently bypassed the mosquito and her deadly donations of yellow fever and malaria.

Scott prevailed and quickly secured the port and, by early April, led his troops toward the capital, outsmarting both Santa Anna and the mosquito. She did not save Mexico from the Americans as she had done previously against Spain. For once, the mosquito was thwarted on her own turf, by Scott's scrupulous preparations and his steadfast insistence on fleeing her miasmic coastal hunting grounds and securing safer inland positions beyond her deadly reach. Mexico City was captured in September, compelling the formal treaty of surrender in February 1848. Although the war was unpopular both in America and abroad, Mexico ceded 55% of its territory to the United States. The wars of Manifest Destiny had conveyed the soaring and coasting civilization of Columbia to the Golden Gate and the sparkling ocean waters of the Pacific.

General Scott's academic mind and meticulous planning to purposefully countermand mosquito-borne disease secured for the US the territories of California, Nevada, Utah, Arizona, New Mexico, most of Colorado, smaller portions of Wyoming, Kansas, Oklahoma, and of course Texas. J. R. McNeill surmises that for these territorial acquisitions, America "owed everything to Scott's determination to avoid summer in the lowlands . . . free from the yellow fever zone." Scott's victory, as McNeill states, led "to the US in 1848, consolidating its position as the greatest power in the American hemisphere." Many Americans believed, however, that Mexico had been bullied and viewed the war as a cowardly act of imperialistic American aggression. Grant later declared, "I do not think there was ever a more wicked war than that waged by the United States on Mexico. I thought so at the time, when I was a youngster, only I had not moral courage enough to resign."

The Mexican-American War was the training ground for many Civil War generals, most of whom were acquaintances, if not friends, including Grant and Lee. On the Union side: George McClellan, William Tecumseh Sherman, George Meade, Ambrose Burnside, and Ulysses S. Grant. For the Confederacy: Stonewall Jackson, James Longstreet, Joseph E. Johnston, Braxton Bragg, Robert E. Lee, and future Confederate president Jefferson Davis.* Grant drew a straight line from the Mexican-American War to the Civil War: "I was bitterly opposed to the measure, and to this day regard the war, which resulted, as one of the most unjust ever waged by a stronger against a weaker nation. It was an instance of a republic following the bad example of European monarchies, in not considering justice in their desire to acquire additional territory. Texas was originally a state belonging to the republic of Mexico. . . . The occupation, separation and annexation were, from the inception of the movement to its final consummation, a conspiracy to acquire territory out of which slave states might be formed for the American Union." Here, Grant enters the debate about the future spread of slavery to this vast, newly conquered territory.

This former Mexican territory having been secured, questions arose as to the admittance of new states and territories into the Union as free or slave states. California became a free state in 1850, appeasing northerners and abolitionists alike. In return, as part of the larger 1850 Compromise, the Fugitive Slave Act was passed by Congress requiring all escaped slaves to be rebonded into slavery. Those helping or harboring runaways were fined the equivalent of $30,000. Bounty hunters were also

* In 1835, Lieutenant Jefferson Davis married Sarah, the daughter of his commanding officer, General Zachary Taylor. Three months into their marriage, they both contracted malaria and yellow fever while visiting family in Louisiana. Sarah didn't survive.

allowed to track and apprehend slaves in free states. In summary, once a slave, always a slave. Roaming "blood-hound gangs" frequently kidnapped any African American, free or not, and "returned" them into bondage. Such is the premise for the brilliant 2013 movie *12 Years a Slave,* which won the Academy Award for best picture. Fugitive slaves and free African Americans in the North now had one option—flee to Canada.

Harriet Tubman's Underground Railroad kicked into high gear, shuttling runaways and those in the north to Canada, to terminuses like Josiah Henson's farm in southern Ontario. Between the passage of the Fugitive Slave Act and the onset of the Civil War in 1861, over 60,000 African Americans found safe refuge and freedom in Canada. Henson was the basis for Harriet Beecher Stowe's influential bestselling 1852 novel *Uncle Tom's Cabin.*

Writing in response to the Fugitive Slave Act, Stowe highlighted in unadulterated, graphic prose the evils and brutality of slavery. The influence of Stowe's book in garnering support for the abolitionist movement cannot be overstated. *Uncle Tom's Cabin* cleaved a deep wound between North and South over the future of slavery. When President Lincoln met Stowe as his honored guest at the White House in 1862, he supposedly greeted her by saying, "So you are the little woman who wrote the book that started a great big war."

During the warring decades prior to the Civil War, clearing land for cotton and other agricultural pursuits in the South and West also led to an explosion of mosquitoes and a broader dissemination of malaria and yellow fever. Malaria was a monotonous fact of frontier life. "By the 1850s, malaria was extensively endemic throughout the United States," reports epidemiologist Mark Boyd in his 1,700-page treatise *Malariology,* "with hyperendemic areas in the southeastern states, the Ohio River Valley, Illinois River Valley, and practically all of the Mississippi River Valley from St. Louis to the Gulf." As population densities increased and port cities along the Gulf Coast and the Mississippi River became hubs for global trade, malaria and yellow fever flourished.

The macabre storyteller Edgar Allan Poe captured the pervasiveness of yellow fever in his 1842 "The Masque of the Red Death": "And now was acknowledged the presence of the Red Death. He had come like a thief in the night. And one by one dropped the revelers in the blood-bedewed halls of their revel. . . . And Darkness and Decay and the Red Death held illimitable dominion over all." New Orleans, Vicksburg, Memphis, Galveston, Pensacola, and Mobile were home to annual epidemics of yellow fever for three decades prior to the Civil War. The epidemic of 1853 was particularly virulent, killing 13,000 people across the Gulf Coast, including 9,000 in New Orleans alone. "Such scenes of mass death, burial trenches, and refugees call to mind parallels with Civil War battlefields," historian Mark Schantz reminds us. "The New Orleans death count . . . from the summer of 1853, for example, would have been far greater than the total number of Confederate dead who fell at Gettysburg in the summer of 1863." In Mobile, Dr. Josiah Nott, who was among the early proponents of an insect-vector cause of yellow fever, reported, "Certain it is that in many villages around the Gulf States, this fearful epidemic committed ravages far beyond decimation."

During this thirty-year reign of yellow fever across the South, New Orleans, as usual, was hit especially hard, with 50,000 people dying of the disease. Across the United States, from its first appearance on the Atlantic coast in 1693 to its curtain call in New Orleans in 1905, when the city was at last freed from its reputation as a crypt of despondency and death, yellow fever claimed the lives of over 150,000 people.* These mosquito-dispensed epidemics and her domination of death was only a dress rehearsal for the looming clouds of war and desolation that would soon shroud the angsty nation.

The solidification of international borders and the new lands conquered and seized during its wars of Manifest Destiny against British Canada, indigenous peoples, and Mexico brought the maturing but insecure United States to a cultural, political, and economic breaking point. The mosquito-ravaged and conflicted nation turned its growing pains inward during its horrendous, monumental Civil War to settle a socioeconomic sibling rivalry between free North and slave South. During this struggle, the mosquito went on an unadulterated feeding frenzy and sponsored a Union victory, finally deciding the issue of "a house

* During this same period, it is estimated that between 500,000 and 600,000 people contracted yellow fever, putting the overall mortality rate at 25–30%.

divided against itself." She was the most skilled stalker on the battlefields and emancipated ghosts by the thousands "that a nation might live." The mosquito ensured President Lincoln's "new birth of freedom—and that a government of the people, by the people, for the people, shall not perish from this earth." Lincoln's definition of people included African Americans. During the Civil War, mosquitoes acted as a third army of sorts, and primarily aided the northern cause of preserving the Union, and, eventually, with the unfurling of Lincoln's 1863 Emancipation Proclamation, aided in abolishing the very institution of slavery she herself helped to create.

CHAPTER 15

Sinister Angels of Our Nature: The American Civil War

On November 21, 1864, a haggard and forlorn President Abraham Lincoln sat slouched at his desk, staring through sunken eyes at a blank piece of paper. Only fifty-four years old, he had been aged by three and a half years of bloody civil war, his face now worn and drawn by too many sleepless nights brooding over the dead. Although he was witnessing the last stumbling steps of the starving Confederacy, he found little solace in knowing that the end was near. The body count had attained horrifying heights no one could have imagined when he mobilized his army on April 15, 1861, to preserve the Union.

How could he put into words the sacrifices made by so many who gave "the last full measure of devotion"? He lifted his head, pressed his pen, and breathed life into the leaf of paper. "Executive Mansion, Washington, Nov. 21, 1864," began Lincoln, before formally introducing his letter to Mrs. Lydia Bixby, a widow of Boston:

> Dear Madam,
>
> I have been shown in the files of the War Department a statement of the Adjutant General of Massachusetts that you are the mother of five sons who have died gloriously on the field of battle.
>
> I feel how weak and fruitless must be any word of mine which should attempt to beguile you from the grief of a loss so overwhelming. But I cannot refrain from tendering you

the consolation that may be found in the thanks of the Republic they died to save.

I pray that our Heavenly Father may assuage the anguish of your bereavement, and leave you only the cherished memory of the loved and lost, and the solemn pride that must be yours to have laid so costly a sacrifice upon the altar of freedom.

Yours, very sincerely and respectfully,
A. Lincoln*

Yet Lincoln, born to humble means at Sinking Spring Farm in the slave state of Kentucky in 1809, had been cultivated and matured by a country that was seemingly always at war. His life shadowed the wars of Manifest Destiny from the War of 1812 to the Mexican-American War. He had even briefly served as a militia captain in 1832 during Black Hawk's War in Illinois, one of President Andrew Jackson's numerous ethnic-cleansing military crusades to force the relocation of indigenous peoples, during his callous 1830s policy of Indian Removal. Lincoln summed up his only military service, which lasted a whopping three weeks, with one brief remark: "I fought, I bled, and came away. I had many bloody struggles with mosquitoes; and although I never fainted from loss of blood, I can truly say that I was often hungry."

Fierce and bloody struggles with mosquitoes, or "gallinippers" as they were called by soldiers, were a run-of-the-mill, everyday part of military life during the Civil War. Skirmishing with single-minded, bloodthirsty mosquitoes was as common and mundane as marching or carrying a weapon and was an unofficial routine duty of soldierly conduct and drill. "For Billy Yank and Johnny Reb the war was as much a story of putrid infections and burning fevers as one of long marches and frontal assaults. . . . Simply stated, had mosquito-borne illness not been part of the South's landscape in the 1860s, the story of the war would be different," points out Andrew McIlwaine Bell in his meticulous and impressive

* It was later revealed that of Mrs. Bixby's five sons, two survived the war, two were killed in action, and one likely died a prisoner of war.

work *Mosquito Soldiers: Malaria, Yellow Fever, and the Course of the American Civil War.* "Soldiers on both sides frequently complained about these annoying insects that fed on their blood, buzzed in their ears, invaded their tents, and generally contributed to the misery of army life. Little did they suspect that these pests were also helping to shape the larger political and military events of the era." Not only did the mosquito play a pivotal role in the outcome of the war, but after two years of fraternal butchery on the battlefields, she also profoundly shifted Lincoln's strategic objectives for the bloodstained struggle itself. In doing so, the mosquito forever restructured and re-formed the cultural and political face of the nation.

During the first years of the war, the mosquito, assisted by competent Confederate commanders, hammered Union forces led by hesitant and ham-fisted generals, effecting an atmosphere of attrition and "total war." Lincoln's initial goal, of preserving the Union and its undivided economic portfolio, was gradually tailored to include a complementary nation-defining war aim—the abolition of slavery. Had the mosquito not prolonged the war and had the Union realized a quick victory, as expected, the Emancipation Proclamation would never have entered the pages of history.

In a twist of irony, the mosquito was not only a cause of the African slave trade, but during the Civil War she also helped put the final nail in the coffin of the institution of slavery itself, unshackling roughly 4.2 million African Americans from their chains of bondage along the way. Bell acknowledges, "By unwittingly serving as soldiers, mosquitoes have done more to shape our history than most people realize." He narrows this assertion by reasoning that "the important role these insects played cannot be ignored by any scholar aspiring to understand the Civil War in all its wonderful and dizzying complexity."

The causes of the Civil War were also complex and certainly not as simple as opposing views on slavery between the North and South. Slavery was undeniably *a* cause but not *the* cause to the exclusion of other instigators. Numerous economic, political, and cultural factors also played their part. With the argument for secession gaining momentum, the election of 1860 delivering Abraham Lincoln to the White House was the crowning blow to southern convictions. While Lincoln repeatedly assured the slave states that he would not abolish the institution where it already existed, he was also adamant that slavery could not spread west into new states and territories. Poor white farmers, like his own father, needed an opportunity to make a decent living farming food crops on "free soil" detached from the no-win wage competition with unpaid slave labor. The simple economics of slavery impoverished all spectrums of American society, slaves and freemen alike. The money-spinning fusion of slavery and cotton could continue as it also fueled northern industrial wealth. The merging of slavery with other unrelated agricultural markets would not be permitted. Not only did the southern states want to expand slavery westward, in the end they also simply did not trust the new president-elect. They believed that once sworn into office, Lincoln would abolish slavery. Between Lincoln's victory in November 1860 and his formally taking office in March 1861, the quilted union of thirty-four "united states" came unstitched.

Prior to Lincoln's inauguration, seven states peacefully seceded from the Union, issuing individual Declarations of the Immediate Causes of Secession. Together, they formed a government with a capital, first at Montgomery, Alabama, and then, as of May 1861, at Richmond, Virginia. They ratified a constitution and elected Jefferson Davis president of the Confederate States of America. Upon his swearing-in on March 4, Lincoln inherited a country on the verge of Civil War. "In your hands, my dissatisfied fellow countrymen, and not in mine," he reflected during his inaugural address, "is the momentous issue of civil war." War arrived a month later, when Confederate troops forced the surrender of Fort Sumter in Charleston Harbor. By June, four more states voted for secession, rounding out the eleven states of the Confederacy. "Both sides deprecated war, but one of them would make war rather than let a nation survive," expressed Lincoln, "and the other would accept war rather than let it perish. And War came." When the first shots of the rebellion ricocheted off the walls of Fort Sumter on April 12, 1861, Lincoln's unwavering war aim was to preserve the territorial and economic integrity of the nation—including southern slavery.

Like the American colonies during the revolution, all that was left for the Confederacy was to win the war. Unlike for the colonists, however, help would not arrive. There would be no genius foreign general like the Marquis de Lafayette to answer the call and no equivalent French fleet to break the garroting Union naval blockade. The Confederacy gambled on two rolls of the dice. The first was that Lincoln would back down. He didn't. The second was that Britain, dependent on southern cotton to fuel its lucrative textile industry, would come to a Confederate rescue and break the Union blockade, or at worst, send military supplies and other resources. It didn't.

Britain had banned the slave trade in 1807 and banned slavery itself in 1833. Its population was fiercely opposed to slavery, an opposition that only intensified after *Uncle Tom's Cabin* became an instant national bestseller in 1852. Britain was also fiercely opposed to yellow fever. There was great consternation among politicians and civilians alike that ships making the Home-Islands-Caribbean-Confederacy-Home-Islands run would be floating carriages of death. "Although the finer points of the discussions taking place," conveys Mark Harrison, professor of the history of medicine at Oxford, "were probably unknown to most of the public, the occurrence of two outbreaks of yellow fever on European soil in the space of a few years created great alarm." The British media speculated that "climate and terrible yellow fever" might allow the Confederacy to defy "all the levies that the North can bring against it." Britain wanted no part of the Confederacy's yellow fever, which, ironically, never materialized.

For decades prior to the Civil War, the southern states were ravaged by mosquito-borne disease. For this reason, unlike in wars of the past, yellow fever did not affect the outcome of this war, for it had already bestowed immunity on the survivors. In addition, at the onset of war, the Union Navy implemented General-in-Chief Winfield Scott's "Anaconda Plan," blockading Confederate ports, putting a stranglehold on southern trade. Foreign ships, specifically those from the Caribbean, could not make port and deliver their cargo or distribute the dreaded virus and its disease-vectoring sailors and mosquitoes.

New Orleans, the heart of Dixie trade, was captured a year into the war in April 1862, followed by Memphis a month later, effectively damming the Mississippi River and choking the flow of blockade runners and Confederate supplies. In doing so, the Union also inadvertently closed river access to yellow fever, saving the occupying forces from the nightmare of disease and death that historically engulfed New Orleans and the Mississippi delta. Confederate planners fully expected New Orleans to be a headache for the Union. A Virginia newspaper predicted that the vital port of New Orleans would be "a prize which will cost them vastly more to keep than the animal is worth, if his Saffron Majesty [yellow fever] shall make his annual visit." Sharing this same fear, a Union surgeon forecasted at the outbreak of war that "throughout both the North and South it was prophesied that the great scourge of the tropics, yellow fever, would decimate any northern armies that might penetrate the 'Cotton States' within the 'yellow fever zone.'"

As it turned out, yellow fever was scarce during the war, especially in New Orleans, where it killed only eleven residents. The Union occupation force maintained stringent sanitation measures and a strict quarantine. During the Civil War, only 1,355 cases and 436 deaths were reported among Union troops. As the Anaconda Plan tightened its stranglehold on the South, yellow fever became increasingly less likely. However, the same cannot be said for its sibling malaria. While yellow fever was kept in check, malaria flourished.

Like yellow fever, malaria was chronic prior to the Civil War, but unlike yellow fever, it continued to stalk the battlefields, debilitating millions between 1861 and 1865. "Mosquitoes," decreed a malaria-stricken soldier from Connecticut, "were the most awful enemies" he ever encountered. The total military mobilization of 3.2 million men during the war allowed malaria to blossom and thrive. Unseasoned Yankee soldiers crossed the Mason-Dixon Line into the South in huge numbers, breaching the epidemiological barrier. "As men from all over the country assembled to settle the issues of federalism and slavery on the battlefield, the mosquitoes of the South were galvanized by the large number of new prey that suddenly appeared in their midst," stresses Bell. "And before the guns fell silent, these tiny insects played a significant, and heretofore underappreciated, role in the events of the Civil War." With the mass movement and migration of soldiers and civilians across our three zones of infection, pulsating mosquito populations took flight and quickened the marching steps of malaria.

Without British aid, the undermanned and undersupplied Confederacy was left to fight it out alone against both mosquitoes and the Union. Lincoln's military machine possessed an overwhelming advantage in everything needed to win a war, from manpower, resources, infrastructure, industry, and foodstuffs to all manner of weapons, as well as quinine, as crucial to victory as bullets and bayonets. The only portfolios that tipped South were raw cotton and slaves and yet on the front lines, the Confederacy controlled the first two years of the war.

Until the concurrent Union victories at Gettysburg and Vicksburg in July 1863, the underdog Confederacy was driving the momentum of the war, and Johnny Reb and the mosquito were getting the better of Lincoln's overconfident blue-clad Yankee boys and their bumbling generals. For the North, which had every military benefit, the war was not supposed to have lasted this long nor stooped and descended into a war of attrition. Forecast to be fleeting and steeply tilted in favor of the Union when the first few harmless Confederate shots were lobbed at Fort Sumter, this rebellion of the southern states was ferociously set ablaze at the First Battle of Bull Run.

On a beautiful sunny day in July 1861, Wilmer McLean sat on his front porch in Manassas, Virginia, listening to the rumble of artillery and the clatter of marching soldiers. His house had been commandeered to headquarter Confederate general P. G. T. Beauregard. In the distance, he could see hundreds of well-dressed, dapper spectators on the surrounding hilltops, sitting in chairs under shade umbrellas, snacking from wicker picnic baskets. These were the enraptured elite and wealthy of Washington, DC, including numerous senators, congressmen, and their families, who had made the twenty-five-mile journey to watch the bloody spectacle and historic event, not wanting to miss the Union crushing the southern rebels in one swift stroke. As the whining grew louder, McLean covered his head and shuddered as a Union cannonball ripped through his kitchen chimney, prompting Beauregard to write that "a comical effect of this artillery fight was the destruction of the dinner of myself and staff." It was the mosquito that had chosen McLean's front yard near

Bull Run Creek as the site for the first significant salvos of the Civil War, although she cannot be held liable for destroying his kitchen.

Winfield Scott, commanding general of the United States Army, was a veteran of the War of 1812, the Seminole Wars, and the Mexican-American War. Having already served for a staggering fifty-four years, he knew firsthand the dangers mosquito-borne disease presented for unseasoned troops. He had outwitted both Santa Anna and the mosquito in Mexico and was not prepared to sacrifice his soldiers to her bite with a southern campaign against Confederate homelands. At the onset of the Civil War, Scott warned both President Lincoln and his immediate military subordinate, Major General George McClellan, that if the Union did not attack the South immediately, the public would grow impatient. By design, however, his Anaconda Plan needed time to starve out the Confederacy. Scott was also aware that the public, shielded by climate from endemic mosquito-borne disease, did not fully appreciate the grim reality of fighting in southern mosquito country. "They will urge instant and vigorous action, regardless I fear of the consequences," he counseled. "That is, unwilling to wait for the slow instruction . . . and the return of frosts to kill the virus of malignant fevers below Memphis."

When the War Cabinet met in June 1861, a month before Bull Run, the decision facing its members was whether to mount the main offensive in Virginia or the Mississippi River Valley. Virginia won the contest because it was resolved that it would be military suicide to "go into an unhealthy country to fight them." Union physicians had also warned Lincoln that "northern troops, in passing now no farther south even than the lower Chesapeake enter a climate entirely foreign to their constitution [with] marsh miasm." On July 21, 1861, at the mosquito-selected site near the McLean house in Manassas, Virginia, on the banks of Bull Run Creek, the two armies finally clashed.

After fierce fighting throughout most of the day, and a stubborn stand by Confederate general Thomas J. Jackson, earning him immortality as "Stonewall" Jackson, the chaotic Union forces and a disorderly mob of shocked and rattled spectators fled in a panicked, rain-dashed retreat back to Washington, somersaulting the nation toward total war. Overconfident Union forces were routed in what was the largest and bloodiest battle in American history up to that point. This distinction and military achievement would be repeatedly shattered during the brutal battles that lay ahead, with names like Antietam, Shiloh, Chancellorsville, Spotsylvania, Chickamauga, and Gettysburg that still resonate through the collective consciousness of the country. Littered with the battered, disfigured, bloated bodies of thousands of Americans, on the blood-soaked battlefield of Bull Run any prospects, delusions, or pipe dreams of a short war went up in smoke. This was going to be a protracted, grisly struggle, and the mosquito would do everything in her power to prolong it.

Following First Bull Run, McClellan dithered for almost a year, allowing the Confederacy to organize a war economy as best it could, mobilize its military resources, and dig in. Aware of an impending assault on Richmond, both Davis and Lee authorized the transfer of troops from the Deep South to Richmond, knowing that mosquito season would prevent Union operations in this southern theater while sparing their own troops from disease. "At this season I think it impossible for the enemy to make any expedition into the interior," wrote Lee. "The troops that you retain there will suffer more from disease than the enemy." President Davis added that "decisive operations are pending here in this section, and the climate already restrains operations on the coast." Davis stressed that these reinforcements come only "from positions where the season will prevent active operations." Lee's Confederate Army of roughly 100,000, burrowed in around Richmond, was ready for McClellan's Union Peninsula Campaign. The next generations of Yorktown's drooling history-making mosquitoes, whose ancestors had fed on the British eighty years earlier, were now flying in wait for McClellan's men.

McClellan was an overly obsessive planner, lacked an aggressive military mind, habitually overestimated enemy strengths, and was apprehensive that defeat or any considerable loss of troops under his command would damage and weaken his designs on the presidency. A frustrated Lincoln and the scathing media clamored for action. McClellan eventually bowed to mounting pressure and began his much-anticipated strike on Richmond in March 1862. "Little Mac" channeled 120,000 men up the peninsula between the now familiar York and James Rivers riven by creeks and swamps—ideal mosquito festival grounds. Having disembarked his numerically superior force, instead of seizing the initiative, the blundering McClellan employed his favored military pastime of hurry up and wait.

Following the Union capture of Yorktown in mid-April, McClellan's nervous jitters, plus a stiff Confederate delaying action, ground the Union advance to a slow crawl among the rising rivers and swamps created by the spring thaw and April showers. A Union soldier testified to being assailed by "an army of Virginia mosquitoes. . . . They were the largest specimens I ever saw and the most blood-thirsty as well." Another complained of being probed by "squads of full-grown mosquitoes." Union surgeon Dr. Alfred Castleman commented, "Everything soaked in rain, chilly, and cheerless. But we are gradually becoming amphibious." Over the next two months, Union forces advanced a mere thirty miles through the Jamestown/Yorktown mosquito colonies. Dr. Castleman summed up the disease environment: "Sickness among the troops rapidly increasing. Remittent fever, diarrhea, and dysentery prevail." Malaria and dysentery were by far the most crippling diseases of the war.

As Union forces crept toward Richmond, malarial sickness began to increase, adding to escalating battle casualties. By the end of May, with his army at the city gates, McClellan was deliriously ill and bedridden with malaria. By this time, 26% of the Union Army was too sick to fight. During his malarial absence, partitioned Union columns floundered in an area the Confederates called the "pestilent marshes of the Peninsula." Union command structure broke down and supplies of quinine were left in the rear to allow for the forward movement of ammunition, artillery, and other supplies. Malaria and dysentery continued their upsurge into June and July.

Confederate soldier John Beall understood the perils of the Union position. "McClellan now encamped . . . being exposed to the malarious and miasmatic winds," he reported home. "His army, with its strength shattered by fatigue, hunger, excitement, and dispirited by defeat, must fall by thousands before fevers and sickness." McClellan's weakened army could not crack Richmond's defensive perimeter and in late June,

Lee launched fierce counterattacks that drove Union forces into a headlong retreat back to the coast. The Union ineffective sick list had reached 40% of their total manpower. "The subtle malaria of the rebel soil," confessed Union surgeon Edwin Bidwell, "destroys and disables more Northern soldiers than all the wounds received from rebel arms." Confederate forces were positioned on higher ground and away from the marshes and mosquitoes. While malaria did diminish southern strength, sickness in the Confederate ranks during the campaign was considerably lower, fluctuating between 10% and 15%.

McClellan's subordinate, Brigadier General Erasmus Keyes, wrote to Lincoln urging the president to withhold reinforcements and extract the army entirely: "To bring troops freshly raised at the North to the country in the months of July, August, and September would be to cast our resources to the sea. The raw troops would melt away and be ruined forever." Although McClellan was begging for reinforcements for another crack at Richmond, he was bluntly told to evacuate the mosquito-plagued peninsula because "to keep your army in its present position until it could be so re-enforced would almost destroy it in that climate. The months of August and September are almost fatal to whites who live on that part of the James River." Just as they had forced the surrender of Cornwallis at Yorktown, Virginia's malarious mosquitoes helped prolong the Civil War by aiding in McClellan's embarrassing failure to capture the capital of Richmond. "The high rate of malaria during the Peninsular Campaign helped expedite the Army of the Potomac's retreat to Washington," reiterates Bell. "McClellan's defeat, in part attributable to disease, triggered a sea change in the North's approach to the war; afterwards it would work to destroy slavery and create a new birth of freedom rather than fight exclusively to preserve the old republic." Harassed by mosquitoes, McClellan failed to deliver Lincoln a victory in the east. Meanwhile, his mosquito-hounded commanders in the west did not deliver, either.

While the malarious mosquito was melting McClellan's army in Virginia, she also prolonged the war in the west by rebuffing the Union's first attempt to take the Confederate stronghold of Vicksburg, Mississippi, between May and July 1862. She also contributed to the decision not to march on Vicksburg from the north after the Union victory at Corinth in northern Mississippi in May 1862. Having maneuvered the Confederate Army under Beauregard out of Corinth, roughly ninety miles due east of Memphis, Union commander General Henry Halleck was wary of pursuing him south of Scott's "Memphis Line" at the onset of yellow fever and malaria season. He rightly believed that a southern advance toward Vicksburg would be suicide by mosquito. "If we follow the enemy into the swamps of Mississippi," he reported to his political masters in Washington, "there can be no doubt that our army will be disabled by disease." His army was already thinning from the tag team of malaria and dysentery. While laid up with malaria, Major General William Tecumseh Sherman, not yet a household name, alerted his superiors that only half of his 10,000 soldiers were fit for duty. Prior to retreating south to fight another day, Beauregard reported that roughly 15% of his men were suffering from malaria. General Halleck stayed put, refusing to give chase for fear of mosquito-borne disease.

Instead, it was Admiral David Farragut who led his men into the malarial trap plotted and prepared by the mosquitoes of Vicksburg. Having captured New Orleans in April 1862, Farragut was ordered to proceed north along the Mississippi. As a communications, supply, and transportation hub, Vicksburg was too important for the Union to pass over and ignore. "Vicksburg," proclaimed Jefferson Davis, "is the nail head that holds the South's two halves together."

Farragut made a halfhearted aborted attempt to capture Vicksburg, or the "Gibraltar of the West," in May. Because Vicksburg was the last Confederate stronghold on the Mississippi, Lincoln and his military strategists were frustrated with Farragut's lackluster effort and were restless to secure source-to-mouth control of the river to entirely cut the Confederate lifeline. Farragut was ordered to renew the Vicksburg offensive in late June with a combined fleet of 3,000 soldiers. "Awaiting them were ten thousand Confederates," Bell weighs in, "and an untold number of anopheles mosquitoes. Both proved to be lethal deterrents." The fortress city of Vicksburg is situated on a high bluff on a peninsula at a horseshoe-shaped bend in the eastern shore of the river, surrounded by clusters of untamed and interspersed swamps and backwater channels. There was no viable access to the towering city aside from the fronting river. The geography prevented Farragut from pressing his naval superiority or landing troops. As a solution, he attempted to dig a canal across the neck of the peninsula to bypass the fortified cliffs. Everything he tried was repulsed by mosquitoes.

Union troops, reported Brigadier General Thomas Williams from Vicksburg, were "yet so affected by malaria as to be good for nothing." When Farragut finally abandoned his operation in late July, 75% of the troops under his command were either dead or hospitalized by mosquito-borne disease. "The only course now to be pursued," it was suggested, "is to yield to the climate and postpone any further action at Vicksburg till the fever season is over." Confederate commander General Edmund Kirby Smith concurred. "The enemy will, I think, attempt no invasion of Mississippi or Alabama this summer," Smith advised his superior, General Braxton Bragg. "The character of the country, the climate . . . are insurmountable obstacles." With McClellan's simultaneous mosquito-chased retreat from Richmond, the Confederate states were winning their war of independence.

Considering the 1862 humiliations in Virginia and at Vicksburg, Secretary of the Treasury Salmon P. Chase, an early advocate of enlisting African Americans, said aloud what most other Union politicians and military minds were already thinking. "We cannot maintain the contest with the disadvantages of unacclimated troops and distant supplies against an enemy enabled to bring one-half the population under arms with the other half held in labor, with no cost except that of bare subsistence for the armed moiety." Although Chase was instrumental in securing the phrase "In God We Trust" on American currency in 1864, during the Civil War, God was on the side of the biggest and best quinine-supplied battalions. The mosquito, in concert with morality and manpower considerations, unseated and deposed the established cultural, racial, and legal conventions of the United States by scripting the environment for the Emancipation Proclamation with its promise of a new birth of freedom for African Americans kept and guaranteed by General Ulysses S. Grant.

Collectively, the Union defeats during the spring and summer of 1862 upended Union strategy. Lincoln and his advisors agreed on a new way forward—the complete annihilation of Confederate armies and a policy of starvation-enforced capitulation of the entire southern war effort and economy through the eradication of slavery. "Those who deny freedom to others," remarked Lincoln, "deserve it not for themselves." The losses and mosquito-induced military blunders of 1862, argues Bell, "helped convince the Lincoln administration that only the complete subjugation of the South, including the dismantling of slavery, would restore the Union and bring peace." Charles Mann agrees that malaria "delayed the Union victory by months or even years. In the long run this may be worth celebrating. Initially the North proclaimed that its goal was to preserve the nation, not free slaves. . . . The longer the war ground on, the more willing grew Washington to consider radical measures." Given the role of the mosquito in prolonging the grinding conflict, he reckons that "part of the credit for the Emancipation Proclamation be assigned to malaria." Following the first Union victory (or more accurately a draw) at the meat-grinding Battle of Antietam in September 1862, Lincoln forever altered the direction of the war and the nation itself by drafting his most celebrated and enduring executive order.*

On January 1, 1863, the Emancipation Proclamation legally liberated (at least on paper) roughly 3.5 million enslaved African Americans in select areas of the Confederacy, specifically those states still in rebellion.† It also officially sanctioned and authorized the enlistment of African Americans to fight in a war that Lincoln whispered "was in some way about slavery." While the impetus for Lincoln's deliverance of the Confederate slave population was a moral one, it was also directly coupled to military pragmatism. As argued by Chase, freed acclimated slaves would

* After scoring a victory at Second Bull Run, Lee invaded the North and clashed with Union forces at Antietam Creek near Sharpsburg, Maryland, on September 17, 1862. Although the battle was really a draw, it was spun as a Union victory as Lee's forces retreated from the North back to Virginia. Combined casualties during the single-day battle totaled almost 23,000, including 3,700 killed (another 4,000 would later die of wounds). Antietam remains the bloodiest single day of combat in American history.

† The Proclamation applied only to slaves in Confederate-held territory and did not include the non-Confederate slave states of Delaware, Maryland, Kentucky, and Missouri, nor Tennessee, which had been previously occupied by Union forces.

strengthen Union numbers, while at the same time depriving the Confederacy of its workforce.

Although this component of the Emancipation Proclamation is generally overlooked, the decree was correspondingly designed as a military measure to reduce Confederate labor, forcing the reassignment of frontline fighting troops to the fields and factories. "The president's decision to emancipate slaves and arm them for the purpose of killing their former masters represented a radical departure from his earlier policies," acknowledges Bell. "The military reversals of 1862, however, convinced Lincoln that emancipation and black enlistment were military necessities. Both policies strengthened northern forces while robbing the Confederacy of its chief labor force." Lincoln also shared the belief of medical authorities and advisors that African American soldiers equipped with their impenetrable genetic defenses to mosquito-borne disease would be invaluable to operations in the seething theaters of the Deep South to "hold points on the Mississippi during the sickly season." According to Surgeon General William A. Hammond, it was a "well-ascertained fact" that Africans were "less liable to the affections of malarious origin than the European." Of the roughly 200,000 African Americans who eventually served in Union forces, two-thirds had formerly been southern slaves. With their newfound freedom, they enlisted to ensure the emancipation of their captive brethren by fighting on the front lines and battlefields of a war that was now being waged to decide the fate of slavery itself.

Along with the primary aim of preserving the economic integrity of the Union, the war was now also about expunging and purging slavery, with its windfall of military expediency. "The Emancipation Proclamation transformed the moral atmosphere of the war," grants distinguished military historian John Keegan. "Thenceforward the war was about slavery." Without a Union victory, however, the Proclamation was nothing more than a paper tiger. The freedom of over four million people hung in the balance, and they clung to the hope of a Union victory and the unconditional surrender of the Confederacy. Ulysses S. Grant, with the aid of quinine and an allied General Anopheles, delivered, bringing the rousing words of Lincoln's Proclamation to life and into legal reality.

Unlike McClellan, who was defeated by Lincoln in the 1864 presidential election, Grant had no political machinations or pretenses and was not afraid to gamble on the battlefield. He was introverted, quiet, awkward, and quirky, but he was also a hard-charger and was willing to sacrifice lives to achieve victory, which earned him the nickname "the Butcher." His campaign at Vicksburg between May and July 1863 was a bold, brilliant, and successful masterstroke of generalship. In later years, Grant scrutinized and commented on his own performance and war record. In his typical self-disparaging manner, he asserted that all his Civil War campaigns could be enhanced and improved bar one: Vicksburg. During mosquito season, Grant ran the Union fleet past the gauntlet of Vicksburg's guns, landing his men south of the city. The press maligned his initial movements. Due to mosquito-borne disease, armchair-general newspaper reporters concluded, "The simple substance of it is, that an army of seventy-five thousand men would find their graves between now and the first of October without ever facing an enemy." General Lee also believed that any Union advance on Vicksburg during the sweltering summer mosquito months was highly improbable.

But Grant wasn't worried about second-guessers nor concerned with Lee's sensible combat estimate. Ulysses S. Grant was a winner, unlike the parade of tripping Union generals before him. "I hope yet to fool the rebels and effect a landing where they do not expect me," he relayed to his staff officers. And he did just that by severing his own supply lines and marching his army through the backdoor swamps surrounding Vicksburg. With his store ships unable to run the river past Vicksburg's elevated guns, Grant's soldiers were forced to live off the land. It was a brilliant stroke of military maneuvering. During his encirclement of the city, he captured several smaller ports as well as the state capital, Jackson.

As a supporting operation to Grant's main thrust, a Union detachment of 30,000 to 40,000 soldiers, including nine recently mobilized regiments of US Colored Troops composed primarily of emancipated slaves, cordoned Port Hudson, located 20 miles north of Baton Rouge and 150 miles south of the besieged river bastion of Vicksburg. A staunch advocate of enlisting African Americans for military service, Grant reminded Lincoln that "I have given the subject of arming the negro my hearty support. This, with the emancipation of the negro, is the heaviest blow yet given to the Confederacy." Having squeezed the Confederate fortifications at Vicksburg with a Union line stretching 15 miles and unsettled by two fruitless yet costly frontal assaults on entrenched defenders, Grant initiated his siege on May 25—directly at the onset of mosquito season.

Grant, however, knew he had an advantage that the depleted and besieged defenders of Vicksburg did not. While he had proven himself willing to leave his rations and supply depots behind, there was no way he was slogging through to muck about the swamps of Mississippi without stockpiles of quinine. One of the most important munitions in the Union's arsenal was its abundant supply of this antimalarial medication. "The advantage this drug gave to Union forces cannot be overstated," emphasizes Bell. "In fact," he says of his own book, "one could argue without too much hyperbole that a more appropriate subtitle for this book might have been 'How Quinine Saved the North.' . . . The Confederacy, on the other hand, experienced quinine shortages for most of the war, which meant that malarial fevers among Rebels went unchecked more often than not. Southern civilians also suffered."

Over the course of the war, the Union dispensed 19 tons of refined quinine and 10 tons of unrefined cinchona bark to its soldiers as both a treatment and a prophylactic for malaria. For the Confederacy, however, "the effectiveness of the Union naval blockade meant that southern surgeons . . . suffered from quinine shortages for most of the war," says Bell. "Given the prevalence of malaria in the South, it is astonishing that any Confederate troops were healthy enough to fight by the end of the war, when Richmond's quinine supplies were extremely low." This precious quinine certainly did not trickle down to the troops on the battlefield. Confederate politicians, including Jefferson Davis, had healthy stocks of quinine tucked away for themselves and their families. Ironically, while the naval blockade halted yellow fever, it allowed malaria to thrive.

The astronomically increasing price of quinine in the Confederacy throughout the war attests to the cumulative effects of the Union blockade. It also signals that the smugglers knew just how crucial and sought-after the diminishing supply of the medicine was to a southern population

"Advantage of 'Famine Prices'": An 1863 cartoon from *Harper's Weekly* mocking the shortage and skyrocketing price of quinine in the Confederacy. "Sick Boy: 'I know one thing—I wish I was in Dixie.' Nurse: 'And why do you wish you was in Dixie, you wicked boy?' Sick Boy: 'Because I read that quinine is worth one hundred and fifty dollars an ounce there; and if it was that here, you wouldn't pitch it into me so!'" *(Library of Congress)*

suffering from unrelenting endemic malaria. In the opening year of the war, an ounce of quinine averaged $4, increasing to $23 by 1863. At the close of 1864, on the black market supplied by blockade runners, the price per ounce ranged from $400 to $600. By war's end, quinine smugglers operating out of the Caribbean were making an incredible 2,500% return on their initial investment.

As the dealing in contraband quinine became increasingly profitable, it was smuggled into the Confederacy by any means possible, including many of the same creative methods used by drug mules or traffickers today. It was sewn into the bustles and skirts of women masquerading as traveling nuns or aid workers. It was stuffed and stitched inside children's dolls, furniture, and upholstery. To clear Union customs and navigate checkpoints, carefully packaged cinchona powder was transported inside the anal canals and intestines of livestock. At the gates of Vicksburg, Grant's sentries apprehended a trio of women carrying contraband quinine under false bottoms of their luggage. The lifesaving drug was confiscated and doled out to Union soldiers, although unlike their malaria-pricked Confederate counterparts, they had plenty of quinine in circulation already.

Grant's medical staff at Vicksburg had enough quinine on hand not only to treat malarial patients but also to distribute daily preventive doses to healthy soldiers. "The hospital arrangements and medical attendance were so perfect, that the loss of life was much less than might have been expected," Grant said in praise. "I venture the assertion that no Army ever went into the field with better arranged preparations." Quinine was so abundant that it was even administered to feverish "sallow-cheeked and sunken-eyed" Confederate prisoners and to local "haggard and care-worn" civilians. Malaria still incapacitated 15% of Grant's force during the campaign as the drug—depending on the dosage, quality, and concentration of the active quinine ingredient—is not perfectly mosquito-proof, and many men refused to take the bitter medicine.

The beleaguered Confederate forces and civilians trapped inside Vicksburg with dwindling provisions and no quinine were not so fortunate and faced a bleak, mosquito-bristling reality. "The dreary wastes of oozy swamp and fen," wrote a British war correspondent, were deadlier "than sword or bullet." Without quinine, "no man alive could have counteracted the effects of that climate," he concluded. Rebel soldiers and hapless residents ensnared by Grant's dazzling strategic designs and bloodthirsty mosquitoes, he confessed, were confronted with an abject existence of "malaria, salt pork, no vegetables, a blazing sun, and almost poisonous water." Under the showering cloudbursts of Union shells, those holed up in Vicksburg were beset by malarious mosquitoes, described by a Confederate physician in a letter to his wife as "the largest, hungriest, and boldest of their kind. May you never know a mosquito!" The same mosquitoes that had served as Vicksburg's guardian angels and driven off Union forces a year earlier now became Vicksburg's own pixies of death. "The enemy's shells annoyed us, but there was another foe we had to contend with," wrote Confederate surgeon Dr. W. J. Worsham from inside Vicksburg, "more annoying than the enemy's shells—the mosquitoes, or, as the boys called them, 'gallinippers.'"

Six weeks into the siege, the situation inside Vicksburg mirrored that of Jamestown's Starving Time. A young Confederate soldier wrote home to his parents, pleading for provisions because abnormally large "Gallinippers" had pinned him "by the throat" and stolen his "Boots, hat, & 5,000 doll[ars] In Green Backs." Ravenous civilians and soldiers ate dogs, rats, leather shoes and belts, and a few reports of cannibalism among the 3,000 huddled civilians surfaced after the war. To avoid the incessant shelling, soldiers and civilians took refuge in over 500 caves dug into the yellow clay hills and mockingly called "Prairie Dog Village" by Union soldiers. Malaria had also killed or sickened 50% of the initial 33,000 Confederate troops, who were depicted as "an army of scarecrows." Union soldiers sympathized with what was described as "the woeful sight of a beaten, demoralized army—humanity in the last stage of endurance. Wan, hollow-eyed, ragged, sore-foot, bloody, the men limped along."

Amid the subdued celebrations of American independence, on July 4, the day after Lee's Confederate Army was routed at Gettysburg, Grant accepted the unconditional surrender of Vicksburg. "The Father of the Waters," announced Lincoln upon hearing the news of Grant's victory, "again goes unvexed to the sea." As Grant predicted, "the fall of the Confederacy was settled when Vicksburg fell." With the crucial port city now under Union control, the Confederacy was split in half, precluding the lifeblood cattle, horses, corn, and other agrarian yields west of the Mississippi from reaching and sustaining Lee's Army of Northern Virginia, while the snaking blockade tightened its grip on an already depleted and resource-starved South. More importantly, as malaria ripped through the veins of the gray-clad southern soldiers, this cordon also denied the Confederacy much-needed quinine. It was only a matter of time before the enslaved peoples "shall be then, thenceforward, and forever free." The name the "Victor of Vicksburg" echoed through the corridors of power. Although most politicians, including Lincoln, had never met Grant in person, in the highbrow social circles and sycophantic cocktail conversations of Washington, he was rapidly becoming something of a celebrity.

Grant's unrivaled battlefield prowess, his lack of political ambition and bureaucratic scheming, and his personal opinions on emancipation and the military employment of African Americans quickly endeared him to the president. Having suffered and endured a succession of inept, maladroit, backstabbing, and politically plotting generals, Lincoln had been desperately scouring his senior ranks for his own Robert E. Lee since the drubbing at the First Battle of Bull Run. "Lincoln had heard that Grant claimed he could not have taken Vicksburg without the Emancipation Proclamation," reports acclaimed author Ron Chernow in his superlative 2017 tour-de-force biography needing only the title *Grant*. "Once again, Grant's sympathy with the broad political aims of the war formed no minor part of his attraction in Washington." Chernow establishes that after Grant's martial showmanship at Vicksburg, the unpretentious and self-effacing forty-one-year-old soldier was "a rising star in the Lincoln firmament, for he was fast becoming the president's beau ideal of a general: one who regularly beat the enemy while endorsing the expanded war aims" of liberating and mobilizing southern slaves.

Not only was Grant personally opposed to slavery, but he also fully supported the moral and military tenets of the Emancipation Proclamation. "By arming the negro we have added a powerful ally," he wrote Lincoln shortly after the fall of Vicksburg. "They will make good soldiers and taking them from the enemy weakens him in the same proportion they strengthen us. I am therefore most decidedly in favor of pushing this policy." Grant's strategic military assessments and personal views were harmonious with those of Lincoln. The two leaders immediately formed an unfailing bond and trustworthy union that would transform the fortunes of the war and the country itself.

In March 1864, Lincoln promoted Grant to lieutenant general, a rank previously reserved exclusively for George Washington. "The

President . . . eight inches taller"—measured by Grant's aide-de-camp Horace Porter during the official ceremony—"looked down with beaming countenance upon his guest." As commanding general of Union forces, Grant was now answerable only to the president, who was enraptured by his new military spearhead. "That man Grant has been of more comfort to me than any other man in my army," Lincoln pledged. "Grant is my man, and I am his the rest of the war." The cigar-puffing, alcoholic, tongue-tied, taciturn, short, and dowdy Grant, who stood in sharp contrast to the tobacco-abstaining, teetotaling, articulate, eloquent, loquacious, towering, and lanky Lincoln, summed up his commander in chief as "a great man, a very great man. The more I saw of him, the more this impressed me. He was incontestably the greatest man I ever knew."* With their unwavering mutual respect, loyalty, and admiration, the like-minded military partnership and faithful personal friendship of Grant and Lincoln, who both had been lampooned and disparaged by detractors as bumpkin hayseeds from the western prairies, would win the war and forge the future of the nation.

Grant's campaign at Vicksburg was a microcosm of the wider war during its final two years. Larger and healthier Union forces were pitted against smaller and sicklier Confederate forces. For the first time in history, quinine helped decide the outcome of a war. The combination of sheer population and healthier soldiers prodded the Union to victory. According to John Keegan, "the Union triumphed in the end only because of larger numbers and greater wealth of resources." Manpower was a serious problem for the Confederacy during the final two years of the war. To fully appreciate the influence of malaria and quinine in breaking the Confederacy, we must first do a bit of number crunching.

Roughly 2.2 million soldiers served in the Union forces from a total available population of 22 million. Approximately 1 million Confederates fought from a total population of 4.5 million, excluding another 4.2 million slaves. By the close of 1864, of men between the ages of eighteen and sixty years, 90% of those in the Confederacy had served or were serving, compared with 44% in the North. But by 1865, desertion became

* Grant was just shy of five feet eight and 135 pounds, while Lincoln was all of six feet four and weighed 180 pounds.

a serious problem for Confederate commanders, with as many as 100,000 troops taking unauthorized convalescence at any given time. As the end of the war drew closer and desertion increased, the arms of Confederate conscription lengthened to embrace males between the ages of fourteen and sixty. Still, this sweeping measure could not shore up the compounding military shortcomings and deficiencies, reverse years of slaughter, offset the fading stocks of human fodder, or dam the bloodletting and the flow of deserters. By February 1865, with 16% of his army astray and unaccounted for, a disheartened General Lee confessed to Jefferson Davis that "hundreds of men are deserting nightly." These numbers were compounded by rampant malarial infection and a severe lack of quinine. Abundantly supplied Union troops and allied malarious mosquitoes had tapped and bled dry the fighting strength and spirit of the Confederacy.

It is worth keeping in mind, as US forces would realize later during the Pacific War and in Vietnam, that a sick soldier is just as useless to the war effort as a wounded soldier, and twice the burden of a dead soldier. A sick soldier needs to be replaced on the line while also continuing to consume resources. The dead do not drain supplies and manpower through medical attention and care. In the case of mosquito-borne disease, the sick also act as a conduit for the spread of infection to their fellow soldiers, continuing the cycle of contagion. This may seem harsh, but pragmatically, sick soldiers are deadweight and a taxing military handicap. "That the Confederacy suffered from a shortage of quinine in the war," stresses Margaret Humphreys, physician and professor at Duke University's School of Medicine, "made a significant difference in the number of men able to render military service. . . . The Union blockade then caused an acute shortage of quinine to the South, leveling the playing field further." Unlike the Union, the Confederacy could not replace combat casualties, and recurrent malarial sickness drained the ranks of already dwindling Confederate field forces. "There can be no doubt," Humphreys continues, "that the Confederacy did not have enough quinine to adequately treat malaria."

By 1864, the Anaconda Plan was 95% effective in strangling southern trade. In the spring of that year, Grant's loyal and dependable friend and

"Before Petersburg—Issuing Rations of Whisky and Quinine," March 1965: This engraving for *Harper's Weekly* depicts a Union "Quinine Parade." Quinine was a war-winning weapon for the well-stocked Union. For the Confederacy, scant and inadequate supplies caused manpower shortages in the face of unremitting malaria. *(U.S. National Library of Medicine)*

subordinate, General William Tecumseh Sherman, began his scorched-earth "March to the Sea" from Tennessee through Georgia and eventually up the Carolinas, cutting a 200-mile-wide swath of wanton destruction. Union soldiers burned crops and farms, impounded livestock, and destroyed railways, irrigation facilities, dams, and bridges. Sherman's controversial tactics unintentionally broadened mosquito habitats and malarial infection across the South. Famine, disease, and deprivation gripped Confederate soldiers and civilians alike. The South was effectively being starved and sickened into submission by General Sherman, mosquitoes, and blockading ships.

Meanwhile, confiscated consignments of quinine, food, weapons, and other vital supplies intended for Confederate troops ended up in the veins, stomachs, and hands of their Union enemies. "While the Union soldier's ration was increased during the war," explains Keegan, "the Confederate's shrank," reckoning that "the Union soldier was the best fed on record." During the war, President Lincoln heeded Napoleon's advice that "an Army marches on its stomach." More importantly, as we've seen, the

Union had ample supplies of quinine. Apart from this lifesaving cinchona powder, however, medical knowledge and practices during the Civil War were still rudimentary and antiquated.

While experimentation with chloroform and ether anesthesia was a Civil War medical breakthrough, amputation was the preferred surgical practice, so mountainous piles of severed limbs littered field hospitals. Treatment for disease remained archaic. Revolutionary-era remedies such as mercury, bleeding, cupping glasses, and other superstitious cures were still common practice. As in the past, soldiers systematically avoided hospitals, viewing them as morgues rather than halls of healing. Hospitals served as the pivot transportation terminal for interchangeable infections, with soldiers swapping out one for another. Those suffering from illness generally sucked it up and soldiered on without seeking treatment. Union cavalryman John Kies, for example, was admitted after a Rebel round shattered his arm at Second Bull Run. He confessed to the doctor that he had been suffering from malaria for two months. Kies survived his battlefield wound. He even survived the amputation of his arm. He did not, however, survive his skirmish with malaria.

As the war dragged on and scarce quinine supplies evaporated or became generally unaffordable, southerners medicated with all sorts of useless tree barks and other quinine substitutes. The Confederate surgeon general instructed doctors to use indigenous remedies "as may be found growing in proximity to every hospital and station." A dense guidebook, *Resources of the Southern Fields and Forests*, was issued in 1863 to Confederate physicians and field commanders, itemizing a vast catalogue of worthless homeopathic replacements for quinine and other medicines. Across the South, ersatz substitutes for all manner of medicines and foods, including coffee, were consumed.

A Union artillery officer later wrote, "Coffee was one of the most cherished items in the ration. If it cannot be said that coffee helped Billy Yank win the war, it at least made his participation in the conflict more tolerable." In fact, the paper bag was invented in 1862 as a lightweight, cheap, and compact way for Union troops to carry their coffee. When Rebel and Yankee soldiers readily mingled and socialized, tops on the Confederate bartering list was coffee. "The Boys," wrote Union sergeant

"Hard Times in Ole Varginny, an' Worse a Cumin'! Scene—Rebel Pickets in Western Virginia," *Harper's Weekly*, January 1862: Two Confederate soldiers griping and grumbling about "gitting another Shake of that Ager [ague/malaria] and no quinine in the 'Federacy! Worser still! Got them Blue Devils after me, an' nary drop o' Whisky!" As the Union naval blockade, dubbed the Anaconda Plan, put a stranglehold on Southern trade, endemic malaria and a dire shortage of quinine shackled Confederate soldiers and civilians throughout the war. *(Library of Congress)*

Day Elmore from Atlanta in July 1864 at the onset of General Sherman's March to the Sea, "have been to gather a number of times . . . traiding [*sic*] coffee for tobacco." The most utilized Confederate coffee replacements were made from acorns, chicory, cotton seeds, and dandelion root. Coffee or not, by 1865, creative substitutes could not feed or cure the civilian population, let alone Lee's shattered army, which was being badgered across Virginia by Grant's robust Union columns. After a dogged nine-month stand around Richmond, on April 2, Lee abandoned the city to its fate.

On April 9, 1865, after 10,000 battles both large and small, the Civil War ended, in a place that Wilmer McLean, whose kitchen had been destroyed in the First Battle of Bull Run, would never have imagined. He had uprooted his family to escape the war after the Battles of Bull Run, relocating in what seemed to be the peace and quiet of a tiny crossroads community in nowhere Virginia called Appomattox Court House. But the war found him there, and, however unlikely, he hosted the terms of surrender between Generals Grant and Lee in the parlor of his roomy Federal-style home. The Civil War was over.

Lincoln prevailed in both his war aims of preserving the union and ending the evils of slavery but at a cost of 750,000 American lives, including roughly 50,000 (predominantly southern) civilian war-related deaths. To grasp the extent of this savagery, the total butcher's bill would today equate to more than 7 million dead. More Americans died in the Civil War than all other American wars combined. Of the 360,000 Union dead, 65% died of disease. More than 1.3 million cases of malaria were recorded by Union hospitals, with 10,000 deaths, although the actual numbers are presumably much higher. In certain southern theaters of the war, particularly in the Carolinas, annual malaria rates reached a nauseating 235% (multiple infections or relapses per man).

Although Confederate records went up in smoke with the fall of Richmond, the chief surgeon of the Confederacy knowledgeably estimated that of the 290,000 military fatalities, 75% were caused by disease. We can only guess at the total malarial impact on Confederate troops. The consensus among Civil War historians is that malaria rates and deaths were roughly 10% to 15% higher than those of Union forces. Given manpower considerations, malarious mosquitoes helped drain southern military strength, promoted a northern victory, preserved the Union, and dismantled the institution of slavery. With the mosquito-supported Emancipation Proclamation, liberated southern slaves refashioned as soldiers helped to safeguard its promises of freedom.

Over 200,000 African Americans served in Union forces during the

Civil War, reporting 152,000 cases of malaria. "I had supposed the black man to be peculiarly exempt from diseases due to malarial influences," reported Union physician John Fish while traveling with a Colored Regiment along the Mississippi from Baton Rouge to Vicksburg, "but I should not expect to have encountered a greater number of cases of intermittent fever." Roughly 40,000 African Americans perished fighting for their freedom, with 75% succumbing to illness. The scientific stereotype of African immunity to mosquito-borne disease was discredited. "Notwithstanding the supposed exemption of negroes from the climatic diseases of the South, I am constantly seeing cases of the same fevers and diarrhoeas [*sic*] among them, which prevail among the soldiers, and apparently of equal severity and frequency," divulged a Union surgeon from Memphis. "I am inclined to think that their power of resisting Southern climatic influences is greatly overestimated, though there is doubtless something to justify the common opinion on the subject." The fallacy of these justifications built on hereditary immunities like Duffy negativity or sickle cell was exposed by the inclusion and participation of African Americans in the Civil War.

High rates of malaria among these country-born African Americans who no longer possessed genetic buffers splintered the prewar pillar of "racial science" and its buttressing pseudoscientific claims that for generations had served as convenient exonerations of slavery. A Union physician bluntly stated that the academic doctrine concerning African resistance to mosquito-borne disease "so often reiterated in our textbooks" was demonstrably unfounded. Not only were 4.2 million African Americans no longer the property of plantation owners, the racial stereotypes of mosquito-borne disease were unraveling.

African American military service as fighting troops in the Civil War also undermined prevailing martial race theories. Following the unprecedented body count at Antietam in September 1862, Lincoln issued a preliminary outline or warning order for the Emancipation Proclamation. That same month, although technically unofficial, the first African American unit, the 1st Louisiana Native Guard, was formally received into the United States Army. Following the official sanction to muster African American contingents composed of freed slaves permitted by the Emancipation Proclamation, a total of 175 segregated regiments of US Colored Troops served during the war. There were, however, less than 100 African American officers across these regiments, none with a rank above captain, and until June 1864, colored soldiers pocketed less pay than their white comrades. While the military legally accepted African Americans, sanctioned desegregation of the US Armed Forces did not occur until President Harry Truman's executive order in 1948 after the Second World War. While the Union allowed for stipulated and controlled African American service, the Confederacy wanted no part of arming its slaves.

Major General Howell Cobb, who had served as president of the Provisional Congress of the Confederate States prior to the election of Jefferson Davis in February 1861, succinctly summed up the Confederate position and questions of racial hierarchy surrounding the conversion of slaves to soldiers. "You cannot make soldiers of slaves or slaves of soldiers," he claimed. "The day you make soldiers of them is the beginning of the end of the revolution. If slaves will make good soldiers our whole theory of slavery is wrong." In late March, with the war all but lost and manpower reaching a critical mass, the Confederate Congress relented and asked slave owners to allow 25% of their human property to be called into service. Only two confused companies of slave soldiers were hastily raised and showpiece-paraded around Richmond before Lee surrendered and the Confederacy, and its culture of slavery, crumbled.

In the opposing trenches, however, African American soldiers fought for the Union with distinction and courage. They skirmished at Port Hudson near Vicksburg, inspiring Grant to extol, "All that have been tried have fought bravely." Colored regiments also engaged Confederate soldiers around Nashville, clashed at the Battle of the Crater during the siege of Petersburg, and were among the first troops to enter the abandoned and smoldering Confederate capital of Richmond in the wee hours of April 3, 1865. The famous but futile assault by the 54th Massachusetts Colored Regiment in July 1863 on the island ramparts of Fort Wagner in Charleston Harbor entered pop culture in 1989 with the Academy Award–winning movie *Glory* (including a young Denzel Washington).

The venerated abolitionist, author, and former slave Frederick Douglass, whose own sons fought in colored regiments, avowed shortly after the Emancipation Proclamation, "A war undertaken and brazenly carried for the perpetual enslavement of the colored men, calls logically and loudly for the colored men to help suppress it." Not only did African Americans rally to Douglass's reasoning that by fighting, "no power on earth [could] deny that he has earned the right of citizenship in the United States," they carried out his larger vision of life and liberty with heroism and valor. Twenty-three African American soldiers were awarded the Medal of Honor during the Civil War. Despite these decorations and accolades, theirs was certainly a different and unique war from that fought by other American troops, both Union and Confederate.

African Americans were fighting for freedom in a segregated and skeptical army against an enemy who offered no quarter and delighted in killing them, all under the microscopic scrutiny of a curious, cross-examining, and judging nation. For African Americans, surrender was not an option. Confederate soldiers were disgusted and appalled at having to fight former slaves in what should have remained a white man's war, and they exacted harsh retribution on the wounded and captured. African American soldiers suffered sadistic violence at the hands of Confederate soldiers and were singled out for torture and execution on numerous occasions.

The worst atrocity and massacre occurred in April 1864 along the Mississippi River at Fort Pillow, Tennessee. "The slaughter was awful. Words cannot describe the scene. The poor deluded negroes would run up to our men fall upon their knees and with uplifted hands scream for mercy but they were ordered to their feet and then shot down. The whitte [*sic*] men fared but little better," penned eyewitness Confederate sergeant Achilles V. Clark. "Their fort turned out to be a great slaughter pen. Blood, human blood stood about in pools and brains could have been gathered up in any quantity. I with several others tried to stop the butchery and at one time had partially succeeded but Gen. Forrest ordered them shot down like dogs and the carnage continued. Finally our men became sick of blood and the firing ceased." Confederate troops under Major General Nathan Bedford Forrest, who was later elected the first

Grand Wizard of the Ku Klux Klan in 1867, mercilessly tortured and killed African American troops and their white officers following their capture or surrender, in what Forrest called "the wholesale slaughter of the garrison at Fort Pillow." "The river was dyed with the blood of the slaughtered for two hundred yards," he reported three days after the horror. "It is hoped that these facts will demonstrate to the Northern people that negro soldiers cannot cope with Southerners." Roughly 80% of African American soldiers and 40% of their white officers were executed. Only 58 African American troops were marched into captivity, which might have been worse than death by execution, as internment was often a prolonged and agonizing death sentence itself.

Confederate prison camps were a graphic nightmare filled with starvation, filth, desolation, squalor, and disease. Death stalked skeletal and emaciated Union prisoners by the thousands. Prior to its liberation in May 1865, at the notorious Andersonville prisoner-of-war camp in Georgia, 13,000 Union troops died from a medical directory of diseases including scurvy, malaria, dysentery, typhoid, influenza, and hookworm in less than a year. The accounts of the suffering and deplorable conditions at Andersonville are so sickening that they are beyond imagination or description.* The prisoner-of-war camps, however, simply replicated and adhered to the larger thematic cogs of the Civil War—massacre, mosquitoes, disease, bloodshed, and death.

And so the Civil War, like so many wars that came before it and so many that came after, was consumed by mosquito-borne disease and deadly pestilence. Unlike most wars, however, the unprecedented slaughter engendered one positive, humanizing, and nation-enlightening effect. Underwritten by the mosquito, Lincoln's Emancipation Proclamation was "dedicated to the proposition that all men are created equal. [and] all persons held as slaves . . . shall be then, thenceforward, and forever free." With the ratification of the Thirteenth Amendment to the Constitution on December 6, 1865, slavery was forever banned in the United States.

The cost of freedom was staggering—750,000 dead Americans. Ever

* The Andersonville commandant, Captain Henry Wirz, was executed for war crimes in November 1865.

the eloquent wordsmith and stirring poet-president, Lincoln tendered the departed of the Civil War, including the sons of Mrs. Bixby of Boston, the consolation that "in the end, it's not the years in your life that count. It's the life in your years." The casualties of the Civil War certainly did not die in vain. Despite all the ghastly horrors and butchery of the war, General Grant concluded, "We are better off now than we would have been without it." He believed, as did Lincoln, that the war was a "punishment for national sins [slavery] that had to come sooner or later in some shape, and probably in blood."

After the mind-boggling carnage of the Civil War, the United States deserved a long vacation from death. There would be no time, however, for the war-torn country to lick its wounds. The mosquito does not respect the grieving period and takes advantage of both petty squabbles and all-out war. Regrettably, while the killing on the battlefields stopped, the mosquito did not recognize the peace-brokering salutes between Lee and Grant on Wilmer McLean's veranda. Millions of soldiers filtered back home with visions of battle burned into their brains and mosquito-borne disease boiling in their veins. During the politically tumultuous and racially turbulent Reconstruction decades, straddling Grant's sullied, scandal-plagued presidency, the mosquito unleashed the worst epidemics in American history upon an already mourning and war-weary population.

CHAPTER 16

Unmasking the Mosquito: Disease and Imperialism

Kentucky physician and leading expert on yellow fever Dr. Luke Blackburn was too old to enlist. But as a Confederate zealot, he was determined to serve the southern cause. He hatched a maniacal plan to defeat the Union by unleashing a biblical plague of yellow fever on the District of Columbia, killing Lincoln in the process. Learning of a nasty black vomit epidemic stalking Bermuda, which was also a haven for Confederate blockade runners, in April 1864, he made passage to the island. Upon arrival, Dr. Blackburn proceeded to fill several trunks with soiled garments and bedding from yellow fever victims. The boxes were loaded onto a steamer destined to spread the dreaded virus and fever-burning death to an unsuspecting population. In August, on instruction from Blackburn, Godfrey Hyams, a coconspirator who was to be paid the handsome sum of $60,000 upon delivery, sold the trunks of "contaminated" items to a trade store a few blocks from the White House. Blackburn had told his messenger that the "infected" clothing "will kill them at sixty yards." This already strange and shocking story of biological mosquito weaponry takes an unexpected turn and enters the bizarre, adhering to Mark Twain's reality that "truth is stranger than fiction."

In April 1865, as Generals Lee and Grant were cordially discussing terms of surrender in Wilmer McLean's parlor at Appomattox Court House, Blackburn was back in Bermuda colluding to unleash a second serving of yellow fever, using the same delivery system. This time, he contracted another agent, Edward Swan, to deliver trunks of tainted clothing and linens to New York City for "the destruction of the masses there." Blackburn, however, had an additional surprise for the city. Once yellow fever had set its hooks and plagued the panicked population, he would unleash a subsequent wave of terror—Blackburn had concocted plans to poison New York's water supply. Chaos and death would consume his "damn Yankees."

On April 12, two days before the assassination of President Lincoln, a resentful and still unpaid Godfrey Hyams casually walked into the United States Consulate in Toronto. He calmly and methodically told authorities the details of his involvement in Blackburn's macabre intrigues. When news reached Bermuda, authorities raided Swan's hotel and found the trunks and their contents, saturated in black vomit. Swan was arrested and convicted of violating local health codes. With his conspiracy exposed, Blackburn too was arrested, but was eventually acquitted.

Like the British-gifted smallpox blankets of Pontiac's Rebellion, and Cornwallis's unrewarding slave-dispensed smallpox ventures during the American Revolution, Blackburn's nefarious but ingenious scheme, despite an honest effort, was also foiled and ended in failure. The botched conspiracies of Dr. Blackburn, one of the nation's foremost authorities on yellow fever, also reveal the limited medical knowledge surrounding mosquito-borne disease. Our apex assassin remained anonymous and her lethal subversion undetected.

Only Aedes mosquitoes, not soiled clothes or sheets, can transmit the deadly virus of yellow fever, and in the decades after the war, she did just that. During the Reconstruction era following the Civil War, the mosquito unleashed one of the worst epidemics in American history. In Memphis, the throngs of sick and dying would be ministered to by none other than the illustrious Dr. Luke Blackburn, earning him the morbid nickname "Dr. Black Vomit." Memphis, climbing from the bluffs of the lazily drifting Mississippi River, was a tired and somber city. The Civil War had drained the vibrant life from the bustling cotton port and railway hub for four major lines. By the spring of 1878, the city was home to a diverse population of 45,000 inhabitants, including freshly emancipated former slaves, sharecroppers, recent German immigrants,

Confederate sympathizers and cotton plantation owners, and northern shipping and business moguls. This eclectic population was almost double that of Atlanta or Nashville, and south of the Mason-Dixon Line was second in size only to New Orleans. The contrasting city of Memphis, sitting at the cultural crossroads between North and South, while acting as the gatekeeper to the new western frontier, had gained the reputation as a den of despondency, filth, and disease. In the immediate aftermath of the Civil War, it was swallowed by murderous, bloodthirsty mosquitoes.

Memphis was not the only city in the South with the melancholy mosquito-orchestrated delta blues, however. Rapacious mosquitoes insidiously, and quite diligently, gnawed the old Confederacy to pieces. During the devastating yellow fever epidemics that coursed through the South during the 1870s, Dr. Luke Blackburn traveled, like the virus itself, from city to city, including Memphis, to treat the afflicted, refusing any form of compensation.

The first major postwar epidemic mushroomed in 1867, with the mosquito eating her way through the Gulf states, killing upwards of 6,000 people. Having never been convicted for his stabs at biological warfare, Blackburn was in New Orleans, the epicenter of the epidemic, tending to the infected. Despite his best, but medically and scientifically blind, efforts, yellow fever claimed 3,200 people in the "Big Easy." Six years later, yellow fever snatched another 5,000 lives, including 3,500 in Memphis, where Dr. Blackburn had hung out his shingle. He then turned his migrant medical road show east to Florida in 1877 during another yellow fever epidemic, which killed roughly 2,200 people. A year later, he was back in Memphis as the mosquito was shredding the Mississippi River Valley and harvesting human souls.

By the close of August 1878, Luke Blackburn was exhausted. Not only was he ministering to thousands of floundering yellow fever victims languishing in the sweltering heat of Memphis, he was also the Democratic candidate in Kentucky's race for governor. An eerie stillness hung over the city while Blackburn, a die-hard Confederate, took some respite to view the historic sights of Memphis, including Jefferson Davis's home on Court Street. There was no foot traffic, save ghosts, gracing Union

Avenue; Beale Street was silent and lifeless; and Main Street was haunted only by windswept trash and a few hurrying, frightened citizens. Nearly 25,000 residents, more than half the city, had already fled in panic. Of the roughly 20,000 remaining, 17,000 would contract yellow fever. The mosquito had besieged Memphis.

In late July, the first case of yellow fever was reported. A sailor on board a ship that had made passage to Memphis from Cuba via New Orleans instigated the epidemic. "Many of those ships in 1878 came from Cuba, where the Ten Years' War for independence was coming to an end and an epidemic of yellow fever had been raging since March," reports Molly Caldwell Crosby in her nail-biting, finely crafted book *The American Plague: The Untold Story of Yellow Fever, the Epidemic That Shaped Our History*, charting the 1878 yellow fever epidemic that frayed the southern United States. "Refugees landed in New Orleans by the hundreds. . . . The harbor was filling with vessels bobbing in the water, the Yellow Jack flying high over their decks." Within a month, the remaining dazed and confused residents of a traumatized Memphis were drowning in the feverish summer sweats of yellow fever. The city was paralyzed in a tomb of death, bereavement, and fear. The average daily mortality rate during the month of September was 200. The mosquito had literally sucked the life out of Memphis and turned it into a city of crypts and corpses. While America was keenly watching the protracted Cuban insurgency against Spanish rule with covetous commercial eyes, the yellow fever epidemic spread unchecked from Memphis, snaking across the Mississippi, Missouri, and Ohio River watersheds.

By this time, Blackburn had traveled to Louisville to attend to its sick and dying victims of "Yellow Jack." The 1878 epidemic thundered across the shuddering South until the chilly winds and first frosts of October killed the unknown mosquito assailant and put an end to more than five months of suffering. Blackburn resumed his political campaign, winning the election by a decisive 20% margin over his Republican opponent. He served as governor of Kentucky from 1879 to 1883 and continued to practice medicine until his death in 1887. His tombstone is emblazoned with the simple slogan THE GOOD SAMARITAN. As a tribute to "Dr. Black Vomit," the Blackburn Correctional Complex, a minimum-security prison near Lexington, Kentucky, was unlocked for tenants in 1972 in his honor. Given his attempted biological terror campaign (including an indirect shot at Lincoln's life), for which he was never brought to justice, in this case irony steals the last laugh.

During the pandemic of 1878, of the 120,000 people infected, yellow fever harvested more than 20,000 souls: 1,100 in Vicksburg, 4,100 in New Orleans, and 5,500 in Memphis—a staggering 28% of those who stayed behind, or 12% of the original population. Imagine the pandemonium and mayhem in our current sociocultural climate if 165,000 people in metropolitan Memphis died from yellow fever or another choice disease over the next few months. The 1878 contagion, the worst yellow fever tragedy in American history, was also, thankfully, the last major outbreak of the disease. The virus rippled through the southern states periodically until the last minor epidemic imported from Cuba in 1905 claimed 500 people in New Orleans.

The epidemics that gripped the battle-scarred and mosquito-bitten country in the 1870s were spawned by the rapid growth of trade and the expansion of markets not only in the United States, but also across South and Central America and the Caribbean. The viral 1878 epidemic, for instance, was traded from the lingering Spanish satellite of Cuba through New Orleans to Memphis. The United States looked on these few loitering Spanish colonies, the remnants of a once dominant empire, with lusting imperialistic eyes to propel its own wielding industry and mercantilist economic system into international waters. When the United States declared war on Spain in April 1898, "Why trade when you can invade?" entered the American playbook. America's first target in this great game of global empire building was Cuba.

During this maiden charge of American colonization in Cuba, the mosquito stood between the United States and mountains of money. Wealth is a powerful motivator, even when daring to joust with and taunt deadly Cuban mosquitoes. A few determined and resolute mosquito fighters commanded by Dr. Walter Reed escorted America's first true flirtation with imperialism during the Spanish-American War. While American soldiers of the Fifth Army Corps set their gunsights on unseasoned Spanish defenders, Reed's US Army Yellow Fever

Yellow Jack-in-the-Box: An 1873 cartoon from *Leslie's Weekly* portrays the state of Florida in the clutches of a yellow fever Gollum-like demon escaping a crate labeled TRADE while Columbia, the personification of the United States of America, signals for help. Behind the trio, frightened Americans flee for their lives. As trade, most notably from the Caribbean, was regenerated and energized after the Civil War, yellow fever went on a serial killing spree across the United States during the 1870s. *(Library of Congress)*

Commission trained their microscope crosshairs squarely on Cuban mosquitoes.

Predictably, as American infrastructure and trade blossomed after the Civil War, so, too, did mosquito-borne disease. Not only were mosquito-reared epidemics, including the 1878 infestation trafficked from Cuba, escalating in breadth and ferocity, she was also biting into the bank accounts of American traders and investors in the process. Prior to the outbreak of the Spanish-American War, she was killing both people and profit at peak rates.

The mosquito carnage of 1878, for example, bit a distressing $200 million chunk out of the US economy. Congress candidly announced that "to no other great nation of the earth is yellow fever so calamitous as to the United States of America." The mosquito swung through the South like a wrecking ball and smashed the economic levees, draining American finance and commercial buoyancy. Congress responded by creating the National Board of Health the following year to remedy these debilitating health and economic concerns. Little could be done, however, as the actual cause of mosquito-borne disease, including yellow fever, was still anonymous. Although it was hiding in plain sight, scientists and researchers were still searching in the dark for the world's most wanted serial killer. Unable to infiltrate and breach the bases of mosquito-borne disease, the newly minted National Board of Health had no way of knowing that it was this same cherished and coveted commerce that sparked the mosquito's postwar rampage. The southern scourge of yellow fever centered on skyrocketing American (and global) trade, its expanding and snaking transportation infrastructure, including a latticework of railways, and the last great spike of immigration to the United States.

While the Civil War had churned up fallow fields, cotton plantations, which had stagnated during the war, were rebooted and enlarged with former slaves, now styled as sharecroppers. The military-industrial complex that had fueled the Union during the Civil War was refashioned and pumped out exportable manufactured goods. Increased global traffic once again descended on southern ports. For the mosquito, and her diseases of yellow fever, malaria, and dengue, the South was reopened for business. The postwar influx of immigrants added to the misery by importing their own brands of the disease. Endemic malaria, for example, which had been absent for decades, was reintroduced across New England.

The Civil War had reinvigorated the mosquito, and while malaria continued its wreckage during the immediate peace, yellow fever was reenergized as well. "American progress was the virus's other ally. A great influx of immigrants—Irish, German, eastern European—had been migrating south since the Civil War," confirms Molly Caldwell Crosby. "They served as fuel for a fever fire, a fresh source of nonimmune blood for the virus. Transportation paved the way for these immigrants. Trains connected every corner of America for the first time—east to west, north to south." By 1878, as the South was heaving and retching with yellow fever, more than 80,000 miles of railway track was operational in the US. At the turn of the century, 260,000 miles stretched across the country, reaching 410,000 miles only fifteen years later. This massive growth of railways and other infrastructure was built to propel swelling American economic portfolios into the global market.

The railways also eased the frontier passage west for land-hungry settlers. In its own backyard, the United States continued its western economic drive of Manifest Destiny and the subjugation of indigenous peoples. The "Iron Horse" ferried increasing numbers of "sod-busting" pioneers, fortune-seeking miners, and their bodyguard US Cavalry to the Great Plains and Rocky Mountains, where they came face-to-face with proud and defiant indigenous peoples who were willing to fight to defend their homelands. Cavalrymen and paid assassins, such as William "Buffalo Bill" Cody, exterminated the bison, their livelihood, and battled, slaughtered, and forcefully removed the starving, straggling remnants to bleak reservations.

Along the wagon trails and train tracks, malaria plodded west with the homesteaders and thrived on the new frontier, making frequent guest appearances in Laura Ingalls Wilder's autobiographical novel *Little House on the Prairie* depicting her childhood in 1870s Independence, Kansas. Roughly 10% of Lieutenant Colonel George Armstrong Custer's 7th Cavalry, for example, was suffering from malaria when they were routed by the Sioux, Cheyenne, and Arapahoe, led by Sitting Bull and Crazy Horse in June 1876 at the Battle of the Little Bighorn. While this encounter may have been "Custer's Last Stand," in a sense, it was also the last stand of American indigenous autonomy. The Sioux won the battle, but with their massacre at Wounded Knee in 1890, they lost the war, sealing the fate of indigenous peoples across the United States. This internal economic expansion of the United States at the expense of indigenous peoples generated a thirst for overseas ports and resources to feed domestic industry and foreign exports.

Rapid escalation of commerce and trade was coupled to the collection of a sprawling American colonial checkerboard. This era of American expansion announced a permanent departure from President James Monroe's 1823 isolationist doctrine.* American imperialism set off a sweeping chain of events, which continued through both world wars. During the century between the conclusion of the War of 1812 and the outbreak of the First World War in 1914, the United States drastically expanded its territorial footprint, securing Florida, the remainder of the west beyond the Rocky Mountains, Alaska, Cuba, Puerto Rico, Hawaii, Guam, eastern Samoa, the Philippines, and the Panama Canal.

As the American economic tentacles of empire reached across the Caribbean, the Pacific Rim, and beyond, Europe took its last clumsy imperialistic steps in Africa and the East Indies. From the defeat of Napoleon in 1815 until the outbreak of the First World War in 1914, European nations generally licked their wounds, remained cordial, and peacefully carved up the rest of the unclaimed world. With the Western Hemisphere being gathered to and embraced by the American sphere of influence, European imperialism, with the aid of quinine, shifted away from the Americas to Africa. A great game of mercantile Monopoly and military Risk was simultaneously played out across the "dark continent," periodically seeping into India, central Asia, the Caucasus, and the Far East.

It was within these final moves of the last global imperial scramble that the mosquito was finally unmasked. The clandestine and murderous agent of filariasis, malaria, and yellow fever, among her other vehicles of assassination, would, at long last, be revealed. Like most scientific invention and technological innovation, exposing the mosquito as the cause

* The Monroe Doctrine, opposing any further European colonialism in the Americas in order for the US to attain a monopoly on trade in the Western Hemisphere, was written by President Monroe's secretary of state, John Quincy Adams.

of contagion was directly tied to capitalism in the British colonies of India and Hong Kong and the French outpost of Algeria, and to conflict with the American invasion of Cuba.

Beginning in the 1870s, American entrepreneurs and capital poured into Cuba, and the island was slowly bought up by American corporations, progressively fraying its economic ties to Spain. As early as 1820, Thomas Jefferson contemplated that Cuba would be "the most interesting addition which could ever be made to our system of States" and reasoned that America "ought, at the first opportunity, to take Cuba." In fact, Spain had rejected offers from five US presidents—Polk, Pierce, Buchanan, Grant, and McKinley—to purchase the island. A similar commercial Americanization was also materializing on the independent Hawaiian Islands. Seeing as both Cuba and Hawaii were not territories of the United States, aggrieved American plantation owners were charged tariffs on their "foreign goods" at American ports. Despite these import duties, by 1877 the United States purchased a staggering 83% of Cuban exports (yellow fever was the one Cuban import that had no tariff).

In the decades following the Civil War, the American industrial economy boomed. By 1900, the United States was the global leader in manufactured goods, which accounted for almost half of total American exports. While American natural resources were certainly richly abundant, and Canada outfitted its southern neighbor with most shortfalls, both countries lacked rubber, silk, a sizable sugar industry, and other tropical commodities. The swelling shipping fleets facilitating this relatively quick expansion of American trade also required coaling stations and naval protection. American capitalism needed mercantilist colonies. Uncle Sam's lusting eyes wandered toward the volatile, wayward Spanish colony of Cuba, which had been consumed by insurrection against imperial rule since 1868.

Cuba benefited directly from Toussaint Louverture's successful mosquito-backed slave revolt in Haiti. The financial price, or punishment, for Haiti's prized freedom in 1804 was the destruction of its plantations and its blacklisting as a global economic pariah. Filling this commercial pecuniary vacuum, Cuba quickly unseated and supplanted

Haiti as the largest sugar producer in the world (half the global supply), while emerging as a main exporter of tobacco and coffee. As investments and wealth flooded the island, Havana with its majestic seafront promenade quickly blossomed into an ethnic melting pot, a playground for multinational elites, and a cosmopolitan mecca rivaling the glitz and glamour of New York. Although numerous revolts against the lingering Spanish rule occurred throughout the nineteenth century, they lacked cohesion and foreign support and were brutally suppressed by the Spanish and their Cuban-born political puppets.

Beginning in 1868, however, protracted insurrection became a mainstay on the island, during which time a large segment of slaves, who accounted for roughly 40% of the population, secured freedom. Spain responded by pumping in hefty contingents of fresh, unseasoned troops. Unlike many other Caribbean islands, Cuba was home to a healthy diaspora of its colonizing Spanish peoples and their descendants, who made up the largest segment of the total 1.7 million population. Between 1865 and 1895, over 500,000 Spanish immigrants settled in Cuba. The high rate of new arrivals, sojourners of fortune, and Spanish soldiers to Cuba kept the notoriously lethal Cuban mosquitoes well stocked with virgin blood. In the closing decades of the nineteenth century, virulent annual epidemics of yellow fever consumed the island, with a death toll reaching 60,000.

When slavery was banned in 1886, the wealthy Spanish-Cuban elite saw their profits plummet. The rise of the global sugar beet industry, founded by Napoleon's France after the loss of Haiti, as mentioned, also cut into sugar revenues. Floundering economically, Spain instituted taxation policies on Cuba similar to those enacted by the British on the American colonies prior to the revolution. Spain put the financial squeeze on Cuba, its last bastion of colonial commerce, by levying augmented taxes and withholding voting and legal privileges from the Spanish-Cuban population. Americans could certainly understand why the Cubans revolted against this tyrannical Spanish rule crowned with burdensome taxation, imposed without colonial consent or political representation. The Cuban plight was something Americans could rally around to serve their own imperialistic agenda. With both foreign and domestic support swelling, the Cuban "Sons of Liberty," many brought up in the shadows and stories of Simon Bolivar's struggles for freedom, slowly began to gather strength and numbers. In 1895, full-scale rebellion broke out in Cuba.

Over the course of hostilities, roughly 230,000 Spanish soldiers led by General Valeriano "the Butcher" Weyler ruthlessly fought to suppress the insurgency. Rural peasants were rounded up for "reconcentration" and quartered in hastily built, overcrowded camps. Crops and livestock were confiscated or cleansed, and the countryside and villages were put to the torch. By 1896, over a third of Cuba's entire population had been relocated to these concentration camps, with 150,000, nearly 10% of the island's population, dying of disease. Of the 45,000 Spanish military deaths, over 90% were caused by disease, primarily yellow fever and malaria. By January 1898, of the 110,000 remaining Spanish troops, 60% were incapacitated by mosquito-borne disease. As mutinous Cuban mosquitoes continued to devour Spanish troops with no tangible military results, opposition to the war intensified on the home front. "After having sent 200,000 men and having spilt so much blood," decried the leader of the Spanish opposition party, "we are masters in the island only of the territory upon which our soldiers stand." Unseasoned reinforcements sent directly from Spain were torn apart by the mosquito within weeks of landing. Spanish hospital admissions for mosquito-borne disease reached 900,000—multiple admissions per man.

The architects of the revolution understood that yellow fever, malaria, and dengue were their formidable allies, praising "June, July and August" as their most distinguished generals, with September and October receiving honorable mention. For the seasoned Cubans, only 30% of their 4,000 military deaths were caused by these same diseases. According to J. R. McNeill, the revolutionary leaders "goaded the Spaniards into unpopular policies, courted foreign support—especially in the U.S.—and, most of all, used their mobility to avoid Spanish forces except when they found patrols in vulnerable situations. Thus they kept the rebellion alive, like Washington, Toussaint, and Bolivar before them, and emerged victorious because time and the 'climate' was on their side."

The American press, led by rival New York media moguls Joseph

Pulitzer and William Randolph Hearst, used Weyler's atrocities to mobilize validation for war against Spain (and sell newspapers), inflaming American public opinion toward intervention. President William McKinley accused the Spanish of waging a "war of extermination." More importantly, American entrepreneurs, drooling at the thought of the annexation of Cuba, pleaded for conflict resolution. The war was increasingly bleeding their personal fortunes and diminishing profit while also draining the larger American economy by slashing plantation production, harrying shipping, and sheering away local labor.

After American arbitration efforts were sneered at by the Spanish, the battle cruiser USS *Maine* was sent to Havana Harbor to protect American shipping, property, profit, and other economic assets. In February 1898, a mysterious explosion, blamed on a Spanish mine, rocked the *Maine* and killed 266 sailors.* The infuriated American public, stirred to a frenzy by sensationalized reporting, demanded action under the popular slogan "Remember the Maine! To Hell with Spain!" By April 1898, the US Navy initiated a blockade of the island, and Congress issued a declaration of war against Spain and her colonies. When the first Americans waded ashore in late June at the onset of mosquito season, only 25% of the Spanish force of 200,000 was healthy enough to fight. "It is something awful to see," reported the Spanish surgeon in chief from Cuba. "Those ignorant, sickly peasants brought here from Spain to defend the Spanish flag are dying by the hundreds every day." The Americans, however, were also bitten by Cuba's legendary mosquitoes.

After his chain of superiors was killed or incapacitated by yellow fever, a fresh-faced and eager Theodore Roosevelt unexpectedly assumed command of his regiment. Roosevelt's fortuitous mosquito-influenced battlefield promotion would thrust him into the national spotlight. "The battle that was to follow at San Juan Hill," writes David Petriello, "was to propel the young Assistant Secretary of the Navy to the presidency, a situation only made possible by the illness that upset the pre-established command structure." In truth, when Colonel Roosevelt and his small detachment of volunteer Rough Riders walked up

* The true cause of the sinking, an accidental boiler-room fire, was not made public until many years later.

the hill, they were greeted by Lieutenant John "Black Jack" Pershing and a group of African American "Buffalo Soldiers" who had already crested the summit and scattered its defenders. Nevertheless, Roosevelt boastingly exaggerated his battlefield prowess to reporters and grabbed national headlines.

The war in Cuba lasted only a few months, attaining a reputation as a "Splendid Little War." The quick American victory was secured by 23,000 total troops at a cost of only 379 servicemen killed in combat. Another 4,700, however, died of mosquito-borne disease. When these shocking casualty returns filtered back to Washington, it was quickly understood by politicians and investors that the mosquito was the paramount obstacle to unlocking the economic potential of Cuba and incorporating its riches into the larger American mercantilist market. This dire situation of life-sucking mosquito-borne disease was not lost on military men with boots on the ground, guiding strategy in Cuba either. Prolonged military involvement on the island would be tantamount to mosquito-inflicted suicide. Dislodging the Spanish was one thing; contesting the mosquito with an army of occupation was quite another. Help, however, would soon be on the way.

America's initial voyages of imperialism during the Spanish-American War were tied to epidemiology and forever altered the global world order. Science and technological innovation gave us new weapons in our war with the mosquito. She could no longer fly below the radar. The ancient miasma theory, which had been the prevailing school of thought for the cause of disease for over 3,000 years, was now expunged and flushed out of circulation. Like most historical events, the discovery of the mosquito as the vector for multiple contagions, including filariasis, malaria, and yellow fever, was tied directly to global empire, mercantilism, and capitalism in Cuba, Panama, and beyond.

By the 1880s, the miasma and humoral models of Hippocratic medicine were being replaced with modern germ theories. Early researchers of mosquito-borne disease were operating under the scientific umbrella of the germ theory postulated and proven by Louis Pasteur (French), Robert Koch (German), and Joseph Lister (British) beginning in the

1850s.* Advancements in science and medical instruments, including the microscope, allowed for a more complete and advanced study of disease. The mosquito and her pathogens could no longer hide in the shadows of scientific simplicity and medical ignorance. Of course, boasting a planet-consuming population of 110 trillion, mosquitoes had never actually attempted to be clandestine or inconspicuous. After all, they have been flying in our face for eternity.

In the decades following the monumental discovery of the germ or microorganism theory of disease, a handful of mosquito hunters finally cornered her and broadcast to the world that at last our ultimate, previously indestructible, enemy had been arraigned for her crimes against humanity stretching back hundreds of thousands of years. With numerous medical bounty hunters pursuing her across the planet, arresting the mosquito was a collective international effort.

After millions of years of discreetly smuggling misery and death, the mosquito was unmasked in a swift series of scientific discoveries. First, in 1877, British physician Patrick Manson positively incriminated the mosquito as the vector of filariasis, or elephantiasis, while stationed at the British outpost of Hong Kong. For the first time in history, Manson had definitively coupled an insect to the transmission of disease. Although lacking corroborating scientific evidence, Manson then postulated that the mosquito also delivered malaria.

Three years later in 1880, while peering through his crude microscope, Dr. Alphonse Laveran, a French military physician assigned to the colony of Algeria, noticed something strange. Small spherical foreign bodies were swimming in the blood sample of a patient admitted with "marsh fever." Upon further study, he correctly identified these bodies as four distinct forms in the life cycle of the malaria parasite. By 1884, he theorized that the mosquito was the method of delivery for this biological killer. Similarly, an American physician and veteran of the Civil War (serving as a surgeon for both sides) with the dazzling name Albert Freeman Africanus King implicated the mosquito in 1882, boldly

* Hence the terms *pasteurization* for removing pathogens from liquids and foods and for Listerine brand antiseptic products.

suggesting, "You can have mosquitoes without malaria . . . but you cannot have malaria without mosquitoes." King's flawless assertion was rejected and ridiculed when he posited that Washington, DC, should be enclosed by a 600-foot-tall mosquito safety net.* The discoveries of Manson, King, and Laveran kick-started the field of malariology, leading to what historian James Webb calls a "trio of discoveries in 1897" by Ronald Ross, Giovanni Grassi, and our germ theorist Robert Koch.

Ronald Ross was a rather uninspiring British doctor born in India to a general in the British Army. Ross was an altogether improbable and dubious candidate to expose the preeminent killer of humankind. To appease his father, he grudgingly attended medical school, but he spent most of his time procrastinating, writing plays and novellas, and otherwise daydreaming. Ross did so poorly on his exams that when he graduated in 1881, his credentials allowed him to practice medicine only in British India, where he spent the next thirteen years bouncing from one assignment to another. On a brief trip to London in 1894, he met Manson, who took the lackluster young doctor under his wing and mentored him on his own malaria research. Given India's endemic malaria, Manson prodded Ross to return to his post to produce concrete evidence of his own malaria-mosquito theory. "If you succeed in this, you will go up like a shot and get any facilities you may ask for," he told his young apprentice and squire. "Look on it as the Holy Grail and yourself as a Sir Galahad." Upon his return to India, Ross immediately made the hospital rounds, stalking malaria patients.

He spent the next three years with his face buried in a microscope, squinting at dissected mosquitoes. His research notes and his descriptions of what he was spying through the lens indicate that, for the most part, he did not know what the hell he was looking at or looking for. He hated the natural sciences and had no clue about the actual biological workings of mosquitoes. His original mosquito experiments, for example, were conducted on species that did not and could not vector malaria. He complained that these mosquito test subjects were "obstinate as

---

* King was in the audience at Ford's Theatre on April 14, 1865, when Lincoln was assassinated by John Wilkes Booth. He was one of the first physicians to treat the dying president and helped carry Lincoln across the street to the Petersen House, where he died the following morning.

mules" for refusing to bite, which is akin to scolding a chestnut as lazy for refusing to fall. In the meantime, an Italian zoologist, Giovanni Grassi, was also persistently poking and prodding mosquitoes to unveil the malaria parasite that inflicted endemic misery and death across his country.

In 1897, both Ross and Grassi finally had their "aha" breakthrough moments. Ross discovered that mosquitoes were the vector for avian malaria and postulated with insufficient evidence from ongoing trials that the same must be true for human malaria. Grassi beat Ross to the finish line by conclusively proving that the Anopheles mosquito was the distributer of human malaria. These simultaneous discoveries set off a professional feud and smear campaign between the two men comparable to that of Thomas Edison and Nikola Tesla in the early twentieth century.* Much to Grassi's anger and resentment, Ross's public relations campaign prevailed, and he won the Nobel Prize in 1902, with Laveran accompanying him in 1907.

The last of the trio of 1897 discoveries belonged to Robert Koch, who won the Nobel Prize in 1905. Working out of the malaria-plagued colony of German East Africa, the distinguished bacteriologist scientifically confirmed that quinine cleansed human blood of the malaria parasite as had been championed for 250 years since it allegedly first cured the beautiful countess of Chinchon in Peru. "These three epochal discoveries struck a destabilizing blow to miasmatic theory," Webb concludes. "In the years after 1897 the theory of miasma was dead in the water."

Mosquito-borne malaria, the cause of limitless and unrivaled suffering and billions of deaths since the dawn of humankind, was exposed. Our nameless archnemesis that had been stalking us since our creation had finally been unmasked. This lethal bond between the mosquito and the scourge of malaria was laid bare by the collective weight of science. With the cause of this affront to humanity revealed, surely a foolproof treatment or vaccine would quickly follow. Or alternatively, this

* In 1915, Tesla and Edison were corecipients of the Nobel Prize. When each man adamantly refused to share the award with the other, it was presented to neither and passed to the father-and-son team of William and Lawrence Bragg for their work in radiology, which Tesla had also pioneered.

verminous abomination, destroyer of worlds, could be exterminated. After all, malaria was caused only by the small, worthless mosquito. Right?

With this realization, the mosquito was the subject of intense study and scrutiny. If she was the sole delivery system for filariasis and malaria, what other deadly poisons did she discharge from her proboscis? And though her lethal yellow fever viral weaponry remained undetected for the time being, with the mosquito attracting so much scientific scrutiny, it too could not hide forever. Embroiled with both the Spanish and yellow fever in Cuba since April 1898, to reap the whirlwind of the island's capitalistic opportunity, the Americans needed to defang the dreaded Black Vomit once and for all.

Witnessing the destructive power of yellow fever on his troops in Cuba, the American commander General William Shafter declared that the mosquito was "a thousand times harder to stand up against than the missiles of the enemy." With the Spanish surrender in August 1898 after only four months of combat, military commanders realized the inherent dangers of maintaining an occupation force in Cuba. Yellow fever and malaria began to spread among US troops. In a letter to President McKinley, Shafter reported that his force was "an army of convalescents" with 75% unfit for service.

A second straightforward letter signed by numerous generals (and Colonel Roosevelt) known as the "Round Robin" candidly forewarned Congress, "If we are kept here it will in all human possibility mean an appalling disaster, for the surgeons here estimate that over half the army, if kept here during the sickly season, will die." The dispatch closed with the blunt caveat: "This army must be moved at once or it will perish. As an army it can be safely moved now. Persons responsible for preventing such a move will be responsible for the unnecessary loss of thousands of lives." While US forces made short work of Cuba's Spanish defenders, they hastily retreated in the face of the mosquito's mauling barrage of malaria and yellow fever. The evacuation of US forces was initiated in mid-August. "Cuba became a U.S. dependency until 1902. Thereafter it was nominally free . . . thanks to yellow fever and malaria," concludes J. R. McNeill. "Cubans have lionized their heroes. Americans venerated theirs, and elected one, Theodore Roosevelt, to the presidency before carving his likeness on Mt. Rushmore. There are no monuments to mosquitoes, far and away the most lethal foe of the Spanish army in Cuba." The mosquito also spared Cuba from outright American annexation, instigating nearly a century of hostile relations and harrowing events.

With mosquito-borne disease hindering any American military occupation, Cuba was given formal independence in 1902 under a puppet government answerable to Washington. Underwriting this token independence were furtive fine-print clauses. Cuba was forbidden to form alliances with other countries, America retained the first right of refusal for all trade, economic portfolios, and infrastructure contracts, maintained the right to militarily intervene at its choosing, and secured perpetual possession of Guantanamo Bay. Under the new American-backed regime, Cuba became a dictatorial banana republic and an American economic and self-indulgent epicurean playground at the expense of the impoverished Cuban people.

In 1959, socialist revolutionaries led by Fidel Castro and Ernesto "Che" Guevara put an end to the US-sponsored authoritarian rule and corrupt regime of President Fulgencio Batista, and quickly aligned themselves as a communist satellite of the Soviet Union. President John F. Kennedy's 1961 Bay of Pigs Invasion using CIA-trained counterrevolutionaries was a disaster. "Victory has a hundred fathers and defeat is an orphan," the president remarked while accepting full responsibility for the fiasco. The botched mission drove Cuba further into the Soviet embrace, leading to the near-apocalyptic Cuban Missile Crisis in October 1962. Although cool heads prevailed, and rational dialogue eventually deescalated the possibility of nuclear annihilation, the global population held its breath for thirteen nail-biting days as the planet teetered on the eve of destruction. It took over fifty years for US-Cuban relations to begin to normalize, under President Barack Obama.

The Spanish-American War, however, was not isolated to Cuba. It seeped across the Pacific to the Spanish colony of the Philippines, where the American Navy crushed its Spanish opponent in Manila Bay on May 1, 1898. American forces simultaneously landed at Puerto Rico, Guam, and Hawaii. Japan, a burgeoning industrial and military power, watched uneasily as America expanded its influence across the Pacific

Rim. President McKinley assured the world that despite its imperialistic veneer, "the American Flag has not been planted in foreign soil to acquire territory but for Humanity's sake." The global Spanish-American War officially ended with the American capture of the Philippine capital city, Manila, on August 13, 1898.

"Hit Him Hard!: President McKinley: "Mosquitoes seem to be worse here in the Philippines than they were in Cuba." The American invasions of Cuba and the Philippines during the Spanish-American War highlighted the perils of foreign imperialistic forays into the tropics. This February 1899 cartoon from *Judge* magazine mocking President McKinley depicts Cuban and Filipino insurgents as lethal and stubborn mosquitoes. The 1898 American invasion of Cuba, however, also led to the unmasking of the Aedes mosquito as the cause of yellow fever by the US Army Yellow Fever Commission headed by Dr. Walter Reed. *(Library of Congress)*

Following the Spanish surrender in the Philippines, President McKinley announced that "there was nothing left for us to do but to take them all, and to educate the Filipinos, and uplift and civilize and Christianize them, and by God's grace do the very best we could by them." Instead, American occupation forces initiated their own brutal and barbaric cleansing and "reconcentration" of Filipino civilians, mimicking the counterinsurgency tactics of General Weyler in Cuba. One American general, who was later court-martialed, ordered his men to execute every Filipino male over the age of ten. The media, however, publicly spun President McKinley's words "that the official mission of the United States is one of benevolent assimilation."

During this forgotten Philippine-American War, Filipino revolutionaries, who had been combating Spanish colonial occupation since 1896, fought a guerrilla war against American forces until 1902. They wanted independence from any and all foreign powers. William Taft, governor general of the Philippines and future US president, argued that it would take a century of blood before the Filipinos could be taught to appreciate "what Anglo-Saxon liberty is." Eventually, reports of American atrocities could no longer be contained or censored. The widely circulated weekly magazine the *Nation* reported on the not so "splendid" or "little" war that had degenerated "into a war of conquest, characterized by rapine and cruelty worthy of savages." During its first deployment of troops outside the Western Hemisphere, the United States poured more than 126,000 men into the Philippines.* Of the roughly 4,500 who died, 75% perished from disease, including malaria and dengue. Over the course of the brutal three-year war, the best estimates place the total Filipino death toll at 300,000 as a result of combat, murder, starvation and disease, and the squalor of the concentration camps. The Philippines remained under American (or Japanese) jurisdiction in some form until it was finally granted complete independence in 1946.†

* I do not count President Jefferson's deployment of sailors in 1801 (and again under Madison in 1815) during the brief and intermittent Barbary Wars against North African Ottoman pirates.

† This hard-won self-rule came only after the 1942 Japanese invasion and American evacuation, a harsh Japanese occupation, and an American reinvasion and return in 1944 during the Second World War.

The Spanish-American War did more than carve out a global American empire. It also led to the unmasking of the mosquito as the vector for yellow fever. When American forces invaded Cuba in 1898, the military men, physicians, and politicians steering the war fully understood the threat posed by yellow fever. Cuba had rightfully earned a notorious reputation as a catacomb for mosquito-borne disease. Given that the mosquito-malaria mystery had been unraveled a year earlier, numerous leading researchers also fingered the mosquito as the merchant of yellow fever. In 1881, Carlos Finlay, a Cuban doctor educated in France and the US, isolated the Aedes mosquito as the vector for yellow fever, though acknowledging at the time that his experiments were inconclusive. The mosquito remained innocent until scientifically proven guilty.

The American architects of the war dissected the medical reports pouring in from Cuba with great interest and anxiety. They recognized that, as in the past, Cuban mosquitoes could manipulate the destiny of American designs on the island. The task of combating yellow fever, an enemy far more lethal than the Spanish, landed on the shoulders of Dr. Walter Reed.

Reed earned his medical degree in 1869 at the age of seventeen. He enlisted in the US Army Medical Corps in 1875 and was predominantly posted to units across the western frontier engaged in pacifying, slaughtering, and relocating indigenous populations. Reed tended both American soldiers and indigenous peoples, including the famed Apache Geronimo. In 1893, as a professor of bacteriology and clinical microscopy, Reed joined the newly created Army Medical School, where he was able to conduct unhindered research of his own choosing. At the outbreak of the Spanish-American War, he was posted to Cuba to investigate an epidemic of typhoid fever, which he concluded was the result of contact with fecal matter or food and drink contaminated by flies. During his stay in Cuba, however, he became more interested in yellow fever, which was buckling American troops at an alarming rate. In June 1900, Reed was appointed to establish and head the US Army Yellow Fever Commission. Reed was an avid fan of Carlos Finlay's résumé, and Finlay's body of work formed the basis for Reed's own research.

Although his four-member team in Cuba, made up of himself,

another American, a Canadian, and a Cuban, received full backing from their military superiors, the media maligned his theory that the mosquito transmitted the disease. An article in *The Washington Post*, for example, mocked, "Of all the silly and nonsensical rigamarole of yellow fever that has yet found its way into print—and there has been enough to build a fleet—the silliest beyond compare is to be found in the arguments and theories generated by a mosquito hypothesis." In October 1900, after conducting trials with human test subjects, many of whom died, including one of his team members, Reed announced that he had scientifically and definitively unmasked the female Aedes mosquito as the cause of yellow fever, while identifying the cyclical time frame of contagion between humans and mosquitoes.* General Leonard Wood, a physician and the US governor of Cuba, acknowledged and applauded that "the confirmation of Dr. Finlay's doctrine is the greatest step forward made in medical science since Jenner's discovery of the [smallpox] vaccination." Walter Reed received credit and fame (and numerous institutions named in his honor) for apprehending the killer Aedes mosquito. Prior to his premature death in 1902 from complications of a ruptured appendix, however, he publicly shared recognition with his team and with his hero and mentor, Carlos Finlay.†

Following Reed's announcement, the chief military sanitary officer in Havana, Dr. William Gorgas, energetically set out to rid the island of yellow fever through a systematic and deliberate mosquito sanitation and extermination program. Gorgas, who survived yellow fever as a youth in Texas, was not connected to the "Reed Board" nor was he a research scientist. He was a military doctor who fanatically carried out his orders to destroy yellow fever in Havana. Gorgas first meticulously mapped the city and surrounds before deploying more than 300 men in six teams working around the clock to execute his equally meticulous war on Havana's mosquitoes. These "sanitation squads" attacked the finicky breeding patterns and limited flight range of Aedes mosquitoes by draining

* Reed's paid test subjects were made aware of the risks and, for the first time in medical history, signed consent forms, setting the precedent for the common and legal use of these documents.

†Although Finlay was nominated for the Nobel Prize seven times, he never won the prestigious award.

ponds and swamps, limiting standing water and open barrels, erecting netting, clear-cutting targeted vegetation, fumigating with sulfur and insecticidal chrysanthemum-pyrethrum powder, and spraying all unreachable or suspect locations with a coat of pyrethrum-laced kerosene on top of other wholesale sanitation measures throughout the city. For the first time since 1648, thanks to the keen determination of Gorgas, yellow fever was completely eradicated from Havana by 1902. After the last American outbreak in New Orleans in 1905, "cleanup crews" reoccupied Cuba and by 1908 the entire country was released from the clutches of yellow fever. Malaria and dengue, however, continued to prowl the island.

The actual yellow fever virus, however, was not isolated until 1927. Under sponsorship of the philanthropic Rockefeller Foundation, successful vaccination was realized a decade later in 1937, courtesy of South African American Max Theiler. In 1951, when accepting his Nobel Prize for this accomplishment, Theiler was asked what he was going to do with his prize money. He answered, "Buy a case of scotch and watch the Dodgers." Yellow fever was defanged and stripped of its monumental impact on geopolitical affairs. The curtain was drawn on its career as a feared and adroit killer and as a mettlesome and influential agent of human history. Malaria, however, proved to be an indefatigable survivor and determined enemy.

Following the American military extraction from Cuba and his own successful Cuban mosquito crusade, Gorgas was superseded as the island's chief health officer by none other than Dr. Carlos Finlay. Gorgas's unique talents and eradication expertise were required elsewhere. He had been summoned to conjure his mosquito-silencing, abracadabra magic on the historically lethal mosquitoes of Panama. Having already overpowered and dispatched the Spanish, English, Scottish, and French, the undefeated Panamanian mosquito next challenged the confident United States, managed by its headstrong president, Teddy Roosevelt, for Canal Zone supremacy. "If we are to hold our own in the struggle for naval and commercial supremacy we must build up our power without borders," announced the dynamic young president. "We must build the Isthmian canal, and we must grasp the points of vantage which will enable us to have our say in deciding the destiny of the oceans of the east and west." To make its newly acquired Pacific colonies, including the Philippines, Guam, Samoa, Hawaii, and chains of smaller atolls and islands, financially viable and to fuse its newly created global empire, America needed to punch a forty-eight-mile canal through Panama. This shortcut linking the Atlantic to the Pacific Oceans would supplant the perilous, time-consuming, big-ticket journey around the tip of South America at Cape Horn. Teddy was adamant that where the Spanish, English, Scottish, and French had failed, the Americans would succeed in constructing an economic superhighway across the isthmus. His demanding order to his engineers was simply "Make the dirt fly!"

This idea was not innovative, but the engineering and mosquito control were. The first Spanish attempt to blaze a trail across Panama at Darien in 1534 was rebuffed by the mosquito. Ensuing Spanish colonial attempts met the same disease-ridden destiny. After they had sacrificed over 40,000 men to the mosquito, their painstaking efforts produced little more than a grubby single-lane mule track through the jungle, bracketed by two languid, fever-drenched villages. The mosquito thwarted an English attempt in 1668 before writing the Scottish script for William Paterson's Darien horror show in 1698, climaxing with the forfeiture of Scotland's independence.

In 1882, Ferdinand de Lesseps, the vaunted French engineer who had completed the Suez Canal in 1869, tried to repeat his success in Panama. He bribed government officials and lured investors to back his project. The French effort foundered in mud and mosquitoes. While battling malaria after a visit to Panama in 1887, French Post-Impressionist artist Paul Gauguin recalled the skeletal bushwhacking workers being "devoured by mosquitoes." The popular magazine *Harper's Weekly* ran the headline "Is M. de Lesseps a Canal Digger or a Grave Digger?" Nearly 85% of the workforce suffered from mosquito-borne disease. Over 23,000 men (25% of the personnel) died, primarily from yellow fever, before the project, nearing 40% completion, was abandoned in 1889 amid bankruptcy and scandal. A total of $300 million from over 800,000 investors had been gobbled up by Panamanian mosquitoes. Numerous politicians and contractors were convicted of collusion and corruption, including Gustave Eiffel, who had recently unveiled his tower at the 1889 Paris World's Fair for the centennial celebration of the Storming of the Bastille.

To procure the rights to the Canal Zone, the United States, using gunboat diplomacy while militarily buttressing local revolutionaries, chiseled out the independent country of Panama from Colombia. In 1903, the United States recognized the sovereign Republic of Panama, and two weeks later, America was granted permanent exclusive domain over the ten-mile-wide strip, the Canal Zone. The Americans took up the gauntlet in 1904, armed with the newly discovered knowledge that mosquitoes spread deadly diseases. In transit to the unfinished French ditch, Gorgas was admonished by a local: "A White man's a fool to go there and a bigger fool to stay." Fresh from his successful eradication campaign in Cuba, Gorgas and 4,100 workers systematically eradicated yellow fever from the Canal Zone.

Gorgas and his sanitation squads used the same systems that had destroyed the Aedes mosquito in Cuba, as well as new trial-and-error eradication techniques. According to Sonia Shah, the sanitation "blitzkrieg" consumed "the entire U.S. supply of sulphur, pyrethrum, and kerosene oil." Twenty-one quinine dispensaries flanking the canal also doled out daily preventive doses to most workers. By 1906, two years into construction, yellow fever completely disappeared, and malaria rates had fallen by 90%. Although Gorgas lamented that "We did not get rid of malaria on the Isthmus of Panama, as we did in Cuba," he understood the immense significance of his work. In 1905, the canal had a death rate three times higher than the continental United States. Upon completion in 1914, it had a death rate half that of the US. Officially, 5,609 workers (out of 60,000 total) died of disease and injury from 1904 through 1914. The canal was unlocked to traffic only days after the outbreak of the First World War on August 4, 1914.

In light of the discoveries made by Manson, Ross, Grassi, Reed, and Gorgas, among others, countries around the world established national health departments, schools of tropical medicine, benefactors for scientific research like the Rockefeller Foundation, departments of military hygiene, army nursing corps, sanitation commissions, public waste

"Make the Dirt Fly!": Innovative and effective mosquito control in Panama under Dr. William Gorgas allowed the Americans to succeed where the mosquito-chased Spanish, British, Scottish, and French had failed in constructing a Panama Canal. American efforts under President Theodore Roosevelt began in 1904, and the canal was opened to traffic in 1914. Here a member of a Sanitation Squad sprays oil on mosquito breeding grounds, Panama, 1906. *(Library of Congress)*

disposal infrastructure, and codified health laws. In his exploration of the impacts of mosquito control during the construction of the Panama Canal, Paul Sutter reports that "it was the commercial and military expansion of the United States into tropical Latin America and the Asian Pacific that most forcefully connected federal entomological expertise to public health campaigns. Indeed, these imperial campaigns helped to build federal public health capacity and to reframe disease control . . . as a federal issue during the early twentieth century." The United States was joined by a host of other countries in framing national health as being not only a civilian priority (or perhaps even a legal right) but a military necessity as well. The mosquito was at the top of everyone's hit list.

The construction of the Panama Canal secured American economic domination and naval supremacy.* "Effective control of malaria and yellow fever," acknowledges J. R. McNeill, "changed the balance of power in the Americas and the world." The scales of global power tipped toward a growing industrial, economic, and military American superpower. While Teddy Roosevelt opened new American economic frontiers, his policies also thrust the United States headlong into the great game of world politics. He personally played a hand at this international gaming table, winning the 1906 Nobel Peace Prize for brokering a settlement to the Russo-Japanese War.

The decisive Japanese victory over Russia in 1905 shocked global observers and marked a turning point in world history. It was the first major military triumph of an Asian power over a European power since the Mongol war machine crafted by Genghis Khan 700 years earlier. Japan seemingly arrived on the world stage out of nowhere. Formerly an introverted and reticent nation, Japan sought to modernize, industrialize, and join the currents of global commerce. The United States was now also positioned as a Pacific power, no longer confined to Atlantic waters since the colonial prize winnings of the Spanish-American War and the Panama Canal. Japan resented American economic encroachment on the Pacific Rim. In need of petroleum, rubber, tin, and other resources, the nation of islands eventually aimed to carve out its own imperial "Greater East Asia Co-Prosperity Sphere" just as the United States had done during the turn-of-the-century era of America. Conflict between the two vying Pacific nations remained dormant, for now.

In addition to the colonial spoils from the Spanish-American War, the United States used the conflict as an excuse to annex Hawaii. In 1893, a group of American plantation owners, entrepreneurs, and

* The US controlled the canal until 1977, when Panama slowly began administration in a joint operation with the US, until a complete handover to Panama was finalized in 1999.

investors, aided by US Marines, overthrew the traditional Hawaiian government and placed Queen Lili'uokalani under house arrest, forcing her to abdicate the throne two years later. The aim of these American conspirators was simple. Like Cuba, Hawaii under American jurisdiction meant foreign tariffs on their sugar bounty unloaded at American ports would no longer apply. Proponents of annexation argued that Hawaii was a strategically vital economic and military bastion and a prerequisite to promote and protect American interests in Asia. Despite the objection from most indigenous Hawaiians, Congress voted to officially annex the Territory of Hawaii in 1898 shortly after the outbreak of war with Spain. The following year, the United States established a permanent naval base at Pearl Harbor.

CHAPTER 17

This Is Ann: She's Dying to Meet You: The Second World War, Dr. Seuss, and DDT

With the Japanese attack on Pearl Harbor in December 1941, over 16 million Americans eventually shouldered the burdens of war and were thrust into combat against both the Axis powers and deadly mosquitoes. That infamous day drove the United States into a maelstrom of total war and set in motion a series of transformative events that rearranged and soldered the circuit board and conductors of global power, including the mosquito's place within this new composite world order. To her own jeopardy, the mosquito was inextricably tangled in these historic global affairs. Like our own life-or-death struggles being mediated by bullets on the bloodstained battlefields of the largest war ever witnessed, for the mosquito these were also troubling, life-threatening times.

At the outset of the Second World War, "the incidence of malaria in the United States was," according to the Office of Malaria Control in War Areas, a wartime predecessor to the Centers for Disease Control and Prevention (CDC), "the lowest in history." As the war unfolded, a very different story emerged. Combating the mosquito, as well as the human enemy, was paramount to victory on all fronts. The Second World War was a watershed for science, medicine, technology, and military hardware, including the modernization and enhancement of our weaponry and munitions against mosquitoes. During the conflict and the immediate Cold War "peace" that followed, effective synthetic malaria drugs like atabrine and chloroquine, and the mass-produced, inexpensive eradication chemical DDT, propelled the mosquito and her diseases into a graveyard spiral and a full-blown global retreat.* For the first time in history, humans gained the upper hand in our eternal war with mosquitoes.

Equipped with the recent discoveries of mosquito-borne disease by Ross, Grassi, Finlay, Reed, and others, during both world wars and certainly more so in the second, governments and their militaries were able to deal more effectively with mosquito control, contagion, and treatment. Having cornered the mosquito, and identified it as the purveyor of malaria, yellow fever, and other debilitating and deadly diseases, humans were finally learning how to scientifically fight her bite.

Our research, development, and experimental trial by fire for innovative mosquito-assassinating ammunition, however, took time. It was punched into hyperdrive when the Japanese awoke the American sleeping giant at Pearl Harbor. The US military-industrial juggernaut placed a high priority on mosquito research and viewed her annihilation as a vital cog in the Allied war effort. Quinine was shelved for more proficient synthetic malaria drugs such as atabrine and chloroquine, and the pesticidal properties of the cheap miracle-chemical DDT unearthed in 1939 proved to be a universal lifesaver.

In a more sinister application of these scientific advances, the mosquito was also ominously added to our military arsenal as a biological agent. The mosquito and her diseases were the substance of bone-chilling experimentation and medical and weapons research by both the Axis and Allied powers. We could now harness her destructive power and her dominion of death to purge our human enemies. In the Pontine Marshes surrounding Anzio, the Nazis deployed malarious mosquitoes as a premeditated biological weapon against Allied forces advancing on Rome.

Although the mosquito had been trapped by science, synthetic drugs, and the panacea insecticide DDT, she was by no means finished with her influential feeding and deadly carnage. Despite the unlocking of her secrets, between the outbreak of the First World War in 1914 and the unconditional surrenders of the Second in 1945, the mosquito continued to incapacitate and kill millions of soldiers and civilians around the

* DDT: dichloro-diphenyl-trichloroethane

planet. During the Second World War, however, American researchers and mosquito soldiers of the classified and top secret "Malaria Project" finally cracked her enigmatic code using the chemical formula of DDT. Hope was on the horizon.

Unlike in the Second World War, although always a willing and enthusiastic combatant, the mosquito was sidelined from the principal and pivotal fields of the First World War. She was all quiet on the Western Front. The frigid European theaters of war were simply too far north for her to enlist and contribute to the futile butchery. She did, however, make frequent guest appearances among significantly leaner troop concentrations in other, much smaller "sideshow" campaigns in Africa, the Balkans, and the Middle East. The influence of the mosquito, however, was generally restricted to personal dealings in death and did not bite into the larger concerns of the war or its outcome.*

Over 65 million men served in the First World War between 1914 and 1919. Roughly 10 million were killed and another 25 million wounded.† An estimated 1.5 million soldiers contracted a mosquito-borne disease, including my teenage malaria-gifted great-grandfather William Winegard. Unlike 95,000 others, he survived, thankfully. Given the sheer number of men who fought and died, these statistics are paltry. Mosquito-borne disease accounted for less than 1% of all war-related deaths—a far cry from her inventory of the past. Given her quarantined isolation in no-man's-land, the lonely mosquito did not alter

* On the Macedonian/Salonika Front, for example, the British and French facing off against the Bulgarians were ravaged by malaria. "Regret that my army is in hospital with malaria," replied the French commander when ordered to attack in October 1915. "One cannot do something with nothing." Roughly 50% of the French force of 120,000 contracted malaria. From a British force of 160,000 men, there were 163,000 admissions for malaria (more than one per man). An embedded journalist described the British soldiers as "listless, anemic, unhappy, sallow men whose lives were a physical burden to them and a material burden to the Army." When the Bulgarians finally surrendered in September 1918, the Allied Army had lost 2 million service days to malaria on this Salonika Front. The British penetration along the Eastern Mediterranean Levant from Egypt north through Palestine to Syria, led by General Edmund Allenby, as mentioned, was harassed by malaria but not as violently as expected, thanks in part to Allenby's hounding insistence on exploiting quinine, mosquito netting, and high terrain. Of the 2.5 million British imperial troops who served across North Africa, the Middle East, Gallipoli, and the southern Russian Caucasus, only 110,000 cases of malaria were reported. Conversely, malaria preyed on the opposing undersupplied and starving Ottoman-Turkish defenders with more zeal, infecting some 460,000 troops.

† Civilian deaths are imprecise and debated but generally fall between 7 and 10 million.

the outcome of this global Great War for Civilization. The conflict was decided beyond her scouring reach by a war of attrition waged in the stagnant trenches on the Western Front, zigzagging like an angry scar for 450 miles from the Swiss Alps to the Belgian coast on the North Sea and, to a far lesser extent, on the Eastern Front prior to the 1917 Russian Revolution and the ensuing civil war.

In the immediate fraudulent peace of the post-Versailles era, however, disease was far more lethal than it had been during the war itself. Abetted by cramped and squalid trench conditions and repatriation centers harboring soldiers returning to all four corners of the globe, the roving 1918–1919 influenza epidemic infected over 500 million people, killing upwards of 75 to 100 million worldwide, five times more than the world war that helped it go viral.* Influenza was not the only disease spread by homeward-bound veterans, although it has overshadowed all others in our collective memory. Australia, Britain, Canada, China, France, Germany, Italy, Russia, and the United States, among numerous other nations, all witnessed spikes of malaria. During the interwar years, the mosquito made up for lost time, unleashing a deluge of disease. Despite our realization that the mosquito caused malaria, yellow fever, filariasis, and dengue, it still proved difficult to stunt her dealings in death, even in affluent Western nations.

The average global malarial infection rate during the decade of the 1920s, for example, was calculated to be an astonishing 800 million per year, producing an annual death rate of 3.5 to 4 million. In the United States, 1.2 million Americans contracted malaria during the 1920s, slackening to 600,000, including 50,000 deaths, the following decade. Dengue was also roaring across the American South, infecting 600,000 Texans in 1922, including 30,000 in Galveston alone. A casual observer imparted the wisdom that attempting to whitewash mosquito-borne disease was as pointless as "a one-armed man [trying to] empty the Great Lakes with a spoon." During the 1930s, mosquito-borne disease was costing the United States an annual average of $500 million, up from

* The whereabouts of patient zero for this epidemic of "Spanish Flu" remains hotly contested among academics. While it certainly did not originate in Spain, theories place its roots in Boston, Kansas, France, Austria, or China. Boston appears to be the most likely.

$100 million at the turn of the century. When the Yangtze River in China flooded in 1932, malaria infections in affected areas reached 60%, causing a body count of over 300,000. Over the next five years, malaria ravaged an estimated 40 to 50 million Chinese. The newly minted Soviet Union, forged by revolution and civil war, was swallowed by mosquitoes.

The 1917 Bolshevik Revolution knocked Russia out of the war and eroded the Eastern Front. The ensuing Russian Civil War devastated populations, landscapes, and health services across the former czarist Romanov Empire. A tragic Malthusian ecological disaster of flooding, famine, and pestilence quickly followed, killing as many as 12 million Russians before the conclusion of the Civil War in 1923. Although the triumphant Red Army of Lenin, Trotsky, and Stalin provided the sweeping introduction of the Soviet Union and communism as a rival political, military, and economic global menace to Western democracies, this historic event was also accompanied by a tidal wave of disease and deprivation.

While Lenin was ruthlessly consolidating his power, *vivax* and *falciparum* malaria latched on to both the Great Famine and a catastrophic eruption of typhus and then thundered across the entire Soviet Union as far north as the glacial port of Archangel, situated roughly 125 miles below the Arctic Circle on a latitudinal line with Fairbanks, Alaska. This 1922–1923 Arctic epidemic reveals that with the perfect storm of temperature, trade, civil strife, suitable mosquitoes, and a vectoring warm-blooded human population, the scourge of malaria has no boundaries or territorial parameters. It is estimated that this peculiar and bewildering flurry of polar malaria infected 30,000 people, killing 9,000. According to historian James Webb, "in 1922 to 1923, the greatest European malaria epidemic of modern times struck." In the hardest-hit areas of the Volga River basin, southern Russia, the Stans, and the Caucasus, regional infection rates climbed between 50% and 100%. In 1923 alone, there were an estimated 18 million cases of malaria across the Soviet Union, with 600,000 deaths. The corresponding flea-borne typhus epidemic peaked between 1920 and 1922, blighting 30 million and killing 3 million Russians before tapering off in 1923, the same year the cyanide-based pesticide Zyklon B was

"Destroy Mosquito Larvae": The statement in the bottom left of this 1942 Soviet mosquito eradication poster references the war on mosquitoes and swamps. The Soviet Union/Russia had a long history with malaria. During the worst recorded European outbreak in 1922–23 following the Russian Revolution and the ensuing Civil War, malaria struck as far north as the Arctic port of Archangel. In 1923 alone, there were an estimated 18 million cases of malaria, including 600,000 deaths in the Soviet Union. *(U.S. National Library of Medicine)*

developed in Germany.* Malaria spiked again across the Soviet Union in 1934 with a caseload of almost 10 million. Given this distressing uptick in mosquito-borne disease during the interwar years, probing medical research and mosquito eradication programs gained momentum. While the meat-grinding conflict of the Great War and its violent aftershocks groaned and staggered to a halt, our battle in the trenches against our mosquito nemesis continued.

Within this ongoing scientific struggle against both mosquito-borne disease and mosquitoes themselves, an altogether strange breakthrough

* Originally invented and promoted as an insecticide, Zyklon B would become notorious for its use by the Nazis as the chemical agent used for the mass murder of Jews and other prisoners during the atrocities of the Holocaust.

occurred in 1917. While researching treatments for neurosyphilis, Austrian psychiatrist Dr. Julius Wagner-Jauregg came up with the half-baked idea of injecting his patients with a nonlethal, but still debilitating, strain of malaria to cure their late-stage insanity-delivering syphilis. It worked. Malarial fevers reaching 107 degrees Fahrenheit (42 Centigrade) charbroiled the heat-sensitive bacteria. Patients traded surefire, agonizing syphilitic death for saddling malaria, which I suppose is the lesser of two evils. The mosquito was now both a killer and a savior, although Jauregg counseled that "malaria therapy was still malaria." His treatment gained prominence and by 1922, malaria therapy was being prescribed to syphilitic patients in numerous countries, including the United States. By 1927, the year Jauregg won the Nobel Prize for his insane yet innovative remedy, American clinics had wait lists to "take" malaria like some kind of quick-fix pill. Thankfully, with the discovery of the world-altering antibiotic penicillin by Alexander Fleming a year later, the demand for Jauregg's malarial antidote fizzled out. Patients could now be cured of syphilis (and other bacterial infections) without being stung with malaria. Global mass production of penicillin began in 1940.

Generally, however, less invasive advances were unearthed during the interwar years to combat our most lethal enemy. Cinchona plantations expanded from South America, Mexico, and Dutch Indonesia to other parts of the world. Small and scattered coppices and thickets of cinchona trees eventually took root in British India and Sri Lanka and in the US territories of the Philippines, Puerto Rico, the Virgin Islands, and Hawaii. Mosquito control boards were established across the United States and other mosquito-infested countries and colonies. In 1924, the League of Nations, a feeble precursor to the United Nations, established its Malaria Commission under the canopy of its larger international health organization. The Rockefeller Foundation, conceived in 1913 by American Standard Oil tycoon John D. Rockefeller, was a revolutionary model of philanthropy replicated by many future charitable organizations, including the exemplary Gates Foundation. By 1950, under the motto of "promoting the well-being of humanity throughout the world," the Rockefeller Foundation had allocated $100 million to mosquito control and malaria and yellow fever research, among a host of other health-related endeavors.

The most audacious and successful interwar mosquito eradication program, however, was carried out on the distinguished Pontine Marshes by Benito Mussolini. The Italian dictator made the eradication of malaria via the draining of the Pontine Marshes one of his top priorities. For his National Fascist Party, it was a means of winning hearts and minds, expanding agricultural development in the uninhabited area, breeding "great rural warriors," and illuminating Mussolini's "second Italian Renaissance" for the world. His integral reclamation program began in earnest in 1929, when the life expectancy of a farmer in Italy's malarial regions was a dismal 22.5 years. A preliminary census of the Pontine Marshes found no permanent settlements and only 1,637 "web-toed, fever-ridden corkcutters" occupying dilapidated thatched huts. The report also warned that 80% of people who spent one day in the marshes could expect to contract malaria.

In the first of three stages, the swamps and tidal waters were drained or dammed. The "battle of the swamps," as the Fascist Party styled it, required an involuntary labor force, which peaked in 1933 at 125,000 men, most of whom were dubbed "racially inferior" Italians. Over 2,000 were also subjected to malaria medical experiments. In the second stage, stone-house homesteads and public utilities were constructed and the land was parceled out among forcefully relocated settlers. The third stage took measures against mosquitoes, such as window screens, sanitary improvements, and health services, and against malaria, by distributing quinine from well-stocked strategically placed depots.

Beginning in 1930, malaria-ridden workers cleared targeted undergrowth, planted over a million pine trees, and assembled hydraulic pumping stations along an astounding 10,300-mile-long checkerboard of newly constructed canals and dikes, including the Mussolini Canal, which empties harmlessly into the Tyrrhenian Sea near Anzio. Mussolini used the decade-long operation as a propaganda crusade, often posing shirtless with a shovel or wheat thresher in hand or atop his red motorcycle for photographs or newsreels among the sickly (but smiling) workers or picnicking lovers. Five architecturally distinct model towns were built between 1932 and 1939, including Latina, Aprilia, and Pomezia, along with eighteen rural satellite villages. Mussolini's advertising aside, his reclamation and eradication program, one of the first of its kind, was a resounding success. Malaria rates in the former marshes, and throughout Italy, plummeted by 99.8% from 1932 to 1939. During a few weeks in 1944, however, in a brazen act of biological warfare, the Nazis systematically reversed years of antimalarial gains.

Although mosquito research hit fever pitch during the interwar years, it would take a covert American Second World War program akin to the nuclear Manhattan Project to finally bite back at the mosquito, using newfangled synthetic antimalarial drugs and the mosquito-slaying services of DDT. Although DDT was first synthesized in 1874 by German and Austrian chemists, it was not until 1939 that German Swiss scientist Paul Hermann Müller recognized its insecticidal properties, earning him the 1948 Nobel Prize "for his discovery of the high efficiency of DDT as a contact poison against several arthropods."

Müller originally worked on organic plant-derived dyes and tanning agents, but his love of the outdoors and the flora and fauna of the natural world (and eating fruit) led him to experiment with plant-protection chemicals, including disinfectants. By observing and studying insects, Müller realized that these creatures absorbed chemicals differently from humans and other animals. He was also stirred to action in 1935 by a dire food shortage in Switzerland caused by insect crop infestation and by the lethal epidemic of typhus in Russia, mentioned earlier, and its extensive diffusion across eastern Europe. Determined to save lives, safeguard farms, and preserve his cherished fruit trees, Müller set out on his mission to "synthesize the ideal contact insecticide—one which would have a quick and powerful toxic effect upon the largest possible number of insect species while causing little or no harm to plants and warm-blooded animals." After four years of fruitless laboratory experiments on 349 unserviceable chemicals, number 350—DDT—was the magic bullet.

Following successful trials on the common housefly and the ruinous Colorado potato beetle, a series of rapid-fire tests on other pests revealed that DDT killed fleas, lice, ticks, sandflies, mosquitoes, and a swarm of other insects with astonishing effectiveness and efficiency—dispatching typhus, trypanosomiasis, plague, leishmaniasis, malaria, yellow fever, and a host of other vector-borne diseases in the process. The insecticidal mechanisms of DDT operate by quickly scrambling the proteins and plasma of sodium ion channels and neurotransmitters, disrupting the nervous system of its target, which leads to spasms, seizures, and death. In September 1939, as the Nazis and Soviets were carving up Poland under the Molotov-Ribbentrop Pact and triggering the Second World War, Paul Müller was in the Geigy AG (now the pharmaceutical giant Novartis) laboratory in Basel, Switzerland, activating the chemical age of DDT.

Despite DDT's German derivation, Hitler, on the advice of his personal physician, who considered DDT useless and dangerous to the health of the Reich, prevented its use by German forces, until it was employed judiciously in 1944. In contrast, by 1942, the United States had already begun mass production for the war effort, in conjunction with a colossal Malaria Project that was afforded the same levels of secrecy, security, and scope as the nuclear Manhattan Project. Both atomic weapons and DDT canisters were added to the Allied arsenal.

The US War Department created the Army School of Malariology in May 1942, and trained specialized cadres dubbed "Mosquito Brigades" or "Dipstick Soldiers," officially known as Malaria Survey Units, within the new military Division of Tropical Medicine. Wielding their DDT-spraying magic wands, these unconventional pioneering mosquito soldiers entered the war in Allied areas of operation in early 1943, hoping to make the mosquito dissolve and vanish. While DDT targeted the mosquito directly, it did not attack the disease of malaria itself. At the onset of war, this honor was reserved exclusively for quinine. An additional catalyst for the creation of the Malaria Project was the Japanese stranglehold on global cinchona plantations and quinine supplies.

The rapid Japanese expansion across the Pacific in early 1942 included the Dutch East Indies and its 90% global share of cinchona production. The capture of this quinine, along with petroleum, rubber, and tin, was key to Japanese military planning, with Germany also benefiting from large shipments. For the Allies, the lack of quinine posed a significant problem and a serious military setback. With limited and inadequate amounts of cinchona trickling in from India, South America, and overseas US territories, artificial alternatives were paramount to the prosecution of the war. Working under the umbrella and patronage of the Malaria Project, American chemists scrambled to action and the hunt for a synthetic cinchona-quinine substitute began in earnest.

Over 14,000 compounds were tested, including derivatives of mefloquine and malarone, which would be shelved until chloroquine resistance first appeared in 1957. Leo Slater explains in *War and Disease*, his study of the biomedical research on malaria, "In 1942 and 1943, the antimalarial program would find itself with three main scientific (and clinical) priorities: Synthesizing new compounds, understanding atabrine, and developing chloroquine. . . . On the heels of atabrine's development as the drug of choice, superseding quinine, would come chloroquine, a drug with newfound promise . . . but it would not emerge from clinical testing until after the end of hostilities." In 1943, atabrine production reached 1.8 billion tablet doses and increased to 2.5 billion in 1944.* While all Allied servicemen received their yellow fever vaccine injection, field commanders could not guarantee that they ingested their partially effective atabrine pills.

Given the side effects both real and rumored, many didn't. It left a bitter taste, caused yellowing of the skin and eyes and off-color urine, and triggered head and muscle aches. In rare cases it led to vomiting, diarrhea, and psychosis.† Atabrine did not, however, cause impotence and sterility, a GI gossip item that was quickly exploited by German and Japanese propaganda to diminish Allied morale, fighting strength, and manpower. By snubbing their atabrine, the enemy hoped, Allied soldiers would swap malaria as casually as they traded and bartered cigarettes, chewing gum, Hershey "D Ration" bars, and the pinup bombshells Rita Hayworth, Betty Grable, and Jane Russell.‡

While mosquito nets were also a mandatory piece of kit, one soldier

* Atabrine was also known as mepacrine and quinacrine.

† Recently, attention has been drawn to contemporary military personnel and permanent psychosis caused by mefloquine, the same antimalarial that gave me trippy, psychedelic dreams in 2004.

‡ During the war, the Hershey Chocolate Company churned out 3 billion "D Ration" or "Tropical" bars. By 1945, the production plant was dispensing 24 million units per week.

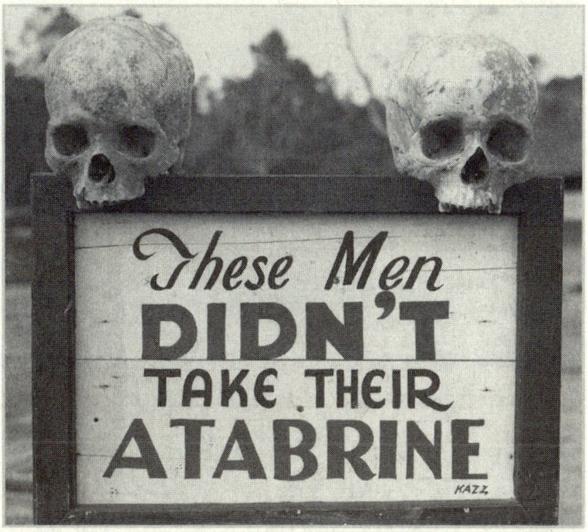

"These Men Didn't Take Their Atabrine": A sign posted outside the 363rd US Station Hospital in Port Moresby, Papua New Guinea, during the Second World War, warning Allied troops to take the antimalarial drug atabrine. Many soldiers did not take their daily dose as it caused yellowing of the skin, eyes, and off-colored urine, and triggered headaches, muscle pain, vomiting, and diarrhea. In rare cases it led to temporary or permanent psychosis, similar to modern-day mefloquine. *(National Museum of Health and Medicine)*

summed up their actual value. The troops, he remembered, "had neither the time nor the strength to bother about mosquito bars and head nets and gloves." Some soldiers purposefully renounced all malarial precautions in order to be taken out of the line, something commanders referred to as "malarial desertion," extremely difficult to prove and prosecute as a military offense. Prudent, switched-on officers went so far as to dole out atabrine tablets during roll call and have troops urinate on sight to produce visual evidence that they were compliant with orders. Generally, however, for combatants of all nationalities in the Pacific theater, malaria was, as one soldier put it, "inevitable and just a part of doing business as usual." Even with DDT and atabrine, the statistics for mosquito-borne disease were shockingly high. We can only guess at what malaria rates would have looked like without these two lifesaving scientific breakthroughs.

There were roughly 725,000 reported cases of mosquito-borne disease among American troops during the war, including approximately 575,000 cases of malaria, 122,000 cases of dengue, and 14,000 cases of filariasis. Mosquito-borne disease equated to 3.3 million soldier sick days. It is estimated that 60% of all Americans stationed in the Pacific contracted malaria at least once. Famous wartime recipients include naval lieutenant John F. Kennedy, war correspondent Ernie Pyle, and Private Charles Kuhl. In August 1943 during the Allied invasion of Sicily, Kuhl was one of two soldiers famously slapped by an enraged General George S. Patton, who accused them of cowardice for faking "battle fatigue" or "shell shock." With a soaring temperature of 102.2 degrees, Kuhl was in fact suffering from and subsequently diagnosed with malaria. The Axis military records are spotty when it comes to statistics on mosquito-borne disease. Based on the best estimates, though, they were comparable to Allied infection rates, if not slightly higher.

Allied servicemen, particularly in the Pacific theater, were drowning in mosquito-borne disease, which prompted a pacing General Douglas MacArthur, commander of US Army Forces in the Far East, to ominously thunder, "This will be a long war if for every division I have facing the enemy, I must count on a second division in the hospital with malaria, and a third division convalescing from this debilitating disease!" The carpet bombing of tiny volcanic atolls during the American island-hopping campaign across the Pacific increased the breeding grounds, and mosquito populations boomed. The 1st Marine Division was gutted by malaria during the 1942 Battle of Guadalcanal, nicknamed "Operation Pestilence," during which 60,000 cases of malaria were reported among US forces. Following the Japanese evacuation in February 1943, it was evident that the Japanese had also been swimming in malarial fevers. Nearly 80% of Australian and New Zealand troops in Papua New Guinea contracted malaria, whereas Japanese troops on Saipan were shredded by malaria during the American invasion in the summer of 1944. In Bataan, the mosquito sided with Japan and reduced the American defenders and their Filipino allies to skeletons, with thousands marching to their deaths on the way to ramshackle POW camps, where many more suffered the same fate.

"Operation Pestilence": A member of the 1st Marine Division (US) being evacuated with malaria during the Battle of Guadalcanal, September 1942. Over 60,000 cases of malaria were reported among US forces between August 1942 and February 1943 during the Guadalcanal Campaign. *(Library of Congress)*

Led by malariologist Dr. Paul Russell, who had MacArthur's ear and backing, blanket DDT spraying in the Pacific and Italy began in 1943. Upon their first meeting, MacArthur stood up and squarely muttered, "Doctor, I have a real problem with malaria." Russell, who only three days earlier was stateside, did not realize that MacArthur had personally summoned him by wiring the chief of staff, General George Marshall, the simple plea, "Find Dr. Russell. Send him to me." Early on in New Guinea, Russell was approached by a hardened infantry commander who snorted, "If you want to play with mosquitoes go back to Washington and stop bothering me, I'm busy getting ready to fight the Japs." Another passerby chimed in, "We are here to kill Japs and to hell with mosquitoes." When Russell informed MacArthur of the exchange, it was the officer who was sent packing.

American Malaria Survey Units were on the ground in MacArthur's areas of operation by March 1943, spraying DDT, sanitizing mosquito breeding grounds, and swamping GIs with atabrine and advertisements. Soldiers joked that if they so much as spilled even a drop of water or spit on the dirt, within seconds "a dipstick" appeared out of thin air to suck it up or spray it down. The "mosquito chasers" also spread almost 12 million gallons of kerosene oil on mosquito breeding grounds across the Pacific, the rough equivalent of the infamous 1989 *Exxon Valdez* oil spill in Alaska. By the end of 1944, more than 4,000 "mosquito-killers" were active at 2,070 camps in over 900 war areas. It appeared DDT was unstoppable. American production increased from 153,000 pounds in

The Malaria Project: An American soldier being showered with DDT, 1945. During the Second World War, DDT was an indispensable weapon in the war against mosquitoes, waged by the US Division of Tropical Medicine and its Malaria Survey Units known as "Mosquito Brigades" or "Dipstick Soldiers." DDT proved to be a lifesaving mosquito-killing chemical. *(Public Health Image Library-CDC)*

1943 to 36 million in 1945. At last we had found our war-winning ammunition against mosquitoes. While DDT targeted mosquitoes, an educational component of the Malaria Project was trained on the troops themselves. Across the Pacific (and other malarious fronts) a torrent of mosquito-driven propaganda complemented and reinforced Russell's eradication teams absorbed in their mission of drowning mosquitoes in DDT.

Walt Disney's 1943 malaria prevention film, *The Winged Scourge*, with cameos by Snow White's Seven Dwarfs, was a howling hit among troops. The lusty mosquito handbook *This is Ann: She's Dying to Meet You* was also released in 1943 to great acclaim and became a favored GI bedtime story. The hypersexualized pamphlet was penned and illustrated by none other

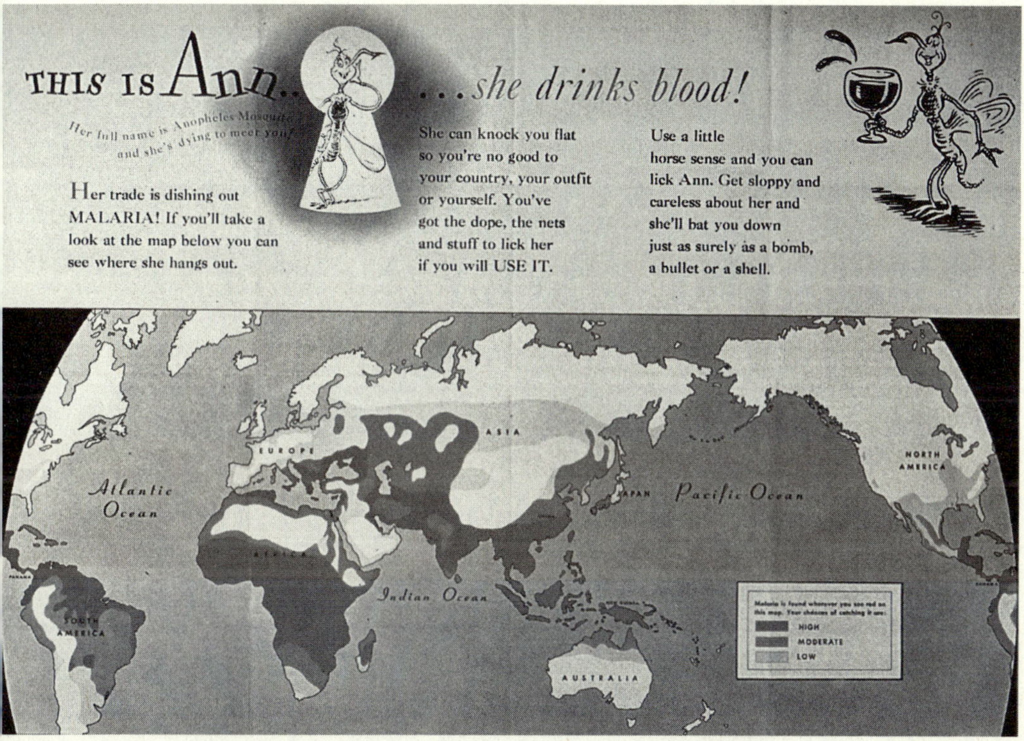

"This is Ann . . . she drinks blood! Her full name is Anopheles Mosquito and she's dying to meet you!": This 1943 flyer was one of many malaria/mosquito posters and pamphlets created for the Special Service Division's war animation department by Captain Theodor Seuss Geisel, our beloved Dr. Seuss, warning troops about the dangers of mosquitoes while promoting protective and defensive measures. The map outlines the geographic range of malaria. Ann, a hypersexualized, risqué mosquito, makes frequent appearances in his wartime print and screen animation. *(U.S. National Library of Medicine)*

than Dr. Seuss. His risqué mosquito was personified as a tangible yet tantalizing succubus, seductress, and local village prostitute who ensnares and feeds on eager, unprotected troops. "Ann really gets around. Her full name is Anopheles Mosquito and her trade is dishing out Malaria. . . . She works hard and Ann—knows her stuff. . . . Ann moves around at night, anytime from dusk to sunrise (*a real party gal*), and she's got a thirst. No whisky, gin, beer, or rum coke for Ann . . . she drinks Blood. . . . By and by Ann wants Just another little drink and off she goes looking for a sap who hasn't got sense enough to protect himself."

During the war, Captain Theodor Seuss Geisel, our beloved Dr. Seuss, created numerous posters, pamphlets, and training films on the dangers of "Ann" for the war animation department.* While she could not compete with the likes of Rita, Betty, or Jane, the pinup mosquito model and actress Ann makes frequent appearances in Seuss's wartime work, including a starring role in three mosquito-themed, sexually stylized episodes of Geisel's comical instructional military cartoon *Private Snafu* (slang GI acronym for "Situation Normal: All Fucked Up"). The popular animated series produced by Warner Bros. was infused with Looney Tunes music and the familiar voice of Mel Blanc, voice actor of Bugs Bunny, Daffy Duck, and Porky Pig.

Hundreds of cartoons, pamphlets, and posters marketing and advertising the dangers of mosquitoes and malaria were produced for Special Services throughout the war. To grab the attention of female-starved GIs, many, like those of Dr. Seuss, were highly suggestive. A half-naked beautiful, buxom woman covered a billboard in New Guinea with a four-word caption REMEMBER THIS, TAKE ATABRINE! Similar billboards depicting naked women with comparable messages greeted troops across the Pacific, Italy, and the Middle East. Others painted mosquitoes as bucktoothed, slanted-eyed Japanese squinting through round glasses. General MacArthur lauded the combined efforts of both the malaria propaganda crusade and Russell's DDT mosquito crews to eliminate disease and curtail its draining effect on his operational manpower. MacArthur "was not at

* Geisel also drew the Seuss-like characters and artwork for the advertisements of the DDT-based insecticide FLIT with the tagline and popular catchphrase "Quick, Henry! The Flit." He also cartooned posters for Esso and Standard Oil.

"Is Your Organization Prepared to Fight Both Enemies?": A highly racist American antimalaria poster from the Pacific theater during the Second World War highlights the lethality of the mosquito and her influence on fighting efficiency and combat strength. There were roughly 725,000 reported cases of mosquito-borne disease among American troops during the war. *(U.S. National Archives)*

all worried about defeating the Japanese," recalled Russell, "but he was greatly concerned about the failure up to that time to defeat the Anopheles mosquito."

Like his American counterpart Douglas MacArthur, while directing British forces battling the Japanese in Burma, Field Marshal Sir William Slim also agonized, "For every man evacuated with wounds we had one hundred and twenty evacuated sick." What Slim didn't know was that his forces actually held the malarial advantage during the brutal Burma campaign, which was defined by slashing monsoon rains, unforgiving jungle terrain, and crippling, untamed disease. Japanese infection rates in Burma rang in at an astounding 90% against a British incidence of *only* 80%. War-ravaged China (and its Japanese occupiers) also continued to suffer, averaging roughly 30 million malarial infections per year during the war.

In the North African and Italian campaigns, the allegiance of the mosquito was fleeting and fickle. Across the ancient desert sands from Morocco through Tunisia and Libya to Egypt, the malarial rate among German and Italian troops was twice that of Allied soldiers, before balancing out in Sicily. With the Germans occupying high-ground defensive positions, malaria (and louse-borne typhus) hit the Allies harder during the mainland Italian campaign, specifically around Salerno/ Naples, Anzio, and the northern Arno and Po Rivers. Overall, however, as DDT-spraying mosquito teams accompanied the plodding Allied advance, malaria and typhus rates continuously decreased among both combatants and civilians on the Italian peninsula. "Cardinal points in the successful execution of the typhus control program," declared Colonel Charles Wheeler, were "the use of a lousicidal [*sic*] powder such as DDT." This same DDT "dusting" applied to mosquito-borne malaria as well.

For all nations embroiled in the Pacific theater and Italy, malaria proved to be the "Great Debilitator." In short, on a strategic scale, mosquito-borne disease was an opportunistic enemy and afflicted all belligerents relatively equally and did not tilt the balance of combat in

"A Day in the Life": Surrounded by ancient desert sands, two British soldiers write letters home through the lens and protection of mosquito netting, Egypt, 1941. *(Library of Congress)*

either the European or Pacific wars in the Allies' favor. The Soviet body count of 25 million dead helped win the wars. The Achilles heel of the Axis powers—dire shortages of petroleum and steel, among other scarce resources—helped the Allies win the wars. Unrivaled and unparalleled American military-industrial output, including petroleum and DDT, and futuristic technology, including nuclear weapons, helped the Allies win the wars.

While Russell's DDT combat units and Dr. Seuss's provocative cartoon propaganda were engaging the "Ann"opheles mosquito, she was also being primed by the Nazis as a contract killer for a sinister cloak-and-dagger operation. At Anzio in 1944, they unleashed mosquito-borne biological warfare against the invading Allies and the Italian people, who had recently renounced their Nazi associates. It was in September 1943 that Italy had substituted the Axis for the Allies. Hitler was enraged. This treason only cemented his delusional prewar suspicions about the substandard Italian racial pedigree. In his view, the Italian traitors needed to be punished. The defense of Italy and the suppression of its insurgent population was left to the Wehrmacht, with an occupation policy of "war against civilians."

After the loss of Sicily in 1943, the Germans successfully defended the Gustav Line south of the Pontine Marshes, necessitating an Allied landing at Anzio in an effort to outflank the German positions. By this time, however, mosquitoes and malaria had been methodically restored to the marshes and subsequently to Italy. In October 1943, Field Marshal Albert Kesselring, or perhaps even Hitler himself, issued the order to purposefully regenerate mosquitoes and disease in the Pontine Marshes—a textbook example of biological warfare. Kesselring had ordered his units to proceed "with all the means at our disposal and with maximum harshness. I will back any officer who in his choice and harshness of means goes beyond our customary limits." Hitler agreed that "the battle must be waged with holy hatred."

For starters, the Germans confiscated and warehoused all quinine supplies and mosquito netting from civilians and compromised the windows and screens on private homes. Moreover, Italian veterans returning from the Balkan Front brought back quinine-resistant strains of *falciparum*. The Germans then reversed the draining pumps and opened the dikes, refilling 90% of the marshes with brackish water interspersed with land mines and defensive obstacles, felling the pine trees so carefully planted during the reclamation project. The Nazi inner circle was being advised by German malariologists that the return of salt water would encourage the proliferation of the deadly mosquito species *Anopheles labranchiae*, which thrives in brackish environments (the mosquito of choice, as it transmits *falciparum*).

The flooding was not only an act of biological warfare against the advancing Allied soldiers, but also revenge against the turncoat Italian civilian population, who would suffer the effects long after the war was over. "In pursuit of these twin ambitions," notes Yale University historian Frank Snowden in his consummate study of malaria in Italy, "the Germans carried out the only known example of biological warfare in twentieth-century Europe. . . . The medical emergency caused by the German plan lasted for three epidemic seasons and exacted a fierce toll in suffering." It was along the Mussolini Canal at Anzio in 1944 that my wife's grandfather, Sergeant Walter "Rex" Raney, your average, archetypal American GI, received his malarial seasoning. What he did not know until I told him seventy-three years later, in the spring of 2017, was that he was a victim of premeditated Nazi biological warfare.

Born in a small farming community in western Colorado, Rex enlisted with the 45th "Thunderbird" US Infantry Division in 1940. In the spring of 1943, he fought his way through North Africa, and participated in the invasion of Sicily in July of that same year. During the five weeks of fighting on the island, there were 22,000 cases of malaria among the American, Canadian, and British troops, and comparable rates among the Italian and German defenders. In September, Rex landed on the Italian mainland at Salerno and battled his way to the gates of Monte Cassino and the German Gustav Line by January 1944. He participated in the amphibious landings at Anzio, to the rear of the Gustav Line, that same month.

From January to June, Rex and the 45th Division were bogged down along the Mussolini Canal. "We dug in along that waterlogged canal and didn't move a heck of a lot until we were taken out of the line in June to prepare for the invasion of southern France in August 1944," Rex recalled. He then recounted the English translation for place names upon his landing at Anzio, suggesting a long struggle with deadly mosquitoes: Field of Death, Dead Woman, Dead Horse, Field of Meat, and, in honor of the underworld ferryman of the deceased crossing the River Styx, Charon. "Those cold-blooded mosquitoes were everywhere at Anzio. I think those critters there were even worse than during our prewar training and maneuvers in Pitkin, Louisiana. Those blasted mosquitoes were more relentless than the German shelling," Rex reminisced to me while reclining in his La-Z-Boy armchair, sipping on his standard after-dinner Scotch. "By the time those mosquito-spraying fellows came around and drenched us and everything else they could aim at with

"Jane's OK—She's Not at Anzio": A British soldier admiring a malaria warning sign on the Anzio Front in Italy, May 1944. To grab the attention of female-starved GIs, many signs like this one were highly suggestive. Similar billboards depicting naked women and comparable messages greeted troops across the Pacific, Italy, and the Middle East. *(Imperial War Museum)*

DDT, I guess, given what you said about those German marsh mosquitoes, it was already too late for me." Rex remembered a sign written and posted in classic GI battlefield humor along the Mussolini Canal: "It said something to the effect of 'Pontine Marshes Fever Company: Malaria for Sale.'" He looked up at me with a wry grin and with his typical dry wit said, "I must have purchased a few rounds of that malaria for myself." During the four-month operations at Anzio, 45,000 American soldiers, including Sergeant Rex Raney, were treated for malaria and other afflictions despite the use of over 500 gallons of DDT. Mark Harrison points out in his intricate study *Medicine and Victory* that, as one might expect, this biological warfare was "a decision which backfired on the Germans, who themselves suffered high rates of malaria as a result of their actions."

Following his malarial seasoning at Anzio, Rex, now a sergeant major, soldiered through his sickness and in August 1944 participated in the Allied landings in southern France, before suffering through the Battle of the Bulge during the wanton winter of 1944–1945. His 45th Division then smashed through the Siegfried Line in mid-March 1945 and crossed the Rhine River into Germany. On April 28, Rex received "puzzling and strange orders for fighting troops." The notice read: "Tomorrow the notorious concentration camp at Dachau will be in our zone of action. When captured, nothing is to be disturbed. International commissions will move in to investigate conditions when fighting ceases. Upon capture of Dachau by any battalion, post air tight guard and allow no one to enter or leave." On April 29, the eve of Hitler's suicide, Rex and his comrades liberated the Dachau concentration camp outside Munich and came face-to-face with the horrors perpetrated by the Führer's now crumbling Third Reich. When I asked Rex to elaborate, he solemnly lowered his tearing eyes and tabled his shaking Scotch. "That was a dark day," he hauntingly whispered. "One I rather wish I could forget." I didn't press him further.

Dachau was home to the Nazi tropical medicine program, and Jewish prisoners were used as human subjects for malaria research. According to the unit histories of Rex's 157th Regiment, there "were 'patients' undergoing experiments of unspeakably inhumane nature. Others were infected with diseases so that effectiveness of various treatments could be tested. . . . A Professor Schilling caused prisoners to be infected with various diseases, such as malaria." At Dachau, Rex contracted his second dose of wartime malaria from an experimental Nazi mosquito. "This second round of malaria was far worse. As much as I wanted to stay with my unit, Doc told me I had to go home," Rex reminisced with regret.

"I Thought I Was a Goner": Sergeant Rex Raney at Anzio, Italy, in May 1944, shortly before contracting malaria, unleashed as a premeditated Nazi biological weapon in the Pontine Marshes to slow the Allied advance. When liberating the Dachau concentration camp in April 1945, Rex was infected with a second round of malaria courtesy of experimental malaria mosquitoes of the Nazi tropical medicine program. *(Raney Family)*

"The Germans couldn't get me, but this malaria sure knocked me flat. I thought I was a goner." His war, after 511 days of combat, was over. Rex spent eleven days in hospital in and out of malarial consciousness and delirium before being invalided home. Sergeant Major Rex Raney peacefully passed away at his home in western Colorado in 2018 shortly before his ninety-seventh birthday and was buried with full military honors.

While Nazi doctor Claus Schilling, the chief resident of the Nazi tropical medicine program at Dachau, was performing chilling malaria research on involuntary test subjects, American physicians of the Malaria Project were conducting experimental clinical trials of their own.* Malaria was such a vexing concern for American military strategists and operational planners that normal codes of ethics and scientific protocols were shelved during this time of total war. Beginning in late 1943, the US Division of Tropical Medicine authorized the use of incarcerated and syphilitic Americans as voluntary human test subjects (in exchange for a reduced sentence or a cure for syphilis) within the larger Malaria Project. American experimentation mirrored the Nazi procedures being carried out on Jewish prisoners at Dachau, "where Claus Schilling went to work every day," relays Karen Masterson in her exquisitely detailed book *The Malaria Project*. "He arrived in early 1942 with a mission not unlike the American Malaria Project's mission—to find a cure for malaria." The *only* difference was that Schilling forced his sadistic trials and tests upon involuntary subjects and, following his capture, was tried by an American tribunal for war crimes.†

Schilling's feeble defense for his ineffably evil and malignant transgressions—that he was ordered to conduct experimental malaria research by Reichsführer-SS Heinrich Himmler—didn't cut it. His legal counsel then asked the court to explain the difference between

* Following the "trio of discoveries" in 1897 by Ross, Grassi, and Koch, during its infancy the international scientific world of malariology was small. Schilling, for example, was the first-ever director of the Tropical Medicine Division from 1905 to 1936 at the Robert Koch Institute, founded by our germ theorist in 1891 as a think tank and research station for the study and prevention of disease. Upon retirement in 1936, Schilling accepted a post in Mussolini's Italy to conduct malaria experiments on the inmates of psychiatric asylums and hospitals.

† Of the roughly 1,000 test subjects used by Schilling, over 400 died from mosquito-borne disease or lethal doses of experimental synthetic antimalarial drugs.

Schilling's work and that undertaken by American wartime researchers on inmates at the Atlanta Federal Penitentiary and the notorious Stateville Correctional Center near Chicago, or at numerous psychiatric hospitals. Schilling's defense team also alluded to Australian malaria experimentation on volunteers, including wounded soldiers and Jewish refugees. This line of twisted reasoning didn't cut it either. While Schilling was hanged for crimes against humanity in 1946, American malarial experiments on inmates continued into the 1960s. This multinational research, however, also served a darker purpose—biological weapons.

In 1941, the America-Britain-Canada Conference (ABC-1) established the joint coordination of wartime resources and strategies with a mission to "cooperate in broad defense." By 1943, ABC biological weapons researchers were working in harmony at Fort Detrick, Maryland, home to the US Army Biological Warfare Laboratories. The international team conducted various projects (some with human subjects, including conscientious objectors such as Seventh-day Adventists) with numerous toxins such as the usual suspects of plague, smallpox, anthrax, botulism, and yellow fever, and the two newcomers, mosquito-borne Venezuelan equine and Japanese encephalitis. "There were innovative efforts to weaponize a number of viruses," reports Donald Avery in his tour of ABC biological weapons, *Pathogens for War*, "yellow fever being considered the most promising." Researchers brainstormed ideas for delivery systems for yellow fever, including the two possible candidates. One was to infect millions of Aedes mosquitoes with yellow fever and then unleash mosquito hordes on Japan. Another was to infect German POWs with disease, possibly yellow fever, and parachute them back into the Reich as instigators for epidemics.

The ABC team was not flying solo in the shadowy world of biological weapons research. The Japanese biological warfare research center in China, dubbed Unit 731, used thousands of Chinese, Koreans, and Allied POWs as test subjects. Unit 731 conducted trials with multiple agents, including yellow fever, plague, cholera, smallpox, botulism, anthrax, and various venereal diseases, among others. Human experimentation and frequent aerial tests on cities, most notably with cholera flies and plague, killed upwards of 580,000 Chinese civilians. This deliberate biological infection was finally acknowledged by Japan in 2002. The culmination of the tests was to be a biological attack on California, using plague bombs carried by one-way flights or by timed balloons delivered on target by prevailing wind currents. Japan surrendered in the face of nuclear annihilation before the biological menace of "Operation Cherry Blossoms at Night" could be put into effect.

Nazi Germany's *Blitzableiter* (Lightning Rod) biological weapons program, operating primarily out of the Mauthausen, Sachsenhausen, Auschwitz-Birkenau, Buchenwald, and Dachau concentration and death camps, conducted human trials on Jewish and Soviet prisoners. German researchers, who shared information and results with their Japanese counterparts from Unit 731, developed similar ideas for yellow fever transmission to those of the ABC alliance. Discounting, but not diminishing, the Japanese biological trials on Chinese villages, the only known purposeful deployment of a biological weapon during the war was the premeditated 1944 Nazi proliferation of malarial mosquitoes to the Pontine Marshes. By 1948, DDT and the restoration of Mussolini's prewar reclamation infrastructure had shored up the damage. Anzio and the Pontine Marshes, or Italy in its entirety for that matter, serve as an excellent statistical example of the mosquito-eradicating magic of DDT.

The Battle of Anzio left the region in a quagmire. Nearly everything Mussolini had accomplished was sabotaged. The cities were in ruin, the steppes depopulated, mosquitoes were frolicking in the marshes, and malaria punched a hole through the Italian population. Malarial deaths in the marshes rose exponentially from 33 in 1939 to 55,000 in 1944. By the end of the war, malaria rates had quadrupled across the country, reaching half a million by 1945. And yet, the fate of the marshes was reversed again. Within a few years, as DDT rained down on Italy, the water diversion and eradication infrastructure of the marshes was restored. The insecticide was so effective it was reported that gleeful Italians "are now throwing DDT at brides instead of rice." The last of Italian malaria was conquered in 1948, with the aid of DDT and the new antimalarial drug chloroquine, which supplanted the now ineffective quinine, to which malaria had become resistant.

The Second World War and its technological terrors and scientific advances opened up a brave, if not scary, new world. "DDT was just one of a multitude of postwar technologies that characterized the modern world," maintains David Kinkela in his book *DDT and the American Century: Global Health, Environmental Politics, and the Pesticide That Changed the World*, tracing the evolution of the insecticide. Within this modern world, for the first time, humanity was unshackling itself from mosquito-borne disease. These innovations, including atomic energy and DDT, could be used to benefit humanity by powering the planet and condemning the mosquito to the ash heap of history.

By 1945, DDT was made commercially available to farmers in the US, and was being used, in combination with cheap and effective chloroquine, by international aid organizations and individual nations alike, to eradicate mosquito-borne diseases. The American wartime Army School of Malariology and Office of Malaria Control in War Areas were expanded and rebranded in 1946 as the Communicable Disease Center (now known as the Centers for Disease Control and Prevention, or CDC) and continued the blitz on the mosquito. Situated at the heart of the southern zone of endemic malarial infection, Atlanta was strategically positioned to headquarter this new branch of the US Public Health Service. With an initial annual budget hovering around $1 million, 60% of the 370 original CDC employees (schematically arranged on a personnel flow chart in the shape of a mosquito) were assigned to mosquito and malaria eradication. By 1949, the agency initiated programs designed to counter biological warfare, which officially converged in 1951 into the Epidemic Intelligence Service branch of the CDC. During its first few foundational years, CDC mosquito control crews, determined to assassinate the deadly vehicle for malaria, sprayed 6.5 million American homes with DDT.

Two years after the establishment of the CDC, the World Health Organization (WHO) was founded in 1948 by the freshly painted and optimistic United Nations. The continuation of the wartime success of mosquito eradication was a top priority. In 1955, with financial backing from the United States, WHO launched its Global Malaria Eradication Programme. Armed with DDT and chloroquine, the war against mosquitoes would be the next world war. Implemented successfully across large areas of the developing world, this effort soon cut the malaria rates in numerous countries in Latin America and Asia by 90% or better. Even for Africa, hope that this age-old scourge would be brought to an end seemed to be in sight. By 1970, it appeared that we had finally turned the tide of battle against our dreaded mosquito foe and were achieving global victory.

Between 1947 and 1970, the year that sales peaked at more than $2 billion, DDT production, primarily based in the US, rose more than 900%. In 1963, for example, fifteen American companies, among them Dow, DuPont, Merck, Monsanto (now a division of Bayer), Ciba (now Novartis), Pennwalt/Pennsalt, Montrose, and Velsicol pumped out 82,000 tons of DDT worth $1.04 billion. Our planet has been bathed in roughly 1.8 million tons (4 billion pounds) of DDT, with more than 600,000 tons (1.32 billion pounds) blanketed across the United States alone.

In 1945, insects caused the destruction of $360 million ($4 billion today) worth of American crops. Between 1945 and 1980, global agriculture was annually spreading 40,000 tons of DDT on ingestible crops, increasing yields and producing bountiful harvests free from the predation of pestering insects. In India, not only did the widespread use of DDT engulf mosquitoes and rout endemic malaria, but during the 1950s, agricultural and industrial productivity increased by an annual average of over $1 billion. Around the planet, harvests increased and consumer costs on staple foods such as wheat, rice, potatoes, cabbage, and corn dropped by as much as 60% in certain regions of Africa, India, and Asia. DDT was a universal success and was lauded as a lifesaving chemical. This compound was the mosquito's Kryptonite, and provided a future for millions of people throughout the world.

Wherever DDT was used in significant quantities, the incidence of malaria declined precipitously. In South America, for example, malaria cases fell by 35% between 1942 and 1946. By 1948, there was not a single malaria-related death in all of Italy. The United States was declared malaria-free in 1951. In India, the number of malaria cases fell from 75 million that same year to just 50,000 a decade later. In Sri Lanka, where the average annual malaria rate hovered around 3 million, DDT spraying was initiated in 1946. By 1964, a mere 29 Sri Lankans contracted

"DDT Is Good for Me!": A 1947 *Time* magazine advertisement for Pennsalt DDT products. By 1945, DDT was made commercially available to farmers in the US and was being used, in combination with cheap and effective chloroquine, by international aid organizations and individual nations alike to eradicate mosquito-borne diseases. During the immediate postwar years, it appeared that DDT was our war-winning weapon against our deadliest predator. *(Science History Institute)*

malaria. By 1975, malaria had been banished from Europe. Globally, between 1930 and 1970, mosquito-borne diseases were reduced by an astounding 90% (in a population that nearly doubled).

Not only had totalitarian regimes been defeated, we were also finally and authoritatively overpowering our deadliest enemy—the mosquito. "This is the DDT era of malariology," declared Dr. Paul Russell, the wartime mosquito crusader, in *Man's Mastery of Malaria*. "For the first time," he announced in 1955, it was possible "to banish malaria completely." The mosquito-killing chemical of DDT, synthetic antimalaria drugs, and yellow fever vaccinations appeared to be unstoppable. We had turned the tide of battle, and the mosquito and her army of diseases were in full retreat. For the first time in our epic and bloody war with our most persistent predator, we were winning on all fronts. As it turned out, that war was far from over. For the mosquito and her malaria parasite, in their struggle for survival against DDT, chloroquine, and our other weapons of extermination, resistance was not futile.

CHAPTER 18

Silent Springs and Superbugs: The Mosquito Renaissance

In 2012, environmentalists around the world celebrated the fiftieth anniversary of Rachel Carson's seminal treatise *Silent Spring*. The villain of Carson's story was of course the "elixirs of death," or DDT. "Few books published in the United States have enjoyed the influence of *Silent Spring*," acknowledges James McWilliams in *American Pests: The Losing War on Insects from Colonial Times to DDT*. "Rachel Carson's attack on DDT and related insecticidal compounds had an impact that has been compared with that of Thomas Paine's *Common Sense* and Harriet Beecher Stowe's *Uncle Tom's Cabin* . . . and sparked the modern environmental movement." McWilliams asserts that "*Silent Spring*, much like *Common Sense* and *Uncle Tom's Cabin*, tapped an emotion deeply embedded in the American psyche, a belief ineradicable and genuine." Following the release of *Silent Spring*, Judy Hansen, former president of the American Mosquito Control Association, remembers that "suddenly, it was fashionable to be an environmentalist." The book remained atop the *New York Times* bestseller list for an astounding 31 weeks. In 1964, only 18 months after publication, Carson died tragically of cancer during her fifty-sixth spring, knowing that she had made a heroic difference.

During the tumultuous protest decade of the 1960s, the seed of the environmental revolution was planted by Carson's 1962 ecofriendly worldview, fertilized by the use of the defoliant Agent Orange in Vietnam, and watered by Joni Mitchell's 1970 hit song "Big Yellow Taxi." As academic findings and field research confirmed Carson's fatalistic philosophy, the Canadian folksinger begged farmers to shelve their DDT in favor of birds, bees, and the beloved spotted apples and fruit trees of DDT's pioneering chemist Paul Müller. With the benefit of looking back at the bygone DDT clouds from both sides now, Mitchell was right to reprimand farmers for paving paradise with the insecticide. It was the widespread, carpeting agricultural application of DDT that created environmental degradation and mosquito defiance, not its relatively limited and surgical use solely as a mosquito killer.

While the toxic and damaging environmental ramifications of the blanketing agricultural use of DDT are well known and generally undisputed, not all recent commentators support Carson's prophecy of gilded paradise cities with estranged DDT spray guns and welcoming jungles of organic roses. "Of note," reported the American Institute of Medicine of the National Academies in 2004, "when used indoors in limited quantities, DDT's entry into the global food chain is minimal." While the current squabble over Carson's scientific evidence and methodology and the reinstatement of DDT as an agent against mosquito-borne disease persists, the reality for most mosquito-infested regions of our planet is that DDT simply doesn't work anymore. The rancorous venom between environmentalists and those ripping on Rachel for her role in the demise of DDT, and the ensuing resurgence of mosquito-borne disease, are spinning their wheels in an endless, futile circle game. Rachel is innocent.

If it is somehow pacifying or soothing to assign blame to anyone or anything, we can point the mollifying finger squarely at the mosquito's evolutionary survival instincts. During her last stand on the final frontiers of the war of attrition between man and mosquito, she withstood the initial shock and awe of our insecticidal onslaught. Borrowing time as an ally, the mighty mosquito gained biological strength and eventually outsmarted and resisted science by genetically counterattacking and defeating DDT. Amid the rallying cries of the fomenting counterculture marches and social revolutions of the turbulent sixties, the mosquito and malaria led their own defiant movements by rejecting the established order of DDT and antimalarial drugs.

In 1972, a decade after *Silent Spring* went viral and America slapped a domestic agricultural ban on DDT, it didn't matter much anyway. The death knell of DDT as the frontline defense against mosquitoes had already been sounded. DDT had overstayed its welcome. The mosquito had outlasted her enemy's effectiveness and utility and no longer feared it. In the face of extermination, the mosquito and her empire of disease struck back and adapted and evolved during the silent springs of the 1960s. Malaria parasites snacked on chloroquine between meals of other antimalarials, and mosquitoes built up a luxurious lather of immunity during their showers in DDT.

In truth, the ban on DDT imposed by the United States in 1972 had more to do with its ineffectiveness against DDT-resistant mosquitoes that were first definitively encountered in 1956 (conceivably as early as 1947) than with some far-reaching environmental political clout or anything Carson wrote. She herself acknowledged in *Silent Spring* that "the truth, seldom mentioned but there for anyone to see, is that nature is not so easily molded and that the insects are finding ways to circumvent our chemical attacks on them." Depending on the species of mosquito, DDT resistance took anywhere from two to twenty years. The average mosquito mutiny against DDT occurred within seven years. By the 1960s, the world was crawling with DDT-immune mosquitoes harboring malaria parasites that were resistant to the best drugs we could launch their way.

The unintended consequence of DDT's resounding initial success was that during its potent reign, research on malaria drugs and other pesticides languished. After all, "if it ain't broke don't fix it." Research and development for alternatives stagnated from the 1950s through the 1970s. Following widespread mosquito resistance to DDT, the world was left without the proper tools to carry on the fight against our reconstituted and resurgent enemy. "Between 1950 and 1972, various U.S. agencies spent roughly $1.2 billion on malaria control activities, almost all of which employed DDT," points out Randall Packard in his well-crafted book *The Making of a Tropical Disease*. "The declaration of the World Health Assembly, terminating the Malaria Eradication Programme in 1969, resulted in a decline in interest in malaria-control activities." As a result, says Packard, this "declining interest in malaria control, combined with a general recognition of the difficulties of demonstrating the economic benefits of control, led to a parallel decline in studies directed at this problem during the late 1970s and the 1980s." During these decades, the birds and bees returned but so, too, did a worldwide onslaught of strutting mosquitoes and a shattering surge of mosquito-borne disease. Her immunity to DDT developed relatively quickly, adhering to Friedrich Nietzsche's 1888 will-to-power proverb that "Out of life's school of war: What does not kill me makes me stronger." Draped in her invincible cloak of immunity, she was resurrected from her hibernating slumber stronger and more starving than ever.

In 1968, for example, Sri Lanka ceased spraying DDT, prematurely as it turned out. Immediately, malaria tore through the island, infecting 100,000 people. The following year infection rates had climbed to half a million. By 1969, the year the WHO ended its fourteen-year Malaria Eradication Programme costing $1.6 billion (roughly $11 billion in 2018 dollars), India reported 1.5 million cases of malaria. In 1975, there were over 6.5 million documented cases of malaria in India. Mosquito-borne disease rates in South and Central America, the Middle East, and central Asia reached pre-DDT rates by the early 1970s. Africa, as always, was consumed by mosquito-borne disease. Even Europe experienced a malaria outbreak in 1995, with 90,000 reported cases. Currently, European clinics and hospitals treat eight times more malaria patients than in the 1970s, and malaria rates in central Asia and the Middle East have increased tenfold.

As DDT-resistant mosquitoes multiplied and expanded their range, given the chemical's poisonous, carcinogenic properties, it was now under siege, peppered by a cloudburst of intense media, academic, and governmental scrutiny. Biologically outflanking our best weapon of extermination, mosquito populations and their diseases had rebounded and made a career comeback for world domination. Not that they ever officially retired from nature's game of evolution or Darwin's eternal struggle of survival of the fittest. "In 1969, WHO officially gave up the goal of eradication for most countries," explains Columbia University professor of history Nancy Leys Stepan, in her comprehensive book *Eradication*, "recommending instead that they return to malaria control—a policy prescription that in many cases turned out to be a recipe for the collapse of antimalaria efforts. Malaria returned, often in epidemic form." General MacArthur's wartime mosquito crusader, Dr. Paul Russell, blamed "resistant strains of Homo sapiens" for the botched program, explicitly calling out corrupt bureaucrats, scaremongering and ignorant environmentalists, and a capitalist crusade that squandered money and resources.

Although the failures of DDT were well documented and America banned its domestic use in 1972, the US, as the largest producer of the pesticide, continued its export until January 1981. Five days before leaving office, President Jimmy Carter issued an executive order prohibiting the export of domestically banned substances from the United States under the Environmental Protection Agency, which had been established in 1970 as a result of Rachel Carson's green revolution. "It emphasizes to other countries," Carter announced, "that they can trust goods bearing the label 'Made in USA.'" Following America's lead, a domino effect of DDT bans toppled the short-lived reign of the insecticide. China ceased production in 2007, leaving India and North Korea as the sole manufacturers (roughly 3,000 tons per year) of the forlorn relic once championed as a miracle cure. DDT, once a matchless mosquito killer and dignified lifesaver, was dead in the water. Unfortunately, so, too, were our frontline drugs to combat malaria.

While the mosquito was reinforcing her armor-plating against DDT, the malaria plasmodium evolved to resist every successive generation of new medications. "Despite the fact that we've known about malaria since ancient times," surmises Sonia Shah, "something about this disease still short-circuits our weaponry." Quinine, chloroquine, mefloquine, and others have all been rendered obsolete, outsmarted by the primal survival instincts of stalwart, stubborn malaria parasites. Definitive quinine resistance was discovered in 1910, although most certainly occurred much earlier. In 1957, twelve years after chloroquine's introduction, doctors in the US encountered chloroquine-resistant malaria parasites in the blood of oil drillers, backpackers, geologists, and aid workers returning home from Colombia, Thailand, and Cambodia. Subsequent tests on local populations confirmed the malariologists worst fears.

In just over a decade, the doughty parasite had refurbished itself to confront and defy the top-tier antimalarial drug chloroquine. By the 1960s, "chloroquine was being consumed around the world on a massive scale," acknowledges Leo Slater, "and the parasites were adapting." By this time, the drug was useless across most of Southeast Asia and South America, while chloroquine-resistant mosquitoes were thriving in the heavily dosed regions of India and Africa. By the 1980s, it was no longer effective anywhere. With no suitable alternatives or new-generation treatments available, cheap stockpiles of chloroquine were administered by aid organizations in Africa until the mid-2000s, making up 95% of antimalarial doses.

The parasite continued to spit out our successive frontline defensive drugs as fast as we could produce them. Resistance to mefloquine was confirmed only one year after its commercial release in 1975. A decade later, mefloquine-defiant malaria cases were being reported worldwide. During the recent combat deployments of coalition troops to malarious zones, including Somalia, Rwanda, Haiti, Sudan, Liberia, Afghanistan, and Iraq, the side effects of mefloquine surfaced like the ghosts of atabrine from the Second World War. In 2012, during a United States Senate committee hearing, researchers listed "vivid nightmares, profound anxiety, aggression, delusional paranoia, dissociative psychosis, and severe memory loss" as common, sometimes permanent, side effects labeled "severe intoxication syndrome." These symptoms are certainly not beneficial to a soldier in combat. Along with post-traumatic stress disorder (PTSD) and traumatic brain injury, the expert testimony entered this syndrome as "the third recognized signature injury of modern war." This mefloquine poisoning has gradually been receiving reinforced media attention, as soldiers and veterans are speaking out about their symptoms and grievances. Although the numbers are relatively small, American troops, and soldiers from other contributing nations of the coalition, have contracted malaria and dengue in all these recent operations.

The best treatments currently available, particularly for the lethal *falciparum* strain, are called artemisinin-based combination therapies (ACTs)—essentially a cocktail of various antimalarial drugs layered around an artemisinin core (think of a jawbreaker with assorted candy coatings surrounding a gumball center). ACTs, however, are relatively expensive, costing roughly twenty times as much as other, less effective antimalarials, including primaquine. Artemisinin-based combination therapies work by bombarding the parasite with multiple drugs that target different proteins and pathways of the malaria plasmodium, essentially overwhelming its ability to fight back on so many simultaneous fronts. Malaria finds it difficult to continue its impressive generative cycle, including its furtive dormancy in the liver, while fighting for its life. The artemisinin component is the knockout punch as it reinforces other drugs by jamming and targeting multiple sites and processes rather than a single protein or pathway.

The medical properties of artemisinin, derived from a common wormwood plant indigenous throughout Asia, have been both known and forgotten by the Chinese for millennia. As you may recall from Chapter 2, tucked away inside a 2,200-year-old Chinese medical text with the uninspired title "52 Prescriptions" is a blunt description of the fever-curing benefits of consuming bitter tea made from the small unassuming shrub *Artemisia annua*. We have come full circle with artemisinin, paradoxically one of the oldest and newest antimalarials in our evolving medicine chest.

Its antimalarial properties were rediscovered only in 1972, by Mao's Zedong's Project 523—a secret, highly classified malaria research venture run by the People's Liberation Army at the request of North Vietnam, which was embroiled in a quagmire of war and disease with the United States. Malaria was a constant burden for all combatants during the protracted conflict. With the insertion of foreign troops popping ineffective chloroquine tablets and the upheaval and mass migrations of unseasoned populations in Vietnam, Laos, Cambodia, and the southern provinces of China, malaria flourished in this tropical "Pearl of the Far East" paradise. "The Vietnamese jungle soon became the world's premier incubator of drug-resistant malaria," reports Sonia Shah in her analysis of Project 523.

Zhou Yiqing, a Chinese physician and member of Project 523, remembered being "ordered to conduct field research on tropical diseases in Viet Nam. China was supporting North Viet Nam and providing it with medical aid. Following orders, my comrades and I travelled along the Beibu (Tonkin) Gulf and through the Ho Chi Minh Trail in the jungle—it was the only way to maintain supplies for North Viet Nam because the United States of America had bombed it so intensely. We were accompanied by showers of bombs during the trip. There, I witnessed rampant malaria that reduced the combat strength by half, sometimes by up to 90% when the soldiers became ill. There was a saying, 'We're not afraid of American imperialists, but we are afraid of malaria,' although in fact the disease took a huge toll on both sides."

During peak mosquito season, North Vietnamese columns pouring down the Ho Chi Minh Trail, snaking south through the jungles of Laos and Cambodia, reported malaria rates reaching 90%, confirmed by Zhou Yiqing's eyewitness account. Only by comparison were the Americans better off. Between 1965 and 1973, there were roughly 68,000 in-country *admissions* for malaria, translating to 1.2 million sick days. It is

Combating the Mosquito Enemy in Hoa Long, South Vietnam, 1968: Corporal Les Nunn of the 1st Australian Civil Affairs Unit sprays a Vietnamese village using a portable swing-fog insecticide machine in a bid to cut down the high rates of malaria among Australian soldiers and Vietnamese civilians. The spraying teams were preceded by mobile loudspeaker vans broadcasting an explanatory message to villagers. *(Australian War Memorial)*

likely that the actual infection rate, including those who did not seek medical attention, was much higher.* Repeatedly, as we have seen, human conflict has been the catalyst for innovation and invention in our war on mosquitoes. The resurrection of artemisinin as a malarial assassin from the pages of antiquity was no different.

In 1967, the father figure and leader of North Vietnam, Ho Chi Minh, appealed for help from Zhou Enlai, a senior Chinese politician who had survived the sweeping purges of Mao's Cultural Revolution. With China already fortifying their Vietnamese ally with military hardware and financial handouts, the call for aid had nothing to do with the South Vietnamese or the Americans. Assistance was requested to neutralize and defuse a far more lethal and debilitating enemy. Malaria was sapping the combat strength and hampering the campaigns of Ho Chi Minh's North Vietnamese Army regulars and his Vietcong communist guerrillas. Zhou Enlai encouraged Mao to initiate a malaria program "to keep allies' [North Vietnam] troops combat-ready." Mao didn't need much convincing as 20 million Chinese contracted malaria during the 1960s. "To solve your problem," Mao responded, acquiescing to Ho Chi Minh's request, "is to solve our problem."

On May 23, 1967, roughly 500 scientists initiated the military-malaria program code-named Project 523 after the calendar day (5/23) of its official launch. "The story I will tell today," began Tu Youyou when accepting the 2015 Nobel Prize, "is about the diligence and dedication of Chinese scientists during searching for antimalarial drugs from traditional Chinese medicine forty years ago under considerably under-resourced research conditions." Ironically, the cutting-edge malaria research conducted by Tu Youyou and her team materialized during Mao's Cultural Revolution, which, like his earlier Great Leap Forward fiasco, was defined by systematic oppression, wholesale famine and starvation, and mass executions. During Mao's sociocultural crusade to install his own perverted brand of socialist industrial and agricultural collectivism, universities and schools of higher education were closed and academics and scientists, among other intellectuals, were targeted for execution or

* By comparison, during the Korean War, there were 35,000 cases of malaria among US troops between 1950 and 1953.

"reeducation." Project 523 likely saved many of these avant-garde malaria scholars from a death sentence. Working in utter secrecy and lockdown conditions, these scientists were divided into two streams of study: one seeking synthetic drugs while the other scoured traditional medical texts and tested organic plant-based remedies.

After four years of unsuccessful trials on over 2,000 "recipes" from more than 200 plants, in 1971, Tu Youyou and her colleagues unearthed the ancient reference to artemisinin wormwood as a fever cure. Having honed down the proper preparations of the plant and refined its heat-sensitive active medicinal compound of artemisinin (*qinghaosu*), in March 1972 she reported that an old remedy was in fact the most promising new antimalarial ever discovered or, in this case, rediscovered. "By the late 1970s, China reported that it had made enormous strides against malaria," reports historian James Webb, "and the infection rate had been cut by almost 97 percent." Malaria, at least in China, had finally met its match. By 1990, only 90,000 cases of malaria were reported in China, down from over 2 million only a decade earlier.

The Chinese initially safeguarded their potent antimalarial weapon. The participants of Project 523 were sworn to secrecy. Following the hurried American flight from Saigon marking the end of direct US involvement in Vietnam, the proof of artemisinin's power was first revealed and published (outside of China) in English in a 1979 academic article in the *Chinese Medical Journal,* authored by the collective "Qinghaosu Antimalaria Coordinating Research Group." Seven years after its lifesaving discovery, artemisinin was finally made public and disclosed to the world. Beyond China and Southeast Asia, however, the international scientific community was not initially captivated by, or particularly interested in, ancient Chinese folklore and homeopathic analgesics. When Project 523 was officially terminated in 1981, artemisinin and Tu Youyou's findings failed to make a global impact or catch the eye of and be courted by any corporate pharmaceutical investors. The only artemisinin production and research taking place outside of China was ongoing at the Walter Reed Army Institute of Research biomedical facility, opened in 1953 near Fort Detrick, Maryland.

Although she had published her work anonymously within China in

"We Are Determined to Eradicate Malaria": With the aid of DDT and the secret antimalarial drug artemisinin rediscovered by Project 523, the Chinese launched a dynamic, vigorous, and highly successful mosquito and malaria eradication campaign from the 1950s through the 1970s. The six images depicted in this 1970 antimalaria poster illustrate the propagation and prevention of malaria. *(U.S. National Library of Medicine)*

1977, Tu Youyou presented her great leap forward with artemisinin to an expert malaria panel at the World Health Organization in 1981. Further delays in mass production were caused by the WHO's refusal to approve the drug unless production was centered in American facilities. After all, it was the United States that supplied the international agency with the bulk of its operating budget and funding. The height of the Cold War also necessitated that production of such a valuable commodity, especially in times of elevated conflict, be housed in a "friendly" nation. The Chinese flat-out refused. By this time, the appeal and the profit of dealing in antimalarials had slowly melted away. Demand and dollar signs were being siphoned away from malaria analysis toward a cutthroat, mad scramble to find a lucrative cure for a new global menace—AIDS.

For wealthy pop-cultured and plugged-in MTV-era westerners, this new bloodcurdling threat hit significantly closer to home than did mosquito-borne disease. With the televised HIV-positive announcement of National Basketball Association (NBA) superstar Magic Johnson to a stunned press on November 7, 1991, followed seventeen days later by the death of Queen's virtuoso frontman Freddie Mercury from AIDS-related pneumonia, there was no real money left to be made in antimalarials. The mysterious, perplexing human immunodeficiency virus (HIV) and its symptomatic counterpart, acquired immunodeficiency syndrome (AIDS), were consuming public commentary, driving cultural fear, and monopolizing medical research budgets. The promise of a cure meant money-spinning prescription payouts.

When the pharmaceutical giants finally acquired the drug rights to artemisinin in 1994, Western governments began the long process of trials and tests on artemisinin-based combination therapies (ACTs), which were launched in 1999, with approval secured from the US Food and Drug Administration a decade later. ACTs quickly became the antimalarial of choice, earning Tu Youyou, the trailblazer of Project 523, her overdue Nobel Prize in 2015 "for her discoveries concerning a novel therapy against Malaria." She shared this honor with William Campbell and Satoshi Omura, who developed the drug ivermectin for eradicating parasitic worm infections, including mosquito-borne filariasis and canine heartworm.

Currently, ACTs are expensive, and marketing campaigns target and chase wealthy vacationers and backpackers—to recoup the costs of research and development, but also because the resistance clock is ticking on ACTs. Drug companies need to make their money before the parasite evolves and adapts, and time runs out on artemisinin as it has on most other antimalarials. "As effective and robust as the artemisinin drugs are today," forewarned the Institute of Medicine in 2004, "it is only a matter of time before genetically resistant strains emerge and spread." Four years later, this statement became a reality.

Unsurprisingly, given its more prolonged usage in Southeast Asia, resistance to the new drug was first confirmed in Cambodia in 2008, and by 2014, artemisinin-impenetrable strains of malaria had spread to the neighboring countries of Vietnam, Laos, Thailand, and Myanmar. As Sonia Shah reports, malaria was big money and numerous drug companies around the world "earned a snappy income selling artemisinin—untethered by a partner co-drug. . . . Exposing the malaria parasite to an artemisinin unfortified with another drug dared the parasite to develop resistance." In other words, when used alone and not wrapped in other antimalarials (think back to our multilayered jawbreaker candy) the parasite could fight back and acclimate. With these cheap drugs being peddled across Africa and Asia, the malaria parasite did just that. For this artemisinin debacle, Paul Russell's "resistant strains of Homo sapiens," chided earlier in relation to the evolution of DDT-impervious mosquitoes, could be modified slightly to "greedy strains of Homo sapiens." At times during our eternal war with mosquitoes, as Russell unabashedly points out, we are our own worst enemy.

By this characterization, we are also guilty of creating resistance through our disastrous mass-cultural behavior as "hypochondriac strains of Homo sapiens." Our ignorant overuse and patent misuse of antibiotics, *which fight bacteria only*, not viruses like the common cold or twenty-four-hour flu, has led to invulnerable and lethal bacterial "superbugs." I cannot sugarcoat this point of truth since this horrible habit or even, perhaps, a genuine lack of understanding, is putting millions of lives at risk. The World Health Organization has repeatedly beseeched our collective that "this serious threat is no longer a prediction for the future, it is happening right now in every region of the world and has the potential to affect anyone, of any age, in any country. Antibiotic resistance—when bacteria change so antibiotics no longer work in people who need them to treat infections—is now a major threat to public health."

Yet people still shamefully rush to the doctor at the first sign of a sniffle and demand their antibiotics for nonbacterial, everyday illnesses. Unfortunately, many doctors, who should know better, pander to these absurd prescription requests. According to the CDC, "Each year in the United States, at least 2 million people become infected with bacteria that are resistant to antibiotics and at least 23,000 people die each year as a direct result of these infections," at an annual cost of $1.6 billion. Unashamed abuse of antibiotics, emerging superbugs, and corresponding death rates are not limited to America: This trend is of global concern to our communal herd immunity. According to estimates from the WHO, if this steep graph continues its ascent, by 2050, superbugs will annually kill 10 million people worldwide.

Like our bacterial superbugs, the mosquito in the closing decades of the twentieth century also underwent a renaissance of sorts. It flourished once more, its parasites and viruses oozed evolutionary creativity, it picked up a few new deadly zoonotic hitchhikers along the way, including West Nile and Zika, all leading to increased levels of human suffering and death. Zoonosis rates have tripled in the last ten years, and account for 75% of all human diseases. The goal of health researchers is to identify potential "spillover" germs before they make the zoonotic jump to humans. One such looming concern is the mutating mosquito-borne Usutu virus originating in birds. Although only three human cases have been identified—in Africa in 1981 and 2004, and in Italy in 2009—the virus is nevertheless capable of clearing the mosquito-vectored hurdle from birds to humans. The Ebola virus is another recent crossover, though vectored by fruit bats and other primates, not by mosquitoes. The first documented cases occurred in Sudan and Congo in 1976. Reminiscent of the 1995 Hollywood blockbuster *Outbreak*, "patient zero" in the recent Ebola eruption was a two-year-old boy from Guinea who was infected while playing with a fruit bat in December 2013.

With a defeatist attitude following the termination of the WHO's Malaria Eradication Programme in 1969, it was easier for the world to forget or ignore the mosquito's resurgent renaissance than to pony up billions of dollars for research and eradication that could never be recouped. After all, 90% of malaria cases occurred in Africa, where most victims could not afford antimalarial drugs anyway. "The increasing costs involved with each new generation of antimalarial drugs threaten to further increase the price of control and the ability of countries to sustain control programs," acknowledges Randall Packard in his thorough history of malaria. "The development and adoption of artemisinin-based combination therapies has already greatly increased the cost of drug treatment." In our modern material world, capitalism, when chained to the cost-benefit profit margin of medical inquiry, can be a cruel master.

"Insecticide-Resistance Testing in Uganda": Entomologist Dr. David Hoel teaching children how to recognize mosquito larvae in northern Uganda, 2013. *(Dr. BK Kapella, M.D., [CDR, USPHS]/Public Health Image Library-CDC)*

Dr. Susan Moeller, professor of media and international affairs at the University of Maryland, also blames the media for this apathetic atmosphere she calls "compassion fatigue." New fashionable designer diseases, such as SARS, bird flu (H5N1), swine flu (H1N1), and especially the dreaded Ebola, could potentially threaten wealthy countries where mosquito-borne diseases have been relatively dormant for decades. AIDS also reminded wealthy nations that epidemic diseases were not historical phenomena or limited to remote continents. Younger generations of Americans, Canadians, Europeans, and other affluent westerners do not live in a malaria world as their bloodlines did, and do not fear mosquito-borne diseases, if they have ever even heard of them.

Thanks to sensationalized media and a steady, nauseating stream of formulaic Hollywood "virus-borne zombie" and "culture of fear" films and shows such as *Outbreak*, *12 Monkeys*, *I Am Legend*, *Contagion*, *28 Days Later*, *World War Z*, *The Walking Dead*, *The Andromeda Strain*, and *The Passage*, to name only a few, our screen-time generations do fear Ebola, SARS, the flus, or some futuristic yet unknown man-eating virus. "Certainly Ebola's entrance into metaphor superstardom had a lot to do with the pop status of the disease," concedes Moeller. "When the admittedly sensational Ebola is represented in such a sensationalized fashion by the media and by Hollywood, other diseases pale in comparison. So, stories of more prosaic illnesses barely register; they're ignored, underreported. The gauge of news values shifts." The *New York Times* reporter Howard French, for example, wrote that "death by the thousands in annual measles outbreaks, or a toll of millions from malaria, are non-events for an outside world that has already moved on to associating Africa with endemic H.I.V. infection and has found an even more spectacularly grim image of a diseased continent: Ebola." If you contracted a mosquito-borne disease on vacation or backpacking (or camping, as in our opening chapter), well, that was your own fault or just plain unlucky. Malaria, contends Karen Masterson, "is probably *the* most studied disease of all time, and yet it persists."

After DDT's fall from grace, nearly forty years elapsed before the mosquito was again pursued as public enemy number one, the world's most wanted criminal. "Out of sight, out of mind" was the attitude for most of the Western world, free from the bondage of mosquito-borne disease. Over the last two decades, a resurgent and increasingly lethal mosquito-mounted offensive waged by her battle-hardened veterans of malaria and dengue and her raw recruits of West Nile and Zika changed all that. Seemingly out of nowhere, in 1999, the mosquito attacked New York City and struck fear into the heart of a panicking superpower. The United States summarily responded with a sustained and surging counterattack commanded by Bill and Melinda Gates.

CHAPTER 19

The Modern Mosquito and Her Diseases: At the Gates of Extinction?

The Bureau of Communicable Disease Control in the New York City Department of Health received an unexpected and strange phone call on August 23, 1999, from Dr. Deborah Asnis. As the infectious disease specialist at Flushing Hospital Medical Center in Queens, Dr. Asnis was baffled and required some immediate, lifesaving answers. Four patients had been admitted presenting mysterious and unique symptoms of fever, confusion, disorientation, muscle weakness, and, eventually, paralysis of their limbs. Her patients were deteriorating quickly. Pressed for time, Dr. Asnis needed to find out what on earth was triggering this alarming illness.

Initial tests on September 3 pointed toward a form of encephalitis, or swelling of the brain. There are numerous causes of encephalitis, including viruses, bacteria, fungi, parasites, and accidental hyponatremia (an imbalance of water and solutes or electrolytes in the brain). Blood and tissue samples of the patients were quickly screened and cross-matched against viruses known to cause brain inflammation and similar symptoms. The results came back positive for mosquito-borne St. Louis encephalitis, which is transmitted from birds to humans by the common Culex mosquito.

Concentrated mosquito and larvicide spraying began in the city and surrounds the following day, but, clinically, something didn't add up. By now, the CDC in Atlanta had entered the dialogue. After a quick scan of their database, the situation and contextual setting became even more puzzling. Since the end of the Second World War, and the creation of the CDC in 1946, there had been only 5,000 reported cases of St. Louis encephalitis in the United States and none in New York City. The CDC was not wholly convinced that St. Louis encephalitis was the culprit. There must be something else that was being overlooked.

Bioweapons experts at the CIA and at the biological weapons research compound at Fort Detrick were also closely monitoring the events unfolding in New York. They were not alone. Hordes of probing journalists were scouring to be the first to get the scoop and break the exclusive story. Having sniffed out the gossip, but still without definitive answers, the media took this opportunity to sell its theories. Reputable global newspapers, trashy tabloids, and a lengthy exposé in *The New Yorker* all pointed the finger at a viral mosquito-borne biological terror attack, courtesy of Saddam Hussein. In 1985, they reported, the CDC had sent samples of a relatively new and rare mosquito-borne virus to an Iraqi researcher. Engaged in a brutal war with neighboring Iran from 1980 to 1988, Iraq was the recipient of billions of dollars' worth of American economic aid, technology, military training, and armaments, including chemical weapons. The delivery of a deadly mosquito-borne virus was certainly not out of the realm of possibility for evidence-starved journalists.

As the story began to take on a life of its own, Mikhael Ramadan, the former body double and political decoy for Saddam Hussein turned Iraqi defector and snitch, claimed that Saddam had weaponized this unusual American-gifted virus. "In 1997 on almost the last occasion we met," Ramadan professed, "Saddam summoned me to his study. Seldom had I seen him so elated. Unlocking the top right-hand drawer of his desk, he produced a bulky, leather-bound dossier and read extracts from it." Saddam boasted that he had engineered the "SV1417 strain of the West Nile virus—capable of destroying 97% of all life in an urban environment."

As these outlandish accusations of Saddam's seditious newfangled West Nile supervirus were infecting media stories across the world, the phones at police stations and assorted health departments in New York and at the CDC began ringing off the hook. The Bronx Zoo reported the peculiar passing of its flamingos and the perplexing fatalities of other captive bird species. Numerous random callers recounted seeing the corpses of birds, predominantly crows, littering the parks, streets, and playgrounds of the city. While the St. Louis virus is vectored to humans by the mosquito directly from birds (not from human to mosquito to human like malaria, yellow fever, and most mosquito-borne diseases), the birds themselves are immune to the virus. It does not harm our feathered friends. Accounts also began to filter in about local horses displaying bizarre and eccentric behavior and becoming abnormally ill. This pandemic was not St. Louis encephalitis or one of the mosquito-borne equine encephalitis viruses, nor was it any of the common and catalogued avian pathogens. This was something very different, and at least for the United States, entirely new. The epidemic infecting birds, horses, and humans was in fact the mosquito-vectored West Nile virus. Saddam Hussein, however, had not unleashed his fabled media-fabricated Chimera supervirus on New York. He was proven innocent on all counts.

During the 1999 outbreak, of the estimated 10,000 people who contracted West Nile, 62 people were hospitalized and 7 died. Twenty cases of West Nile were also detected in horses. Birds suffered the lion's share of casualties. According to estimates, as many as two-thirds of the crow population inhabiting New York City and surrounds may have died from the virus. West Nile also killed birds from at least twenty other species, including blue jays, eagles, hawks, doves, and robins.

Given that our animal comrades bore the brunt of the contagion, hypothetically speaking only of course, if it had been a bioterror attack, it would have been an unmitigated failure. In an era of terrorism, weapons of mass destruction, and paranoia over threats both real and imagined, the mosquito is not immune from registration on the offender list of potential biological weapons. "If I was planning a bioterror event," admitted an anonymous senior FBI science advisor, "I'd do things with subtle finesse, to make it look like a natural outbreak." Secretary of the Navy Richard Danzig added that, while biological terrorism was "hard to prove," it was "equally hard to disprove."

Two years after West Nile infiltrated New York City, the Al-Qaeda attacks on 9/11 put the United States and its rattled population on red alert. If these terrorists could stealthily fund and organize attacks on the

World Trade Center and the Pentagon, what else were they capable of? This fear was heightened in the weeks following the 9/11 strikes when "Unabomber" type letters laced with anthrax bacteria were mailed to several leading media offices and two US senators, killing five people and infecting seventeen others. The shadowy world of American covert institutions, including the various biological weapons agencies housed at Fort Detrick, began to assemble risk assessments for every scenario, including the threat of a biological terror attack. Smallpox, plague, Ebola, anthrax, and botulism headed the list. Serious consideration was also given to yellow fever and a genetically engineered strain of malaria.

In V. A. MacAlister's 2001 fictional biotech thriller, *The Mosquito War*, this is precisely what happens when terrorists nonchalantly release lethal genetically modified mosquitoes in the Washington, DC, mall on Independence Day. This is hardly an innovative idea. The devious formula and sinister strategic design predate Napoleon's Walcheren Fever, Dr. Luke Blackburn's macabre yellow fever missions, and the purposeful restoration of malarious mosquitoes to the Pontine Marshes by the Nazis at Anzio, among other historical samples of biological subterfuge. In his fourth-century BCE book, *How to Survive Under Siege*, Greek writer Aeneas Tacticus, one of the earliest scholars of the art of war, endorsed "releasing stinging insects" into the tunnels being excavated by enemy sappers. In 2010, a group of seventy leading mosquito experts met in Florida to discuss "Countering a Bioterrorist Introduction of Pathogen-Infected Mosquitoes Through Mosquito Control" by asking one simple question, "Consider what would happen if a lone bioterrorist infected with yellow fever infected 500 *Aedes aegypti* by feeding them on his/her blood and a week later released them in New Orleans' French Quarter or in Miami's South Beach." Given the trail of wreckage left by yellow fever in the past, when superimposed on a contemporary unvaccinated and unseasoned general population lacking herd immunity, things would get very ugly, very quickly.

The sudden unannounced and sweeping arrival of endemic West Nile to the United States in 1999 awakened us from our apathetic slumber. We had forgotten who our most dangerous and immortal enemy really was. Iraq did not possess the mobile bioweapons labs the Bush-Cheney administration professed it was secretly shrouding. However, there were legitimate weapons of mass destruction dating back millions of years droning and multiplying across the planet. She was far more lethal than anything in Saddam's armory, and markedly more familiar—our time-honored mosquito foe and her arsenal of diseases.

West Nile virus, closely related to dengue, was first isolated in Uganda in 1937 and popped up occasionally in Africa and India. Beginning in the 1960s, reports of minor outbreaks trickled in from North Africa, Europe, the Caucasus, Southeast Asia, and Australia. By the late 1990s, verifications of West Nile were growing in both geographical breadth and levels of infection. Prior to 1999, however, West Nile flew under the radar of the mainstream media as outbreaks were rare and limited to a handful of reports from secluded pockets. More importantly, West Nile was not in the United States. It was a foreign disease.

That changed when West Nile paralyzed New York City with fear during the summer of 1999. This viral strain, likely originating in Israel (and not from some itinerant Iraqi mosquito factory), is thought to have hitched a ride in migratory birds, immigrant mosquitoes, or visiting humans. The New York outbreak was the first to strike the Western Hemisphere. Scientists at the CDC quickly realized that West Nile was here to stay. When the disease hit again the following summer, the CDC conceded, "We are beyond containment now. We have to live with it and do the best we can." Since 1999, roughly 51,000 cases of West Nile have been diagnosed in the United States, with 2,300 fatalities. The virus inflicted its worst American death toll in 2012. According to the CDC, "A total of 5,674 cases of West Nile virus disease in people, including 286 deaths, were reported to CDC from 48 states (excluding Alaska and Hawaii)." The worst previous year and highest infection rate was 2003, with 9,862 cases and 264 deaths. By comparison, in 2018, there were 2,544 confirmed cases of West Nile, with 137 deaths across every US state, save New Hampshire and Hawaii.

Following New York's 1999 summer scare, West Nile went viral across the United States, southern Canada, and South and Central America, while increasing its intensity in Europe, Africa, Asia, and the Pacific. Within a decade of its debut in the Big Apple, West Nile surfaced as a global disease. Like St. Louis encephalitis, the complicated transmission sequence of West Nile travels from birds to mosquitoes to humans. Roughly 80–90% of those infected (tens of millions of people) will never know and will show no symptoms. The remainder will usually show mild flu-like symptoms for a few days. The unlucky 0.5% will develop full-blown symptoms that can lead to swelling of the brain, paralysis, coma, and death.

With the emerging threat of West Nile, specifically in America, the mosquito was everywhere and became a media darling, although there was certainly no sympathy for this devil. A catchy Microsoft Cloud commercial promoting both Bill Gates's software product and his hunger to rid the world of mosquito-borne disease dominated television screens to help turn our deadliest "enemy into an ally." Discovery Channel launched the film *Mosquito* in 2017 to highlight what it called "the single greatest agent of death in modern human history." While the United States and the rest of the infected world was coming to terms with West Nile, another mosquito-borne disease with an even trendier name centered the mosquito in the global spotlight.

In the buildup and hype to the 2016 Rio de Janeiro Summer Olympics, Zika stunned the world. The virus, resembling West Nile and dengue, was first isolated from a monkey in Uganda in 1947, with the first known human infection occurring five years later. From 1964 to 2007, when Zika showed up on the isolated island of Yap in the Pacific, there were only fourteen other confirmed cases, all in Africa and Southeast Asia. But by 2013, it had slowly spread east from Yap across various Pacific Islands before gaining worldwide attention in Brazil in 2015. This epidemic of 2015–2016 spread to countries across the Western Hemisphere.

In the epicenter of Brazil, roughly 1.5 million people were infected, with more than 3,500 cases of reported microcephaly (babies born with small heads and other fetal brain malformations and impairments) caused by "vertical transmission" from mother to fetus. Even more distressing was the announcement concerning pathways of contagion. The Aedes mosquito acts as the common vector. Unlike all other mosquito-borne diseases, however, Zika can be sexually transmitted between partners of both genders (documented in nine countries) and from mother to fetus as evidenced by the heart-wrenching cases of microcephaly causing a host of neurological and physical complications. The symptomatic characteristics are almost identical to West Nile, with 80% to 90% of those infected presenting no indicators. Those who do get sick show mild symptoms similar to West Nile, dengue, or chikungunya. Akin to West Nile, less than 1% of those infected become seriously ill. Zika is also a cause of the neurological Guillain-Barré syndrome, which can result in paralysis and death.

Zika, like West Nile, has also gone globally viral, while the infection rates of their cousins, dengue and chikungunya, have increased thirtyfold since 1960, at a global economic cost of more than $10 billion per year. In 2002, the city of Rio de Janeiro reported nearly 300,000 cases in a dengue epidemic that lingered on before spiking again in 2008 with another 100,000 cases. Currently, global estimates place annual dengue infection at 400 million people. Sonia Shah contends that "dengue is expected to become endemic in Florida, has emerged in Texas, and will likely spread farther north too, touching millions." In addition to cultivating locally sourced dengue and West Nile, in 2016, Texas hosted the first domestic case of chikungunya in the United States.

From her near-death experience following the Second World War, the mosquito, like a phoenix, has risen from her DDT-laced ashes to become a global force once again. The torch of eradication and extermination that had been extinguished during the silent springs of the 1960s was recently picked up and set alight by a multinational coalition of the willing, led by Bill and Melinda Gates.

A series of international meetings during the 1990s led to the launch of the Roll Back Malaria Partnership in 1998, which unveiled a multiorganization collective, Global Malaria Action Plan, a decade later. Buttressing the international eradication drive was an economic information campaign led by economist and Columbia University professor Jeffrey Sachs, highlighting the financial inequities and burdens posed by mosquito-borne disease. Sachs estimated in 2001 that malaria alone cost Africa $12 billion per year in lost output. In 2000, Bill and Melinda Gates formally opened their foundation and put malaria on the global radar for eradication, as articulated in the "Millennium Development Goals" of both the UN and WHO.

The Global Fund to Fight AIDS, Tuberculosis and Malaria, financed in large part by the Gates Foundation, was established in 2002 to make available large-scale funding to help achieve these mosquito-related millennium goals. In 1998, total spending from all sources on global malaria control was around $100 million. Between 2002 and 2014, the Global Fund approved nearly $10 billion in malaria grants. The Gates Foundation estimates, however, that another $90–120 billion is needed between now and the malaria eradication target year of 2040, peaking at $6 billion for the year 2025. During this same time period, direct economic productivity gains from eradication are expected to be in the ballpark of $2 trillion.

While $10 billion seems like an exorbitant amount of money, it comprises 21% of total funds. Of the total allotments, HIV/AIDS receives 59% and tuberculosis 19%. Over the last decade, annual AIDS-related deaths are less than half those of malaria. These "big three" diseases, however, are contractually partnered and somewhat synergistic. Tuberculosis remains the leading cause of death for AIDS patients, accounting for 35% of fatalities. Unfortunately, Africa bears the brunt of this disease overlap, accounting for 85% of new malarial infections and 50% of new HIV infections. Malaria increases the viral replication of HIV, while HIV, by weakening the immune system, makes carriers more susceptible to malaria. It is a double whammy. Since 1980, researchers estimate that HIV is responsible for more than 1 million malarial infections in Africa, and malaria has donated more than 10,000 HIV infections through its direct role in heightening reproduction. Keep in mind that Duffy negativity, as mentioned earlier, although bestowing immunity to *vivax* malaria, also increases the risk of HIV infection by 40%. Unfortunately for those most tormented and afflicted, malaria (and its genetic safeguard), HIV, and tuberculosis are reciprocal, tag-team miscreants.

Over the last few decades, the Gates Foundation and other philanthropic enterprises and organizations have led the global war on mosquitoes. "The most striking example of the power and influence of philanthro-capitalism is The Bill and Melinda Gates Foundation (GF)," writes Nancy Leys Stepan. "Founded by Bill Gates in 1999 with stocks from his company Microsoft, today the foundation has at its disposal $31 billion of Gates's own money, as well as an additional $37 billion in stocks in Berkshire Hathaway Inc., the hedge fund run by Warren Buffett (given in 2006). Its annual expenditures on health rose from $1.5 billion in 2001 to $7.7 billion in 2009. The GF is, if you like, the Rockefeller Foundation of the global era." The influence of Gates and Buffett extended even further. According to Alex Perry in his book *Lifeblood,* detailing recent eradication efforts, "A fresh high came on 4 August 2010, when Gates and Buffett persuaded forty of the world's richest—among them Oracle founder Larry Ellison, Citigroup creator Sandy Weill, Star Wars director George Lucas, media mogul Barry Diller, and eBay founder Peter [*sic*] Omidyar—to announce they would all be giving away at least half their fortunes." Mr. and Mrs. Gates, and their supporters, deserve a hearty round of applause.

The Gates Foundation is the third-largest underwriter of global health research, trailing only the governments of the United States and the United Kingdom. It is also the world's single largest private donor to the WHO and to the Global Fund to Fight AIDS, Tuberculosis and Malaria. Unlike some governments and corporations, the Gates Foundation has no corrupt or underhanded interests other than the eradication of malaria and other mosquito-borne diseases among a circuit board of other health-related programs. It manages its transparent affairs and conducts its philanthropic administration with no strings attached, save its own good intentions.

On the heels of First Lady Laura Bush's 2007 "Malaria Awareness Day" summit at the White House, even reality television got into the malaria melee. The two-hour *American Idol* malaria-focused "Idol Gives Back" star-studded extravaganza aired in April 2007, complete with guest appearances from dozens of bankable A-list actors and musicians. The show was capped by Canadian songbird Celine Dion performing a duet alongside a hologram of a young, and perhaps bewildered, Elvis Presley. The television gala, watched by 26.4 million Americans, created a viral response on social media and raised $75 million for malaria research. In April 2008, a second Hollywood-encrusted "Idol Gives Back"

A New Hope: Two schoolgirls waiting to be tested for filariasis and malaria in Nord-Est Department, Haiti, 2015. *(Dr. Alaine Kathryn Knipes/ Public Health Image Library-CDC)*

raised an additional $64 million. The war on malaria and mosquitoes is truly international.

While the altruistic efforts of Gates, Sachs, and *Idol* producer Simon Fuller (whose father contracted malaria in Burma during the Second World War) are certainly laudable, the larger global war on mosquitoes still operates under the umbrella of capitalism and the interests of big business. While aid for malaria and mosquito eradication, and corresponding media exposure, has dramatically increased in the last decade, programs are often fraught with administrative complications, corruption, and other impediments. Drug companies spend billions of dollars on research and development on antimalarial drugs and vaccines, and understandably need to recoup their costs, which makes treatments unaffordable to those most in need. "Malaria and poverty," notes Randall Packard, "are mutually reinforcing." Today, for example, 85% of malaria cases occur in sub-Saharan Africa, where 55% of the population lives on less than $1 per day. Southeast Asia houses 8% of the malaria caseload, with 5% in the Eastern Mediterranean region, 1% in the Western Pacific, and roughly 0.5% in the Americas. The masses afflicted by mosquito-borne disease live primarily in impoverished countries.

Underprivileged people in the most heavily affected countries in

Africa and Asia cannot afford drugs and, until recently, did not stimulate commercial medical research and development for "their" diseases. Unlike AIDS, which receives the largest share of global drug funding, malaria and other "neglected diseases" are rarities in the affluent world, so they stealthily fly under the R&D radar. Roughly 10% of private R&D resources targets diseases, including malaria, that account for 90% of the global burden. Between 1975 and 1999, of all the thousands of drugs developed and tested worldwide, only four were antimalarials. There is hope, however, as these pharmaceutical titans have recently been recruited and enlisted in our war on mosquitoes through a sustained multimedia eradication campaign and financial contributions from the Gates Foundation and additional benefactors.

The Gates Foundation and other charitable organizations have funded numerous research ventures for the world's first malaria vaccine. To date, the Gates Foundation has committed $2 billion in grants to combat malaria alone, excluding another total investment of almost $2 billion to the Global Fund to Fight AIDS, Tuberculosis and Malaria, which between 2002 and 2013 spent $8 billion solely on its skirmish with malaria. The Gates Foundation apportions resources to numerous malaria vaccine projects, including the PATH Malaria Vaccine Initiative and the Malaria Research Institute at Johns Hopkins University. By 2004, a diverse collection of independent teams at various universities and research institutes in several countries, all receiving financial support from the Gates Foundation, were serious contenders in the race to complete the magic malaria serum.

The first to the malaria vaccine finish line was the London-based drug giant GlaxoSmithKline. After twenty-eight years of development and $565 million from the Gates Foundation and other backers, its malaria vaccine RTS,S or Mosquirix was finally rolled out for the third and final round of clinical human pilot trials in Ghana, Kenya, and Malawi in the summer of 2018. Based on initial results, however, RTS,S is not a sure thing. Four years after initial vaccination and a series of boosters, the success rate of RTS,S was 39%, harshly sinking to 4.4% after seven years. "The problem with most vaccines is that their effectiveness is often short-lived," explains Dr. Klaus Früh of RTS,S. "With further research and development, it could offer a lifetime of protection against malaria." Other experimental vaccines are also nearing the threshold for the first stage of clinical human trials, including Pregnancy-Associated Malaria Vaccine (PAMVAC) developed by ExpreS^{2}ion Biotechnologies in conjunction with the University of Copenhagen and the live-attenuated plasmodium *falciparum* sporozite vaccine (PfSPZ) engineered by the biotech firm Sanaria. In the summer of 2018, GlaxoSmithKline also unveiled the new radical single-dose treatment of the drug tafenoquine, or Krintafel, which suppresses relapse of *vivax* malaria by attacking the hibernating form of the parasite that nests in the liver. While this ongoing exploration is encouraging, our battle with the shape-shifting malaria plasmodium appears to be far from over or, in the case of vaccines, just beginning.

With these probing advancements in mosquito research and medicine, and the promise of potential malaria vaccines, it is easy to get the impression that humanity has entered a new era. It now seems that all the world's troubles and glitches can be solved with cutting-edge science or a reboot from state-of-the-art technology. Everyday miraculous breakthroughs are achieved by brilliant minds across the vast oceans of academia. Everything is at our fingertips and anything seems possible. Within our many enterprises of discovery, we are exploring strange new worlds, seeking out new life-forms on our sphere and beyond, and boldly navigating the unknown frontiers of space. We talk about populating other planets as though it is just a matter of time.

The stirring visions and rousing horizons of the heroes and legendary figures of history and the curious conquistadors of colonization, including Alexander the Great, Leif Erikson, Genghis Khan, Columbus, Magellan, Raleigh, and Drake, were no different. They also encountered the foreign fringes of Alexander's limitless "ends of the world." During their inquisitive ages of antiquity, as in our own, the trajectory of progress appeared nearly infinite. Even the great, narcissistic genius Sir Isaac Newton gravitated toward the notion that if we "have seen further it is by standing on the shoulders of Giants." To this, Friedrich Nietzsche attached his own illumination, declaring that progress is made possible only by "each giant calling to his brother through the desolate intervals of time." We have advanced to border on, and push the boundaries of, what now appears to be the infinite. It is no longer considered irrational or a lamp-rubbed "I dream of genie" wish to talk about earthly immortality. In our modern reasoning and worldview, "when" has supplanted "if."

Yet, within the whirling, dizzying technologically twittering world around us, the humble mosquito reminds us that in many ways, we are not all that different from Lucy and our hominid ancestors or our African Homo sapiens progenitors. They, too, were embroiled in a war for survival with the mosquito and set us on our collision course with our deadliest historical predator. Indeed, the more the modern world speeds up, the more it replicates those early, accidental encounters between humans, such as our Bantu yam farmers, and deadly mosquitoes. As humans migrated or were forced out of Africa, deadly pathogens, including mosquito-borne disease, tagged along. Over time, our modes of transportation and disease transference broadened from solely our feet to include beasts of burden, ships, wagons, and planes, trains, and automobiles. With these technological advancements we have merely quickened the pace of our first stumbling steps and of the broader dissemination of disease. While the mediums of microorganism conveyance may have changed, the spread of contagion remains relatively the same, except now the travel time has been drastically reduced and diseases are delivered from door to door in hours instead of months and years, or even thousands of years in the case of early human-disease migration and settlement patterns.

As paleopathologist Ethne Barnes observes, "Deadly viruses are being teased out of their slumbering isolation as wars, famine, and greed bring people into contact with them in greater numbers. Migrations and air travel bring people into contact with microbes that they have never encountered before." In 2005, for instance, 2.1 billion passengers flew the friendly skies. Five years later, the number of air travelers increased to 2.7 billion and ballooned to 3.6 billion by 2015. Global airports processed 4.3 billion passengers in 2018, a number expected to rise to 4.6 billion in 2019. A complimentary choice of diseases, including SARS, swine and bird flus, Ebola, and our mosquito-borne maladies as demonstrated by West Nile and Zika, passes through airport security to globe-trot across the planet with an increasing number of passengers to an increasing number of destinations on a cyclical, never-ending, all-expenses-paid world tour. Whether hitchhiking or freight hopping on (or in) the earliest human migrants leaving Africa, on a slave ship bound for the Americas courtesy of the Columbian Exchange, or on a 747 flight or Airbus A380, not much has really changed. Disease is enduring and embedded human luggage.

Ever since 1798 when Thomas Malthus postulated the existence of ecologically imposed limits to human demographics (or perhaps as early as 81–96 CE when John of Patmos penned his apocalyptic Revelation and its pale horse of Armageddon), paranoid doomsday promoters and self-proclaimed oracles have been predicting Malthusian plagues and famines, only to see the supposedly intractable limits to population growth pushed back by technology. And yet, something seems different this time. There were roughly a billion people on the planet when Malthus was writing (more than twofold what it had been consistently for the previous 2,000 years). Today, the proliferating and breeding global population has more than doubled since 1970, to 7.7 billion Homo sapiens. If you are still living by 2055, your global superbug-infested neighbors will be in the range of 10 to 11 million. As our numbers increase, our resources diminish in relation.

Given that the mosquito is far and away our biggest killer, there are many that argue along Malthusian lines against trying to eradicate mosquito-borne disease. Both humans and mosquitoes are part of the global ecology and biosphere, existing within a natural and animate system of checks and balances. Creating a disturbance in the force by eradicating our top predator is playing a dangerous game of Russian roulette. From a Malthusian worldview, given the limitations and sustainability of resources, the repercussions of unbridled human population growth might well lead to unimaginable suffering, starvation, disease, and catastrophic death—a Malthusian check by and of itself.

Alternatively, if it is equality and justice for all we are seeking, it is hard not to appreciate the urgent logic of the counterargument—the unconditional and absolute eradication of the mosquito and her diseases from the face of the earth. Currently, four billion people in 108 countries around the world are at risk from mosquito-borne disease.* As our ancestors can attest, our battle with the mosquito has always been a matter of life and death. At this moment, with disease vectors crisscrossing the globe at record rates, even as our species overshoots the ecological carrying capacity of the planet, it's beginning to look as though our history-shaping confrontation with the mosquito is coming to a head.

Rachel Carson wrote that our attitude toward plants and animals is a singularly narrow one, that "if for any reason we find its presence undesirable or merely a matter of indifference, we may condemn it to destruction forthwith." She could not have anticipated the arrival of CRISPR gene-editing technology, though, which dramatically speeds up the meaning of "forthwith," and even changes the parameters and definition of the phrase "condemn to destruction." By tinkering in a lab, we can now trespass and intrude on natural selection and biological design to impose extinction on any undesirable or indifferent species.

Since its discovery by a team at the University of California Berkeley, led by biochemist Dr. Jennifer Doudna in 2012, the revolutionary gene-altering innovation known as CRISPR has shocked the world and altered our preconceived notions about our planet and our place on it.† The front pages of widely read magazines and journals are currently consumed by the topic of CRISPR and mosquitoes. First successfully used in 2013, CRISPR is a procedure that snips out a section of DNA sequencing from a gene and replaces it with another desired one, permanently altering a genome, quickly, cheaply, and accurately. Think of it as "cutting and pasting" genes at will.

In 2016, the Gates Foundation investment toward CRISPR mosquito research totaled $75 million, the largest single sum backing gene-drive technology. "Our investments in mosquito control," outlines the foundation, "include nontraditional biological and genetic approaches as well as new chemical interventions aimed at depleting or incapacitating disease-transmitting mosquito populations." These genetic approaches include the use of CRISPR machinery to eradicate mosquito-borne diseases,

---

* If global warming trends and predictions hold true, by 2050, add another 600 million people to this total.

† CRISPR: clustered regularly interspaced short palindromic repeats.

most notably malaria. In an article titled "Gene Editing for Good: How CRISPR Could Transform Global Development," published by *Foreign Affairs* in Spring 2018, Bill Gates summarized the tangible benefits of using CRISPR technology and the specific areas of research targeted and funded by his (and his wife, Melinda's) foundation:

> But, ultimately, eliminating the most persistent diseases and causes of poverty will require scientific discovery and technological innovations. That includes CRISPR and other technologies for targeted gene editing. Over the next decade, gene editing could help humanity overcome some of the biggest and most persistent challenges in global health and development. The technology is making it much easier for scientists to discover better diagnostics, treatments, and other tools to fight diseases that still kill and disable millions of people every year, primarily the poor. It is also accelerating research that could help end extreme poverty by enabling millions of farmers in the developing world to grow crops and raise livestock that are more productive, more nutritious, and hardier. New technologies are often met with skepticism. But if the world is to continue the remarkable progress of the past few decades, it is vital that scientists, subject to safety and ethics guidelines, be encouraged to continue taking advantage of such promising tools as CRISPR.

It's not difficult to see why. A team of biologists at Berkeley reported that CRISPR chews through Zika, HIV, and other diseases "like Pac-Man."

The strategic target and goal of the Gates Foundation is, and has always been, the extermination of malaria and other mosquito-borne diseases, not to bring the mosquito—which is harmless when flying solo, untethered from a hitchhiking microorganism—to the brink of extinction. Of the more than 3,500 mosquito species, only a few hundred are capable of vectoring disease. Prefabricated genetically modified mosquitoes rendered incapable of harboring the parasite (a hereditary trait passed down their bloodline) just might end the timeless scourge of malaria. But, as Dr. Doudna and the Gates Foundation are acutely aware, CRISPR gene-swapping technology also has the potential to unleash darker, more sinister genetic blueprints with perilous and dangerous possibilities. CRISPR research is a global phenomenon, and neither Doudna nor the foundation has a monopoly on its limitless designs, its instruments of implementation, or its operational execution.

CRISPR has been dubbed the extinction drive, machine, or gene, as this is precisely what it can accomplish—the extermination of mosquitoes by way of genetic sterilization. This theory has been floating around the scientific community since the 1960s. CRISPR can now put these principles into practice. To be fair, the mosquito altered our DNA in the form of sickle cell and other genetic malarial safeguards; perhaps it is time to return the favor. Designer male mosquitoes, which have been genetically modified with domineering "selfish genes" using CRISPR, are released into mosquito zones to breed with females to produce stillborn, infertile, or only male offspring. The mosquito would be extinct in one or two generations. With this war-winning weapon, humanity would never again have to fear the bite of a mosquito. We would awaken to a brave new world, one without mosquito-borne disease.

An alternative to erecting a mosquito exhibit in the extinct-species wing of museums is simply to make them harmless, a strategy supported and funded by the Gates Foundation. With "gene drive" technology, explained Gates in October 2018, "essentially, scientists could introduce a gene into a mosquito population that would either suppress the population—or prevent it from spreading malaria. For decades, it was difficult to test this idea. But with the discovery of CRISPR, the research became a lot easier. And just last month, a team from the research consortium Target Malaria announced that they'd completed studies where mosquito populations were fully suppressed. To be clear: The test was only in a series of laboratory cages filled with 600 mosquitoes each. But it's a promising start." Dr. Anthony James, a molecular geneticist at the University of California Irvine, who self-admittedly "has been obsessed with mosquitoes for 30 years," CRISPR'd a species of Anopheles mosquito to make it incapable of spreading malaria, by eliminating the parasites as they are processed through the mosquito's salivary gland. "We added a small package of genes," explains James, "that allows the mosquitoes to function as they always have, except for one slight change." They can no longer harbor the malaria parasite. The Aedes breed is more difficult to tackle since it transmits a handful of diseases that include yellow fever, Zika, West Nile, chikungunya, Mayaro, dengue, and other encephalitides. "What you need to do is engineer a gene drive that makes the insects sterile," James said of the Aedes breed. "It doesn't make sense to build a mosquito resistant to Zika if it could still transmit dengue and other diseases." We have reached the point in history where we can choose life-forms to eradicate nearly as easily as we order items from a menu, pick a bingeworthy show on Netflix, or click to buy anything on Amazon.

We have valid, although yet unknown, reasons to be careful what we wish for. If we eradicate disease-vectoring mosquito species, such as Anopheles, Aedes, and Culex, would other mosquito species or insects simply fill the ecological niche and occupy the zoonotic gap, continuing the transmission of disease? What effect would eliminating mosquitoes (or any other animals for that matter, or reintroducing long-extinct species) have on the balance of the force and Mother Nature's biological equilibrium? What would happen if we exterminate species that play an essential but unrecognized role in global ecosystems? Where would it end? As we are just beginning to ask these morally fraught and biologically ambiguous questions, no one really knows the answers.

The only human disease to have been completely exterminated is the *variola* virus or smallpox. During the twentieth century, before it was condemned to extinction and entrusted to history, smallpox killed an estimated 300 million people. The disease was targeted for eradication by the WHO, not only because of its lethal nature, but also because it could not hide. Humans were the sole host, and the virus could not survive independently for more than a few hours at most. The last natural case of this legendary killer was reported in Somalia in 1977. The 3,000-year cycle of smallpox transmission had been forever stamped out. At the same time, however, the still unidentified HIV was slowly making its global rounds out of Africa. One deadly disease was replaced with another. For polio and numerous parasitic worms, including filariasis, the end is also near. But these too are being replaced by other new emerging diseases such as Ebola, Zika, West Nile, and others. Since 2000, for instance, the newfangled mosquito-borne Jamestown Canyon virus, a milder West Nile copycat first isolated in Jamestown, Colorado, in 1961, has spread across North America as far afield as Newfoundland.

With CRISPR, we as a species now have the ability to effect premeditated extinction on any organism we choose. We also have the capacity to bring extinct species back to life, so long as ancient DNA is viable. In February 2017, a team of Harvard scientists announced that "the Wooly Mammoth will be back from extinction in two years." Did I not already watch this movie as a kid? Back then, it was sci-fi and we called it *Jurassic Park*. Hollywood has a dramatic flair for exploiting and capitalizing on our scientific marvels gone awry and our hubris-driven technological miscalculations. The consequences of abusing or misusing CRISPR technology, short of velociraptors terrorizing Times Square or Piccadilly Circus and T. rex window shopping down Main Street USA or the Champs-Élysées, are real. "We can remake the biosphere to be what we want, from woolly mammoths to nonbiting mosquitoes," counsels Henry Greely, professor of law and the director of the Center for Law and the Biosciences at Stanford University. "How should we feel about that? Do we want to live in nature, or in Disneyland?" We as a species are faced with an unprecedented moral dilemma, with repercussions that are immeasurable and almost certainly unintended. The tsunami of cataclysmic change would occur in every sector of civilization. Science fiction would become reality, if it has not already.

According to Dr. Thomas Walla, professor of biology in tropical ecology and my colleague at Colorado Mesa University, "the technology is so easy, cheap, and widespread that graduate students will be able to experiment with new CRISPR applications in the lab with relative ease. The launch of CRISPR might well have unhinged Pandora's Box." With CRISPR, the DNA building blocks of any organism, including humans, can be rearranged endlessly. "What are the unintended consequences of genome editing?" Doudna asked herself. "I don't know that we know enough," she answered. "But people will use the technology whether we know enough about it or not. It seemed incredibly scary that you might have students who were working on such a thing. It's important for people to appreciate what this technology can do." Revolutionary, yes, but frightening at the same time. As J. Robert Oppenheimer, head of the Manhattan Project, lamented after the first successful atomic test in July 1945, "I remembered the line from the Hindu scripture, the Bhagavad-Gita; Vishnu is trying to persuade the Prince that he should do his duty and, to impress him, takes on his multi-armed form and says, 'Now I am become Death, the destroyer of worlds.'"

While this type of genetic manipulation used on humans could eradicate disease, biological disorders, or essentially any traits deemed "undesirable," it could also be harnessed for eugenics, biological WMDs, other depraved purposes, or the eradication of "undesirables," emulating the script of the 1997 movie *Gattaca*. In February 2016, the US director of national intelligence, James Clapper, warned Congress and President Barack Obama in his annual report that CRISPR should be regarded as a viable and potential WMD. "Just as gene drives can make mosquitoes unfit for spreading the malaria parasite," warns David Gurwitz, professor of human molecular genetics and biochemistry at Tel Aviv University, "they could conceivably be designed with gene drives carrying cargo for delivering lethal bacterial toxins to humans." While zoonotic animal vectors, including the mosquito, can be genetically driven to terminate the spread of pathogens, they could also be manipulated to become supercharged delivery systems for these same diseases. Although we have unlocked the secrets of this technology, we have only scratched the surface of its potential. The downside to CRISPR is pretty much the definition of dystopia.

In 2016, the Chinese conducted the first human CRISPR trials, quickly followed by the United States and Great Britain in early 2017. "Everything is possible with CRISPR," says geneticist Hugo Bellen at Baylor College of Medicine. "I'm not kidding." Within the whirlwind of CRISPR genetic reprogramming, there are currently over 3,500 CRISPR human gene-drive experiments under way in laboratories all over the world. While we can remove mosquitoes, we can also remodel humankind. Like any other species, we are the product of millions of years of sophisticated evolution. Now, with CRISPR, we are taking matters into our own hands.

On November 26, 2018, at the Second International Summit on Human Genome Editing, He Jiankui, a Chinese geneticist, announced to the world that he had defied government regulations and guidelines and successfully CRISPR'd the embryos of twin girls, bestowing on one of them, Nana, complete immunity to HIV, while her twin sister, Lulu, was given only partial immunity.* His declaration has stirred up a hornet's nest of controversy, condemnation, criticism, and, most importantly, questions and international dialogue over the future use of CRISPR. Leading geneticists and biologists, including Jennifer Doudna, were appalled by the revelation and issued panning responses that included: "Irresponsible"; "If true, this experiment is monstrous"; "We're dealing with the operating instructions of a human being. It's a big deal"; "I unequivocally condemn the experiment." An article in *Nature* stated that his Chinese colleagues were especially disenchanted, and reproaches were "particularly acute in China, where scientists are sensitive to the country's reputation as the Wild West of biomedical research."

In his "2018 Year in Review" or annual "wrap-up," Bill Gates weighed in on He Jiankui's rogue "CRISPR baby" creations, affirming that "I agree with those who say this scientist went too far." In his hopeful and inspiring vision of the future, however, Gates added, "But something good can come from his work if it encourages more people to learn and talk about gene editing. This might be the most important public debate we haven't been having widely enough. The ethical questions are enormous. Gene editing is generating a ton of optimism for treating and curing diseases, including some that our foundation works on (though we fund work on altering crops and insects, not humans). . . . I am surprised that these issues haven't generated more attention from the public. Today artificial intelligence is the subject of vigorous debate. Gene editing deserves at least as much of the spotlight as AI." For better or for worse, it is widely accepted and acknowledged that CRISPR will soon take center stage and dominate the spotlight, if it has not already.

* Subsequent investigators reported that the "CRISPR twins" might have had their brains inadvertently (or perhaps purposefully) enhanced in the process.

By the time this book is published, I can promise and safely predict that genetically modified CRISPR "designer babies" will have caused a storm of controversy and debate and a flood of international moral and legal soul-searching. As Harvard University geneticist Dr. George Church declared, with CRISPR "the genie is already out of the bottle." Many embroiled in its research and debate want to stuff it back in as quickly as possible. If Dr. He Jiankui's announcement turns out to be true and his results authenticated, this window of opportunity might have already closed.

The idea that we can control these unimaginably complex genetic encodings and ecosystems is like believing we can control the weather. Yes, we can affect it, but we can also certainly make it worse. We have no reason whatsoever to believe that we can engineer a perfectly desired outcome or fabricate a flawlessly designed product *100% of the time.* It only takes one mistake, slipup, inadvertent human error to set us on a disastrous orbit or flight path. The recent uptick in natural disasters, or Malthusian checks, including emerging or reemerging diseases, devastating hurricanes, tsunamis, wildfires, droughts, and earthquakes, reminds us that we are relatively helpless and are not quite as clever or omnipotent as we often believe. We are one of an estimated 8–11 million species that share our planet.* We are no different from any other organism of Darwin's evolutionary design engaged in the continuous struggle of survival of the fittest. Nature always has a way of bringing us, and our Homo sapiens "wise man" hubris, back down to earth.

Charles Darwin stated in his seminal 1859 treatise, *On the Origin of Species*, "Natural selection, as we shall hereafter see, is a power incessantly ready for action, and is immeasurably superior to man's feeble efforts, as the works of Nature are to those of Art." I suppose CRISPR is natural selection by other means, although I am not sure Mr. Darwin would necessarily agree. As drugs and insecticides fail in the face of our vampiric predator, with the silver bullets of malaria vaccines and

* Estimates are tricky and span a wide range. I frequently came across the common numbers of 8.7 million and 11 million. I also found academic research citing 2 billion, 1 trillion, and everything in between, with 40 million insect species alone. Like the living organisms in question, taxonomy is also a work in progress and is continuously evolving.

CRISPR, it appears as though we are approaching the decisive Armageddon battle in our eternal war with mosquitoes.

Now that we can tamper with the mosquito's genome, we finally have the chance to strike back, but there are historical lessons to be mindful of and to heed. As we have seen with DDT, it is never quite that simple. The fate of our species has been tied to that of the mosquito throughout our wild coevolutionary ride from our first clumsy encounters in Africa to Ryan Clark's sickle cells and NFL Super Bowls. We did not get to choose our own adventure. For better or for worse, our destinies and interactive histories have been forever entwined, trapped in a single story of struggle and survival with ultimately the same outcome. We would be naive to think that we can effortlessly and without a catch disentangle them now. After all, in the end, we are both still here.

Conclusion

We are still at war with the mosquito.

Dr. Rubert Boyce, founder of the Liverpool School of Tropical Medicine, bluntly stated in 1909 that the fate of human civilization would be decided by one simple equation: "Mosquito or Man?" This has been the most important survival question asked by both our modern species and our hominid ancestors. In fact, this question was so crucial for the propagation of early Homo sapiens that the mosquito mandated and drove modifications to the genetic sequencing of our DNA. Through natural human selection, hereditary malarial defenses materialized and evolved to meet her lethal bite. With CRISPR gene-editing technology, we now aim to return the favor.

She has ruled the earth for 190 million years and has killed with unremitting potency for most of her unrivaled reign of terror. This tiny but tenacious insect has punched well above its weight class with unmitigated fury and ferocity. Across the ages, she has imposed her will on humanity and has dictated the course of history. The mosquito was the instigator of events, nurturing and mothering the creation of the modern global order. She has consumed virtually every corner of our planet, devoured a vast array of animals, including the dinosaurs, while collecting the corpses of an estimated 52 billion people for good measure.

The mosquito sponsored both the rise and fall of ancient empires, she gave birth to independent nations while callously subduing and subjugating others. She has crippled and even destroyed economies. She has prowled the most momentous and pivotal battles, menaced and slaughtered the greatest armies of her generations, and outmaneuvered the most celebrated generals and military minds ever mustered to arms, slaying many of these men in the course of her carnage. Throughout our history of violence, Generals Anopheles and Aedes were powerful weapons of war, moonlighting as formidable foes or avaricious allies.

Although in recent years we have somewhat dampened her onslaught, she continues to inject her influence on human populations. As natural global warming, hastened by greenhouse gas emissions, consumes our planet, she is expanding the battlefield by opening new fronts and penetrating areas of operation formerly free of her mosquito-borne diseases. Her reach is growing, expanding both north and south and vertically into higher altitudes as previously untapped regions warm up to her presence. Stalwart mosquito-borne diseases maintain a steadfast evolutionary commitment to survival and pose a mounting threat to progressively mobile and mingling human populations. Even in the face of modern science and medicine, she remains the most hazardous animal to humankind.

Last year she killed *only* 830,000 people, but still far outpaced our butchery of our own kind. Recently, our own battle-hardened mosquito warriors, scientific arms dealers, and medical lords of war have added new sophisticated weapons of mass destruction to our arsenal in the form of CRISPR gene extinction drives and malaria vaccinations. We are deploying these ordnances to the most active front lines of the operational battlefield to meet her surging threat, courtesy of her adroit new munitions such as Zika and West Nile, and the upgrading of her historically dependable and seasoned soldiers, including malaria and dengue. In this total war with our deadliest predator, there can be only one outcome—the unconditional surrender of the mosquito and her diseases. There is perhaps only one way to achieve this end state—the utter destruction and extermination of the mosquito and her diseases.

Wiping 110 trillion enemy mosquitoes and their pathogens from the face of the earth would substitute the current continuum of human history, which she painstakingly helped to create, with another divergent reality having unknown repercussions. She would nevertheless still be making history, although it would be her last entry into the archives of humankind. CRISPR may very well write the epilogue to her extraordinary story.

As we have seen throughout history, however, the mosquito has survived the best and worst that nature and humankind have thrown her way, to kill across time with unsurpassed intensity. She outlived the extinction-level event of the dinosaurs and has repeatedly shape-shifted to frustrate all our labors of extermination. Across our existence she has determined the fates of nations, decided momentous wars, and helped design our global arrangement, killing nearly half of humanity along the way. CRISPR, like DDT and other tools of execution, however, may also succumb to her evolving bite. History has shown her to be a dogged survivor. For now, the indefatigable mosquito remains our deadliest predator.

Granted, I sympathize that for most readers, it is understandably challenging to emotionally connect with or attach a human face to the mind-boggling statistics and loss of life surveyed in this book. We have seen the mosquito wreak havoc on humankind since the dawn of our species and kill or pollute a wide swath of populations throughout this bloody journey. For most of this epic adventure we have toured through the past, on a voyage across the ages of antiquity, visited the renowned sites and heroic battlefields of ancient empires and aspiring nations, and flipped through the earmarked pages and highlighted tales of history. The mosquito and her diseases, however, are still feverishly hard at work, writing fresh entries to our human odyssey.

While many of you might live in regions currently pardoned or uninhabited by mosquito-borne disease, if you have read this book, it should come as no surprise that the mosquito still touches the lives of hundreds of millions of people and not just with her infuriating hum-buzz or her irritating yet unreachable itch. Just a hunch, but my guess is, if you ask around, a familiar face might answer with a yes or a nod to dengue, malaria, West Nile, Zika, or, alternatively, be a carrier of a genetic shield such as sickle cell.

Given that my adopted home of Grand Junction, Colorado, is situated in West Nile alley, numerous colleagues and students at Colorado

Mesa University, where I teach, have contracted the disease, some with permanent paralysis and disability. They were infected right in their own backyards, on the surrounding hiking and biking trails, or while rafting or fishing on the Colorado and Gunnison Rivers, which snake through the core of the city that serves as the "grand junction" for the two waterways. I also know of students, friends, and acquaintances who have suffered through the breakbone fevers of malaria and dengue while traveling or volunteering as aid workers. One student described his bout of dengue while backpacking in Cambodia as a two-week vacation in hell. Aside from the vomiting, hallucinatory fevers, and rash, he said that the agonizing pain he experienced "felt like someone was slowly tapping nails into my bones and gradually squeezing my joints and muscles with vise grips." Many soldiers and veterans that I spoke with contracted malaria or dengue during exotic military deployments or when operating as private military contractors (PMC) in Africa. Recently, a mate of mine, who now works as a PMC, called me up from Mali while bedridden with malaria. I also know two people who are carriers of sickle cell trait. While I have experienced vibrant mefloquine-induced kaleidoscope-fantasia dreams, thankfully, I have never contracted a mosquito-borne disease that I know of. I do, however, owe my life, my very being, to an African Anopheles mosquito that fought in the First World War.

For the first time in his life, my fifteen-year-old great-grandpa, William Winegard, left his sleepy Canadian hometown in 1915 to enlist in the army. The outbreak of the First World War in August 1914 awakened his dreams of glory in service of king and country. These chivalrous illusions perished in the industrialized slaughterhouse trenches of the Western Front. In March 1916, William was shot and gassed near Ypres, Belgium. Following hospital convalescence, he was discharged back to Canada for being underage. William never made it back to his idyllically youthful picture-postcard hometown. Disembarking at Montreal, he immediately joined the Canadian Navy, untruthful once more about his age.

William served out the remainder of the war on a minesweeper patrolling the West Central African coast, the ancestral birthplace of mosquito-borne disease. In the summer of 1918, he simultaneously contracted "Spanish Influenza," typhoid, and *vivax* malaria. By the time the ship's medic pronounced him dead and was preparing to toss his corpse overboard, William, a once robust five-feet-ten, 175-pound teenager, weighed a skeletal 97 pounds. As fate would have it, a crewmate saw him blink and he was spared the watery grave of Davy Jones's locker. Like my wife's grandfather, Sergeant Rex Raney, my great-grandfather William also survived his wartime malarial ordeal. After a year in sick bay in Freetown, Sierra Leone, and another year hospitalized in England, he arrived home to Canada in 1920. Almost six years had passed since William left for war. He would again serve in the Canadian Navy during the Second World War and live to the ripe old age of eighty-seven.

The Many Faces of Malaria: Private/Seaman William Winegard was one of 1.5 million soldiers to contract malaria during the First World War. Thankfully for me, unlike 95,000 others, he survived. Here, a sixteen-year-old William poses upon his enlistment into the Canadian Navy in August 1916 after his time (and wounds) as a soldier on the Western Front. *(Winegard Family)*

As a kid, I would sit and listen with reverence and wonderment as he stoically narrated his war stories, including his battles with malaria. He accepted his relapsing malaria as standard seasoning, but stubbornly insisted on blaming the German emperor, Kaiser Wilhelm II, rather than the mosquito. Despite sharing his given name with the German monarch, my great-grandpa William's preferred throwaway line was "Curse Kaiser Bill!" I owe my very existence to that one famished African Anopheles mosquito that fed on him during the war-ravaged summer of 1918. This malarious mosquito and his hydra-headed siren of sickness delayed his repatriation to Canada by almost two years. On his 1920 voyage home, he approached a seasick teenage girl vomiting over the railing and tossed a few snide flirting remarks her way. She lifted her head and, as my great-grandma Hilda told me, she "gave him a tongue-lashing." The quarreling lovers were happily married for sixty-seven years. Yet, mosquito-borne diseases are not a thing of the past or a bygone relic that afflicted only our ancestors. They are still alive and well.

Upon the completion of this epic journey and wild ride, my view and opinion of the mosquito were forever changed. Perhaps your attitude toward the mosquito has also adapted, evolved, or been altered in some way from the common genuine hatred expressed in the introduction of this book. My judgment of her now vacillates between that sincere, loathing revulsion and a genuine respect and admiration. Maybe it can be both. After all, within the ongoing war of our world and the natural law of the jungle, she is no different than we are. Just like us, she is simply trying to survive.

Acknowledgments

Upon the completion of my fourth book, as customary, my dad and I sat down to brainstorm ideas for a follow-up. Although he is an emergency physician, he really should have been an historian. After gently interrupting to tell me to slow down, he simply said, "Disease!" While I was not wholly convinced by his one-word answer, as usual my dad had narrowed my path, and I was now working off a smaller map. With his simple clue of "disease," this book was born, and I began my dogged pursuit of our deadliest predator.

For history geeks like me, this was the ultimate treasure hunt. I could not chart the unknown wilds in search of El Dorado or Cibola like a marauding Spanish conquistador or Nicolas Cage, for that matter, or trek to uncover the Lost City of Z. Nor could I embark on a quest for a *Da Vinci Code* Holy Grail like Robert Langdon, track down the Templar Treasure, emulate any of Indiana Jones's epic adventures, or make the hyperspace Kessel Run in less than twelve parsecs. But, perhaps, I could solve this mystery.

I scoured my bookshelves and grabbed the required student textbooks I assign for my university classes. My multitool teaching portfolio bridges a broad range of topics and spans a wide swath of intersecting themes: American history; indigenous studies; comparative politics; war and politics of petroleum; and the catchall Western civilizations. The books were filled with gallant tales of great battles, decisive wars, and the rise and fall of glorious ancient civilizations, including Egypt, Greece, and Rome. They all recount the genesis and sociocultural explosion of Christianity and Islam. The narratives extoll the genius of influential military leaders such as Alexander the Great, Hannibal and

Scipio, Genghis Khan, George Washington, Napoleon, Tecumseh, and Generals Ulysses S. Grant and Robert E. Lee. They chart the course of explorers, pirates, and characters of colonization, including Columbus, Cortes, Raleigh, Rolfe, and our cartoon Hollywood princess, Pocahontas. The textbooks all seek to explain the evolution of civilization and how our global order came to pass.

This simple notion of how our world of yesterdays fashioned and shaped our todays and tomorrows got me thinking. What and who were the major catalysts of change from our past that shaped our present and future? I judged all the usual suspects of trade, politics, religion, imperial European intrusion, slavery, and war. After scanning everything and everyone in my mental rolodex, I concluded that there was still something missing. When I closed the last book, the answer remained elusive, but my curiosity and the word "disease," which by this time was dominating my thoughts and academic attention, had taken me further down the rabbit hole.

There was, of course, the infamous Black Death of the mid-fourteenth century, wrought by the deadly *Yersinia pestis* bacterium transmitted by fleas on rats, which wiped out 50% of the European population (tallying a global butcher's bill of 200 million). I also knew that of the roughly 100 million indigenous people inhabiting the Western Hemisphere, 95% would be exterminated by a cocktail of disease during successive waves of European colonization kicked off by Columbus in 1492 and the ensuing transference of global ecosystems during the "Columbian Exchange." I was aware of the episodic cholera and typhoid outbreaks of Europe and the American colonies, and the devastating "Spanish Influenza" outbreak of 1918–1919, which killed 75 to 100 million people, five times more than the world war that helped it go viral. These well-known epidemics and their historical repercussions had already been declassified and brought me no closer to my objective. I would ultimately find my prize in the most unlikely of places.

I enjoy doing groceries. I know, it's bizarre, but I find it relaxing. Some people meditate or do yoga. I do groceries. On one outing, shortly after the banter about disease with my dad and browsing through all those books, I wandered the aisles, taking in the astonishing assortment of products. I read the labels and marveled at the fact that I had a selection and choice between 26 different forms of canned tomatoes, 19 different blends or roasts of tinned coffee, 57 varieties of ketchup, and 31 allegedly delicious flavors of food for my dog, Steven. I pushed my cart through the global village of groceries, bumping into produce and sundries from every pocket of our planet. I thought to myself that indeed the world is now a small place and that we are the preeminent species. After placing a bag of Ruffles All Dressed chips in my shopping cart, I looked up. There, standing in front of me, hidden in plain sight, was my answer. My treasure, at last, was emblazoned on a giant billboard in a Safeway in my adopted home of Grand Junction, Colorado.

I read the advertisement again. DEEP WOODS OFF!: REPELS MOSQUITOES THAT MAY CARRY ZIKA, DENGUE OR WEST NILE VIRUS. I shook my head in disbelief and personal displeasure that I had not connected the dots earlier. The topic of my next book, the one that you presently hold in your hand, was now a no-brainer—the mosquito. Nowhere in any of those academic textbooks was there an acknowledgment of her preeminent influence throughout history and her inescapable impact in shaping our human story. At last, I had found my El Dorado. I was determined to set the record straight. This book is the culmination of my treasure hunt.

While catching up with historian Dr. Tim Cook at the Canadian War Museum roughly a year after that fateful grocery shopping run (and devouring that bag of All Dressed chips), I told him about this book idea and of my vast collection of ongoing research. Tim immediately introduced me to his, and now my, agent, Rick Broadhead. Thank you, Tim, for making that quick phone call and, more importantly, for your support and friendship over the years. Rick, you have been with me since the first steps of this adventure and I am so very grateful to have you in my corner. You, my friend, are simply incredible and I cannot thank you enough for all you do. Having finally completed the manuscript in between teaching and coaching the hockey team (I am Canadian, after all) at Colorado Mesa University, I submitted the draft to my editors, John Parsley, Nicholas Garrison, and Cassidy Sachs at Penguin Random House. Thank you all for your keen eyes, stamina, and guidance during the revision and editing stages. Your feedback and dissections were invaluable.

As usual, many friends, colleagues, and new acquaintances offered their expertise, collaboration, and assistance. A special thanks to Sir Hew Strachan, my doctoral supervisor at the University of Oxford, who taught me to see beyond the words on the pages and interact with history as a live creature. I have been extremely privileged to be the beneficiary of your knowledge and mentorship. I would also like to thank in no particular order: Bruno and Katie Lamarre, Dr. Alan Anderson, Dr. Hoko-Shodee, Jeff Obermeyer, Dr. Tim Casey, Dr. Douglas O'Roark, Dr. Justin Gollob, Dr. Susan Becker, Dr. Adam Rosenbaum, and Dr. John Seebach. Adam and John, I enjoyed our numerous mosquito-laced (hominid or hominin?) conversations. John, your erudite answers to my inquiries about early human evolution and migration patterns, overlapping our enjoyable chats about Guns N' Roses and the Tragically Hip, were extremely helpful and beneficial. Thank you also to all those who graciously shared their personal mosquito stories and knowledge. I would be remiss if I did not extend a warm thanks to the library staff at Colorado Mesa University for procuring my endless catalogue of requests, including many out-of-print and obscure titles. You are the true treasure hunters. I also wish to acknowledge Colorado Mesa University for providing funding to offset the cost of procuring photographs.

Thousands of people have spent their entire academic or medical careers within the expansive mosquito world. To these mosquito soldiers and their tireless efforts and to those academics on whose writings this story is partially built, I am indebted and extend my metaphorical hand of appreciation in thanks: J. R. McNeill, James L. A. Webb Jr., Charles C. Mann, Randall M. Packard, Mark Harrison, Jared Diamond, Peter McCandless, Andrew McIlwaine Bell, Sonia Shah, Margaret Humphreys, David R. Petriello, Frank Snowden, Alfred W. Crosby, William H. McNeill, Nancy Leys Stepan, Karen M. Masterson, Andrew Spielman, Jeff Chertack at the Gates Foundation, and Bill and Melinda Gates.

Finally, to my mom and dad, thank you for teaching me the ways of the Force. You are both Jedi Masters and, with my apologies to Alexander the Great, Sir Isaac Newton, and Yoda, you are also tops on my list of heroes. I love and miss you all and our lakefront home in Canada. Jaxson, my beautiful boy, you are too young to understand why I am away for extended periods of time, but trust me I'd rather be having "dude days" with you as well. Who else can save your Wayne Gretzky slap shot, catch your Matthew Stafford passes, or be Darius III to your Alexander the Great? I love you forever and in every galaxy far, far away. To my wife, Becky, thank you for holding down the fort during my work-related absences and my seeming absence while at home, writing. You have taken the sage counsel of "patience" espoused by the esteemed philosopher Axl Rose and mastered it.

Thank you all,
Tim

Selected Bibliography

Aberth, John. *The First Horseman: Disease in History*. New Jersey: Pearson-Prentice Hall, 2006.

———. *Plagues in World History*. New York: Rowman & Littlefield, 2011.

Adelman, Zach N., ed. *Genetic Control of Malaria and Dengue*. New York: Elsevier, 2016.

Adler, Jerry. "A World Without Mosquitoes." *Smithsonian* magazine (June 2016): 36–43, 84.

Akyeampong, Emmanuel, Robert H. Bates, Nathan Nunn, and James A. Robinson, eds. *Africa's Development in Historical Perspective*. Cambridge: Cambridge University Press, 2014.

Allen, Robert S. *His Majesty's Indian Allies: British Indian Policy in the Defence of Canada, 1774–1815*. Toronto: Dundurn, 1992.

Altman, Linda Jacobs. *Plague and Pestilence: A History of Infectious Disease*. Springfield, NJ: Enslow, 1998.

Amalakanti, Sridhar, et al. "Influence of Skin Color in Dengue and Malaria: A Case Control Study." *International Journal of Mosquito Research* 3:4 (2016): 50–52.

Anderson, Fred. *Crucible of War: The Seven Years' War and the Fate of Empire in British North America, 1754–1766*. New York: Alfred A. Knopf, 2000.

Anderson, Virginia DeJohn. *Creatures of Empire: How Domestic Animals Transformed Early America*. Oxford: Oxford University Press, 2004.

Anderson, Warwick. *Colonial Pathologies: American Tropical Medicine, Race, and Hygiene in the Philippines*. Durham, NC: Duke University Press, 2006.

Applebaum, Anne. *Red Famine: Stalin's War on Ukraine*. New York: Doubleday, 2017.

Arrow, Kenneth J., Claire B. Panosian, and Hellen Gelband, eds. *Saving Lives, Buying Time: Economics of Malaria Drugs in an Age of Resistance*. Washington, DC: National Academies Press, 2004.

Atkinson, John, Elsie Truter, and Etienne Truter. "Alexander's Last Days: Malaria and Mind Games?" *Acta Classica* LII (2009): 23–46.

Avery, Donald. *Pathogens for War: Biological Weapons, Canadian Life Scientists, and North American Biodefence*. Toronto: University of Toronto Press, 2013.

Bakker, Robert T. *The Dinosaur Heresies: New Theories Unlocking the Mystery of the Dinosaurs and Their Extinction*. New York: William Morrow, 1986.

Barnes, Ethne. *Diseases and Human Evolution*. Albuquerque: University of New Mexico Press, 2005.

Behe, Michael J. *The Edge of Evolution: The Search for the Limits of Darwinism*. New York: Free Press, 2007.

Bell, Andrew McIlwaine. *Mosquito Soldiers: Malaria, Yellow Fever, and the Course of the American Civil War.* Baton Rouge: Louisiana State University Press, 2010.

Bill and Melinda Gates Foundation. *Press Releases; Fact Sheets; Grants; Strategic Investments; Reports.* https://www.gatesfoundation.org/.

Bloom, Khaled J. *The Mississippi Valley's Great Yellow Fever Epidemic of 1878.* Baton Rouge: Louisiana State University Press, 1993.

Boorstin, Daniel J. *The Discoverers: A History of Man's Search to Know His World and Himself.* New York: Vintage, 1985.

Borneman, Walter R. *1812: The War That Forged a Nation.* New York: HarperCollins, 2004.

Bose, Partha. *Alexander the Great's Art of Strategy: The Timeless Leadership Lessons of History's Greatest Empire Builder.* New York: Gotham Books, 2003.

Boyd, Mark F., ed. *Malariology: A Comprehensive Survey of All Aspects of This Group of Diseases from a Global Standpoint.* 2 vols. Philadelphia: W. B. Saunders, 1949.

Brabin, Bernard J. "Malaria's Contribution to World War One—the Unexpected Adversary." *Malaria Journal* 13:1 (2014): 1–22.

Bray, R. S. *Armies of Pestilence: The Impact of Disease on History.* New York: Barnes and Noble, 1996.

Buechner, Howard A. *Dachau: The Hour of the Avenger (An Eyewitness Account).* Metairie, LA: Thunderbird Press, 1986.

Busvine, James R. *Disease Transmission by Insects: Its Discovery and 90 Years of Effort to Prevent It.* New York: Springer-Verlag, 1993.

———. *Insects, Hygiene and History.* London: Athlone Press, 1976.

Campbell, Brian, and Lawrence A. Tritle, eds. *The Oxford Handbook of Warfare in the Classical World.* Oxford: Oxford University Press, 2013.

Cantor, Norman F. *Alexander the Great: Journey to the End of the Earth.* New York: HarperCollins, 2005.

Capinera, John L., ed. *Encyclopedia of Entomology.* 4 vols. Dordrecht: Springer Netherlands, 2008.

Carrigan, Jo Ann. *The Saffron Scourge: A History of Yellow Fever in Louisiana, 1796–1905.* Lafayette: University of Louisiana Press, 1994.

Carson, Rachel. *Silent Spring.* New York: Mariner Reprint, 2002.

Cartledge, Paul. *Alexander the Great: The Hunt for a New Past.* New York: Overlook Press, 2004.

Cartwright, Frederick F., and Michael Biddis. *Disease and History.* New York: Sutton, 2004.

Centers for Disease Control and Prevention (CDC). *Fact Sheets; Diseases and Conditions; Annual Reports.* https://www.cdc.gov.

Chambers, James. *The Devil's Horsemen: The Mongol Invasion of Europe.* New York: Atheneum, 1979.

Chang, Iris. *The Rape of Nanking: The Forgotten Holocaust of World War II.* New York: Penguin, 1998.

Charters, Erica. *Disease, War, and the Imperial State: The Welfare of the British Armed Services During the Seven Years' War.* Chicago: University of Chicago Press, 2014.

Chernow, Ron. *Grant.* New York: Penguin, 2017.

Churchill, Winston S. *The New World.* Vol. 2 of *A History of the English-Speaking Peoples.* New York: Bantam Reprint, 1978.

Cirillo, Vincent J. *Bullets and Bacilli: The Spanish-American War and Military Medicine.* New Brunswick, NJ: Rutgers University Press, 1999.

Clark, Andrew G., and Philipp W. Messer. "An Evolving Threat: How Gene Flow Sped the Evolution of the Malarial Mosquito." *Science* (January 2015): 27–28, 42–43.

Clark, David P. *Germs, Genes, and Civilization: How Epidemics Shaped Who We Are Today*. Upper Saddle River, NJ: FT Press, 2010.

Cliff, A. D., M. R. Smallman-Raynor, P. Haggett, D. F. Stroup, and S. B. Thacker. *Emergence and Re-Emergence: Infectious Diseases; A Geographical Analysis*. Oxford: Oxford University Press, 2009.

Cline, Eric H. *1177 B.C.: The Year Civilization Collapsed*. Princeton: Princeton University Press, 2014.

Cloudsley-Thompson, J. L. *Insects and History*. New York: St. Martin's Press, 1976.

Clunan, Anne L., Peter R. Lavoy, and Susan B. Martin. *Terrorism, War, or Disease?: Unraveling the Use of Biological Weapons*. Stanford, CA: Stanford University Press, 2008.

Coleman, Terry. *The Nelson Touch: The Life and Legend of Horatio Nelson*. Oxford: Oxford University Press, 2004.

Cook, Noble David. *Born to Die: Disease and New World Conquest, 1492–1650*. Cambridge: Cambridge University Press, 1998.

Crawford, Dorothy H. *Deadly Companions: How Microbes Shaped Our History*. Oxford: Oxford University Press, 2007.

Crook, Paul. *Darwinism, War and History: The Debate over the Biology of War from the "Origin of Species" to the First World War*. Cambridge: Cambridge University Press, 1994.

Crosby, Alfred W. *The Columbian Exchange: Biological and Cultural Consequences of 1492*. New York: Praeger, 2003.

———. *Ecological Imperialism: The Biological Expansion of Europe, 900–1900*. Cambridge: Cambridge University Press, 1986.

Crosby, Molly Caldwell. *The American Plague: The Untold Story of Yellow Fever, the Epidemic That Shaped Our History*. New York: Berkley, 2006.

Cueto, Marcos. *Cold War, Deadly Fevers: Malaria Eradication in Mexico, 1955–1975*. Washington, DC: Woodrow Wilson Center Press, 2007.

Cushing, Emory C. *History of Entomology in World War II*. Washington, DC: Smithsonian Institution, 1957.

Dabashi, Hamid. *Persophilia: Persian Culture on the Global Scene*. Cambridge, MA: Harvard University Press, 2015.

Delaporte, François. *Chagas Disease: History of a Continent's Scourge*. Translated by Arthur Goldhammer. New York: Fordham University Press, 2012.

Desowitz, Robert S. *The Malaria Capers: More Tales of Parasites and People, Research and Reality*. New York: W. W. Norton, 1991.

———. *Tropical Diseases: From 50,000 BC to 2500 AD*. London: Harper Collins, 1997.

———. *Who Gave Pinta to the Santa Maria?: Torrid Diseases in the Temperate World*. New York: Harcourt Brace, 1997.

De Bevoise, Ken. *Agents of Apocalypse: Epidemic Disease in the Colonial Philippines*. Princeton: Princeton University Press, 1995.

D'Este, Carlo. *Bitter Victory: The Battle for Sicily, 1943*. New York: Harper Perennial, 2008.

Deichmann, Ute. *Biologists Under Hitler*. Translated by Thomas Dunlap. Cambridge, MA: Harvard University Press, 1996.

Diamond, Jared. *Guns, Germs, and Steel: The Fates of Human Societies*. New York: W. W. Norton, 1997.

Dick, Olivia Brathwaite, et al. "The History of Dengue Outbreaks in the Americas." *American Journal of Tropical Medicine and Hygiene* 87:4 (2012): 584–593.

Diniz, Debora. *Zika: From the Brazilian Backlands to Global Threat*. Translated by Diane Grosklaus Whitty. London: Zed Books, 2017.

Doherty, Paul. *The Death of Alexander the Great: What—or Who—Really Killed the Young Conqueror of the Known World?* New York: Carroll & Graf, 2004.

Doudna, Jennifer, and Samuel Sternberg. *A Crack in Creation: The New Power to Control Evolution*. New York: Vintage, 2018.

Downs, Jim. *Sick from Freedom: African-American Illness and Suffering during the Civil War and Reconstruction*. Oxford: Oxford University Press, 2012.

Drexler, Madeline. *Secret Agents: The Menace of Emerging Infections*. New York: Penguin Books, 2003.

Dubois, Laurent, and John D. Garrigus, eds. *Slave Revolution in the Caribbean, 1789–1804: A Brief History with Documents*. 2nd ed. New York: Bedford-St. Martin's, 2017.

Dumett, Raymond E. *Imperialism, Economic Development and Social Change in West Africa*. Durham, NC: Carolina Academic Press, 2013.

Earle, Rebecca. "'A Grave for Europeans'?: Disease, Death, and the Spanish-American Revolutions." *War in History* 3:4 (1996): 371–383.

Engel, Cindy. *Wild Health: Lessons in Natural Wellness from the Animal Kingdom*. New York: HoughtonMifflin, 2003.

Enserink, Martin, and Leslie Roberts. "Biting Back." *Science* (October 2016): 162–163.

Faerstein, Eduardo, and Warren Winkelstein Jr. "Carlos Juan Finlay: Rejected, Respected, and Right." *Epidemiology* 21:1 (January 2010): 158.

Fenn, Elizabeth A. *Pox Americana: The Great Smallpox Epidemic of 1775–82*. New York: Hill and Wang, 2001.

Ferngren, Gary B. *Medicine and Health Care in Early Christianity*. Baltimore: Johns Hopkins University Press, 2009.

———. *Medicine & Religion: A Historical Introduction*. Baltimore: Johns Hopkins University Press, 2014.

Fowler, William M., Jr. *Empires at War: The Seven Years' War and the Struggle for North America, 1754–1763*. Vancouver: Douglas & McIntyre, 2005.

Frankopan, Peter. *The Silk Roads: A New History of the World*. New York: Vintage, 2017.

Fredericks, Anthony C., and Ana Fernandez-Sesma. "The Burden of Dengue and Chikungunya Worldwide: Implications for the Southern United States and California." *Annals of Global Heath* 80 (2014): 466–475.

Freeman, Philip. *Alexander the Great*. New York: Simon & Schuster Paperbacks, 2011.

Freemon, Frank R. *Gangrene and Glory: Medical Care During the American Civil War*. Chicago: University of Illinois Press, 2001.

Gabriel, Richard A. *Hannibal: The Military Biography of Rome's Greatest Enemy*. Washington, DC: Potomac Books, 2011.

Gachelin, Gabriel, and Annick Opinel. "Malaria Epidemics in Europe After the First World War: The Early Stages of an International Approach to the Control of the Disease." *Historia, Ciencias, Saude-Manguinhos* 18:2 (April–June 2011): 431–469.

Gates, Bill. "Gene Editing for Good: How CRISPR Could Transform Global Development." *Foreign Affairs* 97:3 (May/June 2018): 166–170.

Gehlbach, Stephen H. *American Plagues: Lessons from Our Battles with Disease*. Lanham, MD: Rowman & Littlefield, 2016.

Geissler, Erhard, and Jeanne Guillemin. "German Flooding of the Pontine Marshes in World War II: Biological Warfare or Total War Tactic?" *Politics and Life Sciences* 29:1 (March 2010): 2–23.

Gernet, Jacques. *Daily Life in China on the Eve of the Mongol Invasion, 1250–1276*. Translated by H. M. Wright. Stanford, CA: Stanford University Press, 1962.

Gessner, Ingrid. *Yellow Fever Years: An Epidemiology of Nineteenth-Century American Literature and Culture*. New York: Peter Lang, 2016.

Gillett, J. D. *The Mosquito: Its Life, Activities, and Impact on Human Affairs*. New York: Doubleday, 1971.

Goldsmith, Connie. *Battling Malaria: On the Front Lines Against a Global Killer*. Minneapolis: Twenty-First Century Books, 2011.

Goldsworthy, Adrian. *Pax Romana: War, Peace and Conquest in the Roman World*. New Haven, CT: Yale University Press, 2016.

———. *The Punic Wars*. London: Cassell, 2001.

Gorney, Cynthia. "Science vs. Mosquitoes." *National Geographic* (August 2016): 56–59.

Green, Peter. *Alexander of Macedon, 356–323 B.C.: A Historical Biography*. Berkeley: University of California Press, 1991.

Greenberg, Amy S. *A Wicked War: Polk, Clay, Lincoln, and the 1846 U.S. Invasion of Mexico*. New York: Vintage, 2013.

Grundlingh, Albert. *Fighting Their Own War: South African Blacks and the First World War*. Johannesburg: Ravan Press, 1987.

Hammond, N. G. L. *The Genius of Alexander the Great*. Chapel Hill: University of North Carolina Press, 1997.

Harari, Yuval Noah. *Sapiens: A Brief History of Humankind*. New York: HarperCollins, 2015.

Hardyman, Robyn. *Fighting Malaria*. New York: Gareth Stevens, 2015.

Harper, Kyle. *The Fate of Rome: Climate, Disease, and the End of an Empire*. Princeton: Princeton University Press, 2017.

Harrison, Gordon. *Mosquitoes, Malaria and Man: A History of the Hostilities Since 1880*. New York: E. P. Dutton, 1978.

Harrison, Mark. *Contagion: How Commerce Has Spread Disease*. New Haven, CT: Yale University Press, 2012.

———. *Disease and the Modern World: 1500 to the Present Day*. Cambridge: Polity Press, 2004.

———. *Medicine and Victory: British Military Medicine in the Second World War*. Oxford: Oxford University Press, 2004.

———. *Medicine in an Age of Commerce and Empire: Britain and Its Tropical Colonies 1660–1830*. Oxford: Oxford University Press, 2010.

———. *The Medical War: British Military Medicine in the First World War*. Oxford: Oxford University Press, 2010.

Hawass, Zahi. *Discovering Tutankhamun: From Howard Carter to DNA*. Cairo: American University in Cairo Press, 2013.

Hawass, Zahi, and Sahar N. Saleem. *Scanning the Pharaohs: CT Imaging of the New Kingdom Royal Mummies*. Cairo: American University in Cairo Press, 2018.

Hawass, Zahi, et al. "Ancestry and Pathology in King Tutankhamun's Family." *Journal of the American Medical Association* 303:7 (2010): 638–647.

Hawkins, Mike. *Social Darwinism in European and American Thought, 1860–1945: Nature as Model and Nature as Threat*. New York: Cambridge University Press, 1997.

Hayes, J. N. *The Burdens of Disease: Epidemics and Human Response in Western History*. New Brunswick, NJ: Rutgers University Press, 1998.

Hickey, Donald R. *The War of 1812: A Forgotten Conflict*. Champaign, IL: University of Illinois Press, 2012.

Hindley, Geoffrey. *The Crusades: Islam and Christianity in the Struggle for World Supremacy*. London: Constable & Robinson, 2003.

Holck, Alan R. "Current Status of the Use of Predators, Pathogens and Parasites for Control of Mosquitoes." *Florida Entomologist* 71:4 (1988): 537–546.

Holt, Frank L. *Into the Land of Bones: Alexander the Great in Afghanistan*. Berkeley: University of California Press, 2012.

Hong, Sok Chul. "Malaria and Economic Productivity: A Longitudinal Analysis of the American Case." *Journal of Economic History* 71:3 (2011): 654–671.

Honigsbaum, Mark. *The Fever Trail: In Search of the Cure for Malaria*. London: Pan MacMillan, 2002.

Horwitz, Tony. *A Voyage Long and Strange: On the Trail of Vikings, Conquistadors, Lost Colonists, and Other Adventurers in Early America*. New York: Picador, 2008.

Hosler, John D. *The Siege of Acre, 1189–1191: Saladin, Richard the Lionheart, and the Battle That Decided the Third Crusade*. New Haven, CT: Yale University Press, 2018.

Hoyos, Dexter. *Hannibal: Rome's Greatest Enemy*. Exeter: Bristol Phoenix Press, 2008.

Hughes, J. Donald. *Environmental Problems of the Greeks and Romans: Ecology in the Ancient Mediterranean*. 2nd ed. Baltimore: Johns Hopkins University Press, 2014.

Hume, Jennifer C. C., Emily J. Lyons, and Karen P. Day. "Malaria in Antiquity: A Genetics Perspective." *World Archaeology* 35:2 (October 2003): 180–192.

Humphreys, Margaret. *Intensely Human: The Health of the Black Soldier in the American Civil War*. Baltimore: Johns Hopkins University Press, 2008.

———. *Malaria: Poverty, Race, and Public Health in the United States*. Baltimore: Johns Hopkins University Press, 2001.

———. *Marrow of Tragedy: The Health Crisis of the American Civil War*. Baltimore: Johns Hopkins University Press, 2013.

———. *Yellow Fever and the South*. New Brunswick, NJ: Rutgers University Press, 1992.

Hunt, Patrick N. *Hannibal*. New York: Simon & Schuster, 2017.

Iowa State University Bioethics Program. "Engineering Extinction: CRISPR, Gene Drives and Genetically-Modified Mosquitoes." *Bioethics in Brief*, September 2016. https://bioethics.las.iastate.edu/2016/09/20/engineering-extinction-crispr-gene-drives-and-genetically-modified-mosquitoes/.

Jackson, Peter. *The Mongols and the West, 1221–1410*. New York: Routledge, 2005.

Jones, Richard. *Mosquito*. London: Reaktion Books, 2012.

Jones, W. H. S. *Malaria: A Neglected Factor in the History of Greece and Rome*. Cambridge: Macmillan & Bowes, 1907.

Jordan, Don, and Michael Walsh. *White Cargo: The Forgotten History of Britain's White Slaves in America*. New York: New York University Press, 2008.

Jukes, Thomas H. "DDT: The Chemical of Social Change." *Toxicology* 2:4 (December 1969): 359–370.

Karlen, Arno. *Man and Microbes: Disease and Plagues in History and Modern Times*. New York: Simon & Schuster, 1996.

Keegan, John. *The American Civil War*. New York: Vintage, 2009.

———. *The Mask of Command: Alexander the Great, Wellington, Ulysses S. Grant, Hitler, and the Nature of Leadership*. New York: Penguin Books, 1988.

Keeley, Lawrence H. *War Before Civilization: The Myth of the Peaceful Savage*. Oxford: Oxford University Press, 1996.

Keith, Jeanette. *Fever Season: The Story of a Terrifying Epidemic and the People Who Saved a City*. New York: Bloomsbury Press, 2012.

"Kill Seven Diseases, Save 1.2m Lives a Year." *Economist*, October 10–16, 2015.

Kinkela, David. *DDT and the American Century: Global Health, Environmental Politics, and the Pesticide That Changed the World.* Chapel Hill: University of North Carolina Press, 2011.

Kiple, Kenneth F., and Stephen V. Beck, eds. *Biological Consequences of the European Expansion, 1450–1800.* Aldershot, UK: Ashgate, 1997.

Kotar, S. L., and J. E. Gessler. *Yellow Fever: A Worldwide History.* Jefferson, NC: McFarland, 2017.

Kozubek, James. *Modern Prometheus: Editing the Human Genome with CRISPR-CAS9.* Cambridge: Cambridge University Press, 2016.

Lancel, Serge. *Hannibal.* Oxford, UK: Blackwell Publishers, 1999.

Larson, Greger, et al. "Current Perspectives and the Future of Domestication Studies." *Proceedings of the National Academy of Sciences of the United States of America* 111:17 (April 2014): 6139–6146.

Ledford, Heidi. "CRISPR, the Disruptor." *Nature* 522 (June 2015): 20–24.

Leone, Bruno. *Disease in History.* San Diego: ReferencePoint Press, 2016.

Levine, Myron M., and Patricia M. Graves, eds. *Battling Malaria: Strengthening the U.S. Military Malaria Vaccine Program.* Washington, DC: National Academies Press, 2006.

Levy, Elinor, and Mark Fischetti. *The New Killer Diseases: How the Alarming Evolution of Germs Threatens Us All.* New York: Crown, 2003.

Litsios, Socrates. *The Tomorrow of Malaria.* Wellington, NZ: Pacific Press, 1996.

Liu, Weimin, et al. "African Origin of the Malaria Parasite *Plasmodium vivax.*" *Nature Communications* 5 (2014).

Lockwood, Jeffrey A. *Six-Legged Soldiers: Using Insects as Weapons of War.* Oxford: Oxford University Press, 2010.

Lovett, Richard A. "Did the Rise of Germs Wipe Out the Dinosaurs?" *National Geographic News* (January 2008). https://news.nationalgeographic.com/news/2008/01/080115-dino-diseases.html.

MacAlister, V. A. *The Mosquito War.* New York: Forge, 2001.

Mack, Arien, ed. *In Time of Plague: The History and Social Consequences of Lethal Epidemic Disease.* New York: New York University Press, 1991.

MacNeal, David. *Bugged: The Insects Who Rule the World and the People Obsessed with Them.* New York: St. Martin's Press, 2017.

Macpherson, W. G. *History of the Great War Based on Official Documents: Medical Services.* Diseases of the War, vol. 2. London: HMSO, 1923.

Macpherson, W. G., et al, eds. *The British Official Medical History of the Great War.* 2 vols. London: HMSO, 1922.

Madden, Thomas F. *The Concise History of the Crusades.* Lanham, MD: Rowman & Littlefield, 2013.

Major, Ralph H. *Fatal Partners, War and Disease.* New York: Scholar's Bookshelf, 1941.

Mancall, Peter C., ed. *Envisioning America: English Plans for the Colonization of North America, 1580–1640; A Brief History with Documents.* New York: Bedford-St. Martin's Press, 2017.

Manguin, Sylvie, Pierre Carnevale, and Jean Mouchet. *Biodiversity of Malaria in the World.* London: John Libbey Eurotext, 2008.

Mann, Charles C. *1491: New Revelations of the Americas Before Columbus.* New York: Vintage, 2006.

———. *1493: Uncovering the New World Columbus Created.* New York: Alfred A. Knopf, 2011.

Markel, Howard. *When Germs Travel: Six Major Epidemics That Have Invaded America and the Fears They Unleashed*. New York: Pantheon, 2004.
Marks, Robert B. *Tigers, Rice, Silk, and Silt: Environment and Economy in Late Imperial South China*. Cambridge: Cambridge University Press, 1998.
Martin, Sean. *A Short History of Disease: Plagues, Poxes and Civilisations*. Harpenden, UK: Oldcastle Books, 2015.
Martin, Thomas, and Christopher W. Blackwell. *Alexander the Great: The Story of an Ancient Life*. Cambridge: Cambridge University Press, 2012.
Masterson, Karen M. *The Malaria Project: The U.S. Government's Secret Mission to Find a Miracle Cure*. New York: New American Library, 2014.
Max, D. T. "Beyond Human: How Humans Are Shaping Our Own Evolution." *National Geographic* (April 2017): 40–63.
Mayor, Adrienne. *Greek Fire, Poison Arrows, and Scorpion Bombs: Biological and Chemical Warfare in the Ancient World*. New York: Overlook Duckworth, 2009.
McCandless, Peter. "Revolutionary Fever: Disease and War in the Lower South, 1776–1783." *Transactions of the American Clinical and Climatological Association* 118 (2007): 225–249.
———. *Slavery, Disease, and Suffering in the Southern Lowcountry*. Cambridge: Cambridge University Press, 2011.
McGuire, Robert A., and Philip R. P. Coelho. *Parasites, Pathogens, and Progress: Diseases and Economic Development*. Cambridge, MA: MIT Press, 2011.
McLynn, Frank. *Genghis Khan: His Conquests, His Empire, His Legacy*. Cambridge, MA: Da Capo Press, 2016.
McNeill, J. R. *Mosquito Empires: Ecology and War in the Greater Caribbean, 1620–1914*. Cambridge: Cambridge University Press, 2010.
McNeill, William H. *Plagues and Peoples*. New York: Anchor, 1998.
McPherson, James M. *Battle Cry of Freedom: The Civil War Era*. Oxford: Oxford University Press, 1988.
McWilliams, James E. *American Pests: The Losing War on Insects from Colonial Times to DDT*. New York: Columbia University Press, 2008.
Meier, Kathryn Shively. *Nature's Civil War: Common Soldiers and the Environment in 1862 Virginia*. Chapel Hill: University of North Carolina Press, 2013.
Meiners, Roger, Pierre Desrochers, and Andrew Morriss, eds. *Silent Spring at 50: The False Crises of Rachel Carson*. Washington, DC: Cato Institute, 2012.
Middleton, Richard. *Pontiac's War: Its Causes, Course and Consequences*. New York: Routledge, 2007.
Mitchell, Piers D. *Medicine in the Crusades: Warfare, Wounds and the Medieval Surgeon*. Cambridge: Cambridge University Press, 2004.
Moberly, F. J. *The Campaign in Mesopotamia, 1914–1918*. Vol. 4. London: HMSO, 1927.
Moeller, Susan D. *Compassion Fatigue: How the Media Sell Disease, Famine, War and Death*. New York: Routledge, 1999.
Monaco, C. S. *The Second Seminole War and the Limits of American Aggression*. Baltimore: Johns Hopkins University Press, 2018.
Murphy, Jim. *An American Plague: The True and Terrifying Story of the Yellow Fever Epidemic of 1793*. New York: Clarion Books, 2003.
Nabhan, Gary Paul. *Why Some Like It Hot: Food, Genes, and Cultural Diversity*. Washington, DC: Island Press, 2004.
Nicholson, Helen J., ed. *The Chronicle of the Third Crusade: The Itinerarium Peregrinorum et Gesta Regis Ricardi*. London: Routledge, 2017.

Nikiforuk, Andrew. *The Fourth Horseman: A Short History of Epidemics, Plagues, Famine and Other Scourges*. New York: M. Evans, 1993.

Norrie, Philip. *A History of Disease in Ancient Times: More Lethal Than War*. New York: Palgrave Macmillan, 2016.

O'Brien, John Maxwell. *Alexander the Great: The Invisible Enemy; A Biography*. New York: Routledge, 1992.

O'Connell, Robert L. *The Ghosts of Cannae: Hannibal and the Darkest Hour of the Roman Republic*. New York: Random House, 2011.

Officer, Charles, and Jake Page. *The Great Dinosaur Extinction Controversy*. Boston: Addison-Wesley, 1996.

Overy, Richard. *Why the Allies Won*. London: Pimlico, 1996.

Packard, Randall M. *The Making of a Tropical Disease: A Short History of Malaria*. Baltimore: Johns Hopkins University Press, 2007.

———. "'Roll Back Malaria, Roll in Development'?: Reassessing the Economic Burden of Malaria." *Population and Development Review* 35:1 (2009): 53–87.

Paice, Edward. *Tip and Run: The Untold Tragedy of the Great War in Africa*. London: Weidenfeld & Nicolson, 2007.

Patterson, David K. "Typhus and Its Control in Russia, 1870–1940." *Medical History* 37 (1993): 361–381.

———. "Yellow Fever Epidemics and Mortality in the United States, 1693–1905." *Social Science & Medicine* 34:8 (1992): 855–865.

Patterson, Gordon. *The Mosquito Crusades: A History of the American Anti-Mosquito Movement from the Reed Commission to the First Earth Day*. New Brunswick, NJ: Rutgers University Press, 2009.

Pendergrast, Mark. *Uncommon Grounds: The History of Coffee and How It Transformed Our World*. New York: Basic Books, 1999.

Perry, Alex. *Lifeblood: How to Change the World One Dead Mosquito at a Time*. New York: PublicAffairs, 2011.

Petriello, David R. *Bacteria and Bayonets: The Impact of Disease in American Military History*. Oxford, UK: Casemate, 2016.

Poinar, George, Jr., and Roberta Poinar. *What Bugged the Dinosaurs: Insects, Disease, and Death in the Cretaceous*. Princeton: Princeton University Press, 2008.

Powell, J. H. *Bring Out Your Dead: The Great Plague of Yellow Fever in Philadelphia in 1793*. Philadelphia: University of Pennsylvania Press, 1993.

Quammen, David. *Spillover: Animal Infections and the Next Human Pandemic*. New York: W. W. Norton, 2012.

Rabushka, Alvin. *Taxation in Colonial America*. Princeton: Princeton University Press, 2008.

Reff, Daniel T. *Plagues, Priests, and Demons: Sacred Narratives and the Rise of Christianity in the Old World and the New*. Cambridge: Cambridge University Press, 2005.

Regalado, Antonio. "The Extinction Invention." *MIT Technology Review* (April 13, 2016). https://www.technologyreview.com/s/601213/the-extinction-invention/.

———. "Bill Gates Doubles His Bet on Wiping Out Mosquitoes with Gene Editing." *MIT Technology Review* (September 6, 2016). https://www.technologyreview.com/s/602304/bill-gates-doubles-his-bet-on-wiping-out-mosquitoes-with-gene-editing/.

———. "US Military Wants to Know What Synthetic-Biology Weapons Could Look Like." *MIT Technology Review* (June 19, 2018). https://www.technologyre

view.com/s/611508/us-military-wants-to-know-what-synthetic-biology-weapons-could-look-like/.

Reich, David. *Who We Are and How We Got Here: Ancient DNA and the New Science of the Human Past.* New York: Pantheon, 2018.

Reilly, Benjamin. *Slavery, Agriculture, and Malaria in the Arabian Peninsula.* Athens: Ohio University Press, 2015.

Riley-Smith, Jonathan. *The Crusades: A History.* London: Bloomsbury Press, 2014.

Roberts, Jonathan. "Korle and the Mosquito: Histories and Memories of the Anti-Malaria Campaign in Accra, 1942–5." *Journal of African History* 51:3 (2010): 343–365.

Rocco, Fiammetta. *The Miraculous Fever-Tree: Malaria, Medicine and the Cure That Changed the World.* New York: HarperCollins, 2003.

Rockoff, Hugh. *America's Economic Way of War: War and the US Economy from the Spanish-American War to the Persian Gulf War.* Cambridge: Cambridge University Press, 2012.

Rogers, Guy MacLean. *Alexander: The Ambiguity of Greatness.* New York: Random House, 2005.

Romm, James. *Ghost on the Throne: The Death of Alexander the Great and the Bloody Fight for His Empire.* New York: Vintage, 2012.

Rosen, Meghan. "With Dinosaurs Out of the Way, Mammals Had a Chance to Thrive." *Science News* 191:2 (2017): 22–33.

Rosenwein, Barbara. *A Short History of the Middle Ages.* Toronto: University of Toronto Press, 2014.

Roy, Rohan Deb. *Malarial Subjects: Empire, Medicine and Nonhumans in British India, 1820–1909.* Cambridge: Cambridge University Press, 2017.

Russell, Paul F. *Man's Mastery of Malaria.* London: Oxford University Press, 1955.

Saey, Tina Hesman. "Gene Drives Unleashed." *Science News* (December 2015): 16–22.

Sallares, Robert. *Malaria and Rome: A History of Malaria in Ancient Italy.* Oxford: Oxford University Press, 2002.

Satho, Tomomitsu, et al. "Coffee and Its Waste Repel Gravid *Aedes albopictus* Females and Inhibit the Development of Their Embryos." *Parasites & Vectors* 8:272 (2015).

Schantz, Mark S. *Awaiting the Heavenly Country: The Civil War and America's Culture of Death.* Ithaca, NY: Cornell University Press, 2008.

Scott, Susan, and Christopher J. Duncan. *Biology of Plagues: Evidence from Historical Populations.* Cambridge: Cambridge University Press, 2001.

Servick, Kelly. "Winged Warriors." *Science* (October 2016): 164–167.

Shah, Sonia. *The Fever: How Malaria Has Ruled Humankind for 500,000 Years.* New York: Farrar, Straus and Giroux, 2010.

———. *Pandemic: Tracking Contagions, from Cholera to Ebola and Beyond.* New York: Farrar, Straus and Giroux, 2016.

Shannon, Timothy, ed. *The Seven Years' War in North America: A Brief History with Documents.* New York: Bedford-St. Martin's Press, 2014.

Shaw, Scott Richard. *Planet of the Bugs: Evolution and the Rise of Insects.* Chicago: University of Chicago Press, 2015.

Sherman, Irwin W. *The Power of Plagues.* Washington, DC: ASM Press, 2006.

———. *Twelve Diseases That Changed Our World.* Washington, DC: ASM Press, 2007.

Shore, Bill. *The Imaginations of Unreasonable Men: Inspiration, Vision, and Purpose in the Quest to End Malaria.* New York: PublicAffairs, 2010.

Singer, Merrill, and G. Derrick Hodge, eds. *The War Machine and Global Health.* New York: AltaMira Press, 2010.
Slater, Leo B. *War and Disease: Biomedical Research on Malaria in the Twentieth Century.* New Brunswick, NJ: Rutgers University Press, 2014.
Smallman-Raynor, M. R., and A. D. Cliff. *War Epidemics: An Historical Geography of Infectious Diseases in Military Conflict and Civil Strife, 1850–2000.* Oxford: Oxford University Press, 2004.
Smith, Billy G. *Ship of Death: A Voyage That Changed the Atlantic World.* New Haven, CT: Yale University Press, 2013.
Smith, Joseph. *The Spanish-American War: Conflict in the Caribbean and the Pacific, 1895–1902.* New York: Taylor & Francis, 1994.
Snow, Robert W., Punam Amratia, Caroline W. Kabaria, Abdisaian M. Noor, and Kevin Marsh. "The Changing Limits and Incidence of Malaria in Africa: 1939–2009." *Advances in Parasitology* 78 (2012): 169–262.
Snowden, Frank M. *The Conquest of Malaria: Italy, 1900–1962.* New Haven, CT: Yale University Press, 2006.
Soren, David. "Can Archaeologists Excavate Evidence of Malaria?" *World Archaeology* 35:2 (2003): 193–205.
Specter, Michael. "The DNA Revolution: With New Gene-Editing Techniques, We Can Transform Life—But Should We?" *National Geographic* (August 2016): 36–55.
Spencer, Diana. *Roman Landscape: Culture and Identity.* Cambridge: Cambridge University Press, 2010.
Spielman, Andrew, and Michael D'Antonio. *Mosquito: A Natural History of Our Most Persistent and Deadly Foe.* New York: Hyperion, 2001.
Srikanth, B. Akshaya, Nesrin Mohamed Abd alsabor Ali, and S. Chandra Babu. "Chloroquine-Resistance Malaria." *Journal of Advanced Scientific Research* 3:3 (2012): 11–14.
Standage, Tom. *A History of the World in 6 Glasses.* New York: Walker, 2005.
Steiner, Paul E. *Disease in the Civil War: Natural Biological Warfare in 1861–1865.* Springfield, IL: Charles C. Thomas, 1968.
Stepan, Nancy Leys. *Eradication: Ridding the World of Diseases Forever?* Ithaca, NY: Cornell University Press, 2011.
Strachan, Hew. *The First World War in Africa.* Oxford: Oxford University Press, 2004.
Stratton, Kimberly B., and Dayna S. Kalleres, eds. *Daughters of Hecate: Women and Magic in the Ancient World.* Oxford: Oxford University Press, 2014.
Stromberg, Joseph. "Why Do Mosquitoes Bite Some People More Than Others?" *Smithsonian* magazine (July 2013). https://www.smithsonianmag.com/science-nature/why-do-mosquitoes-bite-some-people-more-than-others-10255934/.
Sugden, John. *Nelson: A Dream of Glory, 1758–1797.* New York: Henry Holt, 2004.
Sutter, Paul S. "Nature's Agents or Agents of Empire?: Entomological Workers and Environmental Change During the Construction of the Panama Canal." *Isis* 98:4 (2007): 724–754.
Sverdrup, Carl Fredrik. *The Mongol Conquests: The Military Operations of Genghis Khan and Sübe'etei.* Warwick, UK: Helion, 2017.
Tabachnick, Walter J., et al. "Countering a Bioterrorist Introduction of Pathogen-Infected Mosquitoes Through Mosquito Control." *Journal of the American Mosquito Control Association* 27:2 (2011): 165–167.

Taylor, Alan. *The Civil War of 1812: American Citizens, British Subjects, Irish Rebels, and Indian Allies.* New York: Alfred A. Knopf, 2010.

Than, Ker. "King Tut Mysteries Solved: Was Disabled, Malarial, and Inbred." *National Geographic* (February 2010). https://news.nationalgeographic.com/news/2010/02/100217-health-king-tut-bone-malaria-dna-tutankhamun/.

Thurow, Roger, and Scott Kilman. *Enough: Why the World's Poorest Starve in an Age of Plenty.* New York: PublicAffairs, 2009.

Townsend, John. *Pox, Pus & Plague: A History of Disease and Infection.* Chicago: Raintree, 2006.

Tyagi, B. K. *The Invincible Deadly Mosquitoes: India's Health and Economy Enemy #1.* New Delhi: Scientific Publishers India, 2004.

Uekotter, Frank, ed. *Comparing Apples, Oranges, and Cotton: Environmental Histories of Global Plantations.* Frankfurt: Campus Verlag, 2014.

US Army 45th Division. *The Fighting Forty-Fifth: The Combat Report of an Infantry Division.* Edited by Leo V. Bishop, Frank J. Glasgow, and George A. Fisher. Baton Rouge: Army & Navy Publishing Company, 1946.

US Army Infantry Regiment 157th. *History of the 157th Infantry Regiment: 4 June '43 to 8 May '45.* Baton Rouge: Army & Navy Publishing Company, 1946.

Van Creveld, Martin. *The Transformation of War.* New York: Free Press, 1991.

Van den Berg, Henk. "Global Status of DDT and Its Alternatives for Use in Vector Control to Prevent Disease." United Nations Environment Programme: Stockholm Convention on Persistent Organic Pollutants UNEP/POPS/DDTBP.1/2 (October 2008): 1–31.

Vandervort, Bruce. *Indian Wars of Mexico, Canada, and the United States, 1812–1900.* New York: Routledge, 2006.

Vosoughi, Reza, Andrew Walkty, Michael A. Drebot, and Kamran Kadkhoda. "Jamestown Canyon Virus Meningoencephalitis Mimicking Migraine with Aura in a Resident of Manitoba." *Canadian Medical Association Journal* 190:9 (March 2018): 40–42.

Watson, Ken W. "Malaria: A Rideau Mythconception." *Rideau Reflections* (Winter/Spring 2007): 1–4.

Watts, Sheldon. *Epidemics and History: Disease, Power and Imperialism.* New Haven, CT: Yale University Press, 1997.

Weatherford, Jack. *Genghis Khan and the Making of the Modern World.* New York: Broadway Books, 2005.

Webb, James L. A., Jr. *Humanity's Burden: A Global History of Malaria.* Cambridge: Cambridge University Press, 2009.

Weil, David N. "The Impact of Malaria on African Development over the Longue Durée." In *Africa's Development in Historical Perspective*, edited by Emmanuel Akyeampong, Robert H. Bates, Nathan Nunn, and James Robinson, 89–111. Cambridge: Cambridge University Press, 2014.

Weisz, George. *Chronic Disease in the Twentieth Century: A History.* Baltimore: Johns Hopkins University Press, 2014.

Weiyuan, Cui. "Ancient Chinese Anti-Fever Cure Becomes Panacea for Malaria." *Bulletin of the World Health Organization* 87 (2009): 743–744.

Welsh, Craig. "Why the Arctic's Mosquito Problem Is Getting Bigger, Badder." *National Geographic*, September 15, 2015. https://news.nationalgeographic.com/2015/09/150915-Arctic-mosquito-warming-caribou-Greenland-climate-CO2/.

Wernsdorfer, Walther H., and Ian McGregor, eds. *Malaria: Principles and Practice of Malariology.* London: Churchill Livingstone, 1989.
Wheeler, Charles M. "Control of Typhus in Italy 1943–1944 by Use of DDT." *American Journal of Public Health* 36:2 (February 1946): 119–129.
White, Richard. *The Middle Ground: Indians, Empires, and Republics in the Great Lakes Region, 1650–1815.* Cambridge: Cambridge University Press, 1991.
Whitlock, Flint. *The Rock of Anzio: From Sicily to Dachau; A History of the U.S. 45th Infantry Division.* New York: Perseus, 1998.
Wild, Antony. *Coffee: A Dark History.* New York: W. W. Norton, 2005.
Willey, P., and Douglas D. Scott, eds. *Health of the Seventh Cavalry: A Medical History.* Norman: University of Oklahoma Press, 2015.
Williams, Greer. *The Plague Killers.* New York: Scribner, 1969.
Winegard, Timothy C. *Indigenous Peoples of the British Dominions and the First World War.* Cambridge: Cambridge University Press, 2011.
———. *The First World Oil War.* Toronto: University of Toronto Press, 2016.
Winther, Paul C. *Anglo-European Science and the Rhetoric of Empire: Malaria, Opium, and British Rule in India, 1756–1895.* New York: Lexington Books, 2003.
World Health Organization. *Annual Reports; Data and Fact Sheets; Mosquito Borne Diseases.* http://www.who.int/news-room/fact-sheets.
World Health Organization. *Guidelines for the Treatment of Malaria.* 3rd ed. Rome: WHO, 2015.
Zimmer, Carl. *A Planet of Viruses.* 2nd ed. Chicago: University of Chicago Press, 2015.
Zimmerman, Barry E., and David J. Zimmerman. *Killer Germs: Microbes and Diseases That Threaten Humanity.* New York: McGraw-Hill, 2003.
Zinsser, Hans. *Rats, Lice and History.* New York: Bantam Books, 1967.
Zysk, Kenneth G. *Religious Medicine: The History and Evolution of Indian Medicine.* London: Routledge, 1993.

Notes

This book was built on a vast foundation of other books, journals, and publications spanning a wide variety of academic fields. Generally, those authors who provided the main scaffolding and support walls have been thanked in the acknowledgments and referenced in the text itself with numerous direct quotations to highlight their weight and importance. Given the topic of this work, and that at times the historical impact of the mosquito is measured by body counts, statistics are tricky and admittedly many are estimates. That is the inherent nature of historical statistical analysis and there is no way of getting around it. Those used in the book represent the most up-to-date figures or estimates, adhere to the consensus of experts, or find middle ground within data ranges.

Not all sources consulted will be referenced here, although most appear in the bibliography. Many books simply triggered my thought process without being directly employed. The chapter notes below are intended to offer further readings to those who are curious or seeking more detailed explanations, and most importantly, to acknowledge and recognize the authors who provided construction materials for each chapter, while highlighting their exhaustive research and brilliant publications.

CHAPTER 1

The role of the mosquito and other insects in threatening and thinning the reign of the dinosaurs can be found in *What Bugged the Dinosaurs: Insects, Disease, and Death in the Cretaceous* by paleobiologists George and Roberta Poinar. Other sources that offer a glimpse into this theory are *The Great Dinosaur Extinction Controversy* by Charles Officer and Jake Page; Scott Richard Shaw's *Planet of the Bugs: Evolution and the Rise of Insects*; and Robert T. Bakker's *The Dinosaur Heresies: New Theories Unlocking the Mystery of the Dinosaurs and Their Extinction*. Numerous scientific and biological books address the life cycle and inner workings of the mosquito and her hitchhiking microbes. The most readable explanations are offered in *Mosquito: A Natural History of Our Most Persistent and Deadly Foe* by Andrew Spielman and Michael D'Antonio, and in J. D. Gillett's *The Mosquito: Its Life, Activities, and Impact on Human Affairs*. Two exhaustively researched and well-crafted books provided the bulk of information for the coevolution of malaria, our hominid ancestors, and Homo sapiens: James L. A. Webb Jr.'s *Humanity's Burden: A Global History of Malaria* and Randall M. Packard's *The Making of a Tropical Disease: A Short History of Malaria*. These two brilliant accounts also track the global spread and history of malaria across our existence and were referenced or consulted throughout many chapters of this book. My succinct synopses and summaries of mosquito-borne diseases were an amalgamation from a compilation of various sources too lengthy to list here. John L. Capinera's edited four-volume, 4,350-page *Encyclopedia of Entomology* proved to be a tremendous reference and guidebook during the chronology of my writing. S. L. Kotar and J. E. Gessler's *Yellow Fever: A Worldwide History* and David K. Patterson's article "Yellow Fever Epidemics and Mortality in the United States, 1693–1905" provide an excellent and detailed investigation of the deadly virus.

CHAPTER 2

In addition to the splendid works of Webb and Packard, *The Fever: How Malaria Has Ruled Humankind for 500,000 Years* by Sonia Shah provides an excellent chronology of malaria's impact on human affairs, including genetic resistance, as does Sylvie Manguin's *Biodiversity of Malaria in the World*, although with a much more scientific slant. David Reich's book *Who We Are and How We Got Here: Ancient DNA and the New Science of the Human Past* provides a well-written snapshot overview of its title. Numerous other works provided summaries of human genetic immunities to malaria, including Barry and David Zimmerman, *Killer Germs: Microbes and Diseases That Threaten Humanity*; Ethne Barnes, *Diseases and Human Evolution*; Gary Paul Nabhan, *Why Some Like It Hot: Food, Genes, and Cultural Diversity*; Michael J. Behe, *The Edge of Evolution: The Search for the Limits of Darwinism*; and Jared Diamond, *Guns, Germs, and Steel: The Fates of Human Societies*. The connections between coffee (and tea) and the mosquito (and African slavery and revolutions) are highlighted by Antony Wild, *Coffee: A Dark History*; Mark Pendergrast *Uncommon Grounds: The History of Coffee and How It Transformed Our World*; and Tom Standage, *A History of the World in 6 Glasses*, not only in this chapter but throughout the book. The Bantu migrations and their subsequent domination of southern Africa appear in Diamond, Shah, Packard, and Webb. Ryan Clark received a fair amount of media attention during and after his ordeal. Numerous widely available and published interviews, articles, and stories were utilized.

CHAPTERS 3 & 4

Much of these chapters was written from the primary sources of ancient scribes and physicians, including Hippocrates, Galen, Plato, and Thucydides among a host of others. Other valuable sources pertaining to ancient Greece and Rome include J. N. Hays, *The Burdens of Disease: Epidemics and Human Response in Western History*; R. S. Bray, *Armies of Pestilence: The Impact of Disease on History*; Hans Zinsser, *Rats, Lice and History*; J. L. Cloudsley-Thompson, *Insects and History*; W. H. S. Jones, *Malaria: A Neglected Factor in the History of Greece and Rome*; Donald J. Hughes, *Environmental Problems of the Greeks and Romans: Ecology in the Ancient Mediterranean*; Eric H. Cline, *1177 B.C.: The Year Civilization Collapsed*; Philip Norrie, *A History of Disease in Ancient Times: More Lethal Than War*; William H. McNeill, *Plagues and Peoples*; Adrian Goldsworthy, *The Punic Wars* and *Pax Romana: War, Peace and Conquest in the Roman World*; *The Oxford Handbook of Warfare in the Classical World*, edited by Brian Campbell and Lawrence A. Tritle; Adrienne Mayor, *Greek Fire, Poison Arrows, and Scorpion Bombs: Biological and Chemical Warfare in the Ancient World*; Robert L. O'Connell, *The Ghosts of Cannae: Hannibal and the Darkest Hour of the Roman Republic*; Patrick N. Hunt, *Hannibal*; Serge Lancel, *Hannibal*; Richard A. Gabriel, *Hannibal: The Military Biography of Rome's Greatest Enemy*; and two brawny and spanning volumes by A. D. Cliff and M. R. Smallman-Raynor, *War Epidemics: An Historical Geography of Infectious Diseases in Military Conflict and Civil Strife, 1850–2000* and *Emergence and Re-Emergence of Infectious Diseases: A Geographical Analysis*. Egypt and the life and death of King Tut are covered in the works of Zahi Hawass as well as many of those listed above. For

Alexander the Great's malaria-riddled imperial retreat, life, and death, see the numerous sources listed in the bibliography. Throughout history, the Pontine Marshes surrounding Rome have been a regional malaria hotbed and factor in the shaping of early Western civilization perhaps more than any other geographical area outside of Africa. The vast catalogue of primary and secondary literature concerning malaria and Rome spans the Roman Empire to the Second World War. Kyle Harper's *The Fate of Rome: Climate, Disease, and the End of an Empire* is a scholarly gem, as are the works of Hughes, Bray, and Jones mentioned above. Two other invaluable and finely crafted books are Robert Sallares, *Malaria and Rome: A History of Malaria in Ancient Italy,* and Frank M. Snowden, *The Conquest of Malaria: Italy, 1900–1962.* The journal articles of David Soren and Jennifer C. Hume offer archeological evidence of malaria's reign throughout the ancient world; and the works of Webb and Shah also unearth fragments of the mosquito in antiquity.

CHAPTER 5

The correlation between disease, including endemic malaria, and the rise and spread of Christianity is detailed in Hays, *The Burdens of Disease*; David Clark, *Germs, Genes, and Civilization: How Epidemics Shaped Who We Are Today*; Gary B. Ferngren, *Medicine and Health Care in Early Christianity* and *Medicine & Religion*; Daniel T. Reef, *Plagues, Priests, and Demons: Sacred Narratives and the Rise of Christianity in the Old World and the New*; Kenneth G. Zysk, *Religious Medicine: The History and Evolution of Indian Medicine*; *Daughters of Hecate: Women and Magic in the Ancient World*, edited by Kimberly B. Stratton and Danya S. Kalleres; and in the works of Cloudsley-Thompson, Zinsser, Irwin W. Sherman, and Alfred W. Crosby. Webb and Packard provide an overview of the spread of malaria in Europe during the Dark Ages and the Crusades era. Alfred W. Crosby's *Ecological Imperialism: The Biological Expansion of Europe, 900–1900* highlights the role of mosquito-borne disease during the Crusades with brilliant clarity, so much so that I included a lengthy quotation from this work in the text (one of only a handful in the book). His account formed the scaffolding and was drywalled by the works of Piers D. Mitchell, *Medicine in the Crusades: Warfare, Wounds and the Medieval Surgeon*; Helen J. Nicholson, editor of *The Chronicle of the Third Crusade: The Itinerarium Peregrinorum et Gesta Regis Ricardi*; John D. Hosler, *The Siege of Acre, 1189–1191: Saladin, Richard the Lionheart, and the Battle That Decided the Third Crusade*; Geoffrey Hindley, *The Crusades: Islam and Christianity in the Struggle for World Supremacy*; Thomas F. Madden, *The Concise History of the Crusades*; Jonathan Riley-Smith, *The Crusades: A History.*

CHAPTER 6

The best depictions of Genghis Khan and the Mongol era can be found in Peter Frankopan, *The Silk Roads: A New History of the World*; Frank McLynn, *Genghis Khan: His Conquests, His Empire, His Legacy*; Jack Weatherford, *Genghis Khan and the Making of the Modern World*; James Chambers, *The Devil's Horsemen: The Mongol Invasion of Europe*; John Keegan, *The Mask of Command: Alexander the Great, Wellington, Ulysses S. Grant, Hitler, and the Nature of Leadership*; Robert B. Marks, *Tigers, Rice, Silk, and Silt: Environment and Economy in Late Imperial South China*; Jacques Gernet, *Daily Life in China on the Eve of the Mongol Invasion, 1250–1276*; Peter Jackson, *The Mongols and the West, 1221–1410*; Carl Fredrik Sverdrup, *The Mongol Conquests: The Military Operations of Genghis Khan and Sübe'etei.* The works of Bray, Crosby, Capinera, and William H. McNeill also offer insight into the Mongol world.

CHAPTERS 7 & 8

The literature on the Columbian Exchange is extremely vast. Primary sources (including quotations) such as the writings of Bartolome de las Casas, for example, were employed as much as possible. My archival research in Britain, Canada, Australia, New Zealand, the United States, and South Africa for one of my previous books, *Indigenous Peoples of the British Dominions and the First World War*, was utilized for these chapters as well. The most relevant secondary sources for these two chapters are: Alfred W. Crosby, *The Columbian Exchange: Biological and Cultural Consequences of 1492* and *Ecological Imperialism: The Biological Expansion of Europe, 900–1900*; Charles C. Mann, *1493: Uncovering the New World Columbus Created*; William H. McNeill, *Plagues and Peoples*; Mark Harrison, *Disease and the Modern World: 1500 to the Present Day*; *Biological Consequences of the European Expansion, 1450–1800*, edited by Kenneth F. Kiple and Stephen V. Beck; Robert S. Desowitz, *Who Gave Pinta to the Santa Maria?: Torrid Diseases in the Temperate World*; Tony Horwitz, *A Voyage Long and Strange: On the Trail of Vikings, Conquistadors, Lost Colonists, and Other Adventurers in Early America*; Noble David Cook, *Born to Die: Disease and New World Conquest, 1492–1650*; Daniel J. Boorstin, *The Discoverers*; Dorothy H. Crawford, *Deadly Companions: How Microbes Shaped Our History*; Jared Diamond, *Guns, Germs, and Steel*, from whom I borrowed the term "accidental conquerors"; Lawrence H. Keeley, *War Before Civilization: The Myth of the Peaceful Savage*; *Africa's Development in Historical Perspective*, edited by Emmanuel Akyeampong, Robert H. Bates, Nathan Nunn, and James A. Robinson; Robert A. McGuire and Philip R. P. Coelho, *Parasites, Pathogens, and Progress: Diseases and Economic Development*; Peter McCandless, *Slavery, Disease, and Suffering in the Southern Lowcountry*; Margaret Humphreys, *Yellow Fever and the South*; Sheldon Watts, *Epidemics and History: Disease, Power and Imperialism*. For the discovery and influence of the cinchona tree and quinine, see: Fiammetta Rocco, *The Miraculous Fever-Tree: Malaria, Medicine and the Cure That Changed the World*; Mark Honigsbaum, *The Fever Trail: In Search of the Cure for Malaria*; Rohan Deb Roy, *Malarial Subjects: Empire, Medicine and Nonhumans in British India, 1820–1909*. On malaria and the opium trade, see Paul C. Winther, *Anglo-European Science and the Rhetoric of Empire: Malaria, Opium, and British Rule in India, 1756–1895*.

CHAPTERS 9 & 10

Primary source material was consulted when applicable and Mann's *1493* was a wealth of concise, narrative-driven information. Webb, Packard, Kiple and Beck, Spielman, and Petriello outline the spread of malaria within Europe and England and its arrival and dissemination in the Americas in articulate detail. Virginia DeJohn Anderson's *Creatures of Empire: How Domestic Animals Transformed Early America* was also a sturdy reference. The Scottish Darien scheme is outlined in Shah, Mann, and J. R. McNeill, *Mosquito Empires: Ecology and War in the Greater Caribbean, 1620–1914*, among other sources. The concept of the three zones of infection and the Mason-Dixon Line in the Americas is borrowed, modified, and cobbled together from Webb, J. R. McNeill, and Mann.

CHAPTER 11

Masterworks for this period are Fred Anderson, *Crucible of War: The Seven Years' War and the Fate of Empire in British North America, 1754–1766*; Alvin Rabushka, *Taxation in Colonial America*; Erica Charters, *Disease, War, and the Imperial State: The Welfare of the British Armed Services during the Seven Years' War*; Robert S. Allen, *His Majesty's Indian Allies:*

British Indian Policy in the Defence of Canada, 1774–1815; William M. Fowler, *Empires at War: The Seven Years' War and the Struggle for North America, 1754–1763*; Richard Middleton, *Pontiac's War: Its Causes, Course and Consequences.* David R. Petriello's *Bacteria and Bayonets: The Impact of Disease in American Military History* traces the title's theme from Columbus through recent American military campaigns and was a useful reference throughout many chapters of this book. J. R. McNeill articulates the role of the mosquito in colonial wars, including the French disaster at Kourou/Devil's Island, leading up to the rebellions across the Americas encompassing the American Revolution.

CHAPTERS 12 & 13

Two indispensable, exceptional, and exhaustively researched publications pertaining to the mosquito's role in defining the outcome of the American Revolution (and other insurrections against colonial rule in the Americas) are *Mosquito Empires* by J. R. McNeill and *Slavery, Disease, and Suffering in the Southern Lowcountry* by Peter McCandless. A journal article by McCandless, "Revolutionary Fever: Disease and War in the Lower South, 1776–1783," supplements his book. The works of Sherman, Mann, Shah, and Petriello also touch on the mosquito's role in facilitating American nationhood. The ensuing revolutions (and the explosion of yellow fever) across the Americas, including those led by Toussaint Louverture in Haiti and Simon Bolivar across the Spanish colonies, are exquisitely detailed by J. R. McNeill, Mann, Sherman, Cliff and Smallman-Raynor, and Watts; Billy G. Smith, *Ship of Death: A Voyage That Changed the Atlantic World*; Jim Murphy, *An American Plague: The True and Terrifying Story of the Yellow Fever Epidemic of 1793*; J. H. Powell, *Bring Out Your Dead: The Great Plague of Yellow Fever in Philadelphia in 1793*; Rebecca Earle, "'A Grave for Europeans'?: Disease, Death, and the Spanish-American Revolutions."

CHAPTERS 14 & 15

For the War of 1812, see Alan Taylor, *The Civil War of 1812: American Citizens, British Subjects, Irish Rebels, and Indian Allies*; Walter R. Borneman, *1812: The War That Forged a Nation*; Donald R. Hickey, *The War of 1812: A Forgotten Conflict.* The works of J. R. McNeill, Petriello, and Amy S. Greenberg, *A Wicked War: Polk, Clay, Lincoln, and the 1846 U.S. Invasion of Mexico*, highlight the role of the mosquito in the Mexican-American War and in the new American west. Andrew McIlwaine Bell's dazzlingly brilliant *Mosquito Soldiers: Malaria, Yellow Fever, and the Course of the American Civil War* provides a painstaking and erudite account of the interplay between the mosquito, malaria, quinine supplies, and grand strategy during the conflict, ultimately galvanizing and underpinning both the Emancipation Proclamation and a Union victory. Other invaluable Civil War sources are Margaret Humphreys, *Marrow of Tragedy: The Health Crisis of the American Civil War* and *Intensely Human: The Health of the Black Soldier in the American Civil War*; Kathryn Shively Meier, *Nature's Civil War: Common Soldiers and the Environment in 1862 Virginia*; Jim Downs, *Sick from Freedom: African-American Illness and Suffering during the Civil War and Reconstruction*; Mark S. Schantz, *Awaiting the Heavenly Country: The Civil War and America's Culture of Death*; Frank R. Freemon, *Gangrene and Glory: Medical Care During the American Civil War*; Paul E. Steiner, *Disease in the Civil War: Natural Biological Warfare in 1861–1865*; John Keegan, *The American Civil War.* Ron Chernow's superb biography, *Grant*, situates General Grant and President Lincoln within the larger issues and shifting aims of the war, including the Emancipation Proclamation. Other sources that provide context include Mann, McGuire and Coelho, Petriello, Mark Harrison, and Cliff and Smallman-Raynor.

CHAPTER 16

The spread of mosquito-borne disease in the United States during the Reconstruction era after the Civil War, including the yellow fever epidemics of the 1870s, is detailed in both Webb and Packard as well as Molly Caldwell Crosby, *The American Plague: The Untold Story of Yellow Fever, the Epidemic That Shaped Our History*; Jeanette Keith, *Fever Season: The Story of a Terrifying Epidemic and the People Who Saved a City*; Khaled J. Bloom, *The Mississippi Valley's Great Yellow Fever Epidemic of 1878*; Stephen H. Gehlbach, *American Plagues: Lessons from Our Battles with Disease.* The discoveries and eradication programs of Manson, Laveran, Ross, Grassi, Finley, Reed, Gorgas, and others are strewn throughout a vast array of sources, including their own publications. Gordon Harrison, *Mosquitoes, Malaria and Man: A History of the Hostilities Since 1880*, provides a thorough account, as do Greer Williams, *The Plague Killers*; James R. Busvine, *Disease Transmission by Insects: Its Discovery and 90 Years of Effort to Prevent It*; Gordon Patterson, *The Mosquito Crusades: A History of the American Anti-Mosquito Movement from the Reed Commission to the First Earth Day*; James E. McWilliams, *American Pests: The Losing War on Insects from Colonial Times to DDT*; Nancy Leys Stepan, *Eradication: Ridding the World of Diseases Forever?* The influence of mosquito-borne disease in Cuba and the Philippines during the Spanish-American War and in the construction of the Panama Canal is well known and can be found in Ken de Bevoise, *Agents of Apocalypse: Epidemic Disease in the Colonial Philippines*; Warwick Anderson, *Colonial Pathologies: American Tropical Medicine, Race, and Hygiene in the Philippines*; Joseph Smith, *The Spanish-American War: Conflict in the Caribbean and the Pacific, 1895–1902*; Vincent J. Cirillo, *Bullets and Bacilli: The Spanish-American War and Military Medicine*; Paul S. Sutter, "Nature's Agents or Agents of Empire?: Entomological Workers and Environmental Change during the Construction of the Panama Canal," in addition to J. R. McNeill, Petriello, Watts, Shah, Cliff and Smallman-Raynor, Rocco, and Honigsbaum.

CHAPTER 17

The world wars are covered by Karen M. Masterson's brilliant book, *The Malaria Project: The U.S. Government's Secret Mission to Find a Miracle Cure*; Leo B. Slater, *War and Disease: Biomedical Research on Malaria in the Twentieth Century*; Paul F. Russell, *Man's Mastery of Malaria*; Snowden, *The Conquest of Malaria*; Emory C. Cushing, *History of Entomology in World War II*; David Kinkela, *DDT and the American Century: Global Health, Environmental Politics, and the Pesticide That Changed the World*; Mark Harrison, *Medicine and Victory: British Military Medicine in the Second World War* and *The Medical War: British Military Medicine in the First World War*; Donald Avery, *Pathogens for War: Biological Weapons, Canadian Life Scientists, and North American Biodefence*; *Terrorism, War, or Disease?: Unraveling the Use of Biological Weapons*, edited by Anne L. Clunan, Peter R. Lavoy, and Susan Martin; Ute Deichmann, *Biologists Under Hitler*; Bernard J. Brabin, "Malaria's Contribution to World War One—the Unexpected Adversary." The works of Gordon Harrison, Stepan, Webb, McWilliams, Petriello, Cliff and Smallman-Raynor also aided in building these chapters. Archival and secondary research for my previous book, *The First World Oil War*, was also of value for these chapters when looking at mosquito-borne disease rates in the sideshow theaters of the First World War, including the Middle East, Salonika, Africa, the Russian Caucasus, and during the Allied intervention in the Russian Civil War.

CHAPTERS 18 & 19

The postwar eradication decades, the rise of DDT, Rachel Carson's silent springs and the modern environmental movement, and the relatively recent resurgence of mosquito-borne disease are widely covered across the writings of numerous academic fields and mass media. Generally, these chapters were assembled from the works of Slater, Masterson, Stepan, McWilliams, Spielman and D'Antonio, Packard, Cliff and Smallman-Raynor, Webb, Patterson, Kinkela, Russell, and Shah, as well as Alex Perry, *Lifeblood: How to Change the World One Dead Mosquito at a Time*; the extremely detailed *Saving Lives, Buying Time: Economics of Malaria Drugs in an Age of Resistance,* edited by Kenneth J. Arrow, Claire B. Panosian, and Hellen Gelband; Susan D. Moeller, *Compassion Fatigue: How the Media Sell Disease, Famine, War and Death*; Mark Harrison, *Contagion: How Commerce Has Spread Disease*; and reports and publications from the WHO, the CDC, and the Gates Foundation. Specific to the 1999 West Nile outbreak in New York are Zimmerman and Zimmerman, *Killer Germs*; Shah, *Pandemic: Tracking Contagions, from Cholera to Ebola and Beyond*; Madeline Drexler, *Secret Agents: The Menace of Emerging Infections*; and various reports and media releases from the CDC. Given the recent advent of CRISPR gene-editing technology, mainstream media, magazines, and newspapers were vital in producing an up-to-date analysis of our current and ongoing war with mosquitoes and our attempts to eradicate certain mosquito species and their diseases. Academic journals and magazines, including the *Economist*, *Science*, *National Geographic*, *Nature*, and *Discover*, and publications and press releases from the WHO, the CDC, and the Gates Foundation, provided crucial and current information and briefings outlining the ongoing malaria vaccine ventures and the evolving use of CRISPR. Jennifer Doudna, the creator of CRISPR, and Samuel Sternberg just released a book, *A Crack in Creation: The New Power to Control Evolution*. James Kozubek's *Modern Prometheus: Editing the Human Genome with CRISPR-CAS9* was also recently published. With its earth-shattering and mind-bending capabilities, I anticipate a flurry of CRISPR-derived nonfiction (and apocalyptic and dystopian fiction) books flooding the market in the near future.

Index

NOTE: Page numbers in ***italics*** indicate photographs and captions.

About the Author

Timothy C. Winegard holds a PhD in history from the University of Oxford. He is a professor of history and political science and head coach of the hockey team at Colorado Mesa University in Grand Junction. Dr. Winegard served as an officer with the Canadian and British armed forces, and is internationally published, including his four previous books, in the fields of both military history and indigenous studies.